THE THEORY AND INTERPRETATION OF NARRATIVE SERIES

I KNOW THAT YOU KNOW THAT I KNOW

Narrating Subjects from
Moll Flanders to *Marnie*

GEORGE BUTTE

THE OHIO STATE UNIVERSITY PRESS
Columbus

Copyright © 2004 by The Ohio State University.
All rights reserved.

Butte, George, 1947-
 I know that you know that I know : narrating subjects from Moll Flanders to Marnie / George Butte.
   p. cm. — (The theory and interpretation of narrative series) Includes bibliographical references and index.
  ISBN 0-8142-0945-9 (hardcover : alk. paper) — 0-8142-9027-2 (CD-ROM)
  1. Psychological fiction, English-History and criticism. 2. Psychological fiction, American—History and criticism. 3. Intersubjectivity in literature. 4. Consciousness in literature. 5. Motion pictures—History. 6. Narration (Rhetoric) 7. Intersubjectivity. I. Title. II. Series.
  PR830.P75 B87 2004
  823'.08309—dc22
                              2003018678

Paper (ISBN: 978-0-8142-5618-3)
Cover design by Dan O'Dair.
Type set in Adobe Apollo.

Contents

Preface   VII

Part One: Theory

1. STARTING OVER: INTERSUBJECTIVITY AND NARRATIVE   3
   Starting Over   3
   The Disappearance of the Transparent Word   8
   The Subject: Performance or Embodiment?   17
   The New Intersubjectivity: Espousal, Shame, and the Quarrel
       between Merleau-Ponty and Sartre   24

2. REPRESENTING DEEP INTERSUBJECTIVITY: NARRATIVE
   PRACTICES   39
   The Subject Encounters the Other: *Moll Flanders* and *Great
       Expectations*   39
   The Intersubjective Subject: *Pamela* and *The Turn of the Screw*   63
   Others Encounter Others: Intersubjective Omniscience:
       Tom Jones and *Middlemarch*   81

Part Two: Case Studies: Deep Intersubjectivity and Genre

3. COMEDY, FILM, AND FILM COMEDY   105
   Austen, the Intersubjectivity of Anxiety, and *Emma*   108
   Film, Film Comedy, and Deep Intersubjectivity   122
   Hitchcock's Cary Grant Films: Theatricality, Gender, and the
       Intersubjective Gaze   130
   Woody Allen's *Broadway Danny Rose:* The Fool and the
       Mutual Gaze   151

4. DEEP INTERSUBJECTIVITY AND THE SUBVERSION OF COMEDY 163
    The Intersubjective Failure of Intersubjectivity: Henry James's
        The Awkward Age and the Shadow of the Body 163
    Howard Hawks's *His Girl Friday:* Laughter as Comedy's Saboteur 181

5. DEEP INTERSUBJECTIVITY AND MASQUERADE 193
    Masquerade, Monstrosity, and *Jane Eyre* 200
    Hitchcock's *Marnie,* the Maternal Gaze, and Masquerade 219

Epilogue 235
Notes 241
Bibliography 253
Index 263

Preface

This book is about how stories narrate human consciousness. In fact, it is about how stories narrate human consciousnes*ses,* and so in the title phrase, "Narrating Subjects," "subjects" is the *object* of the action of narrating. My real interest is the way narrative interweaves character*s'* perceptions of each other. The special idea here claims that the way stories portray consciousness of consciousness—intersubjectivity—changed fundamentally around the time of Jane Austen. My title is grammatically diverse, perhaps intersubjective, because it allows for two functions of the word "narrating": It can be both verb and adjective. In the first way of reading, to which I've alluded, "subjects" (as the object of the verb) are narrated; in the second, "subjects" do the narrating. Both readings are appropriate for a study of intersubjectivity in narrative, which is a study of the ways human subject*s* narrate and get themselves narrated, and how a new form for representing consciousnesses, what I call "deep intersubjectivity," emerged for us to see, clearly, first in Jane Austen's novels.

This book is also about a kind of reading that allows us to see deep intersubjectivity better. That reading grows out of a tradition in phenomenology that has to some degree been discredited, but which I wish to recuperate in a new form, grounded in what I call a poststructuralist phenomenology. Explaining that recuperated way of reading—and practicing it—are the items on my agenda.

As befits the preface to a book about intersubjectivity, I acknowledge, with deep gratitude, the help of many people over some years who have read parts or all of this work and who often replied with an enormous generosity that I have in turn repaid as well as I could by making this writing better. If I did not, the failure is mine. I wish there were a way to make that hoary cliché of academic writers fresh, because behind the cliché is a real experience. Some of those readers to whom I owe so much are Laura Doyle, Susan Fraiman, Eric Gould, Jonathan Lee, J. Hillis Miller, Beth Newman, Dorothea Olkowski, Constance Penley, Barry Sarchett, Irene Tayler, and Kay Young. Garrett Stewart's final review of the manuscript was exacting and insightful, and I will always be grateful that he understood what this book is about. The editors and staff at The Ohio State University Press have in every case been enormously helpful as well. I must single out the editors of the Theory and Interpretation of Narrative series, Jim Phelan and Peter Rabinowitz, whose elegant and always pertinent criticism pointed toward the more coherent book they believed they could see inside the earlier versions. I cannot imagine better readers for a manuscript being born.

Thanks for permission to reprint are due to *The Hitchcock Annual*, for pages in chapter 3 that it first published, and to Palgrave, Macmillan, for pages in chapters 1 and 3 that originally appeared in *Jane Austen's Business* (St. Martin's Press, 1996).

The film illustrations in this book are frames reproduced from each film. Most film illustrations are actually still photographs taken on the sets during filming and are subtly (or not so subtly) different in framing and mise-en-scène, often in ways that dramatically change the moment's emphasis. For reproducing these frames so well I am most grateful to Andy Hutchison of Alexander Film in Colorado Springs, Jan Enright at Colorado College, and Jennifer Shoffey Forsythe at The Ohio State University Press.

I am also grateful for many kinds of support over all the years from people at Colorado College, from deans to department chairs to library staff to department colleagues, including our department support staff. I want to thank my chair, Barry Sarchett, and my dean, Richard Storey, for time, money, and their belief in this project. Our recently retired department secretary, Donna Gianarelli, helped solve many minor and major difficulties in software, printers, paper trays, and recalcitrant footnotes. Sometimes the support was simply conversation. For example, my colleague Jim Yaffe, also recently retired, with whom I argued many times about *His Girl Friday*, still thinks my views are horrific and probably immoral (but he smiles when he says this). Then there were friends, like Elizabeth, Mike, and Kathryn Leslie, who gave me weekend afternoons to write when the revision had to be done.

But finally it's my family I owe: Billie, Kate, and Reid: We share our lives, and you know the costs of the writer's solitary craft. Thank you—above all to my wife, Billie, who believed in this work and made room for it in our lives for years.

PART ONE
Theory

1

Starting Over: Intersubjectivity and Narrative

The "there" is said to be a wall between us and others, but it is a wall we build together, each putting a stone in the niche left by the other.
—MERLEAU-PONTY, Signs

It did not surprise, but it grieved Anne to observe that Elizabeth would not know [Wentworth]. She saw that he saw Elizabeth, that Elizabeth saw him, that there was complete internal recognition on each side; she was convinced that he was ready to be acknowledged as an acquaintance, expecting it, and she had the pain of seeing her sister turn away with unalterable coldness.
—AUSTEN, Persuasion

STARTING OVER

Fixed as she is in Molland's bakery shop, where only limited movement is possible with the rain outside and where her authorized companions are competing with Wentworth for her allegiance, Anne Elliot must use her keenest skills of navigation in this scene from *Persuasion* (vol. 2, chap. 7). Those skills allow her not only to watch others but also simply to watch those whom the others watch. Anne maps a longer and more remarkable series of exchanged, blocked, anticipated, and denied acknowledgments. Within her gaze, Wentworth and Elizabeth see each other, and they further recognize the sign in the other of being seen and of being seen seeing. As if this maze of perceptions were not intricate enough, Austen turns the screw yet again: Anne is "convinced" she tracks a specific negotiation (II7;176). To the woman whom his courtship of Anne had offended more than seven years earlier, Wentworth offers a compromise fiction that he is an acquaintance, as he leans forward to be acknowledged, but Elizabeth rejects his offer, breaking the chain of gestures. Austen frames each perception with yet another gaze or gesture, each trumping the previous one.

This scene in *Persuasion*, about the observation of observations, gives voice to a profound new way of shaping narrative that takes coherent form, at least in English literature, in the early nineteenth century. When Anne Elliot watches Wentworth and Elizabeth negotiating complex force fields of memory and protocol, the enabling strategy of her story is a new layering of human consciousnesses, or a new representation of those subjectivities as layered in a specific way. Deep intersubjectivity has made its appearance in storytelling in modern culture, and it has altered our sense of self and community and the discourses that construct and reflect them. To conceptualize credibly this sea change in narrative practices requires a different kind of reading of consciousness, a re-formed phenomenological reading, by means of a poststructuralist phenomenology, or at least a phenomenology attuned to poststructuralist questions that also attends to the situating of reader and text in a gendered world of class, race, and political power.

The most helpful theorist of languages, body, and consciousnesses in this project is the French philosopher Maurice Merleau-Ponty, whose intricate reflections on the interfolding of (and gaps within) perceptions and discourses also suggests Mikhail Bakhtin's thoughts about words amidst multiple intentionalities. In Merleau-Ponty, the "chiasm" of subjectivities is a knot that joins and separates bodies and their incarnated subjects. For Bakhtin, we always (and only) find words in the mouths of others, from whom we appropriate them for our own purposes, but without cleansing them of all traces of their source. From both writers we can begin to understand intersubjectivity as an experience of opacities and transparencies. But it is Merleau-Ponty who theorizes the new complex intersubjectivity—more than a hundred years after it altered the nature of narrative—with its dazzling, receding series of blindnesses and insights.[1] Merleau-Ponty enables a kind of phenomenological reading—hence the title of this chapter, "Starting Over"—without the assumptions about transcendental consciousness and transparent texts that characterized and later discredited an earlier generation's "criticism of consciousness."[2]

Reframing our reading of intersubjectivity—more accurately, intersubjectivities—matters because something new in narrative is transpiring in that bakery shop in Bath, among Anne and Elizabeth and Wentworth, something so fundamental that it has been difficult to grasp and describe. My project is to propose a newly useful phenomenology of narrative that can describe these changes in narrative practice and to trace some of the implications of these changes.

STARTING OVER: INTERSUBJECTIVITY AND NARRATIVE

The new conventions of narration presuppose notions of the subject, self, and character that are not only Lockean or Lacanian, but both. The self does not precede others, barricaded inside its senses, so that defending against a potentially isolating solipsism becomes a major, or even impossible, task. Nor is the subject *only* others, a hall of mirrors reflecting images of itself and others that from the "mirror phase" on it internalizes and mimics in the performance (to itself and to others) of having a self. Subjects are both: a body, an experience of that body and its gestures, an intentionality grounded in that body—*and* a mirroring of other bodies, gestures, experiences, and discourses. This mirroring leads to more reflections, and reflections of reflections, often obscured and muddy, always mediated. Yet this mediation leads not to a Lacanian collapse of consciousness into the signifier, but to an experience of an embodied community, of a partial and always partly blinded transcendence of the subject body. Merleau-Ponty is the poet and student of these paradoxes. He moves us beyond our contemporary experience of the stubborn impasse between the claims of the subject and the object, the impasse between defenders of word and world, between claimants for the omnipotence of the signified or, in poststructuralism's heyday, of the signifier. He moves us beyond not by means of transcendence or leaps of faith but by means of the body, as he explains in a chapter (of his last, unfinished book) tellingly titled "The Intertwining—the Chiasm":

> It is said that the colors, the tactile reliefs given to the other, are for me an absolute mystery, forever inaccessible. This is not completely true; for me to have not an idea, an image, nor a representation, but as it were the imminent experience of them, it suffices that I look at a landscape, that I speak of it with someone. Then, through the concordant operation of his body and my own, what I see passes into him, this individual green of the meadow under my eyes invades his vision without quitting my own, I recognize in my green his green, as the custom officer recognizes suddenly in a traveler the man whose description he had been given. (*Visible* 142)

Merleau-Ponty expands on this notion of knottedness in the earlier *Phenomenology of Perception,* with appropriate undertones of the knot as knitting together, reversing directions, and problematic b(l)inding.

> The phenomenological world is not pure being, but the sense . . . where my own and other people's [experiences] intersect and engage each other like gears. It is thus inseparable from subjectivity and intersubjectivity. . . . We witness

every minute the miracle of related experiences . . . for we are ourselves this network of relationships. (*Phenomenology* xx)

Here lurks a new paradigm for narrative and for readings of narrative. This paradigm makes no claims for transparency of consciousness or discourse: The speaker does not possess the other's image or even a representation of the other's image of the landscape, but through the "operation of his body and my own" the speaker recognizes "in my green his green," in a moment of perception that is "imminent" (not *immanent*), and even imminent "as it were." The enfoldings of discourses and gestures point beyond the binary of the lonely subject and the only other. Despite all Merleau-Ponty's emphasis upon discourse, language, and the limits of representation, the signifier nonetheless limps, by way of its own body, toward the signified.

> If my left hand can touch my right hand while it palpates the tangibles, can touch it touching, can turn its palpation back upon it, why, when touching the hand of another, would I not touch in it the same power to espouse the things that I have touched in my own? It is true the "things" in question are my own . . . [but] when one of my hands touches the other, the world of each opens upon that of the other because the operation is reversible at will. (*Visible* 140–41)

As Merleau-Ponty elaborates his gestural, embodied, and yet decoding intersubjectivity, not only does he provide a kind of solution to, or at least respite from, the endless contemporary theoretical inquiry, which is first, word or world? (because he allows us to retain the signifier, discourse, *and* the body, and who is to say which engenders which?), but he also makes it possible to theorize in a new way about the history of narrative. That is, we can now think about a new complex intersubjectivity and note its appearance in the history of storytelling.

The link between complex intersubjectivity and narrative is implicit in Merleau-Ponty's paradoxical approach to consciousness (paradoxical because it combines a postmodern sense of gaps and mediation with a confidence in self-presence that seems almost Cartesian). The paradox of consciousness, in which narrative will play a role, begins with the way the subject, "the tacit *cogito*, the presence of oneself to oneself, being no less than existence, is *anterior to any philosophy,* and knows itself only in those extreme situations in which it is under threat: for example, in the *dread of death*" (*Phenomenology* 404). This given self-presence functions by way of gaps, absences, and the fractures of perceptions of the other and others. But Merleau-Ponty's decentering is not Lacanian. For Lacan, the mirror image a child perceives "situates the agency of the ego, before its social determination, in a *fictional* direction" (2) (my emphasis). Lacan continues,

> [T]he *mirror stage* is a drama whose internal thrust is precipitated from insufficiency to anticipation—and which manufactures for the subject, caught up in the lure of spatial identification, the succession of phantasies that extends from a fragmented body-image to a form of its totality that I shall call orthopaedic—and lastly, to the assumption of the armour of an alienating identity, which will mark with its rigid structure the subject's entire mental development. (4)

Or, as Jonathan Lee explains it, the subject's "fragile and largely illusory identity is essentially bound up with the existence of others" and is "mediated by others, in particular by images of others," so that in a sense "identity" is an "armour that prevents a grasp of anything beyond its inner world" (Lee 23, 26, 23).[3] For Merleau-Ponty, subjectivity is always also intersubjectivity, but not in a way that erases that anterior experience of being a consciousness.

Narrative is intimately linked to subjectivity because the force that finally limits the centrifuge of the shattered cogito of postmodernism in Merleau-Ponty is time experienced in bodies and, more specifically, time in the form of intersubjective narrative. Subjects evolve in sequences, in narratives of recognition (however partial and muddied), espousal, and, yes, sometimes fear (why is that customs officer watching for a particular traveler?). The subject is stories, embodied and exchanged around "the circle of the touched and the touching" (*Visible* 143). Narrative permeates Merleau-Ponty's language itself through and through: If (as I claim) a new shape for representing consciousnesses has made storytelling more intricately intersubjective, this new intersubjectivity is itself, in its constituting structure, narrative: "[M]y own and other people's [experiences] intersect and engage each other like gears." The intersecting and engaging can occur only in time and narrative; there is always a story here. After all, the customs officer did recognize—however fortuitous and absurd the moment of insight—the traveler whom he had been awaiting.

By defining a kind (or kinds) of narrative of complex intersubjectivity, I want to work in two directions: first, to practice a renewed and reframed phenomenological reading that may be germane nowadays, in my concern with the representations of consciousnesses and the profound cultural work they do in stories. Phenomenological criticism has recently attracted more readers because, perhaps, as one response to the stringencies of both deconstruction and cultural studies it returns to the human subject or, in my case to human subjects, even if they are also always already written *and* writing. A renewed phenomenological criticism can posit consciousness as both spoken and speaking, as mediated by and preceding discourses. Second, this reading writes its own story of a fundamental and profound shift in the way narratives are constructed, at least narratives in English, which crystallized at the end of the eighteenth century. In these two senses, my project is about starting over.

THE DISAPPEARANCE OF THE TRANSPARENT WORD

Given how postwar phenomenological criticism lost credibility in the 1970s, I feel the need to protest what this study does *not* assume. The most influential "critics of consciousness" in the 1960s were Georges Poulet and his young colleague J. Hillis Miller, and both approached writing as if language were a transparent medium through which an author's consciousness and a reader's could meet and join in an almost mystical sense. Poulet once described the process this way: "In short, the extraordinary fact in the case of a book is the falling away of the barriers between you and it. You are inside it; it is inside you; there is no longer either outside or inside" (Macksey and Donato 57). In fairness to Poulet, I should add that this joining does not erase the reader's "I" or self-awareness, but when reading, "the subjective principle which I call *I* is modified in such a way that I no longer have the right, strictly speaking, to consider it as my *I*. I am on loan to another, and this other thinks, feels, suffers, and acts within me" (60).

In the almost forty years since the publication of those lines, the shadow of several scepticisms has fallen across Poulet's sunny hopes; his faith in the transparency of the medium is now clouded by our stubborn attention to the signifier's thickness, by rhetoric's refusal to remain invisible, and by our stubborn attention to gendered, sexual, racial, and class identities in author, readers, and their cultural environments.[4] Vivian Sobchack vividly describes the experience of writing a book of phenomenological criticism, published in 1992, in the shadow of these clouds. Little understood and even less read, "phenomenology" was loosely conceived and associated with a multitude of precontemporary sins. It was regarded as idealist, essentialist, and ahistorical. It was also seen as extremely naive, making claims about "direct" experience precisely at a moment when contemporary theory was emphasizing the inaccessibility of direct experience and focused on the constitutive processes and mediating structures of language. (xiv)

The impressions that Sobchack outlines have some justification. It is difficult now to decide which of Poulet's beliefs in immediacy is the more surprising, his belief in the immediacy of the author or that of the unwillful, ungendered, declassed, and anonymous reader. The function of language, whether the author's or the reader's, is not in doubt for Poulet, as Frank Lentricchia observes in *After the New Criticism:* "[I]t is this [inaugurating] cogito [of the author], active and cogent, which somehow makes its way into discourse, through discourse, out the other side, and into the pure receptivity of the critic's 'inner vacuum' " (72). The assumption of the transparency of discourse (for both writer and reader) seems naive now, as Poulet and Miller explore the experience of space and time in, say, Henry James and Gerard Manley Hopkins. Yet Poulet and Miller (and others, like Jean Starobinski) produced work of remarkable generosity, carefully attentive to the writing at hand, as even Lentricchia admits, guided by an admirable ethic of readerly self-effacement before the writer's voice. This self-effacement echoes Lyotard's account of thinking in "Can Thought Go on without a Body?" as a "soliciting of emptiness, this evacuation" so that the body and its world may give themselves to us (83).

Attentiveness and generosity are possible as particular choices, and we can recognize them as part of the critic's performance and defend them as such, without implying that discourse is transparent. Indeed, my topic throughout this study is representation. It is marks on a page whose work I wish to examine. One of my guiding assumptions is a paradox, however, that representation claims to *recover presence,* while confessing to its artificiality as a kind of absence. The representation of subjectivities especially makes claims to presence because subjects, even in texts, famously have a way of desiring, of *intending,* and of focusing action and thought on the future. Hence the ease with which readers, in what has been seen as a kind of naïveté, discuss "characters" as if they were more than marks on the page, with histories, a subconscious, sometimes even a sequel. Complex intersubjectivity, as I describe it, raises the stakes in these controversies even further, as clusters of subjects intend in more and more intricate ways, often disarming even the most ascetically postmodern reader. For me to emphasize a fundamental (and mostly unrecognized) source of this disarming in new resources of *texts* is not a sceptical move. I believe texts matter deeply, and readers must decide for themselves how much and why they and we may need these new stories of complex intersubjectivity to write our lives. I do not seek to demystify the experience of reading the experience of intentionalities. But neither can I make the transcendental step myself, from representation to a space beyond the word where "there is no longer either outside or inside," or where, as Poulet continues, "this *I* who 'thinks in me' when I read a book is the *I* of the one who writes the book" (Macksey and Donato 61).

Another shortcoming of what we might call first-wave phenomenological criticism is its elaboration of idealized and abstracted consciousnesses—in an author, one largely detached from sociohistorical grounding, and in the reader, one free of gender, class, or ethnic experience. The result was sometimes a curiously faceless account of the consciousness represented in texts, as in Poulet's description of loss of self in "Henry James," that identity that all of James's writings add up to: "Nothing is more significant in Henry James than this loss of self caused by the very abundance of memories. If thought is disturbed and gets lost, it is not through diminution, it is through plethora" (*Metamorphoses* 308). In addition, the reading "I" that wills itself into submission to receive the writerly consciousness is as abstract in a way as this Jamesian "thought." This reading "I" is apparently beyond gender, class, or historical location, though its freedoms presuppose extensive privileges, such as the space and time to be will-less, and a considerable confidence in resuming control of the "I" again, that suggest other reservoirs of power. To address the politics of subjectivity and intersubjectivity must now be a fundamental component of a more conscious criticism of consciousness, to ask, what are the ideological moves of certain representations and of the reader of them. Such an address can avoid the occasionally "claustrophobic quality" that Daniel Schwarz, in *The Humanist Heritage,* finds in the readings of deconstruction and phenomenology that failed "to understand the fabric of social institutions, customs and conventions that constitute the context of English and American literature" (226). Nevertheless, a sense of the ways writing and reading are gendered and classed need not alter the wonderful generosity and attentiveness that mark the phenomenological criticism of Poulet and Hillis Miller, among others. The transcendental move is not essential and perhaps is even trivializing. Merleau-

Ponty returns us deeply and profoundly to the body, to subjectivities rooted in the flesh and in time and places.

A couple of instances can illuminate what is at stake in whatever approach we decide to take to what has been a tradition of transcendental intersubjectivity in phenomenology since Husserl. (I refer to the notion in Husserl that perceptions can be communicated to others, that knowledge among consciousnesses is possible, that the barriers of sensory apparatus and language between selves can be transcended.) The first example raises the question, what is the nature and function of desire in narrative? Poulet thematizes desire within the framework of a generalized human narrative (for "generalized" read free of specifics of gender, class, race, and sociopolitical structure), so that, for example, the poetry of Poe writes a story about sleep, dreams, loss, and death: "This is why the moment of awaking is for Edgar Allen Poe of paramount importance. It is the first moment of a new life. It is also the last of an old one" (*Metamorphoses* 184). For Hillis Miller, desire drives the narrative of a writer's body of work, and again the framework for this desire is formed by the broad ontological categories of time, space, and nature. "At the beginning Browning is a huge sea—massive, limitless, profound, but, at the same time, shapeless, fluid, capricious. . . . Browning can convey in his poetry an extraordinary sense of the way consciousness flows out through the senses, plunges into the secret substance of the surrounding world, knows it from the inside, as one's own viscera are known . . ." (*Disappearance of God* 81). A reader now is more likely to ask, "Whose senses, whose world, whose viscera?"

In contrast, students of subjectivity in texts now locate desire and narrative in specific, but also wider, terrain. The common use of geopolitical language, "terrain," "mapping," and "site," for example, points out the interest in providing more precise social and historical referents for any particular account of subjectivity. Another, more Foucauldian, motive for attention to specific cultural terrain is to decode indirect assumptions that guide or even write accounts of the subject, if not the subject itself; such decoding of ideological taken-for-granteds demystifies at least part of that micronetwork of categories along whose grid power is deployed. One assumption of these strategies is the subjection of subjectivity, as at the most extreme a "construction" of cultural forces whose "sites" and operation can be "mapped" and so surrounded, islanded as it were within borders of paper (the map) and so contained.

The most subtle cultural critics allow double roles to the subject, which is both mapped and mapping, both responding to and refining, redrawing, or even subverting ideology. Nancy Armstrong's *Desire and*

Domestic Fiction (1987), for example, deploys all of these strategies in accounting for the role of desire in narrative. For Armstrong, eighteenth- and nineteenth-century narratives rewrite the desiring self to produce powerfully gendered "figures of desire" that promote the sociopolitical agenda of capitalist society. Armstrong's "history of subjectivity" focuses then on very specific historical landscapes for the gendered subject. At the same time Armstrong allows for *some* agency to the writing consciousness, though its power to rewrite the self seems deeply compromised by the "political unconscious" it serves. Armstrong's argument is too complex to untangle briefly, but here is an example of these strategies at work in locating consciousness:

> It is because the Brontes have encouraged readers to seek out the meaning of fiction in a recognizably modern form of consciousness that their novels have played an important part in British history. . . . We can assume their fiction produced . . . figures of modern desire. These techniques have suppressed the political identity along with the knowledge of oneself as such. The production of the political unconscious has accompanied the production of the sexual subject, I believe, and in this way has constituted the repressive power actually exercised by a polite tradition of writing. (191)

The Brontës' fiction then does enormous cultural work, in this view, even if largely to produce a "particular form of consciousness . . . so important to the stability of a capitalist society" (ibid.). Such an approach to subjectivity has certainly rectified the imbalance in first-wave phenomenological criticism, in which gender, race, and political forces were simply not on the radar screen. The issue now is not so much transparency. Cultural critics like Nancy Armstrong and Mary Poovey believe they can read the signifier with a confidence similar to George Poulet's—but they see something else in it, or through it. Abstract, generalized accounts of desire and consciousness that, however specific to one writer, are generalized sociopolitically have given way to concretely gendered and historicized accounts.

My second example elaborates on these issues because it dramatizes how political indeed claims to represent consciousness are. In this example, a different sort of transcendental intersubjectivity raises its head—the claim not to transparency of language and selfhoods, but the claim to locate elements of human consciousness and culture that are "universal," particularly in relation to ethnicity, gender, and social class. This example is the controversy surrounding novelist Charles Johnson's use of phenomenology and Merleau-Ponty, specifically, to frame the problem of racial difference in American and African American literature and culture. For Johnson, fiction like his *Middle Passage* may begin with the experience of a particular "other," in this instance an African American experience of slavery, but it does not end there. Beyond difference is an encompassing humanity, as he explains in *Being and Race:* "To put this bluntly, language is transcendence. And so is fiction. They comport us 'other [sic] there' behind the eyes of others, into their hearts, which might make some few of us squeamish, for suddenly our subjectivity is merged with that of a stranger" (39).

The implications of this position for ethnic identity politics are explosive, as Johnson understands. "Doubters may object that it is racially impossible to strip themselves of their own historically acquired traits. Many black writers claim they cannot imagine what it is like to be white, that all they know is the 'black' experience. For my money, this objection is sheer laziness" (43). Johnson offers as a kind of philosophical authority for this transcendence not George Poulet, whose notion of "merging" is similar to Johnson's, but Merleau-Ponty, whose notion of intersubjectivity is much more complex: "[I]f we go deeply enough into a relative perspective, black or white, male or female, we encounter the transcendence of relativism; in Merleau-Ponty's terms, 'to retire into oneself is to leave oneself' " (44). Johnson then cites—and, as it turns out, significantly mis-cites—part of a paragraph from Merleau-Ponty's *Adventures of the Dialectic* that seems to describe an intersubjective "totality" of perceiving selves, a version of the transcendence of gender and race to which he has just appealed. The citation is useful enough, especially with its omissions silent and explicit, to give in its entirety:

> My own field of thought and action is made up of imperfect meanings badly defined and interrupted [sic]. They are completed over there, in the others who hold the key to them because they see sides of things that I do not see, as well as, one might say, my social back. Likewise, I am the only one capable of tallying the balance sheets of their lives, for their meanings are also incomplete and are openings onto something that I alone am able to see. I do not have to search far for the others; I find them in my experience, lodged in the hollows that show what they see and what I fail to see. Our experiences thus have lateral relationships of truth: all together, each possessing clearly what is secret to the other, in our combined functionings we form a totality which moves toward enlightenment and completion. . . . We are never locked in ourselves. (44)

Johnson flattens Merleau-Ponty's understanding of an intercorporeal "interworld," and it doesn't help that the very language he quotes from

Adventures of the Dialectic is actually a paraphrase by Merleau-Ponty of the thought of his contemporary Sartre, which Merleau-Ponty is criticizing precisely for the starkness of choices that Johnson replicates. Indeed, in a profound mistake, Johnson erases Sartre's voice in Merleau-Ponty's text by omitting the quotation marks around the phrase "imperfect meanings, badly defined and interrupted," words that Merleau-Ponty cites, in a careful footnote, from Sartre's "Reply to Claude Lefort" in *The Communists and Peace* (compare Johnson, p. 44, and Merleau-Ponty, *Adventures,* pp. 138 and 96). Whatever the similarities in Sartre's and Merleau-Ponty's accounts of the subject's phenomenological position, Merleau-Ponty's intention here is to separate himself from Sartre. Johnson misses this intention and quotes Merleau-Ponty's summary of Sartre's thought. For example, this phrase, which modifies the language Johnson cites, follows the last words, "We are never locked in ourselves": "However, the totality toward which we are going together, while it is being completed on one side, is being destroyed on the other" (*Adventures* 139). By omitting the "however" and its succeeding qualification, Johnson distorts Merleau-Ponty's analysis dramatically. And two sentences further comes another complicating reflection: "The open, incompleted meanings that we see in the social world . . . are nearly empty diagrams. . . . These meanings lead an anonymous life among things" (*Adventures* 139). The symmetries of misreading here are remarkable: Johnson has gerrymandered Merleau-Ponty's account of Sartre so that it articulates the transcendentalist position that both Merleau-Ponty and Sartre, for different reasons and in different ways, rejected.

That is, Johnson misreads not only this citation but also Merleau-Ponty's approach to deep intersubjectivity generally. Merleau-Ponty's emphasis on the body, on language as gesture, and on gesture as language ensures the conclusion that although *some* degree of transcendental intersubjectivity between embodied selves is possible, a merging of subjectivities in the realm of universal human experience is not possible. Yes, there is what Merleau-Ponty calls an "interworld" (*Adventures* 200), but our participation in it is fragmentary. Merleau-Ponty articulates this subtle in-betweenness: For two subjectivities, each intending toward the other, "there is woven between us an 'exchange,' a 'chiasm between two "destinies" . . .' in which there are never quite two of us, and yet one is never alone" (*In Praise* 82). Subjectivities are not hopelessly isolated inside body and language, yet neither is an ideal fusion possible. Later on I discuss the function of the image of the wall in Merleau-Ponty, but here I hint at the significance for Merleau-Ponty of a boundary that subjectivities construct together and that both connects and separates.

Because of the politics of multiculturalism in the United States, an appeal to the "universal" or transcendentally human often provokes dismay, anger, and accusations of betrayal. As George Kent observed long ago, the word "universal" has often seemed to be a code word for "white" in American cultural criticism (11). Or to assert the need to "transcend" race can seem to minimize the sufferings and aims of ethnic peoples, whose political efforts and language could be read to concentrate on the less "universal." Molly Abel Travis phrases the challenge to Johnson this way: "Is Johnson's notion of cultural synthesis simply another form of assimilation in which the dominant culture swallows up marginalized cultures?" (191) For Travis, Johnson's use of phenomenology devalues otherness ("Charles Johnson has advised his fellow African American writers 'to move from narrow complaint to broad celebration. . . .'") and sabotages efforts to write the story so that readers must experience the discomforts of difference in African American lives: "Johnson's novel [*Middle Passage*] seeks to transcend race and to suppress the feminine . . . and establishes a middle ground, a neutral space that denies the marginal and offers readers the familiar and the unthreatening" (190, 181, 193). "Intersubjectivity" has become another code word in this debate for "universal" and for a kind of de-differentiated human experience, almost an essence. It has become most definitely a political sign, even, or perhaps most, when Johnson believes he has moved beyond a political sphere.

"Transparency" and "transcendence" are sites, as they say, of powerful ideological contests. One result of the intensity of these contests is the tendency of competing voices to polarize positions, so that for example transparency becomes an all-or-nothing matter: no intermediate shades of opacity allowed. Either one can read and possess the word and the Other, or one is barred from intercourse, left only with Scrabble tiles to shuffle and peer at. It is precisely this stark set of choices about readability that Merleau-Ponty sought so poignantly to complicate, and to the degree he senses this revisionism, Johnson appeals to Merleau-Ponty fairly. Some critics have recognized more recently the dangers of essentializing otherness so completely that white people cannot "read" African American texts, or straight people gay writers, for example (those in positions of apparent power especially are unable to read texts of the marginalized). One thread in Eve Kosofsky Sedgwick's study of the paradoxical articulations of sex/class/gender/sexuality in contemporary culture is the costs and the rewards of "identification with/as"—even when (or if) that cross-reading can with enormous difficulty be achieved—for, say, feminist straight women reading feminist lesbian texts (62). But Sedgwick's work is a testament of faith in the face of that "if," that "as a woman; as a fat woman; as a nonprocreative adult; as someone who is, under several different discursive regimes, a sexual pervert; and, under some, a Jew," she can yet in some competent way read words by nonwomen, non-fat persons, non-Jews (63).

As these two case histories suggest, claims to represent subjectivities carry powerful ideological freight, for several reasons. These claims are usually accompanied by images and their narratives, which offer descriptions of qualities, behaviors, and even what may seem to be "essences" within subjects whose gendered, sexualized, or ethnicized formation is a much-contested topic. These subjectivities used to be situated on the edges of mainstream discourse and power but are no longer, as suggested by the widespread interest recently in what Joseph Boone calls the "crisis in male subjectivity—the crisis that by definition is occidental masculinity itself" (104). Laura Doyle argues eloquently about the gendering effects of hierarchicalized paradigms of subjectivity:

> The ideology of mind over body, as we have seen, keeps the mother in her contained place as bodily producer of racialized bodies which themselves take their fixed places in the mind-body social and labor hierarchy. But if one collapses the distinction between mind and body, between subject and object, one begins to bankrupt the function of the race mother, for one begins to withdraw the capital invested in her differentiating body. (76)

One need not subscribe fully to any particular politics to see and endorse the "disruptive" potential of a "phenomenology of intercorporeality" (ibid.). Claims to represent *inter*subjectivities are also deeply political because they invariably project implications for rapprochement (or its absence) between self and other, between different others, and for community within narrative, with its inevitable analogies to community outside of texts.

Merleau-Ponty provides a model for an approach to subjectivity and intersubjectivity that claims that language and consciousness are neither characteristically transparent nor opaque. That is, I would like to reclaim some of the virtues of first-wave phenomenological criticism, while attending not only to claims for the groundedness of consciousnesses in the body and in cultural contexts and history, but also to traces of these grounded subjectivities that surface in texts, in the writers that write them (or in the communities that construct them, in the case of film), and in their readers (or, in the case of this book's later chapters, their viewers). Merleau-Ponty was probably more interested in resisting the solipsism inherent in Enlightenment empiricism than he was in resisting a kind of transcendental idealism. Nevertheless, his emphasis on chiasm and the mediatedness of perception will be a helpful corrective to the yearning for "union" that is emerging as one thread in efforts to redress what are perceived as the excesses of deconstruction.[5] It will remind us that the Derridian challenge to the transparent Logos, whatever its excesses, has taught us something as well.

In a rough sense, critical movements of the past fifty years have carried us from some notions of discourse's transparency, whether Poulet's, or the New Critics' with their confidence in poetry's rhetorical structure, or the historical positivists', through (so to speak) the opacity of the Derridean signifier, to the body. Thinking the body, writing the body, performing the body, and their inverses, the body thinking and writing and performing, constitute the paradoxes of contemporary literary and cultural studies, especially in their feminist voices. I say paradoxes because the issue of origination is still deeply unresolved: Which is first, word or world, discourse or self, language or the body, performance or consciousness(es)? Does culture write the subject, or the reverse? Or does each manipulate discourse? Merleau-Ponty's rejection of these questions and their enabling binary in his pursuit of a deeper grasp of the embodiment of consciousnesses can be enormously helpful at this juncture, as I suggested before, in at least two ways: by offering another way of reading, now, and by allowing us to decode, through that way of reading, the dramatic rewriting of intersubjectivity in the last two hundred years.

But before I describe the paradigm for a new reading of complex intersubjectivity, the vexed matter of the *subject* requires some attention.

THE SUBJECT: PERFORMANCE OR EMBODIMENT?

Subjectivity, its origins and constituting elements, calls forth the most interesting and problematic reflections of recent cultural criticism. What is this agency, or experience of agency, this force that seems to generate images, conversations, and stories? The initiating (and initiated) narrative emerges: We can see the residue of the act of initiation in the part-issue plans for *Little Dorrit* as a pen scratches out the earlier title, *Nobody's Fault,* and in the storyboards for *North by Northwest,* where another pen draws a line for Thornhill's flight away from the pursuing crop duster. In recent years better understandings and more subtle speculations have evolved about the elements within that initiation: the role of discourse and symbolic systems in the formation of the child's consciousness; the mysteries of the unconscious and its shaping within the psychosexual matrix of the family; the material circumstances of social class and ethnicity that affect writer, publisher, film studios, readers, and viewers; economic constrictions and possibilities; micronetworks of assumptions about sexuality and difference that inform genre and audience—to name only the most significant topics.

For other critics, subjectivity is chimerical, especially in twentieth-century texts. One context for this study is the postmodern uncertainty about or even disappearance of the self. The loss of the self can be cause for mourning or celebration, as Gabriele Schwab writes: "Instead of mourning the loss of the self, poststructuralism and deconstruction privilege experimental fragmentations and (dis)figurations of language as open and dynamic processes of textualization" (5). Schwab distinguishes between the death of the subject and what may be (simply) its decentering. That is, what has been lost is a style (and I would add, a kind of storytelling) and the centering this style gave to the self. "The rhetoric of the end of the subject is, of course, directed against conventional notions of a subject defined as a bounded unity . . ." (ibid.). Schwab's project is to recuperate subjectivity, especially a de-differentiated, fragmented self whose apparent dispersal may in fact "be a precondition for the flexibility and processual development of its boundaries" (11). But for the unbelieving reader, for whom the self is a fiction, or a series of fictions, intersubjectivity, except in the most mechanical, operational sense, must also be fictional, and for that reader this study may be a nostalgic account of a peculiar century (more or less) of faith, with its peculiar and recalcitrant remnant of twenty-first-century believers.

But reports of the death of the subject have been greatly exaggerated. The performance of the body, pressing pen or typewriter key or camera switch, is too difficult to explain, like trying to understand how Pinocchio's carved sticks began to move. The semiotics of performance helps to illuminate the depth of particular gestures and their fields of encoding, as in Erving Goffman's study of microperformances in *Relations in Public,* for example, which clarifies the choreographies of shared spaces. However, the puzzle of agency, of intentionality, remains. I use "intentionality" in a somewhat broader sense than our daily usage;

it incorporates not only the idea of conscious choices and purposiveness, but also the quality of consciousness that leans *toward* the world, that believes something, wishes for, works for. If you will, it is the "aboutness" of consciousness. Because the puzzle of intentionality remains, the body as mapped *and* mapping is a paradox in its roles as cultural, literary, and cinematic agent and product. Bodies display and enact intention, both outside of texts (as when they write them) and inside them; yet bodies are, manifestly, made as well as making—made biologically (out of a host of forces, genetic to environmental) and culturally (fed, schooled, gartered, belted, and trimmed to cues from a series of scripts). Embodiment only extends the double cues signaled by the word *subject* itself, the sign for a center of feeling and consciousness that also signifies subordination, as in subject to law, queen or (more usually) king, or fate.

Because my interest is in the *representations* of subjectivities, I can grant two discrete foundational principles that can be not only discrete but also logically inconsistent with each other. First, representations (and their initiating intentions) do cultural work and are also the products of previous cultural work (and workers). Second, various narratives imply, exhibit, and even articulate assumptions about subjectivities and their origins, assumptions or ideologies or beliefs that may resist or deny the implications of some sociohistorical data about their production. That is, narratives act in the world and may be more than the sum of their apparent environmental causes. I grant the power of circumstances, that stories are to some degree contingent—and contemporary cultural-historical study has written large these contingencies. But my interest is in narratives as agents and in stories' structures and assumptions about subjectivities that give this agency its power.

A specific approach to the origins of the subject underlies this study of represented subjectivities. However powerful the forces of discourse (in the form of class, gender, "race"—power in its myriad expressions), the subject is more than an absence, a series of lacks, to be written by those forces. The subject is always already embodied in the world, as action and speech that incarnate intention, so that the structuralist binary of word versus world, like the binary of subject versus other, is largely deceptive. This principle explains why Merleau-Ponty rejects both questions—does culture write the subject, or the reverse? Merleau-Ponty prepares to articulate this approach when he paraphrases, in his essay "The Child's Relation with Others," the very different approach of Lacan (the immediate topic is the mirror phase):

> To use Dr. Lacan's terms, I am "captured, caught up" by my spatial image. Thereupon I leave the reality of my lived *me* in order to refer myself constantly to the ideal, fictitious, or imaginary *me*, of which the specular image is the first outline. In this sense I am torn from myself, and the image in the mirror prepares me for another still more serious alienation, which will be the alienation from others. (*Primacy* 136)

Lacanian critic Kaja Silverman emphasizes not so much loss, but the absence, the lack, which is the subject initially. She writes in *Male Subjectivity at the Margins*, "the images within which the subject 'finds' itself always come to it from outside," and she cites Lacan's conception of the ego as " 'the superimposition of various coats borrowed from . . . the bric-a-brac of its props department' " (6–7). Later, when she writes about World War II cinema, she returns to images of (violent) loss: "A number of films made in Hollywood between 1944 and 1947 attest with unusual candor to the castrations through which the male subject is constituted—to the pound of flesh which is his price of entry into the symbolic order" (52). But for Merleau-Ponty, the tragic narrative of loss in Lacan is replaced by a comic narrative, or at least tragicomic, of recovery amidst, yes, some experience of separation:

> The body is at once present in the mirror and present at the point where I feel it tactually. But if this is the case, the two aspects that are to be coordinated are not really separated in the child and are in no way separated in the sense in which all objects are separated in adult perception. (*Primacy* 139–40)

Among the enormous intricacies of Merleau-Ponty's reading of Lacan and Freud, a few strands stand out for our purposes: The subject is not an absence, but from the beginning an embodied potential. The problem with Lacan's mirror-phase scenario is that, in focusing on the image in the mirror, Lacan forgets the weight, the presence of the body in front of the mirror. So, the choice between origins of subjectivity in culture or the body is a false choice, and the response "Both" also ratifies the misleading binary. Instead, for Merleau-Ponty, consciousness (however nascent in focus and capacity) is always already embodied in culture, and especially in others, yet is self-sustaining as a stance, as intentionality directed from a place (a body) to the world. In *The Address of the Eye*, Vivian Sobchack gives an extended and extraordinary meditation on Merleau-Ponty, as foundation for her approach to film, and in the course of that meditation observes that Merleau-Ponty transforms the darkness of Lacan by contextualizing the specular alienation of the mirror encounter within a primordial and immanent knowledge the infant always already possesses—a knowledge of the subjective body lived perceptively from within as "mine." . . . That is, the mirror encounter is less an originating act of *meconnaissance* (mis-taken knowledge) than of *reconnaissance* (knowledge re-taken in a different modality). This *reconnaissance* or reflective knowledge is the infant's awareness that the subjective body can be perceived from without as well as lived perceptively from within. (119)

Note Sobchack's emphasis on "immanent" rather than "imminent" knowledge, a difference with essentialist and transcendental overtones. This emphasis reminds us that the siren song, or at least a siren hum, of idealism still lingers seductively in the middle distance of some phenomenological criticism. Indeed, readers hear this tone in the later Merleau-Ponty of *The Visible and the Invisible,* even though this work sought to move beyond the vestiges of Cartesian dualism in his own earlier writing. Fred Evans and Leonard Lawlor see a thread in Merleau-Ponty that speaks for a "univocity of being," a gestalt that reins in the world's chaos (10, 11), and Françoise Dastur quotes Sartre's sardonic comment on Merleau-Ponty: "Reading him at times, it would seem that being invents man in order to make itself manifest through him" (Evans and Lawlor 47). Merleau-Ponty's exposition of the chiasm does sometimes speak of reciprocity between world and subject, as well as between subjects, as if the inanimate world were part of some "immanent," but larger, consciousness. Yet he wished to avoid Husserl's transcendental idealism, though some Husserl scholars see in the later, unpublished, "other" Husserl a more poststructuralist voice, one that Husserl himself hoped would correct the misreading of his phenomenology by those who had fallen back into "the old philosophical naivete."[6]

Whatever the truth about Husserl's work, Merleau-Ponty certainly wished to avoid an appeal to a universal ground of being beyond the embodied subject. He rejected Husserl's transcendental reduction or "bracketing," the well-known notion of separating the *content* of perception from the *experience* of perception, with one effect of eventually identifying a universal field of experience, what he called the transcendental ego, that lies outside individual perceptions. Yet Merleau-Ponty seems to allow for a more limited reduction, one that can identify a kind of "qualified essence" made up of the common "thematic" threads in a community's expression in the bodies of its experiences (Sobchack 45). This edging back toward some universal essence, even if of embodied experiences, allows Evans and Lawlor to speak of an extension of Merleau-Ponty's thought into a notion of the "absolute Other" that would "take advantage of all the religious senses attached to Merleau-Ponty's philosophy" (14).

This version of embodiment allows Sobchack to speak of the phenomenology of film as an exchange of consciousnesses between screen and viewer, by means of a "body" and intentionality that both film and spectator possess: "Although I am not suggesting exact correspondences between the development of the cinema and human lived-bodies, I am suggesting certain broad similarities between them..." (251). Garrett Stewart sees in Sobchack's phenomenology an "absolutist" stance and reminds us again of the tendency for phenomenology to slide back into versions of an older idealism, and not only, I would add, in film criticism (123). I also discussed earlier, in footnote 5, what might seem to be excessively transcendental yearnings in Sobchack and Merleau-Ponty. But I am less interested than Stewart and Stanley Cavell (and André Bazin before them, among others) in the debate over the ontological status of subjectivity and image in visual culture.[7] This debate occurs in the context of what we now call reader-response theory, in the argument over (in Stewart's words) the "phenomenological thrall of cinema, its illusion of existential immanence" for *viewers* (104).

Audience response is one angle of phenomenological inquiry, but it is not my angle, at least not now. The way in which the consumer experiences as "real" the story, the film, the photograph, or the frieze/freeze frame (one of Stewart's major topics) is beyond this book, and my hunch is that lots of different readers and viewers produce lots of different "realities" in their experience. I want to look at narratives and rescue a chiasmic subjectivity (actually, subjectivities), an enfleshed agency, as a credible assumption within those narratives (whatever their ontological frame). It has been difficult to see such subjectivities in recent years, given the discredited essentialisms of the past and the current scepticisms of either Lacanian or Foucauldian readers.

So I prefer the Merleau-Ponty of imminence, ironized by "as it were" (see p. 5 above). My emphasis is quite different from Vivian Sobchack's, but I am grateful for her attentive reading of Merleau-Ponty's phenomenology of the body at a time when such readings in narrative studies were rare and unfashionable. Whatever Merleau-Ponty's true thoughts about immanent transcendence, I choose to concentrate on the language that avoids both the transcendentalism that has discredited so much phenomenological criticism and the narrative of the fragmented self, the Lacanian story of loss and aloneness. Laura Doyle, in her recent book, *Bordering on the Body,* reads the Lacanian narrative and Merleau-Ponty's rereading in a way similar to Sobchack's and mine:

> [Lacanian] theorists are seduced by the tragic drama and heart-breaking romance of [the] split [between mothers and language, mothers and maturity, and mothers and author/ity]. . . . Body and language *must* part, it seems. . . . I suggest, by contrast . . . that this Lacanian drama of splitting is a social mirage which critics sometimes come to believe is fact; and that another phenomenology [of Merleau-Ponty] offers modern critics the terms for narrating another story. (Preface, unnumbered)

In Doyle's view the Lacanian drama, as adopted by many influential Lacanian critics, has proved so powerful an account of subjectivity (perhaps especially in modernist and postmodernist culture) that it has dominated many quarters of cultural studies. There are other paradigms, even other versions of Lacan, though in my view the role of the body never becomes important enough. Nevertheless, Lacan's later thought gives a larger role to "the real," the rupturing force outside any language system that Jonathan Lee identifies with the unconscious. Lee even cites one moment in which Lacan identified it with the body: "[T]he real is 'the mystery of the speaking body' " (135–36). Lee explains: "One way, then, to approach Lacan's later thought is to see him trying to make a philosophically and scientifically satisfying case against the claims of linguistic idealism by showing that any such closed idealistic system simply cannot handle the paradoxical ruptures that crisscross it" (136).[8]

Slavoj Zizek meditates at length on the paradoxes of what Lee calls the "impossible real," how the "answers of the real" function in symbolic systems: "The role of the Lacanian real is, however, radically ambiguous: true, it erupts in the form of a traumatic return, derailing the balance of our daily lives, but it also serves as a support of this very balance" (29). And so, Zizek continues, "This 'answer of the real' is necessary for intersubjective communication to take place. There is no symbolic communication without some 'piece of the real' to serve as a kind of pawn guaranteeing its consistency" (30). But there is not enough of the body, so far as I can see, in Lacan or Zizek or in Kaja Silverman's recent efforts to "flesh out" Lacanian theory.[9] So I turn to Merleau-Ponty, primarily, with occasional cues drawn from other students of the phenomenology of bodies like Bakhtin and, later, Erving Goffman. For my study, the subject in stories begins in a body, where an experience of its agency, intentionality, and enworldedness in culture and discourse *precede* and are already the ground for our work with narrative.

The subject is furthermore already subjects. That is, subjectivity is fundamentally intersubjective. Embodied experience, with its kind of presence and fullness, takes its shape in primordial ways by contact with others. As Merleau-Ponty phrases it, "For we must consider the relation with others *not only as one of the contents of our experience but as an actual structure in its own right*" (*Primacy* 140; original emphasis). Sobchack's summation emphasizes again the contrast with Lacan: "Merleau-Ponty's system accounts for *subjectivity as intersubjectivity*, whereas Lacan's schema accounts for *subjectivity as objectified*" (123). And so the question of origins has taken us, tangoing sideways, from subjectivity to intersubjectivity. There is no clean line to separate the subject and the intersubjective, their origins or consequences, in narratives in fiction and film, or in narratives about the production of these narratives, that is, in stories about writers, audiences, and film studios. In this project our primary "knowledge" about origins will be narratives about origins, whether Lacan's or Freud's or Henry James's. These narratives become more and more intersubjective in a particular and complex way. My subject then is the embedded and embodied consciousnesses of modern narrative—modern, that is, since about 1700—and how their representations have fundamentally and profoundly changed.

THE NEW INTERSUBJECTIVITY: ESPOUSAL, SHAME, AND THE QUARREL BETWEEN MERLEAU-PONTY AND SARTRE

> *I . . . feel myself moved by my appearance in the gaze of others and . . . I in turn reflect an image of them that can affect them, so that there is woven between us an "exchange," a "chiasm between two 'destinies'" . . . in which there are never quite two of us, and yet one is never alone.*
> —MERLEAU-PONTY, In Praise of Philosophy

> *And though there was no second glance to disturb her, though [Henry's] object seemed then to be only quietly agreeable, she could not get the better of her embarrassment, heightened as it was by the idea of his perceiving it.*
> —AUSTEN, Mansfield Park

When Fanny becomes the target of the gaze in *Mansfield Park*, as the victim of Henry's generosity, she experiences a special kind of invasion.

STARTING OVER: INTERSUBJECTIVITY AND NARRATIVE | 25

When Henry looks at Fanny, he endangers her in an extraordinary way: "[S]he saw his eye glancing for a moment at her necklace [his gift]—with a smile—she thought there was a smile—which made her blush and feel wretched" (II, 10; 274). The danger is not only the smile and the arrogance of anticipated possession it probably implies. It is also the residue of that look that Austen traces to decipher a more complex threat in a series of exchanged gestures—exchanged regardless of whether Fanny wants to be part of that commerce. Fanny cannot regain her composure because her embarrassment is extended in the mirror of Henry's eye "by the idea of his perceiving it." Glances are exchanged in the heated air of the ballroom, but they are also exchanged in the interior theater of subjects who embody each other, even against their will or the will of one. Fanny's image of herself is deeply implicated in Henry's first look at her and also in his *second* look, which absorbs and acknowledges her response—her blush—to the first look. The mere idea that Henry continues to observe her response to him paralyzes Fanny, so that she is rescued only when Henry turns away "to someone else" to concentrate on another human subject. The astonishing power of this scene lies partly in Austen's ability to articulate the frightening interiority of the intersubjective. The form of this articulation is extraordinarily significant because it reshapes our narrative of experience.

A sea change in the representation of consciousnesses in narratives in English becomes visible in the time of Jane Austen. It is a change so subtle and fundamental that it has been difficult to conceive and describe. It is a structural change in what we take for granted, like the new articulation of consciousness that Eric Havelock argues for in Plato's language. One aspect of the change has received careful attention in recent years: the move into the interior of the self. Critics as diverse as Erich Kahler, Dorrit Cohn, Elizabeth Ermarth, and, more recently, Carol Rifelj have recounted the strategies by which novels have turned "inward," yet through conventions of what Cohn calls "transparency" simultaneously to triumph over the solipsism that had seemed to separate self and other, a triumph enabled especially by the newly powerful omniscient narrator, and to generate a sort of consensus about the world. The other has still remained in some ways another country, especially when difference is filtered by gender, class, or ethnicity. Nonetheless, it has been possible to imagine the language and story that the other constructs within and to translate that experience as imagined for the privileged reader.

The new conventions of transparency have allowed narrators to calibrate different subtleties of distance and nearness, as narratives modulate their focus from first to third person and chart a range of otherness, close or far from the reader, more or less obscured. Even monstrosity yields to this translation of the interior, as when the novel takes us inside Victor Frankenstein's creation as he learns to read, or inside Dickens's Bradley Headstone as he relives the attempted murder of Wrayburn. What Tristram Shandy yearned for and yet feared, Momus's window onto the soul set like a piece of glass into the body of the other, appears in his century like a dream made real in the body of the novel.

Yearning and fear—these are two of the key responses to the effects of the new complex intersubjectivity. They represent the fundamental disagreement between Jean-Paul Sartre and his contemporary Maurice Merleau-Ponty over the nature of the intersubjective. Because both Sartre and Merleau-Ponty were deeply interested in the phenomenology of the other, this difference suggests, for them and this study, profound implications for the politics and aesthetics of intersubjectivity in narrative. For Sartre, the other is primarily a cause for a deep suspicion, even terror; for Merleau-Ponty, the other is primarily an occasion for companionship, "espousal," in a world people occupy together, however separately. This quarrel over the effects of the intersubjective recurs in many of the narratives in this study.

However, something else deepens the exemplary moments extracted from *Mansfield Park* and *Persuasion* earlier in this chapter. It is a fundamentally different representation not only of consciousness, but also of consciousness*es*, of a newly framed intersubjectivity, which Jane Austen's novels are among the first in English to speak of clearly in this new language within a language.[10] Some further theorizing of intersubjectivity would be helpful at this point. A good place to begin is J. Hillis Miller's description of what he claimed was a new rendering of human experience in nineteenth-century novels:

> In Victorian novels, for the most part, the characters are aware of themselves in terms of their relations to others. . . . The protagonist comes to know himself and to fulfill himself by way of other people. A characteristic personage in a Victorian novel could not say, "I think, therefore I am," but rather, if he could ever be imagined to express himself so abstractly, "I am related to others, therefore I am," or, "I am conscious of myself as conscious of others." . . . A Victorian novel may most inclusively be defined as a structure of interpenetrating minds. (5)

What exactly does it mean to say that the representation of human consciousness had become intersubjective? According to some criticisms of

Hillis Miller's book, its formulations were so general as to apply to virtually all novels.[11] Intersubjectivity does not seem to be a useful formal principle for understanding narrative if it deteriorates into the unremarkable notion that characters and even narrators perceive themselves by way of others. Miller himself admits that intersubjectivity is the stuff of all fiction and argues (only) that there is more of it in nineteenth-century novels, in a form altered by certain forces: the sense of the disappearance of God and the omniscient narrator, to name the two most important (11, 31–34, e.g.). Miller is correct about changed intellectual and formal conditions, but not only the conditions have changed. The fundamental paradigm, the inner matrices and microorganizations of intersubjectivity (to borrow Foucauldian language), have shifted.

Representations and understandings of intersubjectivity are not new. Bakhtin for example offers finely nuanced readings of the ways characters take the word of the other, carrying the traces of the other, and make use of that language themselves: For Bakhtin, the word is never virginal.[12] All language is communal and exchanged. The recent interest in the politics of the body traces in many forms how body or culture as text writes other bodies in another kind of exchange of languages: Frances Burney describing the female body cannibalizing itself at court to follow a demanding script; Jane Eyre's conviction of her own monstrosity.[13]

The new conventions of narration that coalesce into our new paradigm in Jane Austen's time avoid the stark choice between the self of Descartes or Lacan: between the fullness amidst isolation of the former or the absences filled with glittering mirages of the latter. Complex intersubjectivity posits Merleau-Ponty's separated but initiating and embodied subjects, for whom "this circle which I do not form, which forms me, this coiling over of the visible upon the visible, can traverse, animate other bodies as well as my own," so that "the field open[s] for another Narcissus, for an 'intercorporeity' " (*Visible* 140–41). Even a Narcissus can touch another Narcissus in the circle of espousal, and so Merleau-Ponty's gentle irony rebukes both Descartes and Lacan.

The new complex intersubjectivity places groups of these selves, Narcissus and Narcissus (or Narcissa and Narcissa), these centers of perceiving identity, into motion. That motion articulates a new dance of subjects. We can usefully describe the fundamental components of this intersubjectivity as the body and the gaze of one subject and of the Other(s), and then the consequent appropriations negotiated among these consciousnesses and intentionalities, appropriations that the gaze, the body, and their discourses enact. This process of negotiation and embodiment is an enactment of power, and its agenda can be shame or espousal, humiliation and supervision, or mutuality and the passion of generosity. "Shame or espousal": This is the debate as it were between Sartre and Merleau-Ponty over the consequences of the intersubjective. Shame or espousal: Such a binary runs the risk of oversimplifying our problem, but it also emphasizes how much is at stake. Furthermore, Merleau-Ponty's phenomenological paradigm opens the door for us to see more fully what has changed in nineteenth-century narratives, even to frame Sartre's "shame" more clearly.

Intersubjectivity in Merleau-Ponty might be defined as the web of partially interpenetrating consciousnesses that exists wherever perceiving subjects, that is, human beings, collect. This web can "really" exist because of a process that occurs between these subjects, who are embodied users of language. For Merleau-Ponty, the process begins when a self perceives the gestures, either of body or word, of another consciousness, and it continues when the self can perceive in those gestures an awareness of her or his own gestures. Subsequently the self, upon revealing a consciousness of the other's response, perceives yet another gesture responding to its response, so that out of this conversation of symbolic behaviors emerges a web woven from elements of mutually exchanged consciousnesses. This web is too intricate to be the product of only private or mutual delusion. Regardless of whether the gestures exchanged are verbal, the web is evidence of genuine, if imperfect, knowledge of other selves. This is Merleau-Ponty's way of resolving the divorce between subject and object that has bedeviled epistemology since Descartes.

The community of perceiving subjects is not, of course, anything like an exact fit for its members. Merleau-Ponty writes, in the introduction to *Signs*, "There is said to be a wall between us and others, but it is a wall we build together, each putting his stone in the niche left by the other" (19). This language is full of its own revealing clefts. For example, if the "niche" is a blank, a lack to be filled by desire, then the "completed" structure has no space to generate desire and narrative; yet completion seems to be the goal, the smoothing of a surface without a niche. The wall as an image for the intersubjective is indeed deeply paradoxical. It reappears in "The Child's Relation with Others," from *The Primacy of Perception*, again as a boundary that enables the intersubjective:

> [The child's] egocentrism . . . is the attitude of a *me* which is unaware of itself and lives as easily in others as it does in itself—but which, being unaware of others in their own separateness as well, in truth is no more con-

scious of them than of itself. . . . After that the objectification of the body intervenes to establish a sort of wall between me and the other: a partition. Henceforth it will prevent me from confusing myself with what the other thinks, and especially with what he thinks of me; just as I will no longer confuse him with my thoughts, and especially my thoughts about him. (*Primacy* 119–20)

Once again, separateness prevents narcissism and confusion and clarifies intersubjective experience, once "me" is distinguished from "what he thinks of me," and "him" from "my thoughts about him." The circle of the intercorporeal can now be performed. Another poignant reflection on a distance and absence that are also intimate occurs in *Signs*: "For [others] are not fictions with which I might people my desert—but my twins or the flesh of my flesh. Certainly I do not live their lives; they are definitely absent from me and I from them. But that distance becomes a strange proximity as soon as one comes back home to the perceptible world" (15).

The distance between twins is both absence and presence, and the world is both "desert" and "home." We have seen in a few examples with what depth *Mansfield Park* and *Persuasion* render these paradoxes of distance and of the wall, in exactly its qualities as barrier and intimate connection, and we will see similar complexity in *Emma, Great Expectations, Jane Eyre,* Henry James's *Awkward Age,* Woody Allen's *Broadway Danny Rose,* and Hitchcock's *Marnie,* for example. The image that resonates throughout Merleau-Ponty's work is the image of the "chiasmus," the knot of interconnecting, reversible threads, rhetorical and phenomenological, that embodies his sense of bordered separatenesses. Luce Irigaray ponders on precisely this knottedness and its possible duplicities in an essay on the chiasm in Merleau-Ponty, and so reminds us of the dark side to his image:

> According to Merleau-Ponty, energy plays itself out in the backward-and-forward motion of a loom. But weaving the visible and my look in this way, I could just as well say that I close them off from myself. The texture becomes increasingly tight, taking me into it, sheltering me there but imprisoning me as well. (1993, 183)

For Irigaray weaving can separate, like Merleau-Ponty's wall, but without as strong a confidence in the partner on the other side of the wall or at the other end of the loom.

A more detailed analysis of intersubjectivity in *The Primacy of Perception* serves as our paradigm:

> If a friend and I are standing before a landscape, and if I attempt to show my friend something which I see, and which he does not yet see, we cannot account for this situation by saying that I see something in my own world and that I attempt, by sending verbal messages, to give rise to an analogous perception in the world of my friend. There are not two numerically distinct worlds plus a mediating language which alone would bring us together. This is—and I know it very well if I become impatient with him—a kind of demand that what I see be seen by him also. . . . From the depths of my subjectivity I see another subjectivity invested with equal rights appear, because the behavior of the other takes place within my perceptual field. I understand this behavior, the words of another; I espouse his thought because this other, born in the midst of my phenomena, appropriates them and treats them in accord with typical behaviors which I myself have experienced. . . . The body of the other—as bearer of symbolic behaviors . . . tears itself away from being one of my phenomena, offers me the task of true communication, and confers on my objects the new dimension of intersubjective being. (17–18)

The most significant conception here is Merleau-Ponty's account of the intricate exchange of perceptions that occurs between embodied consciousnesses—in a sense, between bodies themselves, as each perceives "this behavior" of "the body of the other." As a result of this interplay of responses, built at each point upon perception of the other's perception, I begin to have some knowledge beyond my own consciousness. Merleau-Ponty would say that I begin to transcend myself, moving toward what Husserl in *Cartesian Meditations* called "transcendental intersubjectivity" (150).[14] I can now begin to learn about myself from a new vantage point and, inductively and imperfectly, about other consciousnesses as their gestures enter the field of my perception. Thus other subjectivities become part of my subjectivity, and I become part of theirs.

The distinction between this model and Hillis Miller's (and Poulet's) is subtle but important. Miller describes the Victorian self as one who "comes to know himself . . . by way of other people," as one who could say, "I am conscious of myself as conscious of others." The self as center of perception bulks too large here and simplifies the network of perceptions. In the formulation growing from Merleau-Ponty's thought, the nineteenth-century self could say, "I am conscious of others' consciousness of me, and even of the way their gestures betray their appropriation of my appropriation of them." Awkward as this formulation is, it describes more adequately the fabric of relatedness that is missing from earlier narrative.

This process of relatedness, however, may produce both terror and intimacy, especially when the body becomes the object of the other's gaze. The gap between these outcomes is the gap between Sartre and Merleau-Ponty and can help us measure both the darker and the more comic strains in deeply intersubjective narratives. For Sartre, in his extended exploration of the Look and the Other in *Being and Nothingness,* the problem of the Other is shame, and shame is necessarily the result of being an object of the Look. "The Other is not only the one whom I see, but the one *who sees me.* . . . He is the one for whom I am not subject but object . . ." (310). The Other excludes, endangers. "In so far as I am the instrument [of the Other] . . . to ends of which I am ignorant—I am *in danger.* This danger is not an accident, but the permanent structure of my being-for-others" (358). The cause of this threat is the Look, which makes one's fundamental, primary experience of the Other that of becoming-a-Thing: " 'Being-seen-by-the-Other' is the *truth* of 'seeing-the-Other.' . . . He is that object in the world which determines an internal flow of the universe, an internal hemorrhage . . ." (345). All of Sartre's images and examples of the Look express shame and fear, often in connection with blood and wounds, or with loss, de-centering: The Other's appearance in my universe "is an element of disintegration . . . ; the world has a kind of drain hole in the middle of its being, and it is perpetually flowing off through this hole" (343). The danger is always already present, even before we can raise our defenses. The Other is *first* "the being toward whom I do not turn my attention. *He* is the one who looks at me and at whom I am not yet looking." This moment is so embarrassing in Sartre because the I *is* looking—elsewhere, stooping at a keyhole, to look up at being spied spying. For Sartre, "Anyone may recognize in this abstract description that immediate and burning presence of the Other's look which has so often filled him with shame" (360–61). The Other always catches you off guard. The Other is Emma watching Jane Fairfax across a crowded ball room.[15]

The Sartrean paradigm in a general sense has characterized discussion of the gaze and gender, especially in film and the visual arts, more widely than any other. In the work of the important film theorist Laura Mulvey, for example, women are the object of the male gaze in just this suspicious, aggressive way (Sartre's analysis is itself innocent of feminist understanding). Mulvey's model is Freud's, whose notion of scopophilia defined a primary sexual drive in "taking other people as objects, subjecting them to a controlling and curious gaze" (16). Mulvey does not discuss shame in the object of the gaze; she is interested primarily in the complex fears, of narcissistic engulfment and castration, for example, in the men who must look. Shame, however, is not the only response conceivable in the person observed. Beth Newman rereads Freud's reading of the Medusa to identify a fear in men of a woman who precisely recognizes and returns the gaze:

> Perhaps the sight that makes the Medusa threatening to the male spectator may be understood as the sight of someone else's look—the knowledge that the other sees and therefore resists being reduced to an appropriable object. (1031)

Newman conceives a project of "defusing the gaze" by resistance and defiance (1037). Charles Bernheimer's analysis of Manet's *Olympia* describes a more ambiguous resistance in the courtesan's gaze, as she faces her client with such scandalous directness: "Is your dominance as bearer of the look [Bernheimer conceives her to be implying] still assured if I return your gaze in full awareness of what it conveys?" (15) Shame, self-defense, aggressive counterattack against the Look—these are the givens of the Sartrean paradigm, gendered, yes, by patriarchy, but perhaps not essentially and always so. As Sartre and Austen's Wentworth know, shame and a feeling of the power of the other to control can be male experiences, too.

Common to all of these critics is the notion that the gaze is a site of struggle. A contest between gazes is exactly what occurs on the stairs from the beach at Lyme, in *Persuasion,* for example, when Anne passes between Mr. Elliot and Wentworth. Wentworth needs the shock of Elliot's "earnest" and "exceedingly" admiring look to see Anne again: "Captain Wentworth looked round at her instantly in a way which shewed his noticing of [Elliot's admiration]" (I, 12; 104). In a sense Elliot challenges Wentworth to see Anne through his eyes. For Anne, who stands between the competing gazes of two admiring men, it is a subtle matter to decide whether she gains or loses dignity and control as the object of their looks.

A very different notion of the gaze appears in Merleau-Ponty, whose thought was so often like and yet distinct from Sartre's. Although the gaze of the Other can be frightening in Merleau-Ponty, it can also be something quite different: a beginning of reciprocity, of espousal. In his view, the poet Valéry could not comprehend how

> I, who am irreducibly alien to all my roles, feel myself moved by my appearance in the gaze of others and that I in turn reflect an image of them that can

> affect them, so that there is woven between us an 'exchange,' a 'chiasm between two "destinies" . . .' in which there are never quite two of us, and yet one is never alone. (*In Praise* 82)

Merleau-Ponty agreed that the gaze can objectify, as when he speaks of the self's experience "under threat: for example, in the *"dread of death"* or of *"another's gaze upon me"* (*Phenomenology* 404), or when he speaks of the possibility that seer and seen can confront each other as "two 'points of view' with nothing in common—two 'I think's,' each of which can believe itself the winner of the trial" (*Signs* 16–17).

But the gaze does not threaten necessarily and always. "In fact the other's gaze transforms me into an object, and mine him, only if both of us withdraw into the core of our thinking nature, if we both make ourselves into an inhuman gaze . . ." (*Phenomenology* 361). Otherwise, especially when gesture and language give context to the gaze, "vision is such that the obscure results of two glances adjust to each other, and there are no longer two consciousnesses with their own teleology, but two mutually enfolding glances, alone in the world" (*Signs* 17). Merleau-Ponty's simplest expression for this mutuality is the architectural image I quoted earlier: "There is said to be a wall between us and others, but it is a wall we build together, each putting his stone in the niche left by the other" (*Signs* 19). The field of mutual consciousnesses certainly includes anger, hatred, and misunderstanding. But Merleau-Ponty's model of the mutual gaze, of "mutually enfolding glances," nevertheless moves us into a world very different from Sartre's. Indeed, Merleau-Ponty's less uniformly oppositional gaze, more multichanneled and polymorphously perverse and playful than Sartre's, suits the evolution of gaze theory in film criticism in recent years, from presuming Mulvey's unitary, commanding spectator (but lacking in the center, in the Lacanian way), to exploring multiple "viewing positions," in Linda Williams's phrase, so that the "spell of classical diegesis" is fractured, as (here Williams quotes Miriam Hansen) "an aesthetics of the 'glance' is replacing the aesthetics of the 'gaze' " (12).

Husserl, Merleau-Ponty, and even Sartre embarked on phenomenology's project of understanding how human perception and the world are imbedded in each other, and Merleau-Ponty traveled farthest in exploring how intersubjectivity spins out from subjects' mutual imbeddedness. Even Bakhtin does not discuss, in the borrowings of language, the *re*exchange of word, the trace upon trace built or erased, the reduplication, the reenactment, and further reenactments. We need another approach that will conceptualize a series of borrowings and tracings, of word, and of body also, so that the writing of the body becomes a writing of bodies gesturing and re-gesturing and yet again gesturing.

Our new understanding performs two tasks. First, it combines both language and body as gestures and encodings, so that complex intersubjectivity includes imbeddedness, words in bodies, and bodies in words.[16] "Imbedding" gestures toward the new and complex field of studies of what might be called "making the body." Since Foucault (or perhaps Kafka's "In the Penal Colony"), the body has come to be read as a kind of text, read and categorized and shaped materially by other textual and cultural agents, especially in relation to its gender and its sexual orientation. Which words or whose words (remembering Bakhtin) and whose bodies are significant matters and will help complicate our understanding of complex intersubjectivity, its opacities and partialities of espousal. It is only fair to admit that Merleau-Ponty's thought seems little interested in the effects of gendering on words, gestures, or bodies, as Judith Butler observed in an important critique in the 1980s: "[T]he potential openness of Merleau-Ponty's theory of sexuality is deceptive. . . . [H]e manages to reify cultural relations between the sexes . . . by calling them 'essential' or 'metaphysical' " (Allen and Young 86). The addition of these elements of intentionality to life in a material world and the framing of gender constructions in that life are inescapable for us now.

Another implication of this claim in our paradigm, that words in bodies and bodies in words help build complex intersubjectivity, is that silence (literally, the absence of spoken or lexical words) is a kind of action and sign, too. I can only gesture now toward the rich work of Elaine Scarry on the body, pain, and silence, in which she reflects on the incommunicability of physical suffering: "Whatever pain achieves, it achieves in part through its unsharability, and it ensures this unsharability through its resistance to language" (4). Scarry traces the escape from "unsharability" in the worked object that contains "within its interior a material record of the nature of human sentience out of which it in turn derives its power to act on sentience and recreate it" (280). That record of human consciousness, like Merleau-Ponty's hands touching hands touching, has space within it for silence, whether the silence of pain and torture or ecstasy.

The second task our model performs is to expand the form of consciousness in the intersubjective, beyond consciousness of consciousness, to the all-important third (and exponentially different) layering, to one's consciousness of the trace in the other of one's own previous and now appropriated gesture, and so on down the long corridor of the embodiments in subjects facing each other. Here lies the dramatic, profoundly structural change in narrative, with implications for topics from narratological rhetoric to the images of community in stories. Because to some degree subjectivity is narrative, the narratives of subjectivities at least cast a shadow on human culture and human lives, and these new narratives cast new shadows. The fundamental differences between Sartre and Merleau-Ponty appear in these narratives, in their approaches to the other as occasion for shame or espousal, or complex combinations and misperceptions of each. And beyond the Sartre/Merleau-Ponty binary, beyond shame versus espousal, other effects of deep intersubjectivity, as it complicates representations of power and community, begin to take shape as well.

Neither this new form of intersubjectivity nor its students are outside history. There is a politics to this complex intersubjectivity, and there is a politics to its reading. The layerings of gazes and gestures are for example gendered in subtle ways and help gender their narratives. Anne Elliott, Fanny Price, Jane Eyre, Esther Summerson, and Pip: All those observers of observation knew this fact of life long before Sartre and Mulvey. No better example in the nineteenth-century novel opens up the doubleness of power than the paradoxes of Fanny Price's experience in *Mansfield Park,* in her use of the look (as unnoticed observer) and yet her vulnerability before the gaze of others like Crawford, who, so to speak, penetrate the fourth wall behind which she has hidden. Now, however, we can see the depth of the paradoxes of power, in the network of ever-moving gestures in which Fanny's look takes its place and in which her fears multiply. Furthermore, Foucault has taught us to wonder about forms of culture and consciousness as themselves scripts that function as agents, as articulations of power. What sorts of power operate in the new scripts of intersubjectivity like Austen's? Power, to follow one track of thought, could hardly ever for Foucault be *comic,* that is, the agent of comedy, although a nostalgia for the festival of execution colors the opening chapter of *Discipline and Punish.* Austen examines the power of power to be comic, measuring by way of complex intersubjectivity barriers to comic renewal and the degree to which they may be circumvented. It is the task of this book to look at some forms of such intersubjective scripts.

This modeling of deep intersubjectivity offers a different framework, a new range of coordinates in which to place the representation of humans experiencing in fiction. Narratives will still represent blindness, stupidity, comic and ironic and pathetic misunderstandings. Misknowing is after all as dramatic a matter for storytelling as knowing.

There will even be an intersubjectivity of scattered, dismantled, and deconstructed—decentered in Gabriele Schwab's terms—selves. But it will be a different dispersion, an absence or disorientation against a different darkness. It will be a deeper failure. James's *The Awkward Age* and Hitchcock's *Vertigo* offer a different absence, a more deeply focused frame for isolation. Mrs. Norris's self-absorption and Fanny's isolation as observer are drawn against new axes. Sartre's shame will appear, in the experience of what Erving Goffman called the stigma, for example, but shame and stigma are staged in a new mise-en-scène. These effects are the result of the fresh narrative strategies that deep intersubjectivity brings with it to model even opacity and narcissism. Elizabeth Ermarth has given us a rich study of the nineteenth-century novel of "consensus," built on a sometimes-fragile belief in community, but "consensus" works on an even deeper foundation of mutuality than Ermarth allows. These new assumptions, perhaps hopes, about selves together, deepen the failures as well as the comic achievements of the will to connect in the narratives of complex intersubjectivity.

The studies that follow trace these assumptions in a variety of ways. In chapter 2 I describe the new networkings of selves in nineteenth-century narrative by contrasting pairs of texts with earlier and later narrative practices. I give accounts of the changing representation of webs of consciousnesses from several vantage points, beginning with the simplest narrative kernel, the encounter between a narrating subject and another (*Moll Flanders* and *Great Expectations*), and then moving inward and outward: inward to the subject's stories of itself (and hence construction of itself) in *Pamela* and *The Turn of the Screw*, and outward to the significance of narrative omniscience (*Tom Jones* and *Middlemarch*), in whose gaze (so to speak) others encounter others.

The implications of this shift in narrative practices for the politics and aesthetics of narrative are enormous, and the second half of the book addresses those implications by way of genre, to examine the effects of deep intersubjectivity in the myths and archetypes of comedy, anticomedy, and masquerade. These case studies track not only the study of power along that continuum from shame to espousal, but also track an aesthetics of multiplicity, duplicity, and excess. For example, the effect of the new intersubjectivity on comedy is to deepen its dark side and to emphasize the strain on community that death, anxiety, and the expulsion of the scapegoat produce. Comedy now focuses on a complex struggle among shame, betrayal, renunciation, and espousal, as Jane Austen's *Emma* and Woody Allen's *Broadway Danny Rose* will show. (My approach to comedy is indebted especially to Freud and

Cornford.) In a different direction, this model of the new intersubjectivity will allow us to see more clearly an aesthetics of duplicity and to trace the body's shadow in the intersubjectively drawn account of the failure of intersubjectivity in Henry James's *The Awkward Age*. James and Hawks's *His Girl Friday* are both examples of the subversion of comedy by way of an aesthetics of the body, whose intersubjective strategies make their subversions all the more troubling. Finally, the webbings of complex intersubjectivity make possible the multiplicities of masquerade in ways we have not understood so well, as I show in *Jane Eyre*'s study of monstrosity as masquerade and in *Marnie*'s mother-haunted narrative of wounded and masked lovers. This model of deep intersubjectivity offers some significant additions to masquerade theory, as well as to feminist narratology, by way of notions of authority in *Jane Eyre*, as developed by Susan Lanser and Allison Case.

In film studies, this paradigm of deep intersubjectivity opens up a new angle on the debate about subjectivities and gazes, about who looks and who looks at looking. I want to move beyond questions about the male or female or bisexual gaze to questions about the mutual gaze, an intersubjective gaze, and the network of embodiments (or failed embodiments) that film narrative can weave in its particular strategies of classical editing and mise-en-scène. The struggle among subjectivities and the intersubjective gaze in Alfred Hitchcock's films take on various tones, to such an extensive and unique degree that Hitchcock looms especially large in this study.[17] I explore in the comedy chapter Hitchcock's study of theatricality in the Cary Grant films, from Alicia's tragicomic gaze in *Notorious* to Frances and Robie's recuperation of duplicity in *To Catch a Thief,* in contrast to the sadly ironic role of disguise and masquerade in *Marnie*, which I explore in the last chapter. Marnie's intricate and deeply intersubjective masquerades offer a useful concluding point from which to measure our distance from Moll Flanders and the masquerades she deploys.

The story I want to tell about the reinventing of representations of consciousnesses will have somewhat different episodes in different national literatures, and my concentration on British fiction and narrative in English—partly strategic, to make the argument manageable, partly a result of my own limitations as a comparatist—determines the specifics of the story in this book. The shift in narrative practices occurs, nevertheless, whether one looks to Laclos and Stendhal in France, or Goethe and Gottfried Keller in Germany, or Cooper and Melville in the United States. Also, the change is more gradual than a "before" and "after" might suggest. Elements of deep intersubjectivity occur in, say, Cervantes, or *Les Liaisons Dangereuses,* or in Sterne and Richardson in England, as I point out in chapter 2.

These refinements do not fundamentally alter the larger argument, that representations of intersubjectivity in Defoe, Fielding, and most earlier novelists are different from those in Austen and Eliot and other nineteenth-century novelists and many twentieth-century writers and filmmakers. The rejection of deep intersubjectivity by modern novelists such as Robbe-Grillet is another story, but one that takes for granted these new ways of narrating subjectivities, which can then be subverted or negated. Subjects now may move in a new network of embodiments and (mis)readings of and by other subjects. Representing this interknitting changes stories, and changing stories affects everything and everyone, from small embodiments of identity to large narratives of community and history. My project is to explore some of these changes in narrative and some of their implications.

2

Representing Deep Intersubjectivity: Narrative Practices

> We look simply to see, see others looking, see we are seen looking, and soon become knowing and skilled in regard to the evidential uses made of the appearance of looking.
> —ERVING GOFFMAN, Forms of Talk

THE SUBJECT ENCOUNTERS THE OTHER: *MOLL FLANDERS* AND *GREAT EXPECTATIONS*

> Such a Man [heated by Wine in his Head, and a wicked Gust in his Inclination] is worse than Lunatick; prompted by his vicious corrupted Head he no more knows what he is doing than this Wretch of mine knew when I pick'd his Pocket of his Watch and his Purse of Gold.
> —Moll Flanders

> My earnestness awoke a wonder in [Estella] that seemed as if it would have been touched with compassion, if she could have rendered me at all intelligible to her own mind.
> —Great Expectations

Moll's encounters with the other, and her consequent constructions of consciousness for the other, launch our investigation, finally, of specific representations of intersubjectivity before and after the great shift in narrative practices. Moll's experiences of other subjects and of their experiences of her are fundamentally different in structure and therefore in substance from Pip's experience of others and of their consciousness of him in *Great Expectations*. Even these brief epigraphs point to the profound shift in what we might call the intersubjectivities of lunacy, passion, sexual desire, loss, and humiliation. My purpose now is to begin to explore the nature of this difference in specific stories. I begin with narratives about encountering the other told by the experiencing subject, because the possibilities of intersubjectivity loom at their starkest in this moment, when the "I" moves toward some kind of engagement with another, in its mysterious promise and terror. In the later sections of this chapter I move inward and outward: inward, to consider the intersubjective fabric of the narrating self, and outward to the intersubjectivity of omniscient narrative and its construction of others encountering others.

Intersubjectivity always poses, at some level, questions about power exercised, negotiated, blocked, or embraced between subjects, between consciousnesses occupying some kind of common space or terrain. Representing these moves, exercises, and negotiations in stories begins inside one center of perception, one subject, one character whose intentionality and experience of self are relatively transparent for the reader, listener, or viewer. I begin with Moll and Pip, to compare narrative conventions and their implications for constructing gendered, classed, intending agents who encounter another. Intersubjective narrative is born as these consciousnesses move across their territory, testing possibilities for control, submission, contest, adaptation, truce, and even collaboration and affection. "Power," as I have suggested before, does not imply in this study only hierarchical relations disciplined by political, economic, or class interests. The force fields amongst subjects that we theorize ought to include espousal, love, recognition, and respect as well as exploitation, cruelty, shame, and violation.

The extraordinary effects of deep intersubjectivity in substantially reinventing these webbings of consciousnesses appear as soon as we enter two such centers of consciousness, two characters in stories written before and after our paradigm shift and observe those subjects' territorial dance with the other. Let us begin with *Moll Flanders* as a first example of earlier narrative, against which we can set *Great Expectations* as an example of the later fiction of deep intersubjectivity. My intention in this chapter is to move back and forth across the shift in narrative practices, comparing images, signs, and narratives of old and new intersubjectivities. My argument begins with the representation of experience in one primary subjectivity perceiving other subjects, and then it moves to the newly intersubjective depths of the experiencing self itself, and finally it addresses the larger canvas in omniscient narrative, the representation of others' experience of others.

REPRESENTING DEEP INTERSUBJECTIVITY: NARRATIVE PRACTICES | 41

What exactly happens, then, in narratives in English before Jane Austen when a "person," that product of words implying a more or less coherent figure of intentions, emotions, and memories, when that consciousness encounters another? To begin with Defoe: What happens "inside" Moll (or in what appears to be her interior consciousness) when we observe her observing others? Several different things happen, the limitations of which are, I believe, characteristic of perception in narratives of simpler intersubjectivity. Most of the time, for example, Moll observes others as objects moving across the screen of her perception. People are different from other objects because they may guard objects Moll wants; they may respond threateningly when Moll attempts to transfer possession. Some readers have suspected that to Moll the difference between husbands, lovers, gold watches, and fine holland is a difference only of degree. But Moll is more perceptive than this analysis allows, as other readers have in defense also argued.[1] On occasion she contemplates others with more insight, and what then transpires demands more of us. "Simple" intersubjectivity is indeed not at all simple rhetorically or politically. Because Moll's text clearly intends to represent her as a human agent, representation necessitates rhetoric, and agency necessitates politics.

Let us begin with a representation of an experience of the other by this centering, primary subjectivity, Moll—primary and centering, that is, for this narrative. A good example occurs when Moll, who has herself been picking pockets and fears being detected, cries out that someone has attempted to steal her watch; in the succeeding uproar, the crowd's anger focuses on another perpetrator, who functions in a way as a double and sacrifice for Moll:

> They cried out a Pick-pocket again, and really seized a young Fellow in the very fact. This, tho' unhappy for the Wretch was very opportunely for my case, tho' I had carried it off handsomely enough before, but now it was out of Doubt, and all the loose part of the Crowd run that way, and the poor Boy was deliver'd up to the Rage of the Street, which is a cruelty I need not describe, and which however they are always glad of, rather than to be sent to Newgate, where they often lie a long time, till they are almost perish'd, and sometimes they are hang'd, and the best they can look for, if they are convicted, is to be Transported. (165)

Moll understands thoroughly the alternative fates awaiting the boy and even comprehends that he would rather die at the hands of the mob. Her understanding grows out of her own experience, transferred to this child, of poverty's social and psychological consequences. Although the "Wretch" has been picking pockets, he nonetheless is a kind of substitute for Moll, a surrogate self, even another lost child (like her children and herself). Moll understands the boy's story, so much so that she can imaginatively reconstruct the chapters of that narrative: imprisonment in Newgate, waiting in hunger and deprivation for trial. Moll even imagines his imagination of the verdict and its consequences: "[T]he best they can look for, if they are convicted, is to be Transported." She conceives a strange paradox, or at least sad resignation, in the boy's emotional calculations—despite the "cruelty" of the "Rage of the Street," the specifics of which Moll's delicacy spares us ("I need not describe"), he is still "glad of" it.

Nevertheless, the "poor Boy" never becomes a specific subjectivity in an intercorporeally framed landscape (or streetscape) for Moll. In fact Moll's reflections are curiously hollow, deflected, and constructed: She does not imagine *this* boy's imagination. Her narrative is exemplary and typical, and the boy's emotion, that wonderfully perceived paradox, is generic: He is a "they," and the gladness is an "always" response. That is, Moll has leapfrogged over the boy's body and consciousness, from "the poor Boy was deliver'd up to the Rage of the Street" to "they are always glad. . . ." The sentence's smooth transition from "the poor Boy" to "a Cruelty . . . which however they . . . ," from *he* to *they*, suggests how deeply this lost child is at best an individual interpreted by reference to a group, and at worst a subjectivity whose interior life Moll *avoids* by retreating to the group. But at least she has broached the possibility of the other's suffering, the other's experience of anticipation, his imagination of outcomes, and his immersion in his own narrative. There is after all an initial sort of exchange here; Moll has become more than the all-consuming ego she verges on being at times. In Merleau-Ponty's language, she has observed the behavior of the other and believes she has understood the symbolic language of his gestures. But Moll's perception is clearly a construction in this instance. The narrative of "these" boys is her summation of her broader experience of street life and has a generic validity. However, Moll applies it *to* her subject. She does not draw it from him. She has not begun to appropriate a particular other's thought or its embodiment.[2]

This limitation is always true for Moll, even when she appears to make a closer approach to others. It is odd, for example, how little we know about her Lancashire husband as a human subject, despite all of Moll's genuine affection. In telling of their mutual deception, marriage, disillusion, hopeless love, and separation, Moll never contemplates

REPRESENTING DEEP INTERSUBJECTIVITY: NARRATIVE PRACTICES | 43

Jemy's self as a center of feeling and intentions from which his actions and words emerge. We have simply his actions and words. For example, note Moll's response to Jemy's farewell letter:

> Nothing that ever befel me in my Life sunk so deep into my Heart as this Farewel: I reproach'd him a Thousand times in my Thought for leaving me, for I would have gone with him thro' the world, if I had beg'd my Bread. . . . [A]fter dinner I fell into a vehement Fit of crying, every now and then, calling him by his name, which was *James, O Jemy*, said I, *come back, come back*, I'll give you all I have, I'll beg, I'll starve with you. (120)

We discover much about Moll here: She has a capacity for sorrow that readers may not have suspected (and some still doubt); even with the emphasis upon "leaving me," Moll betrays some potential for selflessness in her image of herself as beggar with Jemy, willing to be hungry as long as she is with him. Moll is capable of a simple intersubjectivity, registering the evidence of another's consciousness and reflecting shrewdly on that evidence. But has Jemy been more than an image to Moll or a stream of words in the flow of her consciousness?

During the scenes in which they confess their mutual schemes to marry well, Moll and her husband certainly drop their masks, even to the point of admitting wrong. Moll listens to her husband and comes to a judgment about the real man:

> [B]ut he was really a Gentleman, unfortunate and low, but had liv'd well; and tho' if I had had a Fortune I should have been enrag'd at the Slut for betraying me [about his wealth]; yet really for the Man, a Fortune would not have been ill bestow'd on him, for he was a lovely Person indeed; of generous Principles, good Sense, and of abundance of good Humour. (118)

The abdication of the will to manipulate brings these two people closer together, into some sort of intimacy, and I see no hint from Defoe's text, in the editing or shaping of the narrative here, of irony. Moll's response to Jemy is profoundly limited, as indeed is Jemy's subjectivity as she represents it. Moll transcribes the signs of his emotions, for example: "*[H]e said*, I would break his heart"; and from Jemy's letter: "I am a Dog; I have abus'd you. . . . I have been so happy to possess you . . ." (119). But never, in his or Moll's or Defoe's text, does Jemy reflect on Moll as a subjectivity and much less on her consciousness of *him*. Moll's subjectivity, moreover, betrays the same limitation. She registers Jemy's response to her: period. His consciousness of loss and guilt in the words of his letter, for example, does not appear to her as a middle term in a process, in a series of perceptions, either as words preceded by an experience of her whose traces she might meditate on in his letter, or as words whose writing will spark further experience in the writer, as well as in her. Merleau-Ponty's chiasm of exchange is not possible here. Jemy is never, for Moll, a perceiving self whose words and gestures emerge from an intentionality. Moll enters into Jemy's subjectivity, imagining for example the experience that lies behind the need to deceive her, even less than she does the pickpocket's. And so there is never a possibility for the appropriation of appropriation that is the core of Merleau-Ponty's deep intersubjectivity.

In one of the rare instances in which Moll advances toward an intuition of another as a source of intentions, interpretations, and agency, that intuition remains elementary. Here Moll moves from considering the general nature of men intoxicated by wine and lust to reflecting on the inner life of a recent customer:

> For 'twas ten to one but he had an honest virtuous Wife and innocent children, that were anxious for his safety, and would have been glad to have gotten him Home, and have taken care of him till he was restor'd to himself; and then with what Shame and Regret would he look back upon himself? how would he reproach himself with associating himself with a Whore? . . . and hate himself every time he look'd back upon the Madness and Brutality of his Debauch? (177)

Here Moll imagines another center of awareness in a more extended way than before, building upon what is nonetheless a pretty meager treasury of signs: "[H]e seem'd to be a good sort of Man in himself . . . , a comely handsome Person, a sober solid Countenance, a charming beautiful Face" (177). But Moll constructs an interior life, a sequence of thoughts and images for this "poor unguarded Wretch" (177), who will hate himself, in the story Moll spins for him, when he looks back on this present as a memory, "restor'd to himself" by the attentions of "virtuous Wife and innocent Children," who have been anxious for his safety (177). That is, Moll's gentleman is, in her story-telling imagination, the center of a group of perceptions that she details with considerable emotional effort. Furthermore, in a move toward complex intersubjectivity, Moll imagines his perception of her. Perhaps she is to him simply a "Whore, pick'd up in the worst of all Holes," but at least she makes the step to conceive his conception (177).

Moll in fact recommends a deeper and more intersubjective conception: "Would such Gentlemen but consider the contemptible Thoughts

REPRESENTING DEEP INTERSUBJECTIVITY: NARRATIVE PRACTICES | 45

which the very Women they are concern'd with, in such Cases as these, have of them, it wou'd be a surfeit to them" (177). This sober client, a baronet as it turns out, ought, in Moll's view, to attend to the other's perception of him, as Moll attends to his reduction of her to "Whore" that is typical of men under the spell of desire:

> There is nothing so absurd, so surfeiting, so ridiculous as a Man heated by Wine in his Head, and a wicked Gust in his Inclination together; he is in the possession of two Devils at once, and can no more govern himself by his Reason than a Mill can Grind without Water. . . . ; nay, his very Sense is blinded by its own Rage . . . ; picking up a common Woman, without regard to what she is, or who she is; whether Sound or rotten, Clean or unclean; whether Ugly or Handsome; whether Old or Young, and so blinded, as not really to distinguish. (176)

Moll's meditation on the operation of desire here is perhaps her finest moment as a psychologist of the other, observing for example the element of rage that drives such men. This long reflection on the action of desire is particularly startling in its implications for Moll's view of herself as the undistinguished object of a blind, angry inclination. Equally surprising, and satisfyingly symmetrical, is Moll's observation that a similar reduction (of men) by undistinguishing occurs in the thoughts of women so reduced, and she dryly encourages men to be conscious of that consciousness. Thus certain possibilities for the intersubjective surface in *Moll Flanders,* and they serve the complex rhetorical and political ends of Moll's confession (whether they be display, arousal, delight, and/or shame and instruction).

These possibilities, however, fall short of Merleau-Ponty's complex intersubjectivity in important ways and for important reasons. One of Moll's recurring rhetorical strategies is to distance the subjectivity of the other by introducing a generic substitute either for herself or the other. Moll's client the baronet remembers, in Moll's construction, not "this" woman or another image with specific connection to Moll: The "Gentleman" simply regrets his association with "a" prostitute. That is, Moll imaginatively performs this generic move on his image of herself, to reduce her specific selfhood to an "a." She abstracts her client, too, in her meditation on desire: "I was not so past the Merry part of Life, as to forget how to behave, when *a Fop* so blinded by his Appetite should not know an old Woman from a young . . . (176; my emphasis). And later, it is "such Gentlemen" who should conceive how the women they buy think of them. Moll steps away from this specific person in this specific place. In this chapter's opening epigraph from *Moll,* she returns to "this Wretch of mine," but only briefly and as an example of her general principles. Even in her construction of a family romance for the baronet, her frame speculates in a distanced way, again typically in combination with some genuine compassion: "[I]f I could have found out any way to have done it, I would have sent him safe home to his House and to his Family, for 'twas ten to one but he had an honest virtuous Wife . . ." (177). 'Twas ten to one: Probability serves to abstract, so that the following story is to some degree emblematic and generic. Moll's attention to the experience of the other then delivers less than it at first promises to do. The structural reflection of this failure is the absence of the reexchange, the appropriation of appropriation, which Merleau-Ponty understood as the "middle way" of deep intersubjectivity (the middle way between Cartesian idealism and Hume's scepticism).

Moll's sympathy for her client the baronet is impersonal because in her imaginative reconstruction of his life, even of his life when he might have thought of her, she conceives no connection to herself as a consciousness: Moll imagines that her client perceives *her* as she perceives most people, as a creature that may be a source for gold watches or good sex or venereal disease. Moll registers no secondary exchange of perceptions in what would be her consciousness of the client's gestures in response to herself. She abstracts, makes generic others' perceptions (remember the pickpocket, the "poor Boy," who immediately becomes "they"), including their perceptions of her. She is not capable of a reflexive thought by which she might have wondered about and over the nature of the other's consciousness of her own presence. She simply notes that to the baronet she was a "Whore," an image, a role. Even at her most intimate, Moll observes other selves from behind the fourth wall, as if they had become characters in a play. Because she never perceives her self (as a subjectivity) to be present in some other's subjective life, *their* subjectivity never becomes present within hers. The nearest Moll can come to deep intersubjectivity is to observe, from the recess of her mind, the way another mind works. She can see herself only as an image in that mind as in a mirror, never knowing herself as part of an inner life to whose gestures she might respond, mirroring to that consciousness an interpretation of the images it mirrors to her, in anticipation of a yet more extensive series of signs about signs.

Intersubjectivity in *Moll Flanders* is exterior and mechanical and as such has important consequences for the representation of gender and power, negotiation, espousal, struggle, and love. The experience of territoriality for Moll's readers stops, in a sense, at the exchange of experiences of masks, at the representation of stereotypes or generic consciousnesses ("they are always glad of . . . the Rage of the Street"; "such a Man is worse than a Lunatick" when driven by sexual desire). Moll maneuvers among subjectivities as she maneuvers the crowded pavements of London, with an eye to the bodies moving towards her and whatever intentional consciousness drives their immediate gestures (as in the effort to apprehend her). Her strength as maneuverer in such a public world has made her an attractive figure for feminist readers (and many others), and correctly so. Power in that public arena, even the power to look at the other on the street, is deeply gendered as masculine, yet Moll, by adroit mixture of boldness and masquerade, acquires a freedom, economic as well as sexual, that is usually conceived as masculine, while retaining a critical distance from patriarchal assumptions. The significant point for my purposes, however, is the limitation of complexity to this maneuvering consciousness's negotiations with the other. Such limitation may add fuel to critical controversies about Moll's role as heroine and, as she calls herself, "Penitent."

Or perhaps not: To what degree are these limitations Moll's, or Defoe's, or those of narrative in 1720? It is important not to generalize too quickly. Each writer, even each narrative that we study in this project, makes use of the vocabulary and the assumptions of its intersubjective paradigm in an often specific way, so that we find many differences within similarities. Defoe's centering subjects—Moll, Robinson, Roxana—usually approach their worlds with enormous appetite, so enormous that desire works to blind them to the other. Evidence abounds of a canny intelligence that stages Moll's confession (and Defoe's other tellers' performances) in the editor's sly introduction. For example: How do we read the line, "This Work is chiefly recommended to those who know how to Read it . . ."? Or what do we make of the contradiction here, "There is an agreeable turn *Artfully* given [these Incidents] that *naturally* Instructs the Reader . . ." (my emphasis) (4)? Paula Backscheider has recently recounted even more evidence of Defoe's life of multiple voices and identities, anchored in the Dissenter's expectation of social alienation, but decentered by the shame and failure of bankruptcy. Backscheider quotes Defoe, "We live in a general Disguise, and like the Masquerades, every Man dresses himself up in a particular Habit." She continues:

> Assuming, then, willingly or unwillingly, the guise of rising City merchant, the public poet, the bankrupt, the defender of liberty, the pilloried martyr, the spy, the government apologist, the retired controversialist, the elderly sage,

and the betrayed father, he remained intensely aware of the self within, the personality that "precedes and resists alteration," seems "to have existed before events and continues to exist," and that could never be contained in one role. (534)

What kind of anchor do these multiplicities offer for measuring Moll's blindnesses, appetites, and strengths as well as her intersubjective style or competence? For Backscheider, the anchors are Defoe's belief in a coherent "self within" whose essence exceeds any embodying discourse and "his trust in a purpose for his life" (539). Such a confidence in the core self, in combination with Defoe's fascination with multiple performances, ought to open a pathway to deep intersubjectivity, to an interest in tracing the mirroring of mirrorings in the encounter between two subjects. These performances, however, whatever essence they might be seen to perform, presume only a simple practice of the intersubjective. The conventions of this intersubjectivity, in Moll's stories about pickpockets' choices, men in heat, or the baronet's virtuous wife, outline a type of opacity and insight peculiar to Moll, an unusual combination of compassion and evasion by means of generic abstraction. Other specific kinds and degrees of opacity occur in narratives of earlier and later intersubjectivities. As we saw in Moll's relation to the pickpocket, her particular opacity operates through a complex dance of what seems to be approach and withdrawal. Her ability to imagine the life of the other is a function of her fascination with the specific, material world and so seems capable of the phenomenological complexity that Merleau-Ponty describes. But this material imagination, so to speak, is profoundly limited. Moll can approach others in their economic, sexual, and classed specificity, but only in a mode of simple, one-tiered reciprocity of experience.

Can we therefore conclude that Moll's failure is particular to her, in her withdrawal from the other's consciousness? That is, is this simplicity of intersubjectivity particular to this text or even this character? It is these, but it is also more.[3] We have begun to trace a practice for representing consciousnesses that will recur in other early narratives and will continue to recur after the paradigm shift, but in the context of the new, deep intersubjectivity. To clarify what is missing from *Moll*, we need now to study a later narrative in which we can watch a centering consciousness experience the other. Subjects in most nineteenth-century novels become centers of perception caught in the web of other perceiving selves, with secondary and tertiary exchanges of gestures, words, and implication. The effect of this new intersubjectivity is, as I have been arguing, a certain intimacy, a "depth" of layers of perception.[4] A sceptic may now say (and may have been saying for some time), "This is absurd. Characters in earlier narratives understood the perceptions of others. Tom Jones, for example, certainly knows what people think of him—that he'll die of hanging or that Mrs. Waters wants to seduce him. This kind of understanding is fundamental to virtually all characterization." The sceptic's scepticism would be correct, as far as it goes. But the sceptic needs to remember the ways in which Merleau-Ponty's phenomenology is not Locke's. There is more to the web of consciousnesses than the registering of information, even when that information is data about others' perceptions, even other's perceptions of oneself. Once information becomes information about more complex exchanges, among intentionalities that reflect and interpret one's own intentions toward those intentionalities, among signs of appropriation of appropriations, then the mirrorings of self extend in a new order of magnitude and create a new kind of experience among subjects, or at least a new practice for representing experiences among subjects in narrative.

The webbings of complex intersubjectivity make for an extraordinary difference even in the "simpler" narrative structure that concentrates on one subjectivity. What exactly happens when we observe Pip, in *Great Expectations,* observing others? Let's watch how Pip's consciousness functions when he confesses that he will never tell Joe the truth about the purloined pork pie:

> I loved Joe—perhaps for no better reason in those early days than because the dear fellow let me love him—and as to him, my inner self was not so easily composed. It was much upon my mind (particularly when I first saw him looking about for his file) that I ought to tell Joe the whole truth. Yet I did not, and for the reason that I mistrusted that if I did, he would think me worse than I was. . . . I morbidly represented to myself that if Joe knew it, I never afterwards could see him at the fireside feeling his fair whisker, without thinking that he was meditating on it. That, if Joe knew it, I never afterwards could see him glance, however casually, at yesterday's meat or pudding when it came on today's table, without thinking that he was debating whether I had been in the pantry. That, if Joe knew it, and at any subsequent period of our joint domestic life remarked that his beer was flat or thick, the conviction that he suspected Tar in it, would bring a rush of blood to my face. (chapter 6, 71–72)

Here we see how richly a first-person narrative may suggest a web of mutually observed perceptions. For Pip, Joe is not simply a beloved object of observation. Joe is instead already a subjectivity, many of whose motives and feelings Pip can know because their gestures inhabit and shape Pip's life-world, or at least his life-spaces, in what Pip calls "our joint domestic life." More important, those gestures of Joe's inner life become part of Pip's inner life and (apparently) vice versa, or at least in Pip's perception. We discover here Merleau-Ponty's web of exchanging subjectivities, intricately and lovingly described. For Pip, Joe's body, "feeling his fair whisker" at the fireside, speaks a language that communicates an exact consciousness (here, a meditation on Pip's terrific deceitfulness). Joe's words also speak beyond themselves, so that a remark about his beer can become, for Pip, a sign of Joe's memories and interpretations. Even more telling, for the representation of the intersubjective, Pip sees his own body as speaking to Joe. Hence his fear of the blush that would confess to Joe (about what, Pip is unclear, since Joe would already know Pip's guilt: Perhaps the blush threatens to reenact guilt or bring into the open what he and Joe have lost. These bodily signifiers need not be precisely referential.) Simple gestures can send a shiver through the connecting web: Joe looking for his file, or Joe glancing, however casually, at yesterday's meat on today's supper table. In this small room filled with glances, recollections, words, and gestures—all the densely packed signs of collective experience, Pip also has very clear readings of intentionalities: Joe's toward him ("the dear fellow let me love him"), his toward Joe, and most significant, Joe's (feared) appropriation of Pip's response in his blush to Joe's interpretation of his character. This intricate extension of readings marks the change in narrative practices from Defoe to Dickens. In these apparently minute tracings, and tracings of tracings, by consciousnesses of other consciousnesses (Austen's "two Inches of Ivory" could be a definition of this intersubjective terrain), in this small arena a new, fundamental reworking of community, selfhood, and culture takes shape.

Pip's speculations on the future, "if Joe knew," demonstrate most fully the closeness of interwoven perceptions that is now possible. The demonstration is especially telling because it lies in the realm of Pip's imagination, in the assumptions about the intersubjective in the narrative he constructs. Pip conceives a confession to Joe whose effect, Pip believes, would be to alter fundamentally Joe's sense of him. In Pip's story, Joe's appropriation of his behaviors and intentions has consequences more far-reaching than was possible in any circumstances for Moll's own text to represent or for Moll herself to imagine. Pip's consciousness of Joe's altered trust would also and necessarily change the entire texture of their lives, so that their every gesture and nuance, of both body and word, would incarnate Joe's new consciousness of him—and Pip's consciousness of it. The web of connections would shiver, almost fracture, as Pip perceived, painfully and repeatedly, not only Joe's attitude but also his perception of Pip's perception, expressed here in the "rush of blood to my face." Indeed, Pip's deepest fear makes sense only in the terms of our deep intersubjectivity, in combination in this instance with a recognition of the gender of signs: The blush, that gendered mark of the intimate and usually feminine moment, here would signal to Joe Pip's shame, that sign which in itself is only the latest in a series of appropriations.[5] For Dickens, Pip is a center of human feeling to whom the reflections of itself in another consciousness are an intimate aspect of its own existence. Because of his need, Pip is attentive to the languages he perceives to be present for him, reflects on the significance of their communication about both himself and the other, and then responds in a way that he conceives to be part of a continuing series. This perception of perceptions expands until the blacksmith's house seems to fill with two consciousnesses attentive to each other's languages.

This attentiveness carries with it a kind of weight whose impact may be uncertain, threatening to Pip as well as comforting. Deep intersubjectivity increases the risks and the rewards of intimacy, as the traces of betrayal as well as love are retraced again and yet again. From shame to espousal: This range of the intersubjective, a theme from chapter 1, appears dramatically in this scene with Joe and Pip, where the *heimlich* is indeed a site simultaneously of intimate knowledges and secrets, acknowledged or hidden in emotionally charged and repeated gestures.

Our first scene from *Great Expectations* is primarily a study in the possibility of shame, however deep the affection that frames that possibility. Espousal is also a possibility in Dickens, however rare and difficult to achieve, especially in his later novels. The conversation between Pip and Herbert, in chapter 30, about Pip's love for Estella, is a good example of the reciprocity of appropriation between one consciousness and another that is now possible. Dickens's study of these reciprocities is especially remarkable because they traffic so significantly in silences:

"You call me a lucky fellow. Of course, I am. I was a blacksmith's boy but yesterday; I am—what shall I say I am—today?"

"Say, a good fellow, if you want a phrase," returned Herbert, smiling, and clapping his hand on the back of mine, "a good fellow, with impetuosity and hesitation, boldness and diffidence, action and dreaming, curiously mixed in him."

I stopped for a moment to consider whether there really was this mixture in my character. On the whole, I by no means recognized the analysis, but thought it not worth disputing. (XXX, 269)

Part of Herbert's function for Pip is to rename him—Handel, a good fellow curiously contradictory, instead of blacksmith's boy. This renaming emerges from an observation intimate enough that Pip trusts its gesture to return to him some knowledge. That is, Herbert has appropriated, within Pip's view, his words and especially his gestures ("You brought your adoration and your portmanteau here, together. Told me! Why, you have always told me all day long" [XXX, 268]) to lay the ground for an interpretation, that Pip may then interpret for himself and for Herbert. Although in this instance Pip decides not to argue, still, for him, silence is a response to Herbert's appropriation.

Pip's silences indeed acknowledge, perform, and promote espousal. The most poignant instance occurs later in the scene, when Herbert has so fully entered into Pip's dilemma as to speak the unspeakable:

> "Not being bound to her, can you not detach yourself from her? . . .
>
> There was silence between us for a little while.
>
> "Yes; but my dear Handel," Herbert went on, as if we had been talking instead of silent, "its having been so strongly rooted in the breast of a boy whom nature and circumstances made so romantic, renders it very serious. Think of her bringing-up, and think of Miss Havisham. Think of what she is herself (now I am repulsive and you abominate me). This may lead to miserable things."
>
> "I know it, Herbert," said I, with my head still turned away, "but I can't help it." (XXX, 271)

The gesture and countergesture here, in bodies, words, and silences, are now so conventional that it is difficult to see what a remarkable change in conventions this phenomenological crisscrossing, this chiasm, is. It is not that Herbert speaks as if Pip had spoken, as if they share some mystical language beyond the incarnated signifier. This speech in response to silence between intimates will be debased into a sentimentalized transcendentalism in many novels and films, as the new conventions harden. But Herbert has not transcended signs: He has just read them. Out of his reading of Pip's body movement and silence, Herbert fashions another interpretation of Pip, now as the descendant of the so romantic boy, and offers it to Pip as a stimulus to his inner consciousness ("Think of her . . ."), already constructing Pip's response to express yet another movement of his own consciousness, in his compassionate apology ("now . . . you abominate me"). The friends move together and apart, interpreting interpretations. There is a dance of approach and retreat here, on a grid over which class and gendered scripts of male comradeship certainly exert power. This dance is a representation of accommodation, with attendant beliefs about a common language and landscape, even if for these men in this particular lifeworld. The interplay in this room is as dense as that by Joe's fireside, but here *two* intentionalities are turned with a high degree of self-awareness toward each other, gesturing and listening in that "circle of the touched and touching," as Merleau-Ponty called it in *The Visible and the Invisible.*

"The circle of the touched and the touching"; "espousal"; "deep intersubjectivity": The images of intimacy in this phenomenological language—mine, Merleau-Ponty's, Georges Poulet's—should by now suggest a fundamental question about this scene and about the subject of encountering the other in general: How sexualized and/or sexualizing is this language of phenomenology? When does intersubjectivity become intersexuality? What are the sexual agendas in our scene from chapter 30 or in this study, and how do the notions of complex intersubjectivity help us understand them? The intimacy between Pip and Herbert, which I claim reflects and enacts a kind of espousal, is especially suggestive because its topic is romantic passion and its method an exchange that I have not yet mentioned, an exchange of confessions (as Pip bares his secret about Estella, Herbert confesses to Pip *his* engagement to Clara). This intimacy between men, explored through confessions and fantasies about distant women (Herbert can't marry until he encounters more "Capital"), suggests an indirect expression of mutual male sexual interest somewhere in the continuum of sexualized responses that Eve Kosovsky Sedgwick has called homosociality.[6] Perhaps Herbert appropriates Pip's story so deeply, even recommending thoughts to Pip about Estella ("think of her bringing-up . . ."), so as to participate in a kind of three-way erotic engagement.

Appropriation as Merleau-Ponty describes it certainly opens the door to sexual fantasy and (paradoxically) intimacy, as images and language move back and forth between subjects. After all, Herbert wants Pip to "detach" himself from Estella: Is this an effort, even if unconscious, at seduction, only after the failure of which does Herbert confess to his engagement? A recent critic, William Cohen, might say yes, because relations between men in *Great Expectations* are more charged with sexual energy than those between women, or the energy in heterosexual relations is energy deflected from homosocial relations. Cohen points to the recurring altercations between men that are excuses to touch each other, as in the apparently unmotivated combat between Herbert and Pip early in the novel, when Herbert accosts Pip and, without more ado, says "Come and fight." Handshakes are another way men can touch each other, and Cohen discusses hands extensively, as agents of masturbation and of erotic exchange generally, violent between Pip and Orlick, eventually socialized into gentleness between Pip and Herbert. Cohen does not discuss chapter 30, but there is a moment when Herbert turns to Pip, "clapping his hand on the back of mine" (XXX, 269); indeed, the scene is full of what could be seen as homosocial negotiations, from hand clapping to mutual appropriation of erotic hopes and fantasies to confessions of male shame (Clara's class station "is rather below my mother's nonsensical family notions," adds Herbert, "crestfallen" [XXX, 272]). For Cohen, "Herbert's youthful belligerence . . . is rehabilitated as properly sublimated, adult male homosociality," and "both Magwitch and Herbert thus partake of a homoerotic handling [of Pip, which] must be retrofitted in order to discipline those desires," as "the novel attempts to school the men's bodies in normative heterosexual touching" (575–8, 61).[7]

Pip's relations to Herbert, in our scene from chapter 30, clearly are eroticized and sexualized even before the apparatus of deep intersubjectivity is brought into play in our reading. Cohen's and Sedgwick's works therefore contribute to the larger Foucauldian project of describing and demystifying the cultural regulation of erotics, especially by means of normative narratives. Because representations subvert as well as regulate, liberate as well as confine, however, the politics of desire here may be difficult to determine: the work of demystifying—of class, economics, gender systems, and cultural imperialisms—intersects with the unveilings of subjectivities imbedded in bodies and bodies' life-worlds. *Great Expectations* is pretty clear about the links between class and eros (Biddy just isn't going to be the phantom of Pip's desire) and even imperialism (Magwitch stains Pip for several reasons, not the least of which is his place in the circulations of empire). Bodies' life-worlds are deeply classed—Herbert wouldn't be warmly embracing Orlick's hand—and regulated, but is there not an implication, in the intertwining of appropriations, of an energy (including sexual energy) that is not fully regulated? When Herbert asks Pip to think about what he (Herbert) is thinking and about what Estella thinks of Pip and knows that Pip will "abominate" his suggestions, and when Pip responds in this circle of readings, "I know it . . . , but I can't help it," these embodiments of embodiments, it seems to me, reflect some intentionality and agency, and a self-awareness of the Mobius strip of gestures that is not entirely disciplinary.

Without doubt the language of deep intersubjectivity, with its interest in various intimacies and intercourses, carries a powerful erotic component of its own. But the relation of that eros to these other projects of demystification, say, studies of Dickens and gender in 1860, may not always be complementary. Merleau-Ponty seems to choose "espousal," for example, as the strongest image possible for mirroring the other, without the Sartrean fear of shame and abuse. This adoption of the other's signs, as I discuss in chapter 1, occurs in a landscape free of troubling class and gender specifics. The "body of the other" that becomes the "bearer of [my] symbolic behaviors" and so "confers on my objects the new dimension of intersubjective being"—that body is ungendered, without ethnic or class placement (*Primacy of Perception* 18).

Yet Merleau-Ponty's language about complex intersubjectivity valorizes intimacies and subtly sexualizes them to intensify that valorizing. Who exactly is espousing whom in these scenarios? On one hand this discourse inevitably takes on, in the eye of contemporary gender studies, a homoerotic tone, given the traditions of philosophical dialogue as a discourse between men, if for no reason other than the unavailability to women, until quite recently, of formal training in the history and languages of philosophy. The voices in Merleau-Ponty's primal scene in *The Primacy of Perception* are both male: The other is "he," and the "I" is a mask, a persona, for Merleau-Ponty. On the other hand, such a reading foregrounds another kind of historical blindness to the various uses in many traditions of sexual imagery for other kinds of intimacy that, however sexualized by metaphor, are in some sense still not directly sexual. Merleau-Ponty's accounts of hands touching hands and bodies seeing what other bodies see are not immediately sexual narratives; they are in a sense disembodied, or disembodied from *particular* bodies with any particular gendered and sexual—or ethnic or class—experiences. So, the sexualization and *embodying* of intersubjectivity in Merleau-Ponty are curiously contradictory: They seek immersion in the body as a response to Cartesian idealism, but that is a disembodied body. This inconsistency becomes deeply significant once the intersubjectivity of sexual, or sexualized, experience comes under scrutiny, as in *Great Expectations*. How blinding is this contradiction?

The reasonable response to this question seems to me twofold. First, I must admit that the apparatus of complex intersubjectivity is constructed, rhetorical, and image ridden. Second, however, I do not believe our theorizing of deep intersubjectivity is *only* constructed and image driven. These images of intercourse do not determine the specifics of desire in a text that our apparatus for decoding layers of intersubjective mirrorings will help us grasp in the intricacies of evasion or espousal in these new narrative practices. Merleau-Ponty's notions of embodiment, espousal, and appropriation are useful because of the power of these images and micronarratives, so to speak, to illuminate other narratives. The real support for this broad claim, that the genuine element of self-blinding in this apparatus is only partially disabling, lies in the readings that make up this book.

Still, material circumstances do regulate the interplay of subjectivities, even if not as efficiently as Foucault conceived. Under what circumstances, then, does "espousal" or "shame" occur and with what assumptions about power to reveal, protect, or invade subjectivity? What, for example, are the class alignments of experiencing subjects like Pip and Herbert, or Pip and Estella, or, as we examine later, Jane Eyre and Helen Burns, or Emma Woodhouse and Jane Fairfax? "Espousal" seems to imply a level field between negotiating consciousnesses, but not necessarily, whereas "shame" implies inequality, but always and of what kinds? These questions require us to address what we might call the ideologies of embodiment and to move beyond the more neutral, or even naive, language of phenomenological tradition, while recognizing the rhetorical, invested qualities of our own language. If my close reading has been persuasive, then Pip and Herbert in chapter 30 of *Great Expectations* enact a particularly dense narrative of self-constructions in the mirrors of each other, where assumptions about class, sexuality, and gender function profoundly to frame their "interworld" and where our phenomenological apparatus complicates more richly the tangle of body, intentionality, and material world, as I discuss in chapter 1.

The differences in representations of experience in *Moll Flanders* and *Great Expectations* may now begin to emerge. Without the further reciprocities of deep intersubjectivity, encounters with the other lack the confirmations, endorsements, subversions, and revisions of experience, or at least of interpretations of experience, with which literary characters (and who knows, maybe others, too) construct a life-world. And complex intersubjectivity indeed measures subversions and opacities as subtly as it measures appropriations and espousals. So far our

REPRESENTING DEEP INTERSUBJECTIVITY: NARRATIVE PRACTICES | 57

discussion has not entered this sadder territory, but my epigraphs to this section emphasize this direction because they narrate experiences of blindness and looming shame. Pip and Moll are both deeply observant of others' blindnesses, but the nature of their knowledge is fundamentally different. In Moll's instance, it is unconsciousness she registers in "this Wretch of mine . . . when I pick'd his Pocket of his Watch and his Purse of Gold." He knows neither what he is doing (Moll's initial point) nor what *she* is doing, nor of course what she thinks about what he is doing. This blindness has, so to speak, no depth to it. Though Moll reflects at length on the condition of men so heated by desire, that desire is not intersubjectively complex as a *sequence* of consciousnesses gesturing to each other.

In dramatic contrast, the opacity that Pip observes in Estella is lit by the new intersubjectivity:

> "Estella, dearest dearest Estella, do not let Miss Havisham lead you into this fatal step. Put me aside forever—you have done so, I well know—but bestow yourself on some worthier person than Drummle. . . . [T]here may be one who loves you even as dearly, though he has not loved you as long, as I. Take him, and I can bear it better, for your sake!"
>
> My earnestness awoke a wonder in her that seemed as if it would have been touched with compassion, if she could have rendered me at all intelligible to her own mind. (XLIV, 377)

Estella's incomprehension is a failure to grasp Pip's reflection back to her of herself as he has appropriated *her* reflection. Furthermore, Pip perceives her failure to grasp his grasp of her. He defines a kind of intersubjectively framed sterility in this failure: "if she could have rendered me at all intelligible to her own mind." Pip also has a theory about Estella's function for Miss Havisham, and Miss Havisham's for Estella, and pleads with Estella to write her own story, to write her own mothering, rather than to let Miss Havisham edit the story so that it rewrites her own history. But either Estella cannot, or will not, see how Pip sees her, or else she likes what she sees, accepting Pip's language that she is "fling[ing]" herself away on a brute: " 'On whom else should I fling myself away?' she retorted, with a smile." And she comforts Pip, " 'Don't be afraid of my being a blessing to him,' said Estella, 'I shall not be that.' " Even if Estella grasps in part Pip's image of her and signals to him her understanding of its implications, her verdict on the intersubjective enterprise is direct: "We shall never understand each other" (XLIV, 377). Pip concludes with his passionate articulation of Estella's place in his inner life ("You are part of my existence, part of myself"), but Estella "looked at me merely with incredulous wonder" (XLIV, 378).

To reverse Merleau-Ponty's paradigm, "There is said to be a [blindness] between us and others, but it is a [blindness] we build together, each putting his stone in the niche left by the other." Dickens's intersubjective darkness is part of a narrative of failure with more chapters, more footnotes, than Defoe's. Its fabric allows for a more complex study of the politics of desire and for mapping the appropriations and embodiments of despair as well as hope and of cultural scripts and gender systems. The narrative practices of the intersubjective are becoming epic in scale.

Defoe and Dickens are idiosyncratic as well as representative writers. Are the differences I have been describing themselves idiosyncratic or representative? Defoe's protagonists, with their omnivorous appetites, may seem particularly unrepresentative. My argument is that the contrast drawn between Defoe and Dickens is fundamentally true for nineteenth-century narratives and their antecedents: That is, this contrast describes two different phenomenologies in narrative for the encounters between the story-telling "I" and the other. To support this broad claim, I have chosen to read closely a few narratives, rather than attempting an accounting, inevitably thinner, of many more narratives, and I rely on the reader's reading to estimate the degree of special pleading in my examples. As a coda, however, it might be useful to look at two quite different kinds of first-person stories, one epistolary, *Evelina,* and one serially composed of first-person accounts, *The Moonstone,* with different types of negotiation and appropriation between subjectivities. For example, because Evelina is a less confident person than Moll, she is much more attentive to what others think, or at least to their thoughts as they express judgments and approval. This attentiveness to versions of herself in the mirror of the other brings her close enough to some of those others to make possible a more complex interior exchange. *Evelina* seems like a good candidate for an early form of deep intersubjectivity.

One particular sequence of scenes in volume III, letter 5, between Evelina and Lord Orville, which turns on the problematical Mr. Macartney, illustrates the intersubjective possibilities of this text. It is important to examine a moment late enough in the novel for Evelina's friendship with Orville to have been established, but before his avowal of love, after which Evelina's self-conscious embarrassment raises a screen between herself and others, as it does intermittently throughout the novel. Here Evelina is divided between her promise to explain to

Orville her connection to Macartney and her promise to Macartney of secrecy:

> Distressed by this reflection, I thought it best to quit the room, and . . . I ran up the stairs: rather abruptly, I own, and so, I fear, Lord Orville must think; yet what could I do? . . .
>
> Just as we were all assembled to dinner, Mrs. Selwyn's man, coming into the parlour, presented to me [my] letter, and said, "I can't find out Mr. Macartney, Madam; but the post-office people will let you know if they hear of him." I was extremely ashamed of this public message; and meeting the eyes of Lord Orville, which were earnestly fixed on me, my confusion doubled, and I knew not which way to look. (301–2)

Evelina worries intensely about what Lord Orville "must think." Burney dramatizes this worry by a subtle contrast between public and private gazes and spaces: Before the assembled company Evelina meets Orville's earnest look; in consequent shame, with no place to gaze safely, she suffers silently until she can escape to that room of her own. For Evelina, Orville's "thinking" is less the activity of a consciousness than of a conscience, of a force that is somehow an extension of public space and judgment. Evelina, struggling for a kind of survival, wants to know the verdict, not the consciousness that precedes it, and she worries about the evidence on which her trial will be decided. She is powerfully aware of Orville as a mirror in which her outline is traced, and to this extent she does imagine what he is seeing, what occurs within his consciousness: "the appearance of mystery,—perhaps something worse, which this affair must have to Lord Orville . . ." (302). Later she fears his imagination: "We were both silent; yet, unwilling to leave him to reflections which could not but be to my disadvantage . . ." (306).

Evelina's construction of Orville's thoughts is, like Pip's of Joe's, hypothetical, but within her construction, Evelina's encounter with the other never moves beyond a two-layer exchange to multiple negotiations and perceptions. Furthermore, Orville's mirroring, in Evelina's mirror, is flat in the extreme, judgmental, and moralistic. In fact, part of the wonderful irony of Burney's writing is the depth we as readers can see in Orville's concern that Evelina misses almost entirely. It is in Orville's language, reported by Evelina ("I am so much ashamed of myself, that I can scarce solicit your forgiveness" [304]), that his deeper tracing of Evelina, and her blindness, appear. Orville's understanding of Evelina, in other words, is much richer than Evelina understands, and at such moments, when we yearn for Evelina to grasp his grasp of her, Burney may be pointing toward Austen's complex intersubjectivity—or we may simply be remembering Austen.

Even Orville's verdict on Evelina's extraordinary confession—that rare moment in the novel when she actually speaks out—is only marginally, to Evelina, a perception of her inner self. She has for perhaps the first time attempted to reflect that self in her words: "I am new to the world, and unused to acting for myself,—my intentions are never wilfully blameable, yet I err perpetually!" (306) Orville's reply is for Evelina primarily a judgment of her outer shell, exceedingly important as that surface, and perceptions of it, are for Evelina. It is of course the language in which Evelina perceives the verdict that betrays the limits of her appropriation: " 'Would to heaven,' cried he, with a countenance from which all coldness and gravity were banished, and succeeded by the mildest benevolence . . ." (306–7). Evelina reads Orville's face more than his words, and a face whose human intentionality she distances in her anxiety: "a countenance from which all coldness and gravity were banished." Evelina sees no eyes, no agency, only "a countenance": a word whose overtones emphasize judgment (to countenance an act) and deportment and thus drain away the human subject who gestures for the other. Further, the new expression of this "countenance" is the result of a force hidden behind a passive verb ("all coldness and gravity were banished"): What *person* reading her has banished coldness, with what intent for her? Evelina cannot or will not know. At the end of this scene she speaks of her happiness at this reconciliation with Orville and yet still frames that pleasure in terms of judgment deferred: "I cannot express how much uneasiness I have suffered from the fear of incurring his ill opinion" (307).

Orville reads faces, too, and might even identify them as a kind of barrier to intersubjectivity, as in his reply to Evelina's astonishment at his shame: " '[Y]et, if I may be my own interpreter, Miss Anville's countenance pronounces my pardon' " (304). Once again, the countenance speaks. This series of interpretations opens no doors beyond "imputation" (303), judgment, and exoneration. There is no reading of an inner self whose gestures might then be read by the other as part of a continuing series of readings of subjectivities. The meeting here of faces, "countenances," does not lead Evelina to ask about Orville's consciousness or about his perception of her feelings as betrayed in her gestures, which might have contributed to his approach to her. Orville certainly alludes to intentionality and his own history: "I know not what evil genius pursues me this morning, but I seem destined to do or say something I ought not," and his sense of shame ought, in the novel's architectural balance, to mirror Evelina's (304). Here is an open door, so to speak, but neither Evelina nor Orville walks through it. No mirroring occurs. Evelina does not "espouse his thought because this other, born in the midst of my phenomena, appropriates them . . ." (Merleau-Ponty again), nor do we see Orville's espousal of Evelina's thought, though, given his power to look and his freedom of class and gender, we might expect a paternal (if not paternalistic) capacity for seeing what she sees. Here, as elsewhere in *Evelina*, subjects reflect gestures and experiences to other subjects without reflecting on reflections as a series of interpretations gesturing to each other.

With its plot, which turns on characters not knowing what other characters are thinking, *The Moonstone*, published exactly ninety years after *Evelina*, raises barriers of difference—gender, class, colonial experience—as weighty as those in *Evelina*. But difference throws different shadows when lit by deep intersubjectivity. A good example occurs in chapter 7 of the Third Narrative, the chapter in which Franklin Blake and Rachel, meeting in Mr. Bruff's house, begin to understand each other. The early sections of this episode dramatize how miscommunication can be the subject of complex phenomenological study and how a novelist can represent the deep intersubjectivity of misunderstanding. Rachel and Franklin struggle through the mists of memory to understand primarily neither what happened on the fatal night nor their motives conceived as social categories (need for money or family pride), but those feelings that lie behind the languages of body and word by which they have so much misconceived each other. Rachel, even in her anger, questions impulses in herself and in Frank in such a way that he can understand her perceptions and can begin to respond, not only to correct Rachel's errors of judgment, but also to appropriate (and to signal his appropriation of) her behavior. Here is some of their conversation and its perception of perceptions and of being perceived. Frank's narration is a mediation, a limitation, but as in Dickens, more layered a mediation than we find in earlier narratives:

> "Have you come to compensate me for the loss of my Diamond? And have you heart enough left to feel ashamed of your errand? Is *that* the secret of your pretence of innocence, and your story about Rosanna Spearman? Is there a motive of shame at the bottom of all the falsehood this time? . . . Why did you come here to humiliate yourself?" she asked. "Why did you come here to humiliate me?"
>
> . . . I answered, "You have not tried with me to help you." Those words seemed to awaken in her something of the hope which I felt myself when I

uttered them. She replied to my questions with more than docility—she exerted her intelligence; she willingly opened her whole mind to me. (392–94)

When, a few moments later, Rachel's trust ebbs, both characters seem to sense the movements of the other self as intricately as before:

> "You have made me hope something from all this, because *you* hoped something from it. What have you to say now?" The tone in which she spoke warned me that my influence over her was a lost influence once more. "We were to look at what happened on my birthday night, together," she went on; "and we were then to understand each other. Have we done that?"
>
> . . . It wrung my heart to see her; it wrung my heart to hear her. I answered by a sign—it was all I could do—that I submitted myself to her will. The crimson flush of anger began to fade out of her face. (398–99, passim)

Frank sees his world as an interplay between body and word and so reads in others more intricately exchanged levels of mutual knowledge than Moll or Evelina can see in *Moll Flanders* or *Evelina*. "She willingly opened her whole mind to me": The terms or assumptions of Frank's perception are more subtly intersubjective because Collins's text stresses the interplay of appropriations (again, as Frank conceives his interworld). Frank reminds Rachel of her intentions to be a part of his story ("You have not tried with me to help you") and reads her readings of his version of her ("these words seemed to awaken in her . . ."); indeed Rachel's words also seem modeled on the same intersubjective practice: "You have made me hope something from all this, because *you* hoped something. . . ." These characters conceive themselves and the other by way of reversed, reflexive perceptions, as if, in Rachel's anguished questions, there were some link between their humiliations. Frank observes Rachel's adoption of his response to her anger, and even this procedure defines for both of them what it would mean "to understand each other." How different is Evelina's "understanding" of Orville: a reading of his verdicts of her, however warranted by her vulnerability and need to negotiate treacherous waters. With all the humiliation real and threatened in *Evelina,* there is no similar moment of insight into the chiasms of humiliation, no moment of recognition of intertwined violations like the moment when Rachel asks, "Why did you come here to humiliate yourself? Why did you come here to humiliate me?"

There is always a wall between the hearts and minds of subjects in narrative. But in the nineteenth-century novel the wall has become, for its neighbors like Frank and Rachel, "a wall we build together, each putting his stone in the niche left by the other." The encounter with the other has become more deeply threatening and more deeply hopeful because the story of that encounter has more chapters, more recoiling of perception upon perception, and more reading of readings.

The encounter of the I-narrator with the other: That elemental kernel of narrative is a kind of seed for what follows, as the implications of the new intersubjectivity exfoliate into storytelling more widely. This primal encounter is indeed now deeper, more intimate, darker (in the Sartrean nightmare of the eyes that have always already seen me), or less lonely (because, for Merleau-Ponty, I can know that another has more or less seen what I see). However, narrative is also different in two other ways, if we move from the kernel of this encounter either inward or outward: inward to the subjectivity that intends and that has a past and a future in a story, or outward to a broader arena in which subjects encounter others under the sponsorship of a newly intersubjective narrative omniscience. Our first move is inward, to look at the constitution of this "ghost in the machine," the subject in narrative, to see how it presumes and assumes a newly intersubjective stance, even perhaps a "self," a posited "essence," or at least a new kind of performance of what would be a self if a "character" could have a self.

THE INTERSUBJECTIVE SUBJECT: *PAMELA* AND *THE TURN OF THE SCREW*

> I wonder since how I came to be so forward. But what could I do?—My poor grateful heart was like a too full river, which overflows its banks; and it carried away my fear and my shamefacedness, as that does all before it on the surface of its waters!
> —Pamela

> I remember that, to gain time, I tried to laugh, and I seemed to see in the beautiful face with which he watched me how ugly and queer I looked.
> —The Turn of the Screw

Samuel Richardson's Pamela and Henry James's nameless governess make a useful pair to examine the intersubjective subject at this point in our project because neither depends upon a superior omniscience for the portrait of her interior life. For now, I am interested in the self-constitution of the voice, the persona, the character—though a self-constitution that may be unselfconscious, moving according to agendas and powerful magnets it may little perceive or understand. (The arrogance of this approach is in one way unforgivable—as if modern readers like myself have decoded these agendas and hegemonies and write about them with full freedom from or at least with a clear grasp of such agendas that might be writing themselves out through our own work.) There are thus two connected but quite different aspects of this intersubjective subject: its more or less explicit self-description, and the inarticulated assumptions that speak only in behavior and cultural conventions. Because enunciating this latter consciousness of consciousnesses that is performed in the milieux of gesture and ritual is difficult, that is, because the rendering of consciousness as unconscious is inherently paradoxical, this enunciation often requires the added voice or eye of another intelligence, often omniscient. In the third section of this chapter, I look at this other intersubjective subject, often a less conscious intersubjectivity, authorized and shaped by another, exterior framing consciousness. In both arenas, however, to speak of the subject as intersubjective seems, initially, enormously self-evident. But in fact we read backward, I believe, constructing a "depth" of selfhood in Pamela, Robinson Crusoe, and the Princess de Clèves (and even Odysseus and Aeneas), which is a product of this shift in narrative practices that tells new kinds of stories about the subject in relation to other subjects. It is exactly the subjects who can weave together the threads of deep intersubjectivity that have been mostly missing from narratives before Jane Austen.

What is this newly intersubjective subjectivity that tangles and untangles the knots of Merleau-Ponty's chiasm, his crisscrossing of consciousnesses? This self or stance, this potential for agency is not, as I discuss in chapter 1, the absence narrated in Lacanian psychodrama; this subject is not only others, not merely a mirror of other mirrors. Neither is this embodied, enlanguaged consciousness now primarily a self-sufficient intention that encounters others, registering information and acting in a tidy series of negotiations. The opening section of this chapter describes the complex, layered intersubjectivity of this encounter between two intentionalities, two (or more) constantly moving targets of opportunity for crisscrossing perceptions, re-cognitions, shame, humiliation, and appropriation. In the present section I suggest that this center of agency, the subject, has also become newly, deeply intersubjective, but not in a way that reinstitutes an original absence: The body, the potential for intention, and the consciousness *for*—these precede and then are subsequently interwoven with perceptions of perceptions in a web of seeings and a circle of hands touching hands touching. This subject interconnects and exchanges signs with others as a result of its self-articulations and to clarify its multiple self-knowledges. So, to invert the sequence of the opening section of this chapter, the subject queries the image of itself it perceives from another, revises that image for that other, and then yet again reinterprets the other's interpretation, putting bricks into the niches left by the other, but in pursuit, to shift metaphors in Merleau-Ponty, not of the common landscape that both intelligences have seen, but of a clearer grasp of its own subjectivity it knows the other has encountered. The balancing act here is neither to deny the weight of others in shaping subjectivity, nor to deny the reality of that self's power to intend, to experience through its body, and to stand before its mirror and perceive the gap between them (body and mirror).

This intersubjective subject also appears around the time of Jane Austen in British fiction as part of the shift in narrative practices I am addressing. This deeply intersubjective subject may be both cause and effect of this new phenomenology of narrative, and as either or both, it changes the fabric of and raises the stakes in narrative. Because the interior consciousness now records itself by way of others' versions of it, it has more to resist, more to fear, and more to hope; whatever the political and cultural contexts for the appearance of this new agency, its political and cultural consequences are far reaching. My primary project is to identify this sea change in narrative convention to demonstrate what we have come to take for granted. The politics of the construction of consciousnesses, however, looms around the edges of this discussion, modeled by important work on the formation of identity and subjectivity by Nancy Armstrong, for example, Felicity Nussbaum, and Joel Pfister. Nussbaum locates an ideological agenda for the shaping of a *coherent* subject whose essence lies outside class, gender, ethnicity, and history:

> Eighteenth century readers and contemporary readers alike efface these contradictions [of class and gender] to produce the coherent subject of the emergent capitalist society. . . . This ideology of the individual as an instance of a universal human nature distracts attention from the plurality and tensions of identity. In addition, it discourages collective enterprise and accedes to the intervention of church, state and political authority in maintaining the status quo. (1989, 56–57)

Pfister sees a similar naturalizing to be the effect of Eugene O'Neill's "staging of depth" in a new "adult" theater in America in the 1930s.

Pfister sees in O'Neill "the cultural fabrication of a particular kind of individualized self," with "depth," psychic trauma, and significant political implications for regulation of the self and its "transcendence" of mere politics.

Psychologists are important agents of what Foucault called the "disciplinary society," who measure and monitor human "depths" and earmark emotions for judgment and punishment (209, passim), and many critics working in Foucault's tradition have extended the agents of discipline to psychological novelists and their characters. I wanted to distance my project from Foucault in chapter 1, to clear a space for intentionality and a subject that precedes the microorganizations of power. But the new, deep intersubjectivities do live in grids of power, in hegemonic systems. How they do so varies from text to text and genre to genre, however, because, among other reasons, complex intersubjectivity is as interested in representing experiences of subjects, their rhythms, institutions, and possibilities for choice as it is in the isolated, apolitical "individual." In the process of identifying the shift toward deep intersubjectivity as a body of new narrative practices, I look from time to time at the ideological work these new representations do.

Pamela and *The Turn of the Screw* help us do both: see the shift in narrative assumptions more clearly and reflect on the ideological work done by representing different intersubjective subjects. Pamela and Henry James's governess particularly dramatize what is at stake in the intersubjective subject who speaks for and of herself, from powerfully enabling assumptions, however unconscious, about her own consciousness. Pamela and the governess merit pairing because they share many experiences and discourses: They are young, vulnerable women from marginalized classes, they are in love with their masters, they seek to be the heroine of their own tales, they share a predilection for self-dramatizing, and they both see themselves as triumphant in some sense against heavy odds. Because, in other words, the milieux and narrative archetypes in which their subjectivities surface are quite similar, the difference in those possibilities of the inner self are especially significant.

The closure of his courtship brings from Mr. B. a homage to Pamela that focuses conveniently on perceptions of selfhood. " 'I have such an opinion of your prudence, that I shall generally think what you do right, because it is *you* that do it' " (I, 244). Mr. B.'s testimonial is important because it allows us to ask who his "*you*" is for Pamela and how it functions in her self-articulation, in defining her stance in her world. Mr. B. further explains his regard for Pamela at the end of the chariot ride:

"Admirable Pamela!" said he; "excellent girl!—Surely thy sentiments are superior to those of all thy sex!—I might have *addressed* a hundred fine ladies; but never could have had reason to *admire* one as I do you." (I, 243)

Regard is a good word for Mr. B's understanding of Pamela because it is an understanding from a distance, across a gap that both *address* and *admire* confess to and even celebrate. For Mr. B., admiration is pleasure taken from afar, defined in opposition to the intimacies he has previously attempted. Pamela appropriates this version of herself in exactly the same mode, as a kind of metaphor in the discourse of displaced sexuality and the politics of gender. Speaking to her parents, Pamela apologizes for repeating Mr. B.'s praise, whose function for her is to exonerate and even deify *him:*

> I repeat these generous sayings, only because they are the effect of my master's goodness, being far from presuming to think I deserve one of them . . . : and so, with due deference, may [my master's] beneficence be said to be god-like, and that is the highest that can be said. (II, 243)

Pamela continues to stay two steps ahead or to the side of Mr. B., deflecting his constructions of her "you" into her own particular reformulations of social performance. For example, notice her response to my opening quotation, "what you do is right, because it is *you* that do it":

> "Sir," I said, "your kind expressions shall not be thrown away upon me, if I can help it; for they will task me with the care of endeavoring to deserve your good opinion, and your approbation, as the best rule of my conduct." (II, 244–45)

For Pamela, Mr. B.'s interpretation of her either characterizes *his* perspective (by implication, a distorted one) or articulates a *future* version of herself toward which she will strive in the hopes that one day her view of herself will more closely match Mr. B.'s (though, of course, to believe she has arrived at that version of herself would be vanity). At no point does Pamela allow Mr. B.'s "you" to become a live possibility to model her perception of herself *now,* as a person embodied in a specific life-world; instead, that "you" is an agent, welcomed, of social and self-regulation, a kind of training film that "will task me" and serve as a "rule" of conduct. A version of herself, a "you" that might have stimulated intimate self-reflection, instead is flattened, sterilized, desubjectivized, and politicized as "approbation" and "rule" and "task" (even though this last word is a verb). Equally tellingly, Pamela never asks in what kind of consciousness Mr. B.'s "you" originated, in what body and intentionality, in what life-landscape.

Yet in the middle of these deflections of the activity of consciousnesses (hers and Mr. B.'s), Pamela articulates an understanding of her subjectivity in one of her most moving images, cited at the opening of this section: "My poor grateful heart was like a too full river, which overflows its banks; and it carried away my fear and shamefacedness...." She has, after all, "boldly" just kissed Mr. B.'s hand. However controlling and controlled her acts seem to be to some readers, Pamela sees her self-knowledge as deeply flawed, as she admits later, in summarizing her change of heart about Mr. B.: Her "papers" lay out "my free acknowledgement to you, that I found, unknown to myself, I had begun to love him and could not help it" (I, 249). Pamela's images for her own subjectivity are fluid, boundary crossing (overflowing banks), and posit powers beyond her conscious will ("I could not help it"). These images mix tones in a bewildering medley from fullness (no woman-as-lack here) to poorness and gratitude (dependence on male powers to bestow), with the contrariness of waters flooding as loss of control and gaining of potence ("boldness").

So, how well *does* Pamela know herself, or, how well does Pamela's narrative wish us to think she knows herself? More important for our inquiry is the question, not how marginal and flawed might Pamela's intersubjectivity be, but what is the nature of these flaws? What are their implications for the subject's subjectivity? As in Moll Flanders's self-account, several kinds of irony are possible. Pamela's self-construction may serve various ends, which dramatic gaps in her text may reveal to us. For example, Pamela gravitates toward the powerfully patriarchal enunciative powers of Mr. B., perhaps as an anchor for her fluid will-lessness: " 'I have no will but yours,' said I (all glowing like the fire)." Yet this line introduces her criticism of Mr. B.'s plans for their wedding: "It would be better, methinks, in a *holy place*" (I, 246). What dramatic ironies gloss Pamela's self-interpretation, itself a performance before a particular audience (and not always a convincing performance, since her parents disbelieve the letter announcing her marriage)?

The most discrediting possibility is to see Pamela as coy and dishonest (more or less consciously so), as protesting too much that "I repeat these generous sayings, *only* because they are the effect of my master's goodness . . . ; so I hope you will not attribute it to my vanity" (I, 243; my emphasis). By imagining that her parents *might* hear vanity in her recitation of Mr. B.'s praise, Pamela avoids a kind of deadening naïveté but also raises herself doubts about her motives. That is, she is certainly aware that she is the target of interpretation, and she achieves a primary level of perception of others' perceptions of her, an elementary intersubjectivity in her framing of herself. One of the perennial questions about *Pamela* is how are we to read her protestations of unworthiness, given her awareness that she is the target of other's interpretation? A few readers, beginning with Henry Fielding, have suspected a not-so-secret delight in Pamela at both the sweet praise and her pose of renunciation.[8]

Whatever the flaws or bad faith in Pamela's articulation of her own consciousness, however, the curious limitation to me is the simple function of the other's consciousness in her articulation. She is powerfully aware that she is the target of interpretation, but what perceptions, experiences, and tones of feeling give rise to those interpretations in the other? How are they part of the fabric of that consciousness in her parents or Mr. B.? Neither Pamela nor *Pamela* asks these questions of their world. Mr. B. reads Pamela's letters, but she does not read *his* (in this matter *Clarissa* is a step forward). More important, Pamela does not internalize Mr. B.'s perceptions of her—she deflects them—and does not ask what consciousness those perceptions emerged from and to which her responses could be seen to return, as a thread in what could have been a tapestry of responses. So, again to reverse the chronology of the opening section of this chapter, Pamela's subjectivity is not embedded in a sequence of intendings and readings of readings that could illuminate herself to herself, as a network of discourses, embodiments, and gestures. Such a network need not imply mutuality and a sharing of the power to read readings: There is also a complex intersubjectivity of hierarchy, regulation, and supervision. Indeed, the ideological work even of *Pamela*'s simpler intersubjectivity may be the drawing of a boundary around the fluid "feminine" subject by the regulating, approving, and desubjectivized master. An important piece in the dense texture of this ideological work—which may seem ironic only to contemporary eyes—is Pamela's willing and eager contribution to drawing that boundary with her own pen.

One moment that could open into a deeper intersubjectivity occurs at the end of the chariot ride, when Pamela drops to her knees to Mr. B., and he responds to that gesture by kneeling also. But this conjunction of gestures does not serve to open to each the other's perception of her or him. In fact, they hardly acknowledge the moment's physical drama and do so only in terms of a negotiation of raisings and lowerings, of what are signs of power in Pamela's social environment:

> He clasped me in his arms with transport, and *condescendingly* kneeled by me, and kissing me, said, "O my dear obliging good girl, on my knees, *as* you on yours, I vow to you everlasting truth. . . ." "O sir," said I, "how shall I support so much goodness?—I am poor in indeed in *every thing* [sic], *compared* to you!" (my emphases, except as noted) (I, 245)

Condescension is an act of caste confidence whose willingness to soften its exercise of power only dramatizes class confidence in retaining its privilege. Mr. B. lowers himself to confirm his elevation, in his choice to join Pamela, "*as* you" [already] "on yours." And Pamela makes sure Mr. B. knows she knows how to compare their states correctly. These gestures are far removed from the movement of body to body in *Great Expectations,* for example, when Pip and Herbert touch hands. For Pamela and Mr. B., bodies are not signs of mirroring consciousnesses, at least not as Pamela and Mr. B. perceive their bodies and perceive (or do not perceive) the other's perception of their gesture. These bodies are writing a code—a complex, profound code of power and relative status that accurately expresses one kind of (class) generosity and condescension and the reception of these favors. But the movement of consciousnesses to receive, appropriate, and exchange gestures of other consciousnesses is severely limited. Even more important, the limitations of this movement are not themselves mapped against a paradigm of deeper intersubjectivity, so that, again as in *Moll Flanders,* I do not see a structural irony in these phenomenological limitations themselves.

What would such a mapping of the limits of a consciousness against the backdrop of deep intersubjectivity look like? *The Turn of the Screw* gives us a useful and profoundly moving version of a study of such an imperfectly conscious, but still deeply intersubjective, subject. The stakes for self and community, for their narration of freedom, power, and joy by means of complex intersubjectivity, are enormous. James's governess is different from Pamela because she grasps herself, early and often, not only by means of others' (especially Miles's) perception of herself, but also by means of a responding signal to him of her appropriation of his perceptions of her and, to turn the screw again, by means of his grasp of her understanding the implications of his previous appropriation of her. In my study of Merleau-Ponty's chiasm, no better example occurs of the webbing between acting and acted-upon consciousnesses. My point here is that this webbing occurs within the governess's consciousness, so it has no epistemological grounding that would, for example, solve some of the vexed debates in *The Turn of the Screw* criticism about the "reality" of the ghosts and the sanity of the governess. It is precisely this enclosure, however, that makes the governess such a good example of a subject whose self-enunciation is so deeply, thoroughly, dependently, and perhaps fatally intersubjective.

Chapter XIV is a turning point in the labyrinth of consciousnesses in James's novella because it is this confrontation with Miles, outside the Bly church, that gives the governess, as she says a little later, "the sudden revelation of a consciousness and a plan" in Miles, who wants to go back to school (or at least some place in the world where he can "see more life") (XV, 84; XIV, 82). The governess fears these embodiments of Miles's subtlety because they reveal his possession of layers of intentionality, expressed in several performance styles, however deceptive his manipulation of them may be. This opening out of Miles's subjectivity for her is so troubling to the governess because she defines herself by means of his perception of her (or how she thinks he perceives her), as my quotation at the head of this section illustrates: "I seemed to see in the beautiful face with which he watched me how ugly and queer I looked" (XIV, 81). Now her horizon of self-definition is changing vertiginously. When Miles objects that he is "getting on" to be with a lady *"always"* and the governess confesses that behind her performance of "kind" attention she "felt helpless!" Miles "seemed to know that and to play with it" (XIV, 81). Later she decides not to follow him into the church because she would lose the freedom from his "play" that she has temporarily won: "[I]t was too extreme an effort to squeeze beside him into the pew: he would be so much more sure than ever" [now that "I had already, with him, hurt myself beyond repair"] "to pass his arm into mine and make me sit there for an hour in close mute contact with his commentary on our talk" (XV, 84).

But the most extraordinary quality of this moment of desperate struggle, surrounded by the silence of the Sunday morning churchyard, is the extended chain of Miles's perceptions of her (as she constructs them), including her perception of him, by which the governess frames her experience. Miles's question, "When in the world, please, am I going back to school?" is the catastrophic challenge, blocking their way "as if one of the trees of the park had fallen across the road." Here is the kernel of intersubjective negotiation, narrated by the watcher who sees herself watched while she is watching:

> There was something new, on the spot, between us, and he was perfectly aware I recognised it, though to enable me to do so he had no need to look a whit less candid and charming than usual. I could feel in him how he already, from my at first finding nothing to reply, perceived the advantage he had gained. (XIV, 80–81)

As the governess understands this moment of interfolding glances and gestures, Miles is "perfectly aware" that she grasps the seriousness of his challenge to her authority to script his life. That is, James already gives us one "extra" layer of appropriation—Miles's of the governess's response to his question. But James adds another step in this negotiation: Miles, again in the governess's understanding, *wants* her to see that he sees her new sense of their now confrontational relation: "to enable me to do so. . . ." The governess reads Miles's intentionality already at a second level: In that reading, he intends to challenge her authority, and he intends her to see that he perceives how she reacts to his challenge. In the final turn of the intersubjective screw, there are two more moves on the gameboard: the governess's silence in response to Miles's recognition of her recognition, and Miles's subsequent sense of "advantage" gained, which the governess "could feel in him."

In this dazzling labyrinth of perceptions of perceptions, the paradoxical quality of Merleau-Ponty's wall, built by two subjects each placing bricks in the niche left by the other, is especially important because it is not clear how much the attentiveness of each consciousness to the other produces a kind of intimacy or a particularly sad isolation. Does this wall of intersubjective crisscrossing link or separate? It does both, of course. And we cannot trust the governess to quite understand how this linkage and separation work. However "correct" the governess's fears about Miles and the ghosts might be, or in whatever sense they might be correct, it is clear to almost all readers that the governess is not an entirely reliable narrator: that, like Pamela, she misses a few signals in her world and misconstrues every now and then. But the significant comparison to *Pamela* lies here: that the degree of separation, of blindness in the narrating consciousness, is framed by the terms of deep intersubjectivity and by the knotted exchanges of consciousnes*ses*. James's governess is an intersubjective subject in a way fundamentally different from Pamela.

How blind the governess is is the famous, and perhaps irrelevant, problem: irrelevant according to the view that focusing on the "reality" of the ghosts as paranormal phenomena is unnecessary: We see specific traces of the children's wounding—the loss of and abandonment by parents and parent surrogates, the sexualizing by the friendship with Miss Jessel and Quint (what were Flora's words in her illness that so shocked Mrs. Grose? And what were Miles's stories at school that were disturbing enough to cause his expulsion?). Their continuing influence is a psychological reality, whether or not a psychic one.[9] But however blind the governess may be to Miles's "true" motives and innocence, she does not invent his phenomenological sophistication unless we believe she invents events and conversations. So in this same confrontation she gives us reason to believe Miles thinks about thinking in just the way I have been proposing. The frame of deep intersubjectivity, in other words, does not originate only within her consciousness:

> "Does my uncle think what *you* think?"
> I markedly rested. "How do you know what I think?"
> "Ah well, of course I don't; for it strikes me you never tell me. But I mean does *he* know?"
> "Know what, Miles?"
> "Why, the way I'm going on." (XIV, 82–83)

Miles's questions don't delve as intricately into the interfoldings of consciousnesses as the governess does in our earlier scene, but his interest in what he or the governess thinks about what either one knows about what other people think is similar in its structural, phenomenological density. The effect of his careful scrutiny is to reinforce the governess's sense of her self in her world, as a subject whose deeply intersubjective self-framing extends the horizons of conflict and loneliness.

Once the intersubjective subject is framed by another intelligence, usually an omniscient one, the thematic, aesthetic, and ideological impact shifts some, most obviously because the subject now need not have as subtle a sense of relations to the other as Pamela and James's governess do. And those relations can evolve in gestural, ritual codes whose complexities the narrating intelligence can suggest. An intriguing question lurks here: Does deep intersubjectivity need some center of consciousness to render and interpret this intersubjectivity of the body, of gesture, of Merleau-Ponty's incarnation? For narrative, say a text in a theater, simply to present the exchange of touch or to see hands touching hands that touch doesn't adequately open up the spaces of the chiasm. A cynic might say that intersubjectivity, certainly deep intersubjectivity, is always a narrative in the voice of an interpreter, that is, is always a construct, a desire, a type of myth of community ("only connect"). If we accept Merleau-Ponty's rejection of solipsism and Cartesian idealism, then we have a different response: Complex intersubjectivity requires at least one self, one consciousness—one participating in the crisscrossing of perceptions (whatever "participating" might mean)—

with the intelligence and interest to observe the observing, to note gesture responding to gesture, and to trace the receding sequence of mirrorings in the engaged consciousnesses. This "participation" might be open to more than the engaged characters, perhaps also to their narrator and even to an observing, semidetached but talented decoder within the narrative's diegesis, to a Marlow or a Nick Carraway (even if venturing such participation usually reveals deep flaws and blindnesses in this sidelines commentator). In the next chapter I look at the evolving nature of omniscient narrative as it too becomes more deeply intersubjective. But for the moment I am interested in the intersubjective subject inside another narrating frame.

Fielding's *Tom Jones* offers us in Tom a figure whose interest in others promises, despite Tom's simplicities, a genuine intersubjective faculty. This faculty might be conceived as the ability to perceive one's inner experience by way of others' experiences, and Tom possesses this faculty and exercises it in at least some circumstances. One of Tom's most attractive moments occurs when his sympathetic imagination writes the narrative of Molly's future in Book 5. The context is Tom's fear that abandoning the pregnant Molly will expose her to the ignominies that Allworthy has earlier so explicitly described to Jenny:

> [Tom's] own heart would not suffer him to destroy a human creature, who, he thought, loved him, and had to that love sacrificed her innocence. His own good heart pleaded her cause; not as a cold venal advocate; but as one interested in the event, and which must itself deeply share in all the agonies its owner brought on another. (Book 5, chapter 3, 209)

Tom's sympathy allows him to picture the world Molly may soon enter and to narrate her experiences, extending in time the conditions of her condition:

> He now saw her in all the most shocking postures of death; nay, he considered all the miseries of prostitution to which she would be liable . . . ; the ruin of the poor girl must, he foresaw, unavoidably attend his deserting her; and this thought stung him to the soul. (208)

Repeatedly through this chapter the words "saw" and "foresaw" occur to describe Tom's relation to Molly's future suffering, whose possibilities and limits are similar to those of Moll Flanders in relation to the pickpocket's suffering: Tom makes generic Molly's story by his rhetorical appeal to completeness: "all the agonies," "all the most shocking postures of death," "all the miseries of prostitution." Completeness lets Tom off the hook of entering into the difficult specifics of this parable of the fallen woman. He generalizes with other language, too: "the poor girl," one who is both "the object of compassion" and "the object of desire" (209). The result is that Tom does not conceive of himself as the object of another's particular consciousness who can respond *for* him and to whose responses he in turn can gesture.

But perhaps erotic passion can lead Tom deeper than fear and shame. In this and the preceding chapter he has imagined Sophia's imagining and has concluded that one of the aftereffects of his broken arm is the exposure of Sophia's passion for him, in her distraction while playing the harpsichord:

> [A]nd probably she imputed the passionate resentment, which Jones had expressed against the mare, to a different motive from that which her father had derived it. Her spirits were at this time in a visible flutter. . . . [H]e came to reflect on the whole, that all was not well in the tender bosom of Sophia. . . . [H]e had a much stronger passion for her than he himself was acquainted with. His heart now brought forth the full secret, at the same time that it assured him the adorable object returned his affection. (206–7)

Tom's "assurance" is not very deeply assured, however, as he doubts his reading of Sophia. "For first, though he had sufficient foundation to flatter himself on what he had observed in Sophia, he was not yet free from doubt of misconstruing compassion, or, at best, esteem, into a warmer regard" (207). In fact Tom's observation of Sophia is a means of defining and evolving a subjectivity (his) by way of the response to him of another: Tom Jones is most certainly an example of an intersubjective subject. He discriminates subtly among Sophia's possible responses, too: Compassion is not passion, nor is esteem, and he ponders a bit on how easy it is to confuse the gestural signs of one with the other. Perhaps passion does lead Tom more deeply into the life of another than shame did: For eros to open subjects to a superior depth (so to speak) might be a defining difference between comedy and tragedy or satire.

Tom's participation in both Molly's and Sophia's life-world, however, is severely limited in ways characteristic of early, simpler narratives of intersubjectivity. At issue is a lack in Tom's consciousness of a persevering attentiveness to the other's gestures and their originating intentionalities. The webbing of imagined or perceived consciousnesses by which Tom situates himself in the world has no threads leading back to him from a Molly or Sophia who has attended to *his* understanding of her. Molly and Sophia are each "objects" at key moments. Even Tom, amid his passion for Sophia, feels joyful that "the adorable object returned his affection" (207). The limitation of "object" here may seem to originate as much with Tom's narrator as with Tom: Certainly the voice of the free indirect discourse here is Fielding's narrator. But "adorable object" is his translation, with ironic comment, of Tom's feelings about Sophia and reflects that to some degree she remains for Tom a thing as much as a subjectivity: hence the paradox of the phrase "the adorable object returned his affection" (the paradox arising out of the attribution to an *object* of feeling).

Nevertheless, in light of Merleau-Ponty's paradigm of deep intersubjectivity, the major absence here is the crisscrossing of understandings, gestures, and signs. This narrative does not conceive how Tom could care to imagine in Molly's story her perception of his thought or his response to her appropriation of his thought. That is, Tom's story, in an important sense a story about himself, contains no dramatization of Molly appropriating his behavior or words in such a way that he can espouse or even observe her thought of his thought. Remember how different is the intricacy with which Henry James's governess thinks about how Miles thinks about her thoughts about him. The same limitation applies to Tom's efforts to read Sophia. It is her response to him he seeks to read, and his close reading now attends more to body than word, to her "tender bosom" and her "spirits." What is intriguing is the limits that function when Tom tries to move beyond the body. He thinks Sophia might feel "affection towards him" because of "what he had observed in Sophia." But Sophia as a subject with a tone, who sees shadows fall from her own angle, and, most important, who can appropriate Tom's gestures and respond to and *for* him, as her own source of intentionality—this Sophia we never meet in Tom's consciousness. And so Tom cannot be a more fully intersubjective self, one who conceives himself through Sophia's gestures, which articulate his presence in some sense in *her* subjectivity. He does not dramatize his inner life in scripts with more deeply complex networks of consciousness in which his self watches other subjects responding to his gestures, and responds to them, in an expanding series of appropriation and mirrorings.

Again it is significant to note that this absence in *Tom Jones* remains despite the presence of a most articulate, self-aware, subtle narrator. The wonderful consciousness of Fielding's narrator, chef, innkeeper, and ruler of his new kingdom has little effect on the intersubjectivity of the intersubjective self. This narrating consciousness adds a layer of rich rhetoric and commentary over and under that subjectivity. But the chiasm of consciousnesses, the knottedness of perceptions within the subject in *Tom Jones* is not fundamentally different from the constitution of the subject in *Pamela*.

One of the few moments in *Tom Jones*—wonderfully comic but also epistemologically shocking—when a subject observes itself being observed, and which points toward a kind of deep intersubjectivity—occurs only two chapters after the sequence discussed earlier, when Tom happens on the luckless Square in Molly's closet. "He had a nightcap belonging to Molly on his head, and his two large eyes, the moment the rug fell, stared directly at Jones . . ." (215). By emphasizing Square's "large eyes" at this climactic moment, and their object, as they target Jones "directly," the narrator underscores the moment of the shock of recognition that both have of being seen while seeing. It is Sartre's archetypal instant of knowing that one is always already the subject of another's gaze, but here doubled and tangled in comic complications: Jones has of course not "already" seen Square in this position, at least not knowingly, but in fact earlier traces of Square's presence now coalesce into a recognizable story (from Molly's confusion at Tom's arrival a few moments earlier to Square's long-standing defense of "natural" behavior), at the narrative consistency of which Tom laughs as much as at Square's posture in the closet. " 'Right,' cries Jones, 'what can be more innocent than the indulgence of a natural appetite? or what more laudable than the propagation of our species?' " (218). Each man has, in a sense, an edge over the other; the shame of the gaze covers both Tom and Square, letting both off the hook and leaving Molly, the object in an ideologically focused system of male gazes, with no hand to play; her look is of course powerless from the first.

The network of gazes here is enormously complex, describing arcs of supervision, with inversions of power (the teacher taught, the child triumphant) and unchallenged hierarchies (of gender and class). This complexity, however, does not approach deep intersubjectivity. Fielding's effect is comic exposure (of hypocrisies, masquerades, and ideological contradictions), not self-revelation or the opening out of the series of perceptions perceived that would be necessary to ground these exposures in deep intersubjectivity. What does *not* happen here is appropriation of appropriation.

Merleau-Ponty's mutuality is missing because Square does not respond to or for Tom as a subjectivity with his own history and body of gestures that incarnate a consciousness, nor does Tom respond from any center in which he has absorbed Square's observation of *him* observing. A certain kind of exchange about intentionality does occur in this scene, to examine which will help us understand a rhetorical use of limited intersubjectivity that will differ strikingly from the rhetorical uses of deep intersubjectivity. Square *does* grasp the power system in which their gazes—his and Tom's—function, and he negotiates with Tom within that system:

> "Well, sir, I see you enjoy this mighty discovery, and, I dare swear, taste great delight in the thoughts of exposing me; but if you will consider the matter fairly, you will find you are yourself only to blame. I am not guilty of corrupting innocence. . . . ." "Well reasoned, old boy," answered Jones. (218)

Square's notion of the interior subject that can "enjoy" his exposure and "taste great delight" in this moment is not intersubjectively sequential: That is, he conceives no narrative of embodiments, his of Tom's, Tom's of his (even if that narrative were one of blocked, defended embodiments). Instead, his attribution of "delight" to Tom is a counter in a negotiation. The negotiation is the narrative here: Square seeks to neutralize Tom's anticipated pleasure in exposing him by setting against that delight the "truth" of Tom's responsibility for Molly's condition.

This negotiation fails to be deeply intersubjective not only because Square is wrong in his reading of Tom's "delight," but also because Square's "I" and "you" as perceiving consciousnesses make no further effort to construct the other's construction of itself. Jones and Square compare verdicts and negotiate labels: "You was of a different opinion when my affair with this girl was first discovered," says Jones, and Square replies, "The matter was misrepresented to me by that person Thwackum" (219). Fielding's reader never knows either how Square incorporated into his own self-perception his appearance in Jones's gaze or how Tom saw himself as a result of seeing Square or of seeing Square see him. Merleau-Ponty, like Sartre, allows for the alienness of being seen, but even those effects of being seen are missing in *Tom Jones:* "I, who am irreducibly alien to all my roles, feel myself moved by my appearance in the gaze of others and . . . I in turn reflect an image of them that can affect them . . ." (*In Praise of Philosophy* 82)

One of the best suggestions of the interfolding missing here is the *absence* of Molly's gaze, or of her experience of being looked at, or even of Tom's or Square's experience of looking at her looking at them, or of any aspect incorporated into their consciousness of her looking at, or of returning, their looks. Once the curtain falls, Molly simply disappears as a subject or a pair of eyes. Deep intersubjectivity can certainly occur in a patriarchal setting, but Molly's absence as part of an incarnated intergesturing underlines here the *uses* of Square's reading of Tom: not as part of an outfolding of intentionalities but as a tool in an at-most double-layered reading of readings by the Other. Even the shadow of shame here (the shame avoided) is not complex because of its unawareness of the interiority of the violation by the gaze of the Other. This evasion of interiority is part of Fielding's comic rhetoric in several senses of comedy (and I develop this topic more fully in chapter 4): sacrifice (of Molly), the triumph of the vital son, and laughter as both healing and a testament of anxiety. The ideological work of complex intersubjectivity in comedy is less likely to require a sacrifice quite so blithely or to achieve even an ironic negotiated settlement so evenly because of the wariness (in narrators and readers) about subjects that emerges from a more intricate representation of mirrorings of mirrorings. One way of measuring Fielding's fiction against later narrative practice is to note that his social, objective, mythic comedy is, despite its many kinds of richness, flat in this particular human self-conception: When people's eyes meet and remeet, there is little appropriation, espousal, intersubjective gesture and *re*gesturing, and interiorizing of espousal.

Vanity Fair makes a particularly pertinent bookend in this instance because Thackeray's narrator speaks in a voice similar in so many ways—in its combination of cynicism and belief, in its self-awareness as tale-teller and tale-maker, in its zest for his story—to Fielding's narrator. The panoramic arenas of both novels are also similar in reach and, one might say, in the absence of encouragements to intimacy between characters and between them and their narrator. Yet the shift in narrative practice and narrative phenomenology makes its effects felt. The angle of light has shifted. The intersubjective subject is also different in *Vanity Fair*.

Watching watchers, and being seen while seeing, recur in *Vanity Fair*, as one might expect in a novel with so many mirrors, but the depth of these seeings has remarkable importance for the subject's subjectivity and embodies our paradigm shift in an especially dramatic way. Becky's power, for example, resides partly in her ability to respond with equanimity and assertiveness to being seen while seeing. As in *Tom Jones,* eyes meeting eyes is the charged moment of exposure and challenge (as in Sartre's archetypal experience of stooping to the keyhole and glancing backward to discover one is gazing into someone else's eyes):

> "There's not a finer fellow [Dobbin] in the service," Osborne said, "nor a better officer, though he is not an Adonis, certainly." And he looked towards the glass himself with much *naivete;* and in so doing, caught Miss Sharp's eye fixed keenly upon him, at which he blushed a little, and Rebecca thought in her heart, "Ah, *mon beau Monsieur!* I think I have *your* gage." (V, 52)

Even this brief interchange enunciates a more extended, more interiorized negotiation of consciousnesses than we found in *Tom Jones*. George's embodiment of Becky's gaze responds, first of all, to an intentionality the gaze bespeaks ("keenly"), so that his blush is a reading of her reading of his self-understanding as he embodies it before the mirror, and he reads not only her reading, but also her motives for reading and her conclusions. Subsequently, Becky takes George's blush as confirmation of her construction, in yet another response of consciousness to the Other. Thackeray's subjects read, and are read, in a deeply intersubjective way in a complex process that we recognize from *Great Expectations* and *The Turn of the Screw*. This subject (Becky) is capable of reading (sometimes) the Other in an extended, interfolding sequence that complicates even a narcissistic, blinded subject (George Osborne).

Old Mr. Osborne's fury at the premature death of his son is predicated on the same, more intricate, intersubjective subject by way of a similar experience of being seen while seeing:

> There was a chance before of reconciliation. The boy's wife might have died; or he might have come back and said, Father, I have sinned. But there was no hope now. He stood on the other side of the gulf impassable, haunting his parent with sad eyes. He remembered them once before so in a fever, when everyone thought the lad was dying.... [A]fter the crisis of the fever, the lad recovered, and looked at his father once more with eyes that recognized him. But now there was no help or cure, or chance of reconcilement: above all there were no humble words to soothe vanity outraged and furious. (XXXV, 340–41)

This example works even more fundamentally to construct the intersubjective subject because its substance is a narrative Mr. Osborne tells himself about himself, and within it he is watched watching George, whose sad eyes "recognize" him all too well, but the yearned-for response (from George) to being seen watching is silence: The last beat of the narrative in the rhythm of subjects in their dance together is all the more present in its absence, in the empty measure (in the musical sense). In a way, the father and son will continue watching each other across that "gulf impassable" (in the father's internal narrativizing) in an ever-extending mirroring of loss and anger and an ever-reenunciated absence of the words Osborne hungers for, whether, in mutually exclusive and equally tormenting finales to his dream narrative, these words are "his forgiveness, or . . . that apology which his own pride expected . . ." (XXXV, 341). This is the deeply intersubjective subject with a vengeance.

The narrating voice that can authorize layers of perception and reperceivings and misperceivings opens up new terrain for the intersubjective subject: It can represent the operation of consciousness of consciousnesses in George Osborne or Amelia Sedley, for example, that such unselfthoughtful subjects could ill represent themselves. Deep intersubjectivity requires some presence to note the layerings of gesture and discourse, even if what is noted is their absence. But what is remarkable is the continuity of the redirection of narrative practices in narratives of omniscience, too: The representation of the construction of consciousnesses within the experiencing subject is similar in shape in *Pamela, Tom Jones, The Turn of the Screw,* and *Vanity Fair.* The addition of an authorizing narrator extends the playing field for these new narrative practices to allow for a multiplication of complex intersubjectivities, with their more comic, ironic, or tragic implications. It is time now to approach the issues of intersubjective omniscience directly and to move beyond the intersubjective subject to the encounter of others with others, the larger arena in which some of the cultural work of this new paradigm is most explicit, as it exposes and articulates assumptions about community and power.

OTHERS ENCOUNTER OTHERS: INTERSUBJECTIVE OMNISCIENCE: *TOM JONES* AND *MIDDLEMARCH*

Intersubjective omniscience and others encountering others: The important work of two critics prepares the way for both of these topics, or this topic with two faces. J. Hillis Miller links the flowering of intersubjectivity in the Victorian novel to the omniscient narrator in *The Form of Victorian Fiction* and Mikhail Bakhtin's study of heteroglossia in fiction, in *Discourse in the Novel,* devotes extensive attention to the response and counterresponse of voice to voice, language to language, between subjectivities and social classes. Together Miller and Bakhtin trace some of the fundamental elements of intersubjective omniscience and the stories it tells.

For Miller, the new, richer intersubjectivity of Victorian fiction is a product of new conventions of the omniscient narrator, with its "powers of ubiquity in space and time" and especially its "powers of direct access to other minds" and its consequent ability to relive characters' experience from within and to represent them in their words rephrased, or in the narrator's, or in a combination of both (*Form* 3). Of course omniscient narrators before Thackeray and Dickens had such access and power, but the difference—although Miller does not discuss earlier fiction—is that nineteenth-century novelists write in the shadow of the disappearance of God. The form and function of the novel's intersubjectivity have changed: "[B]ecause there no longer seems to be any supernatural foundation for society or the self, Victorian novels are likely to take the form of an incomplete self-generating structure" (33–34), and Miller's book outlines various routes to a new construction of community by way of the newly important narrators, who "are one form or another of a collective mind." As he explains in one instance, "Trollope, like the other five novelists, escapes from exclusion by playing the role of a narrator who coincides not with a god nor with any individual person, but with the general mind of the community" (88). Nineteenth-century omniscient narrators work toward this function, even if they are self-dramatizing voices like *Vanity Fair*'s, but the process is clearest in narrators like Trollope's, who include not only the ironic paraphraser, but also a wider presence surrounding the particular voice (even in Trollope there is such a voice, who occasionally uses the mask of an "I," as in *Barchester Towers*): "[S]urrounding all, like the glass case and its atmosphere, there is the mind which knows all and judges correctly, seeing everything clearly in all space and time, like an immanent god" (86).

Miller's interest in the role of omniscience in articulating an image of connections among others is most helpful to us. Representations of intersubjectivity have important social and political work to do; they are deeply ideological, and our language echoes Foucault in ways Miller's does not. We may have less faith than Miller (in this 1970 text) that "through the act of reading the reader tries to identify himself with another mind and to re-experience from the inside the feelings and thoughts of that mind" (2). But the tracings of narrative on the page remain with us, and their implications are as important now as they were in 1970. An important cluster of implications that is the topic of this discussion is close to the heart of Miller's argument: Our new deep intersubjectivity changes the way narrative represents encounters among others and the assumptions about community (or its absence) that enable those encounters.

Bakhtin's study of heteroglossia in the novel helps us theorize not about narrators, but about the encounters among others themselves or, more precisely, the languages of those encounters. Because for Bakhtin language, as we discussed in chapter 1, is always another's, all conversation is a borrowed and borrowing enterprise. Furthermore, like Merleau-Ponty, Bakhtin sees speaking as directed *to* and *for* another, who will respond:

> In the actual life of speech, every concrete act of understanding is active: it assimilates the word to be understood . . . with the response, with a motivated agreement or disagreement. To some extent, primacy belongs to the response, as the activating principle. . . . The speaker strives to get a reading on his own word, and on his own conceptual system that determines this word, within the alien conceptual system of the understanding receiver. (282)

All words carry the "taste" of another, as Bakhtin sees language, whether it is the "taste" of "a profession, a genre, a tendency, a party, a particular work, a particular person, a generation, an age group, the day and hour"; a subject, however, may appropriate the word, "populat[ing] it with his own intention, his own accent" (293). Nonetheless, the speaker is particularly attentive to the indices of consciousness in the other: "The speaker strives to get a reading on his own word, and on his own conceptual system that determines this word." This model of appropriation anticipates in a useful way Merleau-Ponty's paradigm of appropriations of appropriations, but in a wider social process than Merleau-Ponty's. Bakhtin helps us to conceive of intersubjective encounters among more subjects, with a more tangled skein of class, caste, subject positions, and situations.

Miller and Bakhtin are divergent mentors to solicit for this study, one with deeply metaphysical interests (in *The Form of Victorian Fiction*), the other grounded in cultural materialism, however multiple its forms of carnival. Bakhtin's approach emphasizes difference and contestation among discourses, whereas Miller has a stronger sense of an immanence in the presence of the new narrator that mutes the glossalalia of classes and genres. To Bakhtin, discourse and narrative are fundamentally social, whereas for Miller metaphysical loss is an essential component in Victorian intersubjective narratives. Bakhtin is more interested in the tangle of words themselves than in the construction of subjectivities from whose intentions, memories, fears, and blindness those words issue. Bakhtin's idea, however, that "language, for the individual consciousness, lies on the border between oneself and the other" helps us track the tangle of discourses of intersubjectivities in the larger arena open to the omniscient narrator in our narratives of encounters among multiple others (293). And if dialects and codes are traces of intentions and subjectivity, we can use Miller to think about consciousness of consciousnesses and the assumptions behind its narration. These strategies enable us to make broader and deeper uses of Merleau-Ponty's paradigm of deep intersubjectivity as we examine intersubjective omniscience.

Nevertheless we are left with the fundamental questions, does the shift in narrative practices for the representation of subjectivities that I am proposing affect the nature and function of narrative omniscience? And do they affect the representation of encounters between others in sequences among several others, that final consequence which, as I suggested earlier, requires the enabling omniscient voice to articulate these labyrinths of deep intersubjectivity? If a new narrative of the self, situating it amidst the extended responses to and from other subjectivities, reshapes that subject's relation to the other and to itself, then it is reasonable that this paradigm of complex intersubjectivities will reshape the narration of encounters within larger clusters of others. It will also reshape the voice that narrates those encounters.

It is the new powers of narrating omniscience, I suspect, that nourished representations of deep intersubjectivity. In this instance, life may have imitated art, and texts may have written culture to the extent that our new narrative practices may indeed have written a new psychology and newly intricate forms of material culture, perhaps even the phenomenology that enables this study, in the last two hundred years. Hillis Miller theorized that the disappearance of God gave a purpose to the new voices of omniscience in Victorian novelists, with their compensatory confidence and organ tones of wisdom. Perhaps the newly empowered omniscient voice, with its strategies for tracing complex intersubjectivity, was a device at hand, in the wake of Austen's multiple and far-reaching successes with it, to deepen and ground nineteenth-century narrative amid an array of uncertainties aesthetic, ethical, political, epistemological, and cosmological. This resort to deep intersubjectivity might even have served as a compensation for the losses of, or a defense against, the extending microgrids of surveillance that Foucauldian cultural history has charted, although a pessimist might argue that the camera eye of deeply intersubjective narration could be turned against the subject in a finer technology of supervision. John Bender makes essentially this argument in linking the novel and the penitentiary in eighteenth-century England:

> While it remains permissive in many respects, the novel oscillates between points of view that imply surveillance and enclosure. . . . In this light, it is of

more than incidental significance that Defoe served as a spy and a government agent—the very human medium of surveillance—and that he repeatedly suffered imprisonment. (61)

I prefer to hope that the new deeply intersubjective narration might have been, and might still be, a secret weapon against the panopticon, with its own promises for guerilla action behind the front lines.

To discuss the voice of narrative omniscience as itself intersubjective may provoke in a new form the scepticism I discuss in chapter 1, about "character" as an illusion of depth attributed to a chain of signifiers. I suggested then that insofar as the tracings of a narrative point to agents choosing to act, with intentions (however illusory) and consciousness *for*, to this extent it is justifiable to discuss the construction of intentionality, subjectivity, and "personality." My close readings of Moll Flanders and Henry James's governess seek to clarify the representation of consciousnesses presumed within, traced by, and committed to by those texts. But what sense does it make to speak of a narrative posture, even a dramatized story-telling omniscient character, as a subjectivity? As Wayne Booth and Wolfgang Iser argued years ago, narrators, regardless of whether dramatized and self-identifying, function in complex rhetorical schemes in relation to their readers (that is, the readers they construct, not their real, historical readers, the focus of more recent reader-response criticism as it melds into cultural studies). Part of these rhetorics and relationships is the claim by the text that its narrator is an intentionality, too, a voice with experience and sometimes a history. One might even argue that virtually all omniscient narration claims such a subjectivity, however invisible the narrating fly on the wall is, and that there is a characterizing stance, tone, or enabling world-view, to the narration of *The Return of the Native* or *Gravity's Rainbow* as much as to the narration of (half of) *Bleak House* ("Dead, your Majesty. Dead, my lords and gentlemen. . . . And dying thus around us every day") or *The Mill on the Floss* or *Tom Jones*. Because this omniscient story-telling narrator crosses boundaries of consciousnesses in the world (in its tale), it inevitably takes on some intentionality and consciousness of its own as an agent of transgression and eavesdropping.

Intersubjectivity, either simpler or complex, is of course also part of narration's diegesis, its fabula, and not its only *syuzhet*. Omniscient narration practices intersubjectivity in weaving its tapestry of consciousnesses in two distinct provinces: first, in the tale and its cast of characters; and second, in the frame tale, in the narrative of the narration, so to speak, as the narrative voice implies responses between itself and other subjects within the story, in its own past, or from the audience it conceives for its narration. So narrative omniscience can be intersubjective, whether more simply or less simply, in two different settings. The narrators' self-reflexivity, their thoughtfulness about their own constructedness or that of their tales, interestingly enough, does not itself produce or banish deep intersubjectivity. Conventions of representation, however defamiliarized, have a way of locking into place to tell a story. Thackeray's narrator in *Vanity Fair* identifies Becky and Amelia repeatedly as his puppets, yet readers think of them as consciousnesses interfolding subtly because Thackeray's story imagines them, with whatever self-confessed trickery, as subjects responding and not responding to each other in complex, interlocking sequences of perceptions. The reverse, moreover, is true as well: If self-awareness in a narrator does not banish deep intersubjectivity, neither does it produce it, as we will see in *Tom Jones*. The most obvious arena to study the change in omniscient narrative's intersubjectivity is the first, the tapestry of consciousnesses in the story, and that is the topic of the second half of this discussion. But first I want to spend some time on the second possibility: that omniscience itself, as a consciousness, is capable of intersubjectivity and that this capacity changes with our shift in narrative practices.

Intersubjective Omniscience in Tom Jones *and* Middlemarch

> *If I have been an entertaining companion to thee, I promise thee it is what I have desired. If in anything I have offended, it was really without any intention. Some things perhaps here said, may have hit thee or thy friends; but I do most solemnly declare they were not pointed at them. I question not but thou hast been told, among other stories of me, that thou wast to travel with a very scurrilous fellow: but whoever told thee so did me an injury.*
> —Tom Jones

> *But Fielding lived when the days were longer (for time, like money, is measured by our needs), when the summer afternoons were spacious, and the clock ticked slower in the winter evenings. We belated historians must not linger after his example; and if we did so, it is probably that our chat would be thin and eager, as if delivered from a camp-stool in a parrot-house.*
> —Middlemarch

Tom Jones's narrator is a well-known Mobius strip, residing inside and outside his story at different moments, friend of Allworthy and yet ruler of his new province, the novel. This narrator is ideally positioned to claim intersubjective powers and an intersubjective voice, and he does so in his tale and in what might be called his frame tale, his story about his tale telling and his relation to it and his readers. In this frame tale, our first topic, the extent of his imagination of a life with his readers, for example, is remarkable. To begin with, the *Tom Jones* narrator represents himself as a subjectivity, as a consciousness with feelings, intentions, a memory, and a sense of how others see him. His role as guide and companion on the tale's long journey depends on his construction of his place in the consciousness of his reader. The fact that he has invented this reader himself does not make the assumptions of this construction any less intersubjective.

In this intersubjective space, certain kinds of negotiation occur again, constructed by the narrator for his own rhetorical purposes, as I said before, but the negotiations and interlockings take place nonetheless. In the quotation at the head of this discussion from Book XVIII, for example, our guide conceives a story of anticipation in the reader growing from tales told that reader by the narrator's enemies. In other words, the implied reader is a member of a community, with a circle of influence and friends who might have inadvertently been targets of the narrator's satire. The reader is furthermore a self capable of offense and pleasure, of being angry and entertained, a center of appetite (famously in Book I), who "may be rendered desirous to read on for ever . . ." (53) .The narrator is also a figure who remembers, hears tales, and can be hurt because the "scurrilous" stories that the reader has heard mirror ones in the narrator's memory: "I have had some of the abusive writings of those very men fathered upon me, who in other of their works have abused me themselves with the utmost virulence" (814). Indeed, in an ironic reversal, the narrator has been accused (like Partridge) of fathering offspring that are not his. Both reader and narrator, in that narrator's construction, are consciousnesses that inhabit communities of other subjects who react, perceive, and judge.

The frame tale in *Tom Jones* is manifestly intersubjective. The degree to which Fielding's narrator constructs his readers and *their* narratives of interaction, even the degree to which that narrator knows he is constructing this network and tells his audience he knows he is constructing them, does not alter the intersubjective nature of his fiction. In a sense this labyrinth of intentionalities is similar to the self-enunciation of Mr. Osborne in *Vanity Fair:* It is a drama, conceived within the writing personality, with interfoldings that body forth that personality to itself.

It is also equally clear that Fielding's frame teller is not himself a deeply intersubjective subject, nor, in his stories of response and counterresponse from others, are those others. Those counterresponses are negotiations about actions, decisions, and verdicts ("scurrilous fellow") on a single plane of consciousnesses. There is no circulation of the gestures of subjectivities whose imperfect mediations between boundaried selves could allow some appropriation of the body and intentionality of the other, to ground (or block) a grasp of self or other in a mutual network of perceptions. Fielding's narrator wishes to "entertain" his reader, for example, and never meditates on what that entertainment builds from in the reader's (supposed) consciousness or how that experience could mirror back to him his own project in a series of further mirrorings. Merleau-Ponty spoke of a kind of "intercorporeity" of subjects touching each other touching, speaking to each other speaking: Perhaps this appropriation of gestures and words, in extended mirrorings of response in a new kind of narrative time, is too much to expect within a narrator's own space in the narrative of the narrative.

The narrative of the narrative in *Middlemarch*, however, *is* deeply intersubjective. In the space for movement the narrative voice makes for itself, these mutually acknowledging gestures of attentive consciousnesses are imagined to occur. At the center of the frame tale in *Middlemarch*—the effort by this "historian" to weave her remarkable web—is indeed the consciousness of the storyteller, who conceives herself as a complex intersubjective self. For example, in the parallel citation from *Middlemarch* at the head of this discussion, the voice tells us about its own history, its experience in time as a reader of a Fielding from a different time. This voice is not suprahuman because its contrast with Fielding's world implies that *its* summer evenings are less spacious, *its* clock ticks faster. This is a consciousness already with a landscape, an experience of seasons, a life narrative that includes time to read *Tom Jones*. This subject seems to be less explicitly dramatized than Tom Jones's narrator, but in fact its story and setting, though drawn more indirectly, are well situated and outlined. This voice even has a circle of intimates, as she describes in chapter 27: "An eminent philosopher among my friends, who can dignify your ugly furniture by lifting it into the serene light of science, has shown me this pregnant little fact" (and what follows is the often-cited discussion of candlelight on "your" finely scratched pier glass) (297). This situated story-telling voice, attending to others and speaking out of that attention, becomes more and more deeply intersubjective in the mental life it leads within this landscape and history. The voice's exchange with other subjects is, of course, constructed within its own text's imagined space for the life of its consciousness, encountering (or imagining the encounter with) readers, remembering its life, writing its novel. These encounters presume in various ways the activity of various consciousnesses: for example, the readings of the narrator's audience (their judgment as listeners that "belated historians" who try to imitate Fielding will deliver only "thin and eager" chat as from a "camp-stool in a parrot-house"). Eliot's narrator even imagines her reader's imagination, tacking in the wind of a willful narration toward the sort of subject a reader can really enjoy: "Thus while I tell the truth about loobies, my reader's imagination need not be entirely excluded from an occupation with lords" (XXXV, 375).

Even so, do these negotiations between consciousnesses, storyteller and reader, or novelist and eminent scientific friend, entail the adoptions of perceptions, espoused between selves, of deep intersubjectivity? The mirrorings do not extend as intricately as they will in the novel this narrator's narrative frames, but the storyteller does appropriate implied readings by her audience, imagines the source of those readings, and reinterprets them back to her interlocutors. So the narrator will not imitate Fielding, to be derided as a sideshow crier; she recycles her friend the natural philosopher's understanding of a pier glass as an image for her egoism and ours; she imagines the process of her reader's reading to suggest, however sarcastically, an escape from "loobies" to lords.

Middlemarch's storyteller becomes most deeply intersubjective, however, in her collapsing of the distance between frame tale and tale, so that she and her readers understand the interweaving of consciousnesses in her story as their experience, too, their mutuality of responses in a circle of, if not exactly "intercorporeity," at least of adoption (or refusal) of the other's absorption of our gestures to them.

> This was not what Mr. Bulstrode said to any man for the sake of deceiving him: it was what he said to himself—it was as genuinely his mode of explaining events as any theory of yours may be, if you happen to disagree with him. For the egoism which enters into our theories does not affect their sincerity; rather, the more our egoism is satisfied, the more robust is our belief. (LIII, 565)

Eliot's narrator moves outward from a character to the "you" of the reader and to the "our" that includes herself, in order, among other rhetorical purposes, to construct a complex intersubjectivity in which reader's and narrator's perceptions of the mind(s) of others tangle, intersect, separate, and respond to each other in this space freed by the narrator's address. "Our needs," for example, which measured time and money earlier, are part of a sequence of interfoldings in this frame-narrative space, which may include our disagreement with Mr. Bulstrode, the unplanned pleasures of our egoism, and the responding deepening of our beliefs. That is, even readers respond to response and have imaginations to insert themselves into the play of appropriations and denials in Bulstrode's effort to interpret comfortably Riggs's sale of his estate. As she imagines the world of consciousnesses within her text that live out her story, Eliot's narrator sets into play a company of intelligences, however generic in texture of mind, that listen, internalize, interpret, and bring to bear memories and beliefs in a sequence of responses to each other. Characters of course do not know they are part of this company and do not penetrate their fourth wall to respond to readers' responses. But the remarkable quality of the Eliot narrator's strategy in *Middlemarch* is the degree to which she constructs her subjectivity and that of her readers with memory and imagination, so that her frame tale is represented as inhabited by a community of acknowledging and reacknowledging consciousnesses living out their own deeply intersubjective time ("*while* I tell the truth about loobies, my reader's imagination . . ." [my emphasis]).

Middlemarch's particular structure of complex intersubjectivity that interlocks implied readers, narrator, and characters in a network of intending consciousnesses with an especially remarkable space for mutual reading around the story-telling voice is rare in narrative after our redirection of narrative practices. This rarity reminds us that not all deep intersubjectivities are born equal or the same, nor do they all serve the same aesthetic or cultural purposes.

Our second topic moves us from the frame tale to the tale itself to see how deeply intersubjective omniscience affects the interworld of others. Our new narrative practice has profound ideological implications for the representations it promotes of otherness, class, privilege, illusion and enlightenment.

Others Encounter Others in Tom Jones *and* Middlemarch

> [Tom] well knew, that fortune is generally the principal, if not the sole consideration, which operates on the best of parents in these matters [of a daughter's marriage]: for friendship makes us warmly espouse the interest of others; but is very cold to the gratification of their passions. Indeed, to feel the happiness

> which may result from this, it is necessary we should possess the passion ourselves.
> —Tom Jones

> Lydgate] wanted to pierce the obscurity of those minute processes which prepare human misery and joy, those invisible thoroughfares which are the first lurking-places of anguish, mania, and crime, that delicate poise and transition which determine the growth of happy or unhappy consciousness. . . . Poor Lydgate! or shall I say , poor Rosamund! Each lived in a world of which the other knew nothing.
> —Middlemarch

A key to the functions of simpler intersubjectivity among groups of consciousnesses in *Tom Jones* is the narrator's thoughtful limitation of the work of "espous[al]," a word he uses here almost in Merleau-Ponty's sense. In the narrator's understanding, the subject's ability to appropriate the gestures and signs of the other is limited, as he thinks of Western's friendship for Tom, which will advance Tom very little toward marrying Sophia, given Western's principal qualification for suitors: fortune. A friend may espouse the *interest* of others but not their passions; in order to feel the happiness of gratification, "it is necessary we should possess the passion ourselves" (208). To limit espousal to "interest," here conceived clearly as external, as a contingent and mechanical benefit, is powerfully ironic, given the undertow of "spousal" in the verb. The narrator explicitly rules out an appropriation of the signs of the other consciousness as an interiority, so of course reappropriations of Tom by way of the other become impossible, too. Deep intersubjectivity is not an option here, and even simple intersubjectivity is explicitly limited in *Tom Jones*.

Instead, clusters of subjects see each other as players on a gameboard, the origins of whose movements in anterior perceptions are not of interest, and whose origins in a wider arena of consciousness of consciousnesses are not conceivable. Nevertheless, what is left of human subjectivity is now manageable in fairly clear systems of desire. Groups of subjects seek to navigate their phenomenological environment by mapping the desire of the other, but desire not as the other's interior experience but as an observable, externalizing mechanism: Lord Fellamar's pursuit of Sophia, Thwackum's need for consolidating his identity as pedant, and Jenny Waters's generosity of body and spirit, which is a kind of desire for externalized closeness, if not the intimacy of mutually appropriating subjects. Jenny indeed comes closer than any other character in *Tom Jones* to revealing an inner life that could appropriate the signs of another's inner life. Her moment of intimacy comes in her letter:

> O Mr. Jones, little did I think, when I past that happy day at Upton, the reflection upon which is like to embitter all my future life, who it was to whom I owed such perfect happiness. (816)[10]

Tom's response, and Partridge's, however, never move beyond the externalized. The dark possibility of incest wipes from their minds any attention to Jenny's perceptions of Tom, to which he could respond in a maturing chain of mirrorings (and no character in *Tom Jones* would be as capable of this sequence of embodiments as the generous Jenny). For other characters, the only mystery of desire is the revelation of its theater of operation, not its origins. So Dowling, Blifil, and Bridget are exposed. But no depths of the intersubjective are exposed at the same time. Large scenes of mutual misreading, like the bedroom scene when Allworthy is thought to be dying, map only these single-layered operations of desire, hypocrisy, affection, and deception (think of the doctors, and compare the tracing of their mentality to that of the doctors in the scene from *Middlemarch* below).

Tom Jones's particularly limited intersubjectivity, more limited than that in *Pamela*, for example, or *Clarissa*, or even *Moll Flanders*, serves particular purposes aesthetic and ideological. The threads that link people and events across Fielding's panorama are not phenomenological but mythical or providential, or perhaps both at the same time. Fielding's narrator claims as much authority as Eliot's, for example, even while disclaiming it: "[T]hough we insist upon as much authority as any author whatever, we shall use this power very sparingly . . ." (822). So the issue is not the narrator's powers of intrusion into consciousness, but rather what the narrator chooses to exercise power for. For Fielding's narrator, the threads of connection are evidence of the powers of the myths of comedy or the powers of providence, either aesthetic or divine. The aesthetic, mythical connections cluster around the novel as the saga of the son of Summer, or the odyssey of Telemachus, as J. Paul Hunter emphasizes, not the odyssey of the Odysseus that the text's epigraph cites, for Fielding's "comic epic vision . . . does not ask Tom to be Ulysses but only a modern imitation of a modern version of his lesser son" (1975, 139). Even this reduced comic epic, however, traces a journey home, the return of the prodigal son to Paradise Hall, albeit a postlapsarian paradise.

If the threads of connection are providential, then whose providence (the narrator's or God's) is not entirely clear. Leopold Damrosch cannot be sure whether *Tom Jones* is the end of one tradition or the beginning of a new one, imitating a providential order or creating one within the dream world of art. Hunter traces the text's use of Milton and asserts that "Fielding's conscious intention to reflect a providential order is clear," yet he also sees the text's subversion of that order in its almost aggressively identified artifice: "The radical symmetry of *Tom Jones* at once asserts the absolute order and calls all into doubt" (189, 191). Perhaps what Damrosch calls the "resolute de-psychologiz[ing]" of *Tom Jones* is part of an inquiry into the power of narration as myth and providence (298). Otherness as intersubjective in any extended form would cloud that inquiry.

Otherness as intersubjective, and deeply so, is at the heart of *Middlemarch*'s inquiry. *Middlemarch* is an especially appropriate narrative for study in this project because to untangle the webbings of consciousness, "to pierce the obscurity of those minute processes which prepare human misery and joy," is a desire for one of its characters, Lydgate, as well as for its narrator and indeed is one link, as critics have often noted, between Lydgate and his historian, as if character and storyteller could exchange places in the gallery of Saint Theresa's. But it is a tracing of the webbings of consciousness*es*, the "invisible thoroughfares" of "happy or unhappy consciousness[es]," that gives *Middlemarch* such weight as an achievement of Victorian deep intersubjectivity. The particular power of *Middlemarch* is to set the mirrorings and appropriations that Merleau-Ponty theorized spinning into action in groups of entangled subjects, where the often binary images of Merleau-Ponty, as in that wall two people build together, are insufficient to express Eliot's version of complex intersubjectivity. The result in Eliot, especially in this novel but elsewhere, too, is a rendering of othernesses in a strange dance together, without compromising their separateness, so that her use of complex intersubjectivity helps to render an understanding of social and political community as fractured, yet held together by webs of both misperception and dimly glimpsed and dimly shared appropriations. The special effect in *Middlemarch* is the intense interiority of its representation of the fissures within intersubjective experience and of the depth of being other(s), without warming up or making comfortable that interiority. For Eliot, Merleau-Ponty's wall is about its niches more as gaps than as opportunities to grasp the offering of the other. Loneliness, shame and fear of shame, and aggression are more common here than appropriation in good faith, compassion, and espousal.

Eliot's particular style of complex intersubjectivity appears powerfully in chapter 18 of *Middlemarch,* in the boardroom where the election for the new hospital's chaplain takes place. The election brings together a dozen personalities to evaluate the claims of Mr. Tyke and Mr. Farebrother to the newly salaried position of chaplain. This group includes Mr. Hackbutt, the "rich tanner of fluent speech"; Bulstrode; the two doctors (Minchin and Sprague); the two surgeon-apothecaries, Mr. Wrench and Mr. Toller; Mr. Hawley, the attorney and town clerk; Mr. Brooke; and Lydgate. This moment pulls together many threads of personal and communal histories, beliefs, prejudices, misunderstandings, and deceptions. It is the intersubjective depth of these threadings that is so remarkably different from *Tom Jones, Peregrine Pickle,* and other earlier omniscient narratives and that requires an omniscient narrator to navigate, focus, and control.

The narrator's grand strategy in chapter 18 is to establish, briefly or at length, a framework of experience, metaphors, and blindnesses for most of the hospital electors and then to set them in motion together in a series of interpretations and reinterpretations of gestures that mask or reveal (or both) a skein of intentionalities for others (*for* in the sense of intended to be perceived by others, even if what is to be perceived is a disguise). These consciousnesses interconnect along force fields governed by intentions to deceive, inabilities to understand difference, a desire to express deep beliefs, some interest in perceiving others' perceptions, and a desire to make political use of perceived differences. Dr. Minchin is a wonderful example of this last form of deep intersubjectivity, one that mingles and interplays blindness and perception in dazzling comedy. Minchin tacks tactfully into his patient's prejudices by appearing to confirm them but actually steers slightly to the side in comic non sequiturs that promote a misreading of Minchin's beliefs:

> If Mr. Bulstrode insisted, as he was apt to do, on the Lutheran doctrine of justification, as that by which a church must stand or fall, Dr. Minchin in return was quite sure that man was not a mere machine or a fortuitous conjunction of atoms; if Mrs. Wimple insisted on a particular providence in relation to her stomach complaint, Dr. Minchin for his part liked to keep the mental windows open and objected to fixed limits; if the Unitarian brewer jested about the Athanasian Creed, Dr. Minchin quoted Pope's *Essay on Man*. (XVIII, 211)

The threefold repetition here suggests some design by Dr. Minchin to placate his patients, but in an oddly ironic way, as if upon reading their ideological stance he responds with tangential glosses that promote the patient's comforting misreading of Minchin (comforting to both the patient and the good doctor, who dislikes disagreeing with clients). Here the appropriation of gestures *intends* confusion in the overlapping threads of the intersubjective.

Indeed, the nature of professional life for both established physicians in Middlemarch is a tapestry of interpretations, grounded in patients' bodies, that loop back and forth in a comic tangle of purposive and accidental misunderstandings between doctor, patient, and patient's family. Eliot's microworld dramatizes Merleau-Ponty's intercorporeity with wry humor. Each doctor's body for example becomes a resource (*not* a metaphor in this superstitious community) for his medical practice: Dr. Minchin is "soft-handed" and "might be better able to detect [a disease] lurking and to circumvent it." Sprague, however, is "superfluously tall" and "had weight," for "you heard him go in and out, and up and down, as if he had come to see after the roofing," and therefore he "might be expected to grapple with a disease and throw it" (XVIII, 212).

At some level Minchin and Sprague grasp the current of perceptions in their market and play with and against it, "conceal[ing] with much etiquette their contempt for each other's skill," and "regarding themselves as Middlemarch institutions, they were ready to combine against all innovators" (XVIII, 212). Chapter 18 may be the first, and still best, analysis of the subtle interworld of professional life (not limited to medicine) in which intimate perceptions of perceptions and layers of un/consciousnesses and intentionalities interweave with classed and gendered material conditions in the struggle for reputation, clients, prestige, and income. Here is the vortex of perceptions, superstitions, and assumptions of which Dr. Sprague is the center:

> The Doctor [Sprague] was more than suspected of having no religion, but somehow Middlemarch tolerated this deficiency in him. . . . It was perhaps this negation in the Doctor which made his neighbours call him hard-headed and dry-witted, conditions of texture which were also held favorable to the storing of judgments connected with drugs. At all events, it is certain that if any medical man had come to Middlemarch with the reputation of having very definite religious views, of begin given to prayer, and of otherwise showing an active piety, there would have been a general presumption against his medical skill. (XVIII, 211)

Middlemarch in other words has constructed its view of Dr. Sprague's "texture" of mind. What is at issue is not his character, his good will, or even his medical skill as such, as perceived by those others who consider offering their bodies to his care, but the mode of operation of his intending consciousness, as a sort of warehouse for his specific judgments, say, about drugs, as a doctor.

Other circulations of the reading of readings occur besides these weavings of threads to, from, and around the figures of Minchin and Sprague. Lydgate, for example, despite his passionate interest in the origins and "minute thoroughfares" of human consciousness, is himself unable to map those thoroughfares when their horizon is unfamiliar to him. His ability to read word and gesture in order to stand where another is standing is severely limited. On Farebrother's billiard playing, for example:

> [Lydgate] had always known in a general way that he was not rich, but he had never felt poor, and he had no power of imagining the part which the want of money plays in determining the actions of men. Money had never been a motive to him. Hence he was not ready to frame excuses for this deliberate pursuit of small gains. (XVIII, 209)

Nevertheless, Lydgate is learning to read others' readings and to consider the contours of those consciousnesses among which he must live. As he ponders his vote, he recognizes that a vote for Tyke will be a sign to be interpreted, with troubling implications for Lydgate's view of his own inner life, because the mirror of others' perception of that inner life exacerbates his own confusions about it. "Lydgate did not like the consciousness that in voting for Tyke he should be voting on the side obviously convenient for himself. But would the end really be his own convenience? Other people would say so . . ." (XVIII, 210). Lydgate remains paralyzed in his confusion, amidst this traffic of interpretations of interpretations, mostly because he perceives more intricately than most the web of contradictory perceptions and its politics.

In this scene the comic knottedness lies in the threads of interpretations—maudlin, outrageous, even right for the wrong reasons—by board members of each other's guiding intentions and mentalities, in a sequence of mock embodiments. Mr. Powderell is interested in " 'the souls of the poor sick people'—here Mr. Powderell's voice and face had a sincere pathos in them. . . . 'I should vote against my conscience if I voted against Mr. Tyke.' " Mr. Hackbutt resents the implication that he has asked anyone to vote against his (only men are voters here) conscience but suggests that a vote for Tyke is "incompatible with genuine independence" and more likely a symptom of "a crawling servility"

(XVIII, 213–14). Mr. Plymdale proposes to vote for Mr. Tyke, despite this rendering of his motive. " 'I shall vote for the appointment of Mr. Tyke, but I should not have known, if Mr. Hackbutt hadn't hinted at it, that I was a Servile Crawler.' " These responses to responses, insult trumping insult, are a wonderful example of deeply intersubjective farce.

The climax of the scene's interplay of readings by subjects of others and their otherness is, of course, Lydgate's late entrance and his ever deeper embeddedness in the versions of himself offered by other consciousnesses:

> "The thing is settled now," said Mr. Wrench, rising. "We all know how Mr. Lydgate will vote."
>
> "You seem to speak with some peculiar meaning, sir," said Lydgate, rather defiantly, and keeping his pencil suspended.
>
> "I merely mean that you are expected to vote with Mr. Bulstrode. Do you regard that meaning as offensive?"
>
> "It may be offensive to others. But I shall not desist from voting with him on that account." (XVIII, 217)

Motives get misconstructed by a subject who appropriates the language, tones, and gestures of another subject, who then responds to the first appropriation with another reading of intention and interiority. Furthermore, the readings are intercorporeal, as Merleau-Ponty assured us they are: Lydgate's raised pencil is as clear a challenge to Wrench as his words. Lydgate's resistance to Wrench's appropriation of course does not free him from the operations of surveillance by others, or—more intimate a threat than Foucault's panopticon—from their construction of an interior consciousness for him from which they believe his behaviors emerge. And only one of this text's many ironies is that Wrench's construction is not entirely a misperception. Lydgate *doesn't* like voting "with" Bulstrode. Wrench and Lydgate stand before the same landscape, so to speak, and each does see it to some degree with the other's eyes.

The effect of this tracing of some partial appropriation of perceptions across significant barriers of power, class identity, and economic interest is Eliot's particular coloration of deep intersubjectivity: a vision of community in which the presence of some common ground does not necessarily solve problems, make love possible, or soften enmities. Merleau-Ponty described a knottedness of threads reversing across each other, a chiasm in which two subjects are neither quite fully present to each other, and "yet one is never alone." In Eliot, the chiasm of partial presence of subjects to each other is one effect of her webbing of consciousnesses; yet a deep loneliness is still possible. Mapping the wall we build together may only clarify how different our stones are, even if we learn to recognize and measure the stone of the other. It is not certain what exactly the ideological work of this recognition is, as Eliot criticism makes clear: Is it resignation to the slowness of change, akin to one of Dorothea's renunciations of hope, or is it a spur to greater efforts, fueled by the evangelical warmth of Saint Theresa, to serve the most powerless and the loneliest?[11]

Eliot's narrative of embodied, culturally embedded intersubjectivities, with their failures to grasp the other's gestures of appropriation, still traces a cluster of others with *some* limited access to their mutual life-world, what Merleau-Ponty called their interworld. The climactic examples of this limited access of course occur at the end of *Middlemarch,* when Harriet and Bulstrode see together without exactly seeing together ("She could not say, 'How much is only slander and false suspicion?' and he did not say, 'I am innocent.' " [LXXIV, 808]), and Rosamund's encounter with Dorothea's generosity (however self-punishing) "made her soul totter all the more with a sense that she had been walking in an unknown world which had just broken in on her" (LXXXI, 854). The interworld that emerges from the novel's ironic, compassionate intersubjectivity is similar to the realm of "consensus" that Elizabeth Ermarth finds to be fundamental to Eliot's "realism." Ermarth pursues the "intersubjective nature of narrative consciousness" (77) in (conscious) continuities between minds, and sees in Eliot "moments of possibility where the saving continuities of consciousness might be sustained across the gaps that threaten them" (247). For Ermarth, the "consensus" among characters and narrator in Eliot about time, plot, and identity is "tenuous," dependent upon sorting through different experiences in and of time (249). Ermarth's intersubjectivity is indeed precarious because it never escapes realism's epistemological double bind: "[T]he realistic consensus produces and supports the existence of an objective world. . . . What is so, *is* so, because many different viewpoints *agree* it is so. . . . On the other hand . . . , all consciousness is epiphenomenal: a reflex from, a response to an objective, invariant world . . ." (77–78). In other words, the perceptions of subjects guarantee the world, but the world guarantees the constituting perceptions of subjects. Ermarth suggests, furthermore, that Eliot "qualifies the conventions of realism by calling attention to the fact that the invisible community of consent literally objectifies the world" (255).

The assumptions in Eliot's narrative, however, are not so deeply constructionist. What Ermarth calls "the density of the mental continuum" in Eliot is not only a shell game of consciousnesses (255). Merleau-Ponty allows us to discard these dualities of Cartesian thought, as we discussed in chapter 1, and to remember what he said Lacan forgot, the weight of the body of the child *to* the child, in the child's consciousness, before the mirror at that moment of self-recognition (and not only the misrecognition of Lacan's thought). Eliot's paradigm for the intersubjective grounds perception in a network of consciousnesses, themselves not only braided together, but living as bodies in the world. Consensus in *Middlemarch* is deeply partial and always fracturing, but its continuities, in the narratives of deep intersubjectivity, are deeper and more rooted in experiences in an interworld than Ermarth allows.

It is possible, as Derrida wrote, to try to think about the "structurality of structure," and this study is an effort to do that kind of thinking (249). Nevertheless, the assumptions of deep intersubjectivity have so fixed themselves in and on us that neither Eliot nor I can really think outside them. And there would certainly be no point in trying to write outside them, at least to write any writing directed for another's attention. Eliot's narrative of deep intersubjectivity, of interlocking mirrorings and perceptions of perception, is an astonishingly intelligent and nuanced version of our taken-for-granted world of human interconnections where these narrative practices for stories and subjects are now foundational.

The encounters among others, under the supervision of narrative omniscience, raise a further theoretical topic: What are the implications of the confidence, at least in *Middlemarch,* with which that narrative voice speaks for others, often paraphrasing as well as interpreting? One aspect of the omniscient narrator's godlike access to others that Miller discusses is access across gender and caste boundaries. Eliot's narrator suggests some human-scale limitations to her abilities or her endurance: "I at least have so much to do in unraveling certain human lots, and seeing how they were woven and interwoven, that all the light I can command must be concentrated on this particular web . . ." (chapter 15, 170). "All the light I can command": There is some limit to her light and perhaps even insight. This limit, however, is not a limit inherent in otherness: Eliot's narrator moves with confidence across boundaries of class and region, dialect and education. The assumptions enabling this confidence have moved out of the shadows in recent years, in for example the controversy surrounding William Styron's *Confessions of Nat*

Turner and in Gayatri Chakravorty Spivak's essay "Can the Subaltern Speak?" which challenges the assumptions of speaking *for,* of representing, with whatever politically correct aims, those without privilege, voice, and access themselves to the dominant venues of representation. In his meditation on these issues of authority, Andrew Lakritz notes, as Spivak has herself, the transgression her own essay commits, in speaking on behalf of illiterate or silenced others (Roof and Wiegman 7). Linda Martin Alcoff ponders, in relation to the same question, whether silence is the alternative, with its implied abdications: "If I don't speak for those less privileged than myself, am I abandoning my political responsibility to speak out against oppression, a responsibility incurred by the very fact of my privilege?" (ibid., 100)

Silence is clearly not an option for Eliot's narrator either. She believes in the storyteller's power to will a transparency for consciousnesses that is not available to Lydgate or Rosamund or Dorothea (we remember her serious misconstruction of Casaubon's inner life before their marriage). Boundary crossing in pursuit of her story is not problematic for this narrator because she articulates complex social and economic contexts for consciousnesses as different as Caleb Garth's impoverished sister, Raggles, and Mrs. Vincy, or Mr. Casaubon, Farebrother, and Sir James. Issues of transgression do not cloud this narrative confidence, as they do James Agee's, in Lakritz's account of *Let Us Now Praise Famous Men:* "[T]he subaltern does not speak in Agee's text. . . : Agee has unlearned his privilege" (Roof and Wiegman 16). Or as they should have done in Zora Neale Hurston's construction of a nostalgic African American community that functions, in Lakritz's view, as "an idealized folk origin for Hurston and for an uneasy academy wishing to assert social change as achieved before it is earned . . ." (20). Speaking *for,* even as an omniscient narrator, requires careful explanations now, as writers and critics struggle between the dangers of a transcendentalism that comfortably invades any attractive story or community and an essentialism that locks a speaker into a narrow identity (or slices of identities, as Linda Alcoff wonders; must one choose to write only as a woman, or a New Yorker, a heterosexual, a first-generation intellectual, a second-generation Italian, daughter of an alcoholic . . . ?).

George Eliot of course did not presume to enter communities of difference without effort, as her intense research on the Renaissance for *Romola,* on Jewish history and thought for *Daniel Deronda,* or on the history of science for *Middlemarch* demonstrates. The confidence of her narrator's intersubjective omniscience is nonetheless a significant cultural effect. It may blind us to some caste imbalance in *Middlemarch:*

We do not hover as attentively over the consciousnesses of Freeman's End as over the more articulate inner lives of Lowick. But the transparency of Eliot's deep intersubjectivity is a major achievement and a profound act of faith in *Middlemarch*. The story it tells is one kind of work that our new narrative practices can do.

PART TWO
Case Studies: Deep Intersubjectivity and Genre

3

Comedy, Film, and Film Comedy

The notions of deep intersubjectivity that I have been proposing offer valuable new avenues along which to approach narrative, and I begin now a series of case studies in narrative genre to explore some of these new avenues. The intersections of genre and subjectivity are especially fruitful, given the richness of recent genre theory, at both a microcosmic and macrocosmic level. The most naive notion of classical genre criticism to avoid is the assumption (conscious or not) that genres actually exist "out there," rather than admitting to their complex functioning at an intersection of text, writer/director/producer, audience, and marketplace practices. Rick Altman provides a helpful corrective to traditional genre theory's positivisms in his view of genres as discourses: "Instead of utilizing a single master language, as most previous genre theoreticians would have it, a genre may appropriately be considered multicoded. Each genre is simultaneously defined by multiple codes, corresponding to the multiple groups who, by helping define the genre, might be said to 'speak' the genre" (208).

For Altman not only are genres *not* stable categories, whether conceived as ritual or as ideology, but as they find new purposes they "may have multiple conflicting audiences" (ibid.). Altman is suitably ironic in particular about the move by critics to align genre with myth and to note "the *essential* quality" of a form that then links "with archetypes and myths . . . [that express] broad and perdurable human concerns" (20). Altman's focus on the ways film genres get generated by multiple studio, marketing, and audience behaviors and reception/display technologies across different historical moments is an important qualification of Aristotelian taxonomies. My own approach to genre, which leans toward the mythical, as in comedy's roots in Attic ritual, needs Altman's skepticism to avoid a naïve essentialism.

Altman finds film genrification to be more naive than the formation of genres in literary criticism. But David Perkins sees a similar innocence in much scholarly writing about printed texts: "[L]iterary classifications have generally been constructed by an intuitive synthesis of multiple considerations" by literary historians who "have worked naively and *ad hoc*" (267). As Perkins summarizes the process neatly, genre concepts, like historical periods, are the products of taxonomic observations (that often suppress difference) and positivist "information" external to texts (such as—these are my examples—when Victoria came to the throne or when the Hays office sought to forestall Congressional threats of film censorship in the 1930s). The sceptic views these concepts as overdetermined products of tradition, ideological agendas, and the politics of professional careers and academic institutions (interestingly, to Perkins the "overwhelming role" is tradition's, in the "taxonomizing process" [254]). To me, genre is indeed an overdetermined network of practices and traditions that nonetheless affect the cultural production and reception of stories. The challenge is to use notions of genre without reifying them into positivist categories that become their own myth and therefore to struggle against various kinds of innocence and nostalgia that tempt the critic.

In this vein, then, my investigations of genre seek to show the value of considering the practices, so to speak, of complex intersubjectivity in connection with what one might call various genre matrices. In this first section I take up genre in two specific applications of the word: I look at the genre called comedy, then at the genre called film, and then at film comedy to see what difference those practices of deep intersubjectivity make.

Indeed, deep intersubjectivity's investigations of shame and espousal, and the continuum of embodiments of power between them, which I have grounded in the phenomenologies of Jean-Paul Sartre and Maurice Merleau-Ponty, change what is possible in modern comedy, that is, comedy after about 1800. I demonstrate those changes in case studies of Jane Austen, Alfred Hitchcock's Cary Grant films, and Woody Allen's *Broadway Danny Rose*. By "comedy" in this book I refer predominantly to a thread of myth that runs continuously through genre practice, a thread first identified and conceptualized in the late nineteenth century by the Cambridge ritualists. In this tradition, comedy is the narrative of the *komos* of Attic drama. The ritual of this ancient comedy has a double character, acknowledging death and denial in order to erase or at least defuse them. Comic celebration has always had its dark side, as F. M. Cornford has described better than anyone else (except maybe Woody Allen). What Cornford grasped, from his sources in Frazier (*The Golden Bough* and *The Scapegoat*), is the fundamental doubleness of the scapegoat and the implications of that doubleness for comedy.

In the narrative of renewal that Cornford calls the "carrying out of death," the scapegoat's doubleness appears twice: First, it is paired with the *eiresione*, the olive branch of promised fertility; second, its own images suggest both death and rebirth:

> The bringing in of the new wealth of the harvest['s] other and darker side, the driving out of hunger, sin and death, was expressed in the expulsion of the *Pharmakoi*. On the 6th of Thargelion two men, with strings of figs hung on them, black and white to show one was for the men, the other for the women, were led out of the city and "set in an appointed place...." Finally, it is said, they were burnt, and their ashes were scattered to the winds and into the sea, for a purification. (10–11)

The scapegoat's mysterious connection to health appears even in its name in Greek, *pharmakos*, because the Greek root *pharmakon* is both a poison and a healing drug. In fact, Liddell and Scott's *Greek-English Lexicon* repeatedly mentions three notions for this family of nouns and verbs: medicine/healing, poison, and enchantment, since potions (like our "drugs") may work in all three ways (1,917). Cornford concludes about this puzzle or knot of images:

> The point we wish to emphasize is that the *Pharmakos*, by some primitive conjunction difficult for us to grasp, is a representative both of the power of fertility and of the opposite powers of famine, disease, impurity and death. (11)[1]

Woody Allen's version of this conjunction is the joke he tells at the end of *Annie Hall:* "This guy goes to a psychiatrist and says, 'Doc, my brother's crazy, he thinks he's a chicken.' And the doc says, 'Well, why don't you turn him in?' And the guy says, 'I would, but we need the eggs.' " This knotting of eggs and insanity, of a life-drive and its opposite, characterizes comedy at its most profound, from *The Odyssey* to *The Clouds, Tristram Shandy,* and *His Girl Friday*. The confusions and crisscrossing of genders (the crazy brother-in-law lays eggs) are, in some strange way, also a part of the struggle between the life-drive and its dark opponent. Furthermore, shame may not be a cloud on comedy's horizon, but instead an integral component of its ritual. Orsino sends after Malvolio at the end of *Twelfth Night,* but it's not clear what place this scapegoat could have in Illyria, and Shakespeare ends the play with no response from him.

Deep intersubjectivity makes the contest between shame and espousal more problematic, as the representation of their experience becomes more intricate and their interfolding more compromising. The new paradigm for intersubjectivity is appropriate for an age in which the relationship between humor and anxiety, comedy and despair becomes closer. The intricate mutual embodiments that we have been tracing in this book become a strategy for articulating comedy's experience of limits, claustrophobia, and exposure, and also its carnivalesque release.

Each section of this chapter traces one cluster of these strategies, beginning with Jane Austen's probing phenomenology of anxiety and its profound working through to espousal by way of shame, in a process of which *Emma* is the final exemplar.

AUSTEN, THE INTERSUBJECTIVITY OF ANXIETY, AND *EMMA*

> *To such perseverance in wilful self-deception Elizabeth would make no reply, and immediately and in silence withdrew; determined, if [Mr. Collins] persisted in considering her repeated refusals as flattering encouragement, to apply to her father, whose negative might be uttered in such a manner as must be decisive, and whose behavior at least could not be mistaken for the affectation and coquetry of an elegant female.*
> —Pride and Prejudice

> *Yes, he [Wentworth] had done it. She was in the carriage, and felt that he had placed her there, that his will and hands had done it, that she owed it to his perception of her fatigue, and his resolution to give her rest. She was very much affected by the view of his disposition towards her which all these things made apparent. . . . He could not forgive her,—but he could not be unfeeling. . . . [I]t was a proof of his own warm and amiable heart, which she could not contemplate without emotions so compounded of pleasure and pain, that she knew not which prevailed.*
> —Persuasion

Elizabeth's experience of anxiety has something in common with Anne's, indeed with the experience of all of Austen's thoughtful women (and some men). Their anxiety has to do with claustrophobia and the gendering of subjectivities, and both are keys to understanding the phenomenology of anxiety in these novels. Austen's readers have long recognized that anxiety is a fundamental experience and subject in her novels. Lionel Trilling's essay on *Mansfield Park* is only the best-known argument for the importance of that experience as a product in Austen of modernity's new understanding of moral responsibility accompanied by a concomitant fragmentation of the self. Other readers locate the origin of Austenian anxiety elsewhere, in the discontents civilization is heir to (Tony Tanner), in the threat to traditional order (Stuart Tave), in the absence of a room—and income—of her own (Virginia Woolf), and in women's need to navigate complex political and intellectual contradictions (Claudia Johnson).

Some of the most important contradictions for this study emerge in late-eighteenth- and early-nineteenth-century efforts to guide the formation of the self, especially the bourgeois female subject. The web of expectation and guidance was intricate and deeply political, as Mary Poovey and Nancy Armstrong argue, and one question for Austen readers is the degree of rebellion possible for a writer like Austen in 1812. How scripted is subjectivity, not to mention intersubjectivity, for *Pride and Prejudice* or *Emma*? Claudia Johnson cites James Fordyce, author of the book of sermons Mr. Collins bores the Bennet family with and author of a popular conduct book for young women, who admires the "amiable reserve" of "elegant females" (76). Susan Fraiman cites John Gregory, another conduct book author, who seeks to "render [my daughters] most amiable and worthy of esteem in the eyes of my own sex" (152). Even more telling is Gregory's advice to perform a kind of masquerade: "If you happen to have any learning, keep it a profound secret" (Fraiman 26). The internalization of the gaze and of such masqued performances leads to an articulation of subjectivity, guided by modesty and the need for approval, that we see traced and resisted in my opening Austen quotations and that I discuss again in chapter 5.

Resistance is a thread of response in Austen, however muted and deflected; in Johnson's words, "Austen eludes rather than reiterates conventional moral codes . . ." (77). Fraiman describes a profound doubleness within the guidebook tradition itself, especially in texts written by women, who offer an indirect critique of the dominant gender system in their "doubts about the legibility of male character" (picking out good men is terrifically chancy, husbands stray, and wives must be patient) in their celebration of friendships among women and in their wistful promotion on occasion of education for women in traditionally male domains like the Greek and Latin authors. For Fraiman, "conduct books, like novels, are often profoundly inconsistent in relation to female formation . . . , characteristically contest[ing] the dominant narrative as it appears in both their own and other works" (15).

Reading resistance is problematic, as Fraiman acknowledges in her account of the differences between herself (and one might add Claudia Johnson), on the one hand, and Nancy Armstrong and Mary Poovey on the other: What is the texture of Austen's response to the panopticon's supervision? Fraiman's contribution to this debate is her exploration of Ann Murry's 1778 book of advice, *Mentoria*, which Austen gave to a beloved niece and which promotes women's ambitions to read, know, learn, and write across traditionally gendered boundaries (23ff). The scripting of subjectivity in Austen is profoundly contested and anxious. The scripts of the intersubjective are also intricate demonstrations of those struggles for power. Equally profound, in my view, are the differences in the effects of those struggles—at their most dramatic the difference between shame and espousal. It may seem to be almost impossible, under the spotlight as it were of deep intersubjectivity and gender politics, for readers now to accept as authentic a comedy, in the Greek or Shakespearean sense, written in 1812. Yet Austen's narratives are comic, I believe, precisely because of their attention to deep intersubjectivity and gender politics.

Enclosedness has many shapes, but all of them for Austen's women contain peepholes through which the gaze of others, whether powerful women like Lady Catherine, or men with varying degrees of power, from Wickham to Mr. Elliott to Mr. Knightley, may evaluate the young female subjects of their gaze. Austen's strong women observe their being observed, and this experience of observing being observed can produce a continuum of responses: terror, unease, shame, even arousal, and also, but only in perhaps rare and difficult circumstances, intimacy and espousal. The differences among these outcomes remind us of the quarrel between Sartre and Merleau-Ponty and can help us measure both the sad and the more comic strains in Jane Austen's novels. Let us begin with our two paradigmatic scenes, from *Pride and Prejudice* and *Persuasion*, in preparation for a closer, more extended discussion of *Emma*.

Both of these scenes begin with observation and in fact in each instance with observation of observation. Austen's favorite observers, who are often less privileged women, are finely tuned to the network of perceptions that surround them. Elizabeth Bennet is a good example of this attentiveness, even if she is one of the more fortunate of Austen's less-privileged women. Because *Pride and Prejudice* is Jane Austen's least claustrophobic novel, looking at its representations of the tensions between intersubjective shame and espousal has special weight; in this instance the binary conflict between shame and espousal works because Elizabeth is so explicitly the target of an effort to humiliate.

Skill in navigating the other's treacherous misreadings of her selfhood is one of Elizabeth's most remarkable talents, and Mr. Collins calls forth Elizabeth's skill in an especially sparkling display. His efforts to appropriate and rewrite Elizabeth's gestures to him, and their originating consciousness, have produced an impasse in the Bennet drawing room. In saying her "No" means "Yes," Collins constructs his own fantasy subject—in both senses of the word "subject"—whose desires enable his fantasy narrative. "I shall chuse to attribute [your rejection of me] to your wish of increasing my love by suspense, according to the usual practice of elegant females" (I, 19; 108). By foregrounding his "choice," however, Collins confesses, indeed flaunts, how tendentious his version of Elizabeth's consciousness is, and his choice, so announced for Elizabeth to observe, gives her space to retreat into conventionality. His face-saving interpretation of her rejection as the "usual practice of elegant females" would cover her retreat. It might appear that the face Collins wishes to save is his own, but in fact he has no shame; his response is a counteroffer to Elizabeth in a negotiation of deeply intersubjective responses between embattled consciousnesses. We measure Elizabeth's courage by her willingness to forego such a rescue from embarrassment.

Even more important is the gendering of this deeply intersubjective struggle for control of interpretations of perception. Elizabeth diagnoses Collins's final move ("You are uniformly charming . . .") as "wilful self-deception," but her own resort to fatherly authority suggests her understanding that more is at stake here—and more threatens. Collins's gestures are self-aware, more designed to humiliate and control Elizabeth than she is willing to admit to herself. Earlier he has said, as his efforts to persuade grow more hostile, "It is by no means certain that another offer of marriage may ever be made to you" (I, 19; 108), and now he resorts as well to further pressure: "I am persuaded that when sanctioned by the express authority of both your excellent parents, my proposals will not fail of being acceptable" (I, 19; 109). Elizabeth's response foregrounds the gendering of interpretations of subjectivity, not only because her father's word carries more weight than a daughter's, as the patriarch's and as *her* father's, with the power traditionally articulated in kinship systems of exchange between men, but also because her father's *body* will incarnate an interpretation of her consciousness and of his reading of Collins's, that Collins cannot, in his game of intersubjective misreadings, pretend to misread: "[H]er father['s] negative might be uttered in such a manner as must be decisive, and whose behavior at least could not be mistaken for the affectation and coquetry of an elegant female." Mr. Bennet's body embodies an authorized version of Elizabeth's consciousness (authorized by her), attentive to her intentions, not her suitor's.

This dangerous dance of misappropriations in subjects' readings of subjectivity exposes both Elizabeth's vulnerability and her power of canny resistance, and reveals assumptions about gender that Elizabeth understands well enough to use as her best defense in the circumstances. She observes the observing observer, defuses Collins's narrative and gaze, and avoids the shame that, according to Sartre, one who has always already been seen should feel. Her defiance, intersubjectively framed, suggests the power of our new narrative practices.

Of our two scenes, Anne's offers the real possibility of espousal. Wentworth's behaviors toward Anne, speaking to the Crofts so that they insist on relieving her fatigue and then turning to Anne, "without saying a word," and shepherding her into the Croft carriage, all constitute a text that Anne reads as a reading of her (I, 10; 91). Austen sets all of this reading inside Anne's consciousness, so that it is the deep intersubjectivity of *Anne's* understanding of herself in her life-world and her assumptions of consciousnesses mirroring each other that we see here. But Austen's narrator intervenes enough for her readers to know Anne's consciousness of another's reading of her body is not entirely fantastical: "Captain Wentworth cleared the hedge in a moment to say something to his sister.—The something might be guessed by its effects" (91). The mutual espousal, in other words, is guaranteed, as I discuss in chapter 2, by a narrating omniscience. But how does this mutuality work? How fragile and partial is the comic process of appropriation of appropriation in Austen?

It is partial, and difficult, but not necessarily fragile, partly because Anne's skills at observing observation, even observations of herself, are finely honed. What she perceives—believes is "apparent" in Wentworth's behavior—is a "disposition towards her," an intentionality that speaks in more than one voice. Indeed, words are absent here. Wentworth's language is "his will and his hands."[2] At this moment his body is movement *for* her, that is, on her behalf. And the narrative source is, for Anne, without doubt. "She owed it [the rescue] to his perception of her fatigue"; "he could not see her suffer, without the desire of giving her relief." His movement of desire is necessary, and so the movement of appropriation is not remarkably fragile. It *is* partial, as Merleau-Ponty always insists. We learn later in the novel that Anne exaggerates, in her self-abnegation, Wentworth's distance from her ("perfectly careless of her"), and he is not "becoming attached to another" (91). The reading of bodies and the reading of their reading of previous incarnations of selfhood is of course imperfect. Anne and Wentworth struggle with these fleshly imperfections throughout *Persuasion*, from the Dalrymple party in the octagon room to the Musgrove apartments at the White Hart. But the body *can* be "proof of [a] warm and amiable heart." This appropriation of Wentworth's gesture to Anne of his consciousness of her triumphs against the odds, even inside the panopticon that is Bath: "There could be only a most proper alacrity, a most obliging compliance for public view; and smiles reined in and spirits dancing in private rapture" (II, 11; 240).[3] Anne's remarkable experience, then, in the Croft carriage is fear and absence *and* espousal. Austen's comedy at its richest interfolds all of these in the chiasm of gesture, words, and consciousness of consciousnesses.

These two exemplary scenes can help us investigate the new comedy of anxiety in Austen. As I also ask in chapter 1, what sorts of comic power operate in Austen's new scripts of intersubjectivity? For theorists of power like Foucault, intersubjectivities in whatever form could hardly ever be the agents of comedy, although one wonders about that nostalgia for the festival of execution in *Discipline and Punish*. But the komos wields a complex power in Austen, acknowledging, as Cornford argues, the weight of the scapegoat's outsiderliness in its ritual. One part of Austen's wisdom is her use of deep intersubjectivity to examine intimately anxiety's barriers to comic renewal and the degree to which they may be circumvented. These new assumptions about selves deepen the failures of Fanny or Sir Walter as well as the comic achievements of Elizabeth and Anne; they extend and complicate the triumphs of the comic will to connect in Austen's novels.

Bodies and gazes negotiate the tightly organized spaces of Austen's houses and gardens in wonderfully funny and sometimes brutally painful ways. The weight of the funniness and the suffering and thus the power of Austen's comic vision are products of the new manipulations of complex intersubjectivity. The possibility that espousal will fail is particularly sharp in *Emma*, raising the stakes for deeply intersubjective comedy and reminding us of the pharmakos, which is both poison and healing potion. Our new practices for narrativizing the extended interfoldings of gaze, gesture, and embodiments are just such an ambiguous gift.

The presence, even pressure, of the other and of others produces both anxiety and intimacy in *Emma*. In a sense, it is the intimacy of anxiety that a phenomenology of perception and misperception in narrative can grasp so usefully. In *Emma* that peculiar intimacy is a motive for many characters to screen, block, or subvert the demand, implicit according to Merleau-Ponty in the relation between self and other, that what self and other see should impose itself as real for each. Austen's study of such screenings and subversions, however, is itself thoroughly intersubjective, especially in the terms in which Knightley and Emma both recognize the dangers in a lowering of barriers between separate, possibly hostile, minds. During the Box Hill outing, Frank, wishing with Emma to spark some life into a dull, sullen group, announces that she "desires to know what you are all thinking of." Knightley responds sharply, "Is Miss Woodhouse sure that she would like to hear what we are all thinking of?" Emma, who perceives at least some of the animosities and anxieties simmering in the afternoon heat, replies, "laughing as carelessly as she could," "Oh! no, no . . . ; it is the very last thing I would stand the brunt of just now." Such knowledge would indeed be a blow. She can imagine only one or two friends "whose thoughts I would not be afraid of knowing" (III, 7; 369–70). Knightley's question and Emma's denial imply layers of perceptual exchange: Knowing what others really perceive one to be risks a responding honesty, and in the ensuing network of hostile responses, the fragile civility upon which Hartfield's world depends could be damaged beyond repair.[4] Furthermore, the anguish of an intimate mutuality of perceptions is not only social. Merleau-Ponty speaks of the knowledge of the "presence of oneself to oneself" that occurs only when one is threatened: "for example, in the dread of death or of another's gaze upon me" (*Phenomenology of Perception* 404).

That dread and the defensive screening consequent to it consistently surface in many of *Emma*'s characters. Their feelings of vulnerability arise from specific social causes: One has something to hide, as Jane and Frank do, or one feels guilt and seeks solitude, as Emma does after the Box Hill reprimand from Knightley, or characters feel a peculiarly Austenian social claustrophobia, as Emma does in the coach after Elton's proposal, or as Harriet does most of the time. But enough characters feel this dread to suggest it is a feeling broader than specific social circumstances. Jane voices the yearning to escape the constant pressure of others' gazes when she speaks to Emma on fleeing the Donwell Abbey strawberry party: "Oh! Miss Woodhouse, the comfort of being sometimes alone!" (III, 6; 363). The dread of not being alone is that the other's gaze must be returned and one's return will be observed in a manner that, yet again, one must observe and react to. To paraphrase Merleau-Ponty, one *must* see oneself being seen and signal that one has performed this seeing with equanimity.

Austen understands well how intersubjective blocking occurs to avoid such a sequence of invasions of the vulnerable self. Frank proposes precisely such a sequence of invasions to Emma, to be observed in a triangle with Jane, as he offers Emma the seductive pleasures of the voyeur in witnessing Jane's exposure. Yet he then stands in front of Emma, blocking her gaze and denying her the knowledge he has tempted her with. "Emma soon saw him standing before Miss Fairfax, and talking to her; but as to its effect on the young lady, as he had improvidently placed himself exactly between them, exactly in front of Miss Fairfax, she could absolutely distinguish nothing" (II, 8; 222). Frank's position across the room between two gazes (Emma's and Jane's) explores the paradoxical nature of power (typically more available to men) here: He can both screen and expose, frustrate and protect, for Jane and Emma simultaneously.

A similar scene occurs later, also consisting of a contradictory pattern of avoidance and approach among three people, but although here we again have two watchers targeting Jane (initially), it is Jane who foils both invading gazes. The watchers are Knightley and Frank, and the tension arises out of Frank's knowledge that Perry had for a moment thought to buy a carriage (since Frank could not have obtained his knowledge himself, he has betrayed, to knowing ears, a private source—Jane—within the Bates household):

> Mr. Knightley's eyes had preceded Miss Bates's in a glance at Jane. From Frank Churchill's face, he had involuntarily turned to her's; but she was indeed behind, and too busy with her shawl. . . . Mr. Knightley suspected in Frank Churchill the determination of catching her eye—he seemed watching her intently—in vain, however, if it were so—Jane passed between them into the hall, and looked at neither. (III, 5; 346–47)

The situation is already exponentially more intricate than our previous example because one watcher's targets are *both* the woman to whom so many eyes are turning and the man who seeks to trap—"catch"—her gaze. That is, a watcher watches another watcher in pursuit to compel the telltale look. Knightley understands thoroughly the contest in the doorway and, by means of his sympathy for Jane's vulnerability, also what is at stake. Austen maps a subtle and desperate struggle, with response and counterresponse, and in Jane yet a further counterresponse: "[She] looked at neither."

Both of these scenes carefully and intricately reverse our paradigmatic process of intersubjective exchange. Rather than allow "the thing" one looks at to "impose itself . . . as real for every subject who is standing where" the observer is, to repeat Merleau-Ponty's words, Frank in the first scene and Jane in the second stand precisely so as to disallow the observing other any grasp of what Jane is experiencing as "real." "Impose" raises fundamental questions of power: Who or what imposes, and under whose or what regime? Not only are gazes in both scenes threatening and thus to be avoided, but they are also part of a series of signals, of intended and expected exchanges. Thus the refusal in each scene to be observed observing (especially in the second scene, where Jane avoids meeting anyone's eye) resonates through several layers of denied responses. Knightley does not see Frank seeing Jane's reaction to his knowing glance to her. Emma does not see Frank's gestural "pun" that would have displayed Jane's "colour" to two different observers (Emma and himself) with two different codes of interpretation. The kinds of perception and misperception denied in each scene are subtly different, but what is unmistakable is the deeply intersubjective character of each scene's denial of a *sequence* of observations. The blocked or deflected gaze within a complex human network of expectations is a brilliant example of the intersubjectivity of fragile, imperfect human intercourse in Austen.

Austen's intersubjective comedy also moves inside to shape Emma's experience of who she is. In Austen the comedy of reciprocities occurs within the theater of the inner consciousness, too. This inward theater of the intersubjective opens out in Emma's self-narrativizing at the beginning of volume II, chapter 13, when Emma indulgently imagines Frank's return to court her, in every version of which she refuses him. Even Emma's pride enacts itself in intersubjective plots. Initially Emma's reverie of storytelling seems private, narcissistic, and deaf to Merleau-Ponty's "demand" of the other to be heard. "[S]he sat drawing or working, forming a thousand amusing schemes for the progress and close of their attachment, fancying interesting dialogues, and inventing elegant letters . . ." (II, 13; 264). But "dialogues" and "letters" suggest a fantasy of exchange. Then Emma, to play out the game of self-conceiving, takes another step, a step into Merleau-Ponty's layered, deep intersubjectivity: "Upon the whole, she was equally contented with her view of his feelings" (II, 13; 264). Wayne Booth emphasizes Austen's control of narratorial distance in words like "contented," which describe Emma's self-comforting (Booth, chapter 9, especially 257–58). But inside that narratorial frame the new intricacy of characters' consciousnesses (*within* Emma's fantasy) is remarkable. Emma's reveries need an idea of Frank's idea of her to be rewarding, so she considers at some length the nature of his love for her. The deeply intersubjective climax to this scene is Emma's further effort not only to imagine Frank's feelings (however comically in error and self-servingly) but also to imagine his imagination of *her* feelings:

> Not that I imagine he can think I have been encouraging him hitherto. No, if he had believed me at all to share his feelings, he would not have been so wretched. Could he have thought himself encouraged, his looks and language at parting would have been different. (265)

Emma has an assumption of what it means to know the other and be known as she develops her sense of self by means of imagined stories. Emma's implied sense of self requires a series of subtle, mutual readings (in, one must remember, her mind's eye). That is, Emma imagines herself as the subject of Frank's meditation, as he is at the moment the subject of hers. Furthermore, each reading that she imagines, hers of Frank and Frank's of her, proceeds according to each consciousness's canny (or so each thinks) notations of the other's behavior, including both the physical and verbal ("looks and language," says Emma). "No, if he had believed me at all to share his feelings, he would not have been so wretched" represents Emma's interpretation of Frank's interpretation of her in his gestures *for* her.

Emma also sees herself as the mistress of perception who embodies her understanding in a behavior for the other, which she arranges in order to limit the degree to which the other, Frank in this instance, can appropriate her consciousness. She is able, she believes, to control the extent of her and their mutual espousal: "[W]hen he comes again, if his affection continue, I must be on my guard not to encourage it . . . but I do not know that I expect [his affection] will [continue]" (I, 13; 265). The novel's wonderful irony, of course, lies in the final reversal of this fantasy, when the reader and Emma learn that she has been the "object" of exactly such control of espousal. The larger significance, however, of this scene in volume II, chapter 13, and of much of Emma's inner life in the novel is that Emma's self-misunderstanding is framed as intersubjectively multiple appropriations that open a door to a deeply intersubjective redirecting of her intelligence. Meanwhile, Emma misperceives Frank's gestures (dancing with her at the home of the Coles, standing by her chair) and his word (all the repartee about Dixon and things Irish), misperceives his appropriation of her responses to him, and therefore misunderstands herself. Emma's failure to know herself is a new kind of failure, the misappropriation of another's embodied perceptions of one's own perceptions. We discover in the newly intersubjective comedy fresh depths of opacity.

But Austen's comedy would not be a version of the komos if fiction's new process of self-defining measured in *Emma* only self-evasion or blindness. It also measures some movement toward more complex perceptions of herself in her world. Whatever one thinks of Emma's moral growth, and critics have differed widely on this subject, she manifestly changes to some degree, and demonstrably comes to perceive herself more exactly as imaged through others. Knightley's anger at the Box Hill incident produces just such a demonstration of moral, epistemological, and intersubjective illumination. Having delivered his lecture to Emma, Knightley leaves, believing that Emma's pride has armed her against his criticism, and indeed it has made her angry, but not with him. Emma's reaction demonstrates how much she has learned to gauge the connection between herself and the gestures of others by which she in part knows who she is:

> He had misinterpreted the feelings which had kept her face averted, and her tongue motionless. They were combined only of anger against herself, mortification, and deep concern. . . . [T]hen reproaching herself for having taken no leave, making no acknowledgement, parting in apparent sullenness, she looked out with voice and hand eager to show a difference; but it was just too late. (III, 7; 375–76)

Emma's effort to respond to Knightley's gestures with her own gestures, of both "voice and hand," is really her effort to espouse his behavior, as it embodies his view of her, both for herself and for him.

There is an also evasive undercurrent in Emma's effort, yes, that seeks Knightley's approval, rather than the more painful knowledge of her errors. But her gesture is predominantly one of self-clarification, a process whose enabling assumptions and narrative structure in Austen's fiction are deeply intersubjective. Emma fails now to acknowledge and be acknowledged by Knightley, but she will not in volume III, chapter 13, when, courageously, she asks him to walk again around her garden. For Emma to understand better the intricate relations of her fantasies to her perceptions of the other's perception and embodiment of her gestures (and so on, in the receding series of mirrorings): for her to know herself more fully in this way is a morally and epistemologically difficult act and a remarkable achievement.

Emma's education in the intersubjective opens the door to the lovers' embodiment of embodiment that blooms in her garden and fulfills the promise of the komos. To clarify that achievement, Austen returns immediately after the climactic garden encounter to our previous subject, a character's misimagination of another character's imagination of a romantic attraction, but in this case the misimagining character is Frank, not Emma. The remarkable sequence, in volume III, chapters 14–15, not only mirrors Emma's errors, but also does so in an even more extended mirroring of mirrorings, as Frank writes Mrs. Weston what *he* thought Emma thought he thought, and Emma reads what Frank wrote Mrs. Weston, and Mr. Knightley reads—mostly aloud—to Emma what Frank wrote Mrs. Weston, accompanied by his commentary to Emma and her commentary on his commentary. This comic chiasmus begins with Frank's account of his thoughts about Emma's thoughts:

> Amiable and delightful as Miss Woodhouse is, she never gave me the idea of a young woman likely to be attached; and that she was perfectly free from any tendency to being attached to me, was as much my conviction as my wish.— She received my attentions with an easy, friendly, goodhumoured playfulness, which exactly suited me. We seemed to understand each other." (III, 14; 397–98)

Of course Frank's retrospective account of his reading of Emma has a rhetorical purpose: He knows the Westons have misread Emma's interest in *him,* and he seeks to exonerate himself as far as possible: He has deceived everyone at Hartfield about his engagement to Jane, he admits, but at least he is not guilty of soliciting Emma's affections when he could not reciprocate. They were simply partners in play. Flirtation was a convention, as Frank claims to have believed both of them believed. "From our relative situation, those attentions were her due, and were felt to be so" (III, 14; 398). Frank's narrative, with its reconstruction of his motives and his perception of others' motives, provokes some raised eyebrows among his readers, and not only Mr. Knightley, and that skepticism is the point. This narrative of the intersubjective has occurred before: The imagining of imaginings is Frank's here, but the reader remembers Emma's, too, and how distorted by self-interest hers were as well. Frank of course is closer to the truth than Emma was: He is right that Emma is not in love with him, but he is wrong that she sees his flirtation as simply "attentions" that were "her due." But now the readings of readings get aired in another series of readings of readings, and the result is a degree of clarity, at least for Emma and Knightley, that for example eludes all the characters in Henry James's *The Awkward Age*.

The deepest point of the labyrinth in volume III, chapter 15, occurs when Knightley reads aloud, for Emma's further comment, Frank's account of Jane's account of her wish to break off their engagement, given the "misery" of their masquerade before the Eltons, the Westons, Emma, and all the others. Knightley's remark reconstructs exactly as Merleau-Ponty would have wished the landscape of Jane's life as she must have experienced it: "What a view this gives of her sense of his behavior!" (III, 15; 406) In this brief moment, the near miraculous, in a world that includes the Eltons, has occurred: Compassion and attentiveness to the other's gestures of feeling have triumphed.

The warmth of Knightley's exclamation lights up the cold corners of Hartfield. His ability to track people's perceptions and their perceptions of how others perceive them is indeed the core of Knightley's wisdom in *Emma* and helps him help Emma—to understand what the Box Hill episode meant for Miss Bates, for example, and here to grasp, as he did in the episode we discussed earlier of Perry's carriage, the implications of Jane's embeddedness in a web of perceptions and misperceptions about which, given her dependencies, she can do little except block the occasional invading gaze. Knightley's compassion is intricate, deeply intersubjective, and warmly embodied (whatever Mark Twain and D. H. Lawrence had to say about Austen's inability to live the body). And so, too, now is Emma's.

The web of gazes and perceptions leads to many errors, and anxiety still remains. But Emma and Knightley speak for an idea of community in which words and gestures respond to other words and gestures, not perfectly, but as if one is putting a brick in a niche in our wall left by the other. Knightley even defines a piece of his ideal when he tells Emma, as he sits down to read Frank's letter, "It will be natural for me . . . to speak my opinion aloud as I read. By doing it I shall feel that I am near you" (III, 15; 404). Here Knightley's notion moves in a significantly different direction from his more famous line about language, from the proposal scene, when he says, "If I loved you less, I might be able to talk about it more" (III, 13; 390). But language *is* important in the interworld of human understandings and is even *natural,* says

Knightley, when he finds himself between texts, Frank's letter on one side, Emma on the other; they are joined in a deeper network as he reads Frank aloud, responding to his words and Emma's as she reads his reading of Frank and herself, those deeply intersubjective embodiments extending throughout this little world, "two Inches wide," of Hart-field.[5]

Human disclosure, as a famous paragraph in *Emma* observes, is always limited because of the nature of its process, working as it does from incarnated gesture and language:

> Seldom, very seldom, does complete truth belong to any human disclosure; seldom can it happen that something is not a little disguised, or a little mistaken; but where, as in this case, though the conduct is mistaken, the feelings are not, it may not be very material.—Mr. Knightley could not impute to Emma a more relenting heart than she possessed, or a heart more disposed to accept of his. (III, 13; 431–32)

"Impute" is the key word here: There is no glass onto the soul, as Tristram Shandy once dreamed there might be. Merleau-Ponty's deep intersubjectivity always works by indirection. One reads, or, if others stand in the way of our gaze, fails to read the body, gesture, and the eye's word, as well as the tongue's word. But the network of exchanged indirections and embodied signs is not hopelessly solipsistic. In Austen this network of readings results in some kind of genuine community on rare occasions. We know they are rare because measuring the genuine requires, for Austen, complex representations of the more common and misleading imitations, even forgeries, of community.

That Emma successfully revises her sense of self in the midst of this deeply intersubjective field of consciousnesses and languages is not clear to all readers of her novel. At least we can probably agree that readers are able so thoughtfully to disagree because of the intricacy of Austen's phenomenology of anxiety and misperceptions (and perceptions). But other issues in the controversies over Emma's self-knowledge remain. For me the comic strain in Austenian deep intersubjectivity predominates, despite her emphasis upon the imperfection of discourse and disclosure. Emma and Knightley, and Frank and Jane together place stones in that wall, in the niche left by the other, not so that any of them achieves full presence to the other, but so that, in Merleau-Ponty's words, there is woven "an 'exchange,' a 'chiasm between two destinies . . . ' in which there are never quite two of us, and yet one is never alone."

FILM, FILM COMEDY, AND DEEP INTERSUBJECTIVITY

> *The world is already constituted, but also never completely constituted; in the first case we are acted upon, in the second we are open to an infinite number of possibilities. But this analysis is still abstract, for we exist in both ways at once. There is, therefore, never determinism and never absolute choice.*
> —MERLEAU-PONTY, Phenomenology of Perception

> *[T]he images within which the subject "finds" itself always come to it from outside. In Seminar II Lacan describes the ego as "the superimposition of various coats borrowed from . . . the bric-a-brac of its props department."*
> —KAJA SILVERMAN, Male Subjectivity at the Margins

Austen and Hitchcock and Allen: These storytellers and their work illuminate the disarray of modern comedy and its dependence on deep intersubjectivity for its affect and disturbance. It was always possible for the komos to fail and for sterility to triumph. Much of what is called modern comedy is not comic at all in the classical sense: It offers laughter without redemption, humor without health or healing. Or comedy's ritual may offer more uncertain rewards. In Bakhtin's archetypal comic narrative, carnival, which is the festival of being and of the suspension of time, paradoxically endures only a season. Official time returns, and how deep are the traces of carnival's disorder? The battle between winter and summer and between the self as display or the self as generously and deeply intersubjective lies at the core of Austen. They also are fundamental to the contestation about community in *His Girl Friday,* as we will see in the following chapter, and in *Broadway Danny Rose,* two paradigmatic films, one comic and one anticomic. I argue in the next chapter that *His Girl Friday* is modern "comedy" without hope or healing and that *Broadway Danny Rose* recovers balance and feeling in a world of anxiety and death. But both films dramatize the significance of deep intersubjectivity as form and subject in modern comedy.

Hitchcock's important corpus of films also breaks into at least two contrasting modes, one deeply carnivalesque, the other profoundly ironic and sad—and it is the depth and reach of these films by the same director (and often the same team of writers, assistant directors, and editors) that explain the extensive attention to Hitchcock in this book. Even more important, Hitchcock's abiding interest in articulating subjectivities in film requires his presence here because his narrative modes—carnivalesque and ironic and other voices that lie between these poles—depend intimately on a tracing of those complex embodiments that are fundamental to deep intersubjectivity. So Hitchcock and Allen both function horizontally and vertically in this study: to illuminate, in this chapter, the deeply intersubjective character of modern comedy, and by contrast, in the next chapter, the intersubjectively framed subversion of comedy. Hitchcock and Allen thus open up a new topic about genre practice: how to talk about the representation of consciousness, not to speak of consciousness*es* in film.

Film narrative offers special opportunities and problems for a study of representations of intersubjectivity and especially of intersubjectivity in comedy. Throughout this book I tend to see the narration of consciousnesses as fundamentally parallel in structure in the stories told in print and in film, but this approach will seem counterintuitive to some readers, and indeed important new strategies do appear in film stories, especially in what I discuss in the next chapter as film's intersubjective gaze. Meanwhile, to read film, that medium of surfaces, in light of my phenomenologically interior model, may seem perverse. To prepare for such readings, especially of deep intersubjectivity in film comedy, I want to discuss two issues, one of which appears also in chapter 1. The first has to do with the cultural production of narratives and their consumers, and the second has to do with film's, and in particular film comedy's, generic inhospitability (or what may seem to be a resistance) to representations of consciousness, not to speak of intersubjectivity.

Although in theory I see narrative as both culturally produced and producing culture, the weight of the new paradigm of deep intersubjectivity that I am proposing, at least as I am proposing it, tilts toward narrative's power to produce culture. In contrast, film studies has for some time concentrated on two different linkages: on the industrial and cultural origins of film texts in a matrix of star, studio, distribution, and display systems; and on the production by these systems of real viewing subjects or consuming subjectivities in the world outside the film text. Examples of the first linkage range from Douglas Gomery's work on the studio system to studies of the effect of marketing "adult" movies in the 1950s on Sirk melodrama (Klinger, chapter 2), and the effect of the Steadicam on the enunciation of identity and agency in film since 1976 (Geuens 1993). This linkage, however, tends to bleed into the second because the industrial origins of the film text shape its versions of selfhood, as in Geuens's note about the effects of the Steadicam: "With the Steadicam, visuality is commodified even further: the uncanniness of the gaze not only depersonifies and dematerializes perspective, it also perfectly embodies the recent transformation of capitalist technology identified by Ernest Mandel and illuminated by Frederic Jameson within a context of post-modernism in the arts" (16).

The second linkage, in which film systems construct real viewing subjects, characterizes many approaches to cinema and subjectivity. For example, *New Vocabularies in Film Semiotics* (Stam, Burgoyne, and Flitterman-Lewis) describes in telling terms the significance of the move in early film to shot/reverse-shot editing:

> This is not to say that one-shot actualities (early newsreels) were devoid of meaning. . . . But along with editing came the privileging, channeling and directing of those relations in the production of a viewing subjectivity that is markedly different from one-shot actualities. Classical editing implies subjectivity—or its negotiation—by guiding the subjective processes toward a meaning-effect. (166)

The next step is Baudry's, summarized in this way: "For [Baudry], the reverse-shot structure renders the discursive construction of the film invisible, thus producing a mystified subject who 'absorbs an ideological effect without being aware of it' " (170). Another version of this linkage makes use of the Lacanian notion of the fractured or absent self, in which the plenitude of the film image irresistibly attracts the viewer to the "coherence of its fictions" (170).[6]

Emphasizing these linkages leads to a notion of the function of narrative that is quite different from the ones that have characterized these pages. I have paid some attention to the cultural conditions in which narratives emerge, though these conditions have not been the primary interest here, but the second linkage that is typical of film studies points to a significant absence in this study, of attention to viewing or reading consciousnesses implied in a story or real in the history of its reception and consumption.

This is an appropriate moment to admit that narratives intend *for*, just as individual consciousnesses represented within them enact or embody intention, and a thorough phenomenological criticism would allow for the construction and effects of that intentionality. Furthermore, the interest in its audience in, say, a romantic comedy like *To Catch a Thief* or *Broadway Danny Rose,* both reflects and shapes the audience it conceives for itself and that it intends for; their role in the shaping of classical Hollywood genres and the star system, for example, is a fundamental component in the production of film texts, as Dickens's experience with and imagination of his readers shaped his production of *Great Expectations,* even as it redirected the imagination and consciousness of class and erotic paradox in those readers. However, the concentration of film studies and cultural studies of narrative in general on the two bookends I described earlier—narrative as a culture's product, and film narrative, especially, as producer of consuming subjectivities—has tended to eclipse the significance and power of what is left between the bookends, the narrative itself, intending *for* an audience that it often seeks not to "construct" but to play to as another receptive intelligence. My interest in representations of intersubjectivity in narrative bears a trace of what may seem an ancient formalism, but it also reflects a belief in the slight agency of storytellers and their audience to shape together what is not entirely already shaped in our lifeworld. Hence my invocation of a similar belief, in the epigraph to this section from Merleau-Ponty: "[T]he world is already constituted, but also never completely constituted" (1962, 453).

Film studies' interest in the second linkage I outlined earlier, in the power of film narrative to construct and direct desire in the viewing self, seems reasonable in a particularly commonsensical way, given the experience of the viewing subject in a dark space, emptying (apparently) its consciousness before a paradoxically full yet absent image, projected in a most transitory and fleeting sequence of shadows. The cinematic apparatus, moreover, promises plenitude across a range of the senses, in comparison to written narratives. It sutures the viewing subject into a mise-en-scène in a complex series of strategies, from shot/reverse-shot sequences to point-of-view camera seductions to soundtrack music cues. In this approach to film narrative, like Kaja Silverman's in one of the epigraphs to this section, Lacanian models of the subject have been understandably powerful. If the self knows itself by donning almost randomly abandoned garments from its prop closet, then the cinematic apparatus will hypnotize and overwhelm the deeply lacking gazer.

Nonetheless, as I argue in chapter 1, the Lacanian notion of the self, at least as popularized in gender and film studies, presumes a tragic narrative to which there are alternatives. The power of film narrative to construct consciousness may not be altogether imperial. Feminist and activist critics have noted for some time the tendency of ideological contradictions to disturb the surface of (apparently) faithful productions of the dominant paradigms—or at least such critics assert some freedom of the viewer from the imperial cinematic apparatus, a freedom to read "against the grain" of an ideology whose presentation seems to be "intended" as seamless. So Hollywood's women's films, especially melodramas from *Now, Voyager* to *Written on the Wind,* have been widely read as problematizing the dominant gender system that they seem to underwrite.⁷ It is time then for critics and scholars to write more emphatically for and about that audience for narrative that not only recognizes the often trivializing citations of shots from film history (yet another baby carriage tumbling down the Odessa steps), but also recognizes more significantly the suturing itself, even in the seamless, suture-mystifying studio film. This audience recognizes and decodes the assemblage of narrative in its consumption of defamiliarizing narratives, whether *Vanity Fair, Breathless,* or *Pulp Fiction,* and even in its consumption of less self-reflexive narratives like *Pride and Prejudice,* Nora Roberts's romances, or *E.T.*

The film writing in this book presumes the reception of film narrative by such active, ideologically astute viewers with at least a nascent grasp of film's formal languages, regardless of whether they are what Peter Rabinowitz has called the authorial audience: If such astute viewers are not the filmmakers' ideal audience, at least they are mine.⁸ Murray Smith has recently critiqued in a similar vein the influence of thinkers like Christian Metz, whose notion of the " 'credulous spectator' (who believes in the reality of the represented action)" emphasizes the power of the apparatus over the viewer. Smith admits that Metz sees film consumption as deeply paradoxical, combining credulity and incredulity, and I do not share Smith's dismissal of Metz's paradox: I see film (and indeed printed text) audiences as living a combination of active consciousness moving perhaps parallel to the narrative with a simultaneous yearning to submit, forget the self, and submerge in the narrative. I do not think the "spectator must be aware of the representational status of a representation *at all times* in order to respond appropriately to it" (my emphasis) (42). Nevertheless, even a paradoxical view of spectatorship returns some agency to the hapless film viewer, who need not then be blindly sutured by the apparatus or the star system (or even studio marketing) into a seamlessly edited spectacle. Smith's book is an important study of the ways film texts require and expect audiences to understand and adopt a complex variety of positions in response to film narratives.

The second theoretical issue about intersubjectivity in film narrative asks, how can one talk about a representation of an interior flow of experience in film, itself a picturing of surfaces, much less talk about representing the layered interplay of complex intersubjectivity as posited in this book? The question applies with particular force to film comedy, especially to rapid, highly verbal screwball comedies like *His Girl Friday* (the conventional view of this film, despite my argument for its subversion of comedy). Although I am not making this case for early, more screwball Allen films (like *Take the Money and Run* or *Sleeper*), the question still applies to many later, "deeper," but still "superficial" comedies like *Broadway Danny Rose* or *Bullets over Broadway*: How can these films be deeply intersubjective, with their speed, attention to surface and to behavior rather than character, their stereotypes, and their reduction of experience to the physical?

The narrativizing of consciousness, and even more so of consciousnesses in film, is not as paradoxical as it at first may appear. Film might seem to lack the narrative voice, especially the voice of omniscience, which enables the representation of gestures of consciousness, and especially the web of gestures responding to each other in that receding series of mirrorings that I call deep intersubjectivity, and whose flowering in omniscient narrative I describe in chapter 2. But in fact film narrative does presume an enabling presence, a guarantor of consciousness that is articulated through the movement of the camera and the selection of shots. The rendering of consciousness in film, whether characters' or the narrating intentionality's, depends upon many choices, from the elemental gaps that continuity editing elides, to the explanation of motives with eyeline matches (a victim screams, looking offscreen, and the film cuts to a looming figure, which was likely photographed on another day, at another place). The viewer is sutured into a film narrative most particularly through editing, as we construct linkages between shots to suggest cause and effect (as Lev Kuleshov's workshop explored in their well-known experiments), participate in point-of-view shots, and follow the rhythm of a conversation through shot/reverse-shot conventions.

The content of the frame, however, and the substance of a film's mise-en-scène also articulate consciousness and intersubjectivity. The interplay among these elements—dialogue, the dance of bodies, the display (or masking) of intentionalities and appropriations, the frame's activity itself, for example—produces a rich fabric of mutually attentive consciousnesses. Let me stress again that the product of film discourses is a deeply articulated series of embodiments, of bodies moving to, from, and around other bodies in complex networks of intention and mistaking. (One very brief example, from Spike Lee's *Do the Right Thing*: Think of the two brief architecturally balanced sequences, at about twenty-five minutes into the film, that introduce the comic conflict—worthy of Hawks and Capra—between Da Mayor and Mother/Sister, in pairs of canted frames, oppositely and complementarily angled, and the web of intendings, promised appropriations, and blockages they expose.)

Film can take advantage of the extraordinary resources opened up by our shift in narrative practices as fully as any other narrative form has since the early nineteenth century. However, storytellers in film, as in other genres in the twentieth century, have typically doubted more than nineteenth-century storytellers the achievement of their narratives: They can construct deep intersubjectivity but may not believe in it. Images and myths of community attract rigorous sceptics now. But film is as capable of constructing the fictions of complex intersubjectivity as written narrative and is even better able to track the appropriations of appropriation in the embodiments of Merleau-Ponty's watchers. The fiction of the suture between embodied consciousnesses is no more (or less) problematic here than in *Middlemarch* or, as we will see later, in *The Awkward Age*.

But can film *comedy* trace such deeply intersubjective, intricately sutured characters? Deep intersubjectivity in film comedy may acquire a different style and use of implication but is no less significant than it is in dramatic films. Comedies, however fast, depend on readings of intentions, on bodies responding to and interpreting other bodies, and on misreadings and rereadings. The web of gestures within, say, doorframes and mirrors in *The Lady Eve* presumes as deep a network of consciousnesses reading each other and reading the other's reading as those webs in *Citizen Kane* or *Vertigo*. Sturges's Charley and Jean/Eve misconstruct the other's constructions of themselves with consequences in matters of class, power, and identity that are similar in shape and weight to the consequences that affect Welles's Kane and Susan or Hitchcock's Scottie and Madeleine/Judy. Comedy sometimes attends to surfaces and reduces consciousness to the physical, but so do other genres, and that very attention to the surface and the physical lays the groundwork for exactly the responses among embodied consciousnesses this book traces and seeks to understand.

However, as we move from Austen to Hitchcock and Allen, modern and now modernist (or postmodern) comedy offer an environment for deeply intersubjective narrative radically different from classical comedy. If the komos is a ritual exploration of the boundaries of community, then complex intersubjectivity in comedy now explores the struggle between shame and espousal at considerable risk. After all, in modern "comedy," the failure of the comic ritual is always a possibility. That is, a narrative whose conventions are comic may function, in generic or mythical terms, as anticomedy. The speed, hostilities, and focus on the self as brittle performance in screwball comedy are examples of the underside of comedy. The power of death may *not* be exorcised by the sacrifice of the scapegoat, and the scapegoat may even not go quietly, especially when the dark forces lurk with great staying power in screwball comedy's perverse lovers. Ed Sikov describes the archetype in complementary terms:

> In screwballs, unmarried people are put through a sort of courtship by ordeal. . . . But what makes the genre strange, what gives it its lasting punch, is that the ordeal continues for married people as well. One could even say that in screwball comedies people's lives deteriorate terribly under the strain of conjugal love. (32)

But the peculiar result, the thoroughly modern comic ambiguity is, as Sikov phrases it, that "men and women never really come to terms with each other, but neither do they find themselves broken down beyond repair" (34).

The strains of modern comedy nowhere appear with such clarity as in Hitchcock's film comedies, from the screwball spin on masquerade in *To Catch a Thief*, to the profound tragicomedy of *Notorious*. And the dark side of screwball comedy triumphs in *His Girl Friday*, as we will see in chapter 4. Film narrative offers a special version of complex intersubjectivity in what I call the intersubjective gaze. As I discuss in the following section, the gaze has a special place in film theory, and the notion of a deeply intersubjective gaze subverts and redirects some of that theory. More important, the intersubjective gaze clarifies what matters most about film comedy. It helps to give these films their powerful understanding of what is at stake in the komos (and at least on the surface these stakes seem to be either/or): appropriation or loss, espousal or shame. Even if "modern" to "modernist" to "postmodern" is shorthand for an increasingly secular, eccentric (that is, decentered), self-referential narrative in which signifiers dominate the signified, what is at stake for the komos in such narratives is still enormous: perhaps not healing and life making themselves, but the rituals of healing and life making, which as metaphors still have considerable power.

HITCHCOCK'S CARY GRANT FILMS: THEATRICALITY, GENDER, AND THE INTERSUBJECTIVE GAZE

The Intersubjective Gaze

The films of Alfred Hitchcock illustrate how thoroughly the conventions of deep intersubjectivity had permeated narrative practice by the mid-twentieth century. Of course many films and novels function without the series of succeeding gestures that mirror, distort, or seek to erase preceding gestures of consciousness in the fabric of narrating selves that I have been tracing. This occasional absence of complex subjectivity, however, is less surprising in a way than its sometime presence, in the renewing of a different and difficult representation of consciousnesses, one that requires strenuous attention to the languages of body and word and to their attention to each other. This attention marks Hitchcock's films so significantly across their broad range that Hitchcock's works loom large in this book. It marks with special complexity his comic films—a category that will surprise some readers, since only a few critics like Lesley Brill have understood how fundamental the possibilities of the komos are for what Brill calls the Hitchcock romance.[9] Hitchcock's films have long figured significantly in film theory's work on the gaze and constructions of subjectivity; my project is to link the resources of deep intersubjectivity to what I am calling the intersubjective gaze, in order to explore in this chapter Hitchcock's remarkable comic vision.

Deep intersubjectivity has its most profound effects in Hitchcock's films in their extraordinary studies of theatricality and the masquerade. These studies have both a comic and a tragic mode, or if "tragic" doesn't suit a postmodern age, a bitterly ironic mode that estimates human imperfection and its costs severely. The discussions that follow concentrate on the comic, in the Cary Grant films, and then, in my last chapter, on the darkly ironic voice, in *Marnie*. The building blocks in film for Hitchcock's narrative meditations on power and intersubjectivity are similar to those we have followed in storytelling throughout this book, within a grammar of film form: the language of gestures responding to and against other gestures; the appropriations of words and movements by embodied, intending consciousnesses moving within the dynamic lines of the film frame; and narrative structure working within the film's rhythms of editing and camera movement.

The special element in Hitchcock's subtlety is the way power shapes the movement of perceptions of being perceived: Authority seeps deeply into these selves or into the play that performs the self, and that process appears on screen in the movement of the camera, in the placing of the frame and what it frames, and in the suturing of subjects in shots.[10] Hitchcock's special interest in the role of looking as an extension of power is old news in film criticism. But the gaze (the camera's as well as the characters') in Hitchcock criticism, as in film criticism generally, has become much more than Laura Mulvey's original gesture of the imperial male. The evolution of thinking about the gaze's gendering complements my emphasis on the intersubjective gaze in Hitchcock and on its fundamental role in his treatment of the theatrical and the masquerade. I need to theorize briefly this intersubjective gaze before working with its comic mode in Hitchcock's Cary Grant films.

That evolution of thought about power and the gaze has complicated the role of the look as the gesture of the colonizing male (within the frame, behind the camera, or in the audience), as gender has become less and less essentialized and subject positions less fixed. That is, it has become less clear what is "masculine" in the look: For example, whose gaze is typically more aggressive and confrontational, Marlene Dietrich's or Jimmy Stewart's? Nor is the effect of power so clearly gendered along party lines, as audiences cross gender boundaries, whether women who delight in the surrogate and surreptitious exercise of power by fantasizing with Jeff in *Rear Window* (or indeed finally with Lisa, who gets the last look, as Tania Modleski argues), or teenage boys, the dominant audience in the '70s and '80s for slasher films, who, according to Carol Clover, cheer for the triumph of the Final Girl in *Halloween* or *The Silence of the Lambs*.[11]

The exercise of power in the gaze may also be subverted, ironized, or problematized, as in films like Michael Powell's *Peeping Tom*. What "real" audiences want and what characters within films do is not gendered nearly as straightforwardly as Laura Mulvey first thought (if straightforward can apply to the dense and elegant argument in her 1975 essay), as Mulvey herself has long agreed. In fact it may now be possible to discuss the gaze in a framework that includes, but is not limited to, the framework of gender. Issues of power and identity that Hitchcock's stories and camera articulate can now include a range of hierarchies and privileges conferred by class, education, or political institutions, for example, though gender remains a fundamental problematic for Hitchcock.

My investigation of the intersubjective gaze in Hitchcock develops from the reflections on film in the preceding chapter. Hitchcock's films are wonderful examples of texts that fall into the middle ground between the bookends of those cultural determinisms I posited earlier (films produced by a social/industrial system, for subjectivities constructed by those films). Confident that they are not only products of that industrial regime, Hitchcock's films play thoughtfully and self-consciously to their ideal audience, which sees itself also as not fully constructed by film and media culture and which is able to read, at some level of consciousness, the conventions and sutures of film narrative.

Also, to reprise some of the argument of chapter 1, I use the language of gazing in an effort to shape an understanding of intersubjectivity that is attuned to poststructuralist scepticism but is *not* Lacanian, at least as commonly rehearsed in literary and film studies. My paradigm for the construction of self and gender in a phenomenology of film as well as literary narrative emerges from Merleau-Ponty, for whom the fissures within the self and between the self and the "real" are not so radically unbridgeable, nor the self and the world so deeply unknowable as the dominant Lacanian model presumes. Barbara Freedman's recent Lacanian study of the gaze and Shakespearean comedy illustrates the degree to which, under the influence of Lacan's thought, even comedy becomes an illusion; in works of comic theater like *Twelfth Night*, "recognition must be a misrecognition" for Freedman, and "loss [is] that which cannot be mastered" (234). Such Lacanian logic has been deeply influential in Hitchcock criticism, from Laura Mulvey's famous essay of 1975, through Slavoj Zizek's playful and rich readings of Hitchcock's tracking shots and vanishing ladies. This logic also guides Robert Samuels's book *Hitchcock's Bi-Textuality*, as in this example: "Linked to this profound awareness of the barred subject of language is Lacan's notion that if consciousness is always consciousness of another object, image or person, the ego is itself pure nothingness" (9–10).

Such moves erase agency and simplify the nature of action in Hitchcock. Yes, absence looms, and the self can empty with results both terrifying (*Vertigo*) and comic (*North by Northwest*: Thornhill's unmooring that leads to his reinvention). But absence is not the truth behind the mask in Hitchcock. Murray Smith has also criticized the influence of Lacanian notions of subjectivity on film criticism in conjunction, Smith believes, with Althusser's "deterministic rhetoric," which together "locat[e] ideological subjection in the most basic awareness of self" (45). Recognition is not always or entirely misrecognition in Hitchcock, nor is the recovery from loss simply an illusion or self-deception. The gaze is not always or only imperial and lonely.

Instead, Hitchcock's films explore the labyrinth of gazes that interconnect and reciprocate, that exchange (or subvert) signals by means of gestures and words that, in deep intersubjectivity, reinflect and reinterpret previous gestures in the ongoing embodied discourses of lived subjectivities: That is, Hitchcock's films explore the deeply intersubjective gaze. Throughout this book I am tracing the representation of this network or labyrinth of neighboring consciousnesses in narratives that are a sequence of appropriations and contestations among consciousnesses and their embodied intentions. Hitchcock's cinema of complex intersubjectivity tells stories in many keys, from major to minor, but they almost always enunciate and exploit what Ann Kaplan in another context only hoped would evolve someday, a cinema of "mutual gazing" (1983, 205). But this mutual gaze, even when complicated structurally into what I call the deeply intersubjective gaze, need not be an espousal, as it would be in Kaplan's wish for a cinema imitating the generous and reciprocal gaze between mother and child that would move beyond patriarchy and dominance.[12] "Mutuality" in intersubjective narratives can be a contest, an exchange of poses, or even a form of violence. The intersubjective gaze is Thorwald's defiance of Jeff's supervision, across the courtyard at the end of *Rear Window,* as well as Devlin's confession to Alicia in her sickroom in *Notorious,* "I couldn't see straight. I was a fat-headed guy full of pain."

Violation, shame, deception, as well as comic appropriation and espousal are all possible effects in Hitchcock's profoundly intersubjective narratives. Hitchcock's films explore with particular intensity forms of theatricality and masquerade, and because by their nature theater and masquerade are labyrinths of performance of "self," intersubjectivity would seem to become especially brittle in a series of mirrors reflecting other mirrors. In such a setting, what would it mean to claim the mirrors reflect versions of the komos?

The Cary Grant Films

> *You're like an American character in an English movie. You just don't talk the way an American tourist ought to talk.*
> —Frances, To Catch a Thief

> *I don't like the way Teddy Roosevelt is looking at me.*
> —Roger Thornhill, North by Northwest

Hitchcock's Cary Grant films consistently destabilize conventional assumptions about hierarchy, gender, and power in a profound study of a particularly complex form of mutuality, a deeply intersubjective theatricality within which characters move toward the mutual gaze, and its consequent effects in common projects of staging and scripting. The Grant films are comedies, in contrast to the much sadder and more troubling *Marnie*. Because the komos is also about death and expurgation, theatricality functions in these comedies as a dark force of shame and deception as well as a force of espousal. My subject now is how these films make *comic* use of a deeply intersubjective theatricality to study gender and sexuality.

By the theatrical I mean the staging and scripting by subjects in a film within spaces that they conceive in some way to be public, where subjects' intentions are to be seen. Theatricality is inherently intersubjective because gestures and language in "performance" embody for or against the other the framer's intentions or imposture of intentions. Theatricality becomes deeply intersubjective when its narrative tracks the embodiments of gestures responding to gestures that are themselves interpretations or distortions of yet prior signs: The network, knotting, or chiasmus (as Merleau-Ponty conceived it) of consciousnesses builds an "interworld" of stories, façades, signifiers, and gazes. Hitchcock's camera records such interworlds with special clarity and complexity. It is the erotic stagings, or the stagings of eros, that matter in these Grant films. In order to track the elements of a komos of the intersubjective gaze, I examine particularly the gestures of naming, scripting, and erotic play. Theatricality as form and image permeates

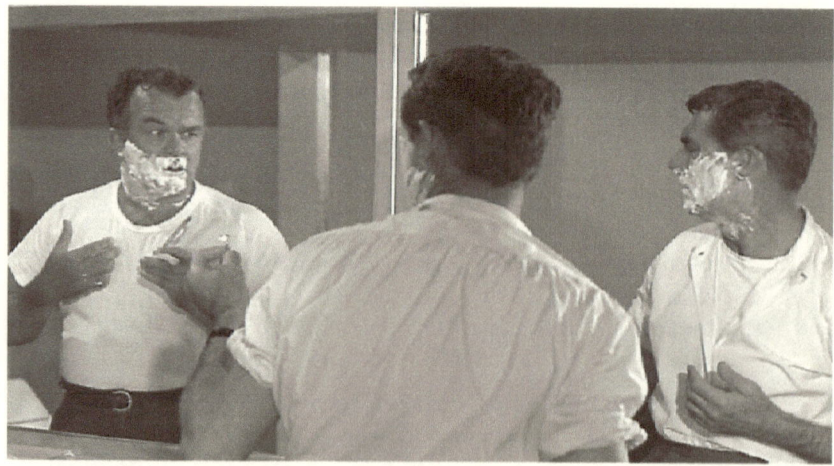

FIG. 1 *North by Northwest*. MGM 1959.
DVD © 1959 Turner Entertainment and Time Warner.

Hitchcock's work, of course, from *Murder!* to *Stage Fright,* and it provides an organizing metaphor in the Grant stories for the politics of intersubjectivity. It also provides metaphors that serve the comic myth of these films.[13] As I explain more fully in chapter 5, my discussion detects a presumption of agency and intentionality within the actors in our narratives. To see these presences as more than *only* ideological effects is perhaps an act of faith that will sabotage my reasoning for some readers.

Subjectivity is performance in Hitchcock because the screen is a stage, and the effects of the politics of looking are everywhere. If subjectivity becomes only performance, however, the results in Hitchcock's world are especially unfortunate. Intersubjectivity is partly about negotiating the boundaries between public and private, and those negotiations are gendered in Hitchcock in ways that are similar yet different for women and men. Masculinity becomes a particular kind of performance because men are the subject of someone's gaze, especially in Hitchcock's Cary Grant films, whether it's the gaze of the audience for that English film that Frances casts John Robie from, in *To Catch a Thief,* or Teddy Roosevelt's stony regard of Roger Thornhill in *North by Northwest.*

Indeed, everyone is looking at or for Thornhill's face in *North by Northwest,* in a way that raises complex issues of power. His control of how others see (and see him) diminishes through the film, particularly in his relation with Eve Kendall, whose authority directs the rituals of erotic foreplay, as in the dinner sequence on the Twentieth Century Limited. She seats Thornhill at her table, sees through his glasses and story, and is always two steps ahead of him. She ranks *his* face. Men get looked at all through *North by Northwest:* the monumental faces on Mount Rushmore, the craggy face of Thornhill (of that monument Cary Grant?), and the redcaps in the Chicago train station. A major aspect of Thornhill's education is his experience as target of the gaze, whether Teddy Roosevelt's or that unseen gazer's (the pilot of the crop-dusting plane) or Eve Kendall's. He learns about (relative) powerlessness and humiliation (demoted to redcap when his train arrives in Chicago; forced to shave in public—albeit in hiding—with Eve's diminished and diminishing razor). This public bathroom scene is especially rich as an example of the deep intersubjectivity of embarrassment, as Thornhill sees himself being seen, miniature razor in hand, and registers, in the gesture of the man next to him, *his* recognition of Thornhill's acknowledgement of seeing himself watched (see figure 1). The intimate network of gestures tightens the noose of embarrassment.

The discomfort of the gaze to its male object, a sexually authoritative male reduced (to his face) to a "nice face," is a fundamental experience in *North by Northwest* and in Hitchcock's other Grant films. Not only is the gaze decentering here, but it also disorients in a particular, deeply intersubjective way that sharpens the threat of shame and exposure. The threat is allied to a characteristic *staging* of the intersubjective, in what amounts to erotic stagings, or the staging of eros. This focus on the theatrical brings to light what is important about Alfred Hitchcock's Cary Grant films: the recuperation of espousal in complex comedies of posturing and deception (the comedy deepens to tragicomedy in the instance of *Notorious*).

Theatricality and Power: Naming, Scripting, and Staging Erotic Play

The Cary Grant films of Hitchcock came in four editions: *Suspicion* (1941), *Notorious* (1946), *To Catch a Thief* (1955), and *North by Northwest* (1959). In the last three films, the focus of my discussion, the fundamental issue of power and gender is the same: How does power circulate in the relation between a sexually aggressive, experienced woman of warmth and sympathy and a man of charm accustomed to exercising authority in sexual relations and elsewhere? In these three films the same dilemma arises and so defines the special politics of these comedies: If a woman makes a claim (even if only implicitly) to the greater sexual experience and the authority it confers—a claim that men have traditionally made—it is extraordinarily difficult for both the woman and the man to transcend parochial notions of power inherited with the sexual double standard. Authority is exactly the contested faculty. In *Notorious, To Catch a Thief,* and *North by Northwest* Cary Grant is the mature, attractive, available man who would expect to write the script of romantic play with an attractive woman but who is puzzled, then angry, when the woman claims the writer/director's role with an authority drawn from sexual knowledge traditionally reserved to men. Grant's character falls back on the traditional male critique of such women—that they are morally soiled in ways no man would be for similar knowledge—as a means to recuperate power, that is, to recapture the apparently dominant role in the interplay of gestures.

In these films, however, women and men partially transform the cycle of humiliation and retaliation and its assumptions about gender. Alicia, Frances, and Eve are not primarily victors in a battle, nor are Devlin, Robie, and Thornhill. These lovers struggle, finally, to revise together conventional understandings of authority as it constructs intersubjectivity. This conventional authority had claimed power over gestures, languages, and the intersubjective narrative that lovers write together. Authority for gazing, naming, and plotting becomes problematic indeed, in a hopeful way, because it is no longer (only) patriarchal.[14]

The study of authority in these four films echoes beyond Hitchcock's Grant group. *Suspicion*'s story reappears, for example, in *Marnie* (1964), whose heroine is certainly not timid and sheltered but whose fragile emotional balance is powerfully threatened by Mark Rutland's sexuality. On the other hand *Notorious*'s archetype appears as early as *Blackmail* (1929), where again the uncertainty about a heroine's sexual virtue leads to a painful struggle over the authority to gaze and name. Nevertheless, Hitchcock's Grant films, especially the last three, constitute a coherent body of work investigating in a special way how the theatrical forms intersubjectivity. They are coherent because, among other reasons, the characters Cary Grant enables Hitchcock to create make claims to sexual authority that are quite different from those made by other Hitchcock leading men, especially the less erotic James Stewart, the younger Farley Granger, and the more confused Henry Fonda or Gregory Peck.[15]

To examine theatricality is to begin with staged selves, staged for the other, in response to that other's staging, in the intertwining of gestures that constitutes the chiasmus. Characters' relations in public space build on the fundamental components of words and gestures, exchanged and reexchanged in the webbing of the characters' interworld. In the Grant films, the most fundamental components for understanding gender and sexuality in this webbing of intentionalities are naming and scripting, especially the scripting of erotic play. These strategies of theatricality do two kinds of work: They expose gaps, parodies, and silences that suggest a metacommentary about the nature of power, and they educate their actors in life in their theater, so that they become able to imagine a new kind of script and gaze. Theater and theatrics provide Hitchcock with the images for a profound study of the performance of authority, especially sexual authority, in all its intersubjective complexity.

Naming for example arises as a problem at the very beginning of *Notorious*, in a silence that is in retrospect intensely dramatic: The word "notorious" never occurs in the film itself. Its equivalents do: "Once a tramp, always a tramp," for example, in Alicia and Devlin's first scene at the sidewalk cafe in Rio. But "notorious" carries connotations that differ from the synonyms. It's a gendered word about audience: A woman can be sexually "notorious," that is, scandalous, as a man cannot be, and she is notorious to an implied audience in the film of worldly but respectable arbiters (they must be worldly or they wouldn't know the stories about the marked woman). The agents of this audience in the film are primarily the FBI, and thus men. The other North American voices we hear, most prominently at Alicia's party, hardly enforce the moral judgments of respectable society. And no one in Brazil (except, again, Americans like Prescott) has heard about Alicia's "notoriety"—surely Alex's mother would have used that reputation against the marriage if she knew of it. Interestingly, neither Prescott nor any of his team uses the word itself. It belongs only to the film's frame; indeed, it occurs in only one frame, and it is claimed as the object of an intention when the title reads: "Alfred Hitchcock's *Notorious*." Naming circulates outward, as it were, from the title frame and powerfully affects the consciousness of others' perceptions of oneself: Alicia knows well what people say about her. But she has little authority over this sign: Its gesture functions without interest in her response to it. Naming here is a model for an intersubjectivity of powerlessness.

Naming sometimes becomes renaming, which reveals a kind of struggle between different postures before an audience, whose reflection to the subject has a powerful effect upon that subject. Consider a sequence of shots in *North by Northwest* that links renaming specifically (and probably not ironically) to a cleansing by convention (and patriarchy). A man holds a woman by her hand as she hangs over one or another granite president (a forefather, in any event) and calls out, "I've got you. Come along." She cries, "I'm trying—I can't make it." Fade to the interior of a train compartment, where the same man pulls the same woman up to a bunk, saying "Come along, Mrs. Thornhill." The renaming of Eve Kendall serves convention in at least two ways: It signals Roger Thornhill's replacement of mother by wife—the only previous "Mrs. Thornhill" in the film and his companion of choice to the theater at the film's opening was his mother. That is, the naming of Eve marks Thornhill's growth beyond fixation on mother and fear of women.[16] Second, the renaming also legitimizes Eve, woman of ambiguous sexual status. Eve is "saved" from other fathers (Vandamm, the professor, and Teddy Roosevelt, or whichever president was returning the gaze to the visitors' balcony at Mt. Rushmore) by a man who can, and finally will, grant her his name and signal to other men that this woman carries his mark.

Marital naming is especially significant in a deeply intersubjective play of signifiers among possessing males, who want to see that others see the marked woman as theirs and to see their woman see that seeing, so she too knows her place in the circulation of powers. Eve's place in Thornhill's Oedipal drama seems clear enough: She functions to illuminate the male's inner journey and to measure his power. Given the rhetoric of these final shots in *North by Northwest*, with the celebratory sound track (timpani sounding triumphantly as the train enters the climactic tunnel), surely Hitchcock's understanding of Eve and Roger's naming ritual is celebratory, too. If so, the conventional (patriarchal) power to name functions in contradictory ways in Hitchcock. It is, at different moments, a power to be subverted and a power to be celebrated.

Nevertheless, *North by Northwest* also parodies patriarchal naming in all its play with Thornhill's initials (ROT). They link name and body (or whatever part of Thornhill is afflicted with rot) in a witty pun that is a good example of how poststructuralist play with signifiers (even if they are bodies) can occur between and within consciousnesses at play. It is symptomatic of the film's multiplicities that it is the signature "ROT" (on the matchbook) that, even while parody, rescues Eve—with the revelation that her disguise is no longer a disguise—at Vandamm's home. In *Notorious* as well, patriarchal naming carries less weight than one might expect. Sandy Flitterman-Lewis criticizes *Notorious* for diminishing Alicia's independence so that in the conclusion she is merely part of a "legalized romantic couple" (12). But Hitchcock cut a final scene from the screenplay that specifically renames Alicia and Devlin as "Mr. and Mrs. Devlin," a scene that would emphatically have replaced Alicia's "notoriety" with the authoritative sign of marriage (154).

If naming is a kind of embodiment whose shaping authority is contested in Hitchcock, so also is scripting—writing scenes and devising plots—even more so a contested narrative practice, especially as complicated by deep intersubjectivity. Hitchcock's women stake serious claims over this practice: Alicia inside Sebastian's house is on her own to make certain things happen (seducing Sebastian; plotting the welcome-home party; securing the cellar key); Frances stages her encounters with "Conrad Burns," whom she knows from the first is Robie; Eve pays the train's steward to seat Thornhill with her at their first lunch. Frances in *To Catch a Thief* may be the best example of writerly authority: She seizes control of her mother's romantic script when she kisses Robie goodnight (the camera emphasizes the mark as sign inscribed on that face); she tracks Robie and plans (or at least fantasizes) their career together in a kind of remake of *Cat People* crossed with *His Girl Friday* in which she will be Robie's new "kitten." Also, Frances is a film critic. Her grasp of film conventions helps her understand Robie's "Conrad Burns": He's like an English actor playing (unconvincingly) an American in an English film, she says in the cliffside picnic scene. Indeed, women in Hitchcock have the most acute perception of narration as a code, particularly as a film code: Remember Marnie's reply to Mark Rutland when he seeks deeper revelations from her in their free-association game: "You want to play doctor. OK, I'm a big movie fan, I know the scenes." With such knowledge in heroines, these films necessarily end with at least some shared authority for scripting the embodiments that will enunciate the subject: the "little drama" (as Vandamm calls it) at the Mt. Rushmore cafeteria and the new and better plot for Francie and Robie in the masquerade ball in *To Catch a Thief*. This newly embodied authority requires circulation back and forth and across the fourth wall, so to speak, as writers exchange pens, names, and plots and embody these exchanges with their audiences (Hughson becomes Robie in *To Catch a Thief*'s masquerade, for example).

The problem of the power to direct the gaze and the performances staged for it is implicit in contests over scripting, but it becomes explicit in these films in the contests over erotic play (which is therefore often not playful). For example, in *To Catch a Thief* Frances claims an authority over flirtation and foreplay that subverts Robie's assumptions about that authority (that it is his). When Frances opens the basket at the cliffside picnic, she offers the urbane Robie the choice, "Leg or breast?" Hitchcock has placed Frances well above Robie in the frame through this sequence, with Robie looking up rather awkwardly until the last moments, to intersect her gaze, which focuses directly on him throughout. Women do not control this interknitting of gesture and gaze in the conventional narrative of foreplay, at least in 1950s' Hollywood movies, especially when their partner is an older, worldly, charismatic male (it is almost impossible not to say, when their partner is an elegantly graying Cary Grant). Frances's authority to direct also expresses itself when she mans the wheel during the automobile chase; in contrast to Alicia, who also takes the wheel in *Notorious,* Frances remains fully in control. In each sequence the camera makes much of Robie/Devlin's unease, with shots of his hand beginning to reach for the steering wheel or nervously tapping his leg. Robie's hands particularly seek to (but know they cannot) displace Frances's hands, as his body reads her body, and she his: Frances's smile is precisely her gestural reading of Robie's anxiety, as Hitchcock's use of graphic matches in his editing highlights: hands matched to hands, frown to smile. Robie's tense face and body, however, show that his unease is more uneasy, less safely masculine than Devlin's because Frances is not a drunk, embittered woman vulnerable to reassertion of male control. Hitchcock intercuts this series of images of Robie's discomfort with shots of Frances at the wheel to underline intersubjectively her power: Robie's eyes shifting from Frances to the rear-view mirror, while Frances smiles, her eyes calmly focused ahead, her body open to the wind.

Frances demonstrates her control over the display of her own body in the fireworks scene when she positions herself headless in the shadows, in strapless evening gown and diamonds, before Robie, and commands, "Hold them." The elements of this image are significant because Frances's eyes are hidden, but she can watch where Robie's are looking and tells him so: The interplay of gestures takes on a remarkable subtlety with Robie playing to Frances, who is wearing a sort of mask. Her motives for the self-exposure are clear: So long as Frances thinks Robie robs women of their jewels, she thinks he might take hers, especially under her guidance. Frances's fascination with being robbed does not mean that she has never slept with a man. Robie certainly does not approach her as if she were sexually innocent. To the contrary, he has been angered by her kiss in the hotel corridor, a kiss whose erotic potential he defuses by admiring what he names its "efficiency" in the car on the way to their picnic. Frances's sexual precocity and aggressiveness of gesture decenter this hero of the Resistance who clearly expects to direct the play of erotic gestures in which his body will mark hers, not vice versa.

Authority for the erotic gesture is also problematic in *North by Northwest,* even though Roger Thornhill is noticeably less angry than either Robie or Devlin about this experience of decentering by a woman's erotic agency. Another pair of rhyming scenes, in this film and *Notorious,* establishes the difference: the long kiss in Alicia's apartment in Rio and the long kiss in Eve's train compartment (both on woman's territory). In *Notorious* Devlin is guarded and tense at every moment (and this scene occurs *before* he knows that his assignment is to help Alicia seduce Sebastian). In this famous sequence Hitchcock positions his bodies in the frame asymmetrically, so that they move across Alicia's apartment with Devlin's stiff spine resisting her gentle posture and so that the phone intervenes physically as well as emotionally. Devlin doesn't return Alicia's kiss because he is responding more to the world on the

FIG. 2 *Notorious*. American Broadcasting Companies 2000. DVD © RKO-Radio, 1946. American Broadcasting Companies, 2001.

other end of the telephone or to Alicia through the filter of that world. This supposedly intimate moment is deeply fractured (note, for example, the line in deep space in figure 2 that divides the frame and separates Devlin from Alicia and Devlin's shadowed, averted gaze), and the length of its shots only deepens its tensions. How ironic that this scene is so often cited as one of the most romantic in cinema, when a close reading of its network of gestures and blockages reveals mostly anxiety.

In contrast, Thornhill is happy and in a sense submissive, even when Eve tells him he must sleep on the floor (though neither he nor Eve may take this command seriously: Is it a nod to the MPAA code?). Thornhill has placed her in the category of women of uncertain virtue: He says in the lunch scene, "Honest women frighten me" (a line that echoes both *Notorious* and *To Catch a Thief*), and Thornhill and Eve are each pleased to admit they are not honest. But at this moment Thornhill is not angry or resentful. He will be both later. In the auction scene his anger at Eve explodes—not over her sexual proficiency, or even her political betrayal, but over her sexual betrayal. His echo of Devlin's constraint occurs in the Ambassador Hotel room, after the crop-duster sequence, when he refuses to hold Eve. In a peculiar example of a kind of intersubjective transference, Thornhill's lifted hand(s) in this scene become Vandamm's in the next, when he removes them from Eve's neck in that ominous close-up in the auction scene; the transference draws even closer parallels between the two elegant graying men competing for Eve's heart (or at least her body). In that scene Thornhill articulates his anger by escalating Eve's infidelity, when Leonard asks Eve whether Thornhill was in her room, and Thornhill responds, "Sure. Isn't everybody?" In other words, Thornhill carries within him seeds of the special contempt men have felt for women whose sense of their sexual authority exceeds conventional boundaries. At the end of this conversation, Thornhill goes so far as to invoke woman as archetypal demon when he suggests that, for his next murder attempt, Vandamm simply ask Eve to kiss Thornhill—to dispatch him with poison. However justified his anger is by his recent experience in the cornfield, the excess of Thornhill's imagery connects him to Devlin and Robie.

Devlin, in *Notorious,* is in fact more deeply tormented by a woman's authority over the interplay of lovers than the other Cary Grant figures in Hitchcock. Devlin comes to us with even less of a past than Eve has in *North by Northwest*. The meager information is nevertheless richly suggestive: "I've always been scared of women, but I get over it." The fear predates Alicia, and neither its origin nor its passing is explained. It seems simply to be repeated. Even Devlin's language admits as much: His "always," along with the present tense of "get over it," tells us that this experience recurs in Devlin's life; in some sense he certainly has not "gotten over" his fear. He therefore picks up immediately on Alicia's anger not only at "cops" but also at men who position her as the other from their own secure superiority. She, however, wants to position herself and to direct her own play. She proposes the picnic and car ride with "handsome" at the first party, for example. During the midnight drive Alicia says, "I'll wipe that grin off your face. I don't like gentlemen who grin at me." Devlin continues to be afraid of Alicia's anger (note the bite of her sarcasm about class in "gentlemen," instead of "men") and of her intelligence and her sexual knowledge, especially as they express themselves with the authority to touch and to ask to be touched.

Relations in Public

The implications of these aspects of theatricality—naming, scripting, and staging erotic play—expand even further in a profound and deeply intersubjective strategy of these Hitchcock films: the use of complex scenes that juxtapose private and public words and gestures in order to threaten espousal, the chiasmus of responding consciousnesses, with shame. In such scenes a public conversation both conceals and exposes a private conversation that transacts its business by way of double meanings to public language and gestures. The tensions in these scenes expose the politics of intersubjectivity. This exposure may seem funny, as when Roger Thornhill bids small, decreasing sums for a valuable antique in the auction sequence of *North by Northwest,* but the undercurrent of anger is unmistakable, as Thornhill renders (while trying to save his life) a complex comment by way of social ritual on Eve's virtue (or lack thereof, as he perceives things).

The conflict between public and private discourses can produce a suffering all the more intense because suppressed, as in the brilliant racetrack scene of *Notorious,* when Devlin and Alicia accuse each other of betrayal while playing the scene as a chance encounter (when they, despite Alicia's binoculars, have in fact been on stage to Sebastian, who has been watching them through his). The network of embodiments offered and refused in this sequence choreographs the tangle of perceptions and misperceptions that connect and separate Devlin and Alicia. Within Hitchcock's frame, eyes glance to and then away from eyes, faces take rigid postures at right angles to each other, and no mutual, intersubjective gaze is possible. Twice Alicia looks to catch Devlin's eye, turning to look offscreen to the left, at a kind of blank space, as it turns out to be, when Devlin looks stonily across Alicia's gaze. At the center of this scene is a sequence of three shots that is edited with stunning speed, as anger and a responding anger ignite when Alicia tells Devlin her news, that Sebastian is now one of her "playmates." The first shot is a close-up of Devlin, who says bitterly, "Pretty fast work." The second shot cuts rapidly to a close-up of Alicia, who turns to (our) left in angry self-defense, "That's what you wanted, wasn't it?" The third shot is the remarkable payoff, a point-of-view shot, so that we see what Alicia sees: Devlin refusing to meet Alicia's gaze, looking also out of the frame to the left. The editing is as fast as the bitter anger, as eyes and bodies deploy in what each character sees to be a defensive response to the other's betrayal. And these bodies are themselves always conscious of the larger framework of their pretense at a casual encounter at the racetrack. Hitchcock sutures his three rapid close-ups to diagram, in Austen-like precision, the failure of reciprocities. Yet these bodies and intentionalities respond to each other's response from behind their masks. Devlin's eyes harden when he hears Alicia's news, and Alicia's tears leak down her face from behind the binoculars.

This juxtaposition between private and public also appears in scenes where heroine and hero, although alone together, act out their (mis)understandings of the other's embodiments of their own gestures, so that we see them still "on stage," performing before the other. The comic quarreling between Robie and Frances throughout *To Catch a Thief*, in the tradition of screwball comedy, is a good example of this kind of theater in duet scenes. Frances and Robie spend plenty of time alone together in these solitary duet scenes, but they still act as if on stage, sparring and playing a role for and against the other, at least in the first half of the film, before Mrs. Stevens is herself robbed. The agenda of private discourse bubbles up through the "public" performance, especially as Robie and Frances walk over the Sandford villa, Robie eyeing the roof and gutters, Frances puzzling over the visit (since she knows the house is not to let), each keeping the conversation turning like a gyroscope with little nudges, while carrying on their quarrel. The real business for them, however, on both levels, is anger about who wields authority over erotic gestures in their intimate theater. This conflict underlies even Robie's battle with the new Cat, since—as he may already suspect—this contest concerns an effort at a kind of seduction by embodiment by Danielle, who now inhabits Robie's Cat-skin, mirroring his moves and skill. The skirmishing in the scene at the Sandford villa climaxes with Robie's bitter retort to Frances, "What you need is two weeks with a good man at Niagara Falls." Frances's response, the enactment of her anger, surfaces in the car chase that immediately follows, when she, smiling happily at the wheel, indeed "wipe[s] that grin off [his] face," as Alicia had wanted to do in *Notorious*.

If *To Catch a Thief* is paradigmatic, and a deeply gendered theatricality seems to control intimacy in these Grant films, what happens to espousal and a mutually inflecting intersubjectivity? Indeed, if the Riviera in the film is a stage where the wealthy play under lights, on the beach, or in costume, watched by the thieves, Resistance cadres, police, and tourists, then what possibility exists for new kinds of interknitting sexual authority? Two sequences in *To Catch a Thief* suggest at least a beginning. The first is Frances's roadside meeting with Robie after Foussard's funeral; the second is the final masquerade ball. Both examples counterpoint theatricality against a fitfully glimpsed interior life and point to a further education of these two accomplished actors (Frances and Robie, that is) in the complexities of the mutually embodying script.

The first scene occurs after a particularly dramatic staging: Danielle's graveside outburst at Robie, as if he really were the Cat (though I suppose at some level she does blame Robie for her father's death). After the graveside scene, Frances's confrontation of Robie outside the cemetery walls seems intimate. Yet the mood of sour anger is similar to the earlier scene's, and so is the apparent inability to move beyond words ("just playthings to you," accuses Robie) and beyond the other as the origin of the objectifying gaze. The astonishing image that organizes this scene and that echoes throughout Hitchcock's work is Frances's hand stretched out to grip Robie's arm, an image underscored by the camera's close-up shot of the arms (twisted together like the fibers of a rope) and Robie's dismayed glance downward (see figure 3). It is a fundamental sign of the gesture intending for and against the other's gesture in a network of embodiments between these quarreling lovers.

The line of arms is horizontal, not vertical (as it will be on the roof's edge at the film's end and as it has been from *Saboteur*'s Statue of Liberty scene to *North by Northwest*'s Mount Rushmore), and the image is newly uncertain, perhaps because for the first time in Hitchcock the agent of the reach is a woman: not God to Adam or Eve, but Eve to the authoritative male. What sort of binding do we see? The last time Frances saw Robie, she had just called the police to arrest him. Just before the close-up, Frances has said, "I'm in love with you." For Robie the loner, love may be as confining as prison, and anyway he doesn't trust her. He ends the cemetery scene by confining her to the role of onlooker, as a "tourist." Nonetheless, the binding is horizontal; the

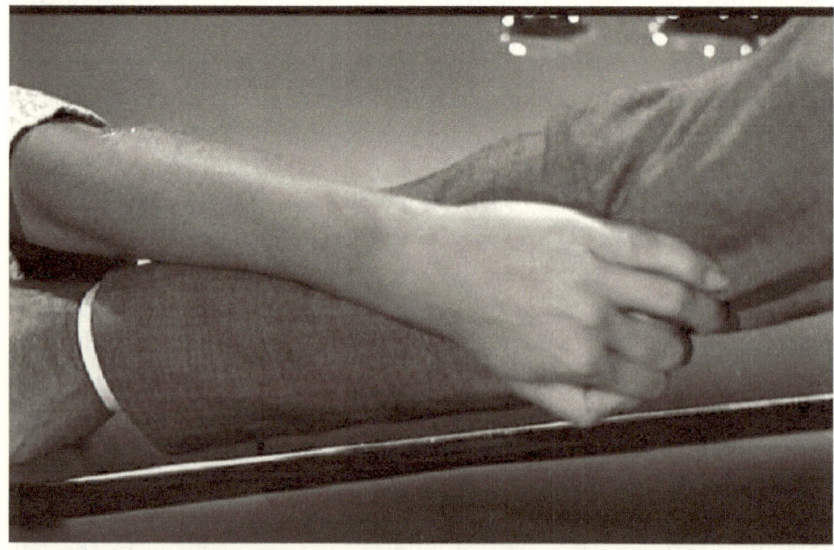

FIG. 3 *To Catch a Thief*. Paramount Pictures 1955.
DVD © Paramount Pictures 2002.

image is an example of how Hitchcock can subvert hierarchy. The shot/reverse-shot sequence here emphasizes the lateral look of Robie: not down or up at Frances, but across. After all, Robie and Frances begin in this scene to plan together their masquerade script, perhaps a better story than Frances's earlier fantasy about John and herself, in which she was going to be his new "kitten." I doubt that these two powerful personalities ever transcend their embodied resistances, whose narrative and assumptions are patriarchal. Certainly the world around them does not transcend these terms: Bertani, the restaurant owner, tells Robie during the funeral to be content with winning Francie's wealth, for example.

The second sequence, the masquerade ball and its aftermath, powerfully articulates the surge toward mutuality in these two authoritative characters, as well as the limitation on their achievement. The masquerade signals some growth beyond parochial assumptions about erotic authority. Robie and Frances write a scene that will hide his absence from the dance floor, a scene in which "John" is represented as the Black servant of an eighteenth-century lady. In this submissive part, "John" is center stage for all to see, the object of others' gaze as the couple dances endlessly in a curiously distanced image of intimacy. Frances and her mother must speak for "John," and they improvise fluently in their parts, as all the powerful women do in these Grant films. This play within a play rescues Robie, and perhaps both Frances and Robie learn from their parts, from a kind of incarnation in the bodies of their surrogate selves. The linkage of the masquerade to the film's last scene at Robie's villa is direct: Frances is still in costume. The very public partnership now becomes a private one: Robie's lair (to extend his "lone wolf" image) will no longer be a male sanctuary, no longer one person's "travel-folder heaven," as Hughson the insurance agent described it when he lunched there.

Yet these linkages of public to private in *To Catch a Thief* also raise the question, does a fundamental evolution toward espousal occur here? Is not Frances still a tourist at the end of the film? And what about Robie, the expatriate American? The problem of "tourist" as another sort of outsider echoes through the film, in Frances's possibly ironic name, for example, and in the travel-poster setting behind the film's titles. Are we the audience also tourists, gazing *at*?[17] Or have Frances and John understood their masquerade? Perhaps Frances's costume, retained in this last scene, is simply another of her elaborate "outfits," another "natural" sign in the code of femininity and deception. Does she in some sense betray Robie in her last line, "Mother will love it up here"? The final sequence of the film emphasizes how problematic the intersubjective gaze is: Frances looks sideways out of Hitchcock's frame (anticipating her mother's pleasure in Robie's home) as Robie stares directly at her, faces resolutely disengaged from each other. The tone of uncertainty in this frame deepens when we remember those three close-ups in the much darker racetrack scene in *Notorious* that rhyme with this shot, but with the male and female roles reversed. *To Catch a Thief* recognizes Frances's knowledge and consequent authority and how her powers evoke deep resentments in Robie. Even in the film's last scene, Frances is rewriting Robie. When she forces him to repeat her line, that he needed the help of "a 'good' woman" (though Robie conveniently omits "good"), Frances is extracting penance for Robie's angry remark about Niagara Falls and a "good" man. *To Catch a Thief* may claim our attention exactly for its final tangle of disguise and revelation, submission and domination, resisted and adopted embodiments. This tangle defines Hitchcock's comedy at its richest, in its study of the relation between shame and espousal.

Theatricality's intersubjective indirections function with a special force in *Notorious* because here the network of interpretations of interpretations must educate more deeply, and it has more to accomplish. It must help Alicia and Devlin strip away layers of presentation of self and constructions of the other if any romance of the mutual gaze is to be possible. As in *To Catch a Thief,* two kinds of indirection of staging occur throughout the film. The first is again the duet scene, in which Alicia and Devlin accuse and counteraccuse. A really poignant example of deep intersubjectivity surfaces in the way each acts out the script the other has written for him or her, as a way of challenging that script and asking for another story. So Devlin is the tough "cop," always suspicious, wheels always turning, as Alicia says, because that is how he sees that she sees him. At the sidewalk cafe in Rio Alicia accepts the description "tramp," which she attributes to Devlin's thoughts—but the quotation marks are hers, in her voice—because she is angrily one-upping Devlin's degradation of her. Toward the end of the film she doesn't attempt to explain her illness to Devlin but only tells him she's been drinking again: Her revenge is to visit on him the triumph of his own story about her (the spots don't change). These duet scenes are in a way a vindictive performance of each lover's perceptions of the other: a curious triumph of intersubjective narrative practices.

In contrast, the performances of Alicia and Devlin before others are curiously intimate. The best example, the film's play within a play, is the kissing scene outside the wine cellar, when the mock embrace becomes a real one for Alicia. Devlin doesn't kiss back (as he does not in the apartment kissing scene earlier), but he nonetheless embodies a profound and deeply angry impulse here.[18] It is not accidental that, even in a moment of improvisation, he writes *this* scene for Sebastian to see. He wants Sebastian to see another man kissing his wife and to feel the violation, as Sebastian does intensely, after Devlin leaves. Sebastian cannot get over the immediate physical sense that, whatever Alicia says about the circumstances, "He *kissed* you." And at some level Sebastian knows that Alicia has responded to Devlin. So the script Devlin writes externalizes into moving bodies the brooding anger that has kept him dark and menacing in most of the film. Because this moment of amateur theatrics is also an education in deep intersubjectivity, what Sebastian perceives is a crucial mirror for Alicia and Devlin, as they see him seeing them perform for him.

In other words, the wine-cellar play is the turning point in which Alicia and Devlin move toward shared authority. But it depends on two especially important earlier scenes of complex theatricality: the racetrack scene and the sequence in Prescott's office when Alicia reports on Sebastian's desire to marry her. In both instances public discourse must function for private ends. In the racetrack scene, the medium of public discourse is the movement of bodies, which must hide the pain Alicia and Devlin both display in their words. In Prescott's office, words and gestures must both be public; yet Devlin and Alicia are fully aware that she is really asking him whether he loves her, and he responds by rejecting her again. This scene stages a particularly powerful example of a special form of the intersubjective in Hitchcock: watching watching—that is, watching another watcher, the act of following the other's look, always with the fear (or hope: This is Merleau-Ponty, not Sartre) that the other may turn to see the watcher's gaze, as if a closet door has opened to reveal the voyeur. It happens in *To Catch a Thief* when Frances watches Robie's eyes going over the roofline at the Sandford villa. It happens in Prescott's office when Alicia looks at the eyes looking at her and looking at each other, especially Prescott's and Devlin's, to read the signs they are exchanging about her. As many critics have observed, *Notorious* constructs a subjectivity for Alicia through the camera; we see often what she sees, whether it's the vision blurred by her hair blowing across her face or the clear vision of the wine bottle that upset Emil. With all this tense watching of watchers and given the authority of Alicia's gaze, the climactic compromise in the education of Alicia and Devlin is all the more remarkable.

The compromise is Devlin's, as he revises his posture of control and (masculine) authority. Crouching beside Alicia, Devlin's posture breaks the tight line of his back for the first time with her, in powerful contrast for example to the straight-arrow profile that, carrying the glass of milk the morning after the first party, retains its linearity as it swirls around in Alicia's eyes. In the Sebastian bedroom Devlin explains his failure in language whose confessional intensity is unique for a man in Hitchcock: "I was a fat-headed guy full of pain." Equally important, Devlin compares himself as watcher to Alicia's condition during that hangover early in the film: "I couldn't see straight." To "see straight" is not just to perceive accurately, of course, but also to understand and to judge accurately. This confession and this posture renounce claims to authority in a profound way for a man of Devlin's assumptions. In this self-understanding Devlin can begin to imagine with Alicia a story of the mutual gaze, even a story in which they try to see with the other's eyes in a triumph of deep intersubjectivity's appropriations.

Sometimes in Hitchcock there is no cinema of the mutual gaze, and that absence, as in *Psycho* or *Frenzy,* can be a cruel revelation. Intersubjectivity then is a masquerade, as my discussion of *Marnie* in chapter 5 emphasizes. Sometimes subjects can bridge the gaps between performances and connect the tears in the intersubjective fabric with only a tenuous filament at first, if at all, and even then only with great difficulty. *Notorious* is Hitchcock's great tragicomedy in its somber emphasis on this reality and on the difficulty of change when it does occur. A sense of miraculous recuperation is essential to the practice of tragicomedy and to *Notorious*. (The archetypal tragicomedy is Shakespeare's *The Winter's Tale*, which swivels on a dime from *Othello*'s tragedy of jealousy to the green world of *As You Like It*.) The final image in *Notorious,* the door that has closed on Sebastian, defines the home as the prison that Alicia and Devlin have escaped. Think how different the film would be if its last sequences were reversed, if its final shot were Devlin's car speeding out of the frame, an image of deliverance and mutuality like *North by Northwest*'s final image.

Hitchcock's comedies, especially our three Grant comedies, complicate and subvert authority's embodiments with an intelligent optimism that deserves broader recognition. These Grant films dramatize deep intersubjectivity as theater with enough detail and complexity to make credible the recuperation of espousal from shame for Alicia, Frances, Eve, and their lovers.

WOODY ALLEN'S *BROADWAY DANNY ROSE:* THE FOOL AND THE MUTUAL GAZE

Woody Allen's *Broadway Danny Rose* is a good companion text to Hitchcock's Grant films because it explores similar kinds of darkness within very different genre traditions, yet both filmmakers depend upon the resources of deep intersubjectivity to tell their tales about discovering how mutually performed lives might be possible in a world of deeply—and intersubjectively—shadowed anxiety and death. Thematically *Broadway Danny Rose* is closest to *Notorious* in its near-miraculous recuperation of love from loss, but this Allen film has few of the genre markers traditionally associated with tragicomedy. Indeed, tragicomedy is not a genre practice in Allen: Perhaps only *Another Woman* could be *The Winter's Tale* of Allen's films. Instead, Allen approaches the profound issues of the komos by way of a different cluster of traditions and assumptions, many of which collect around the figure of the fool. As outsider and boundary crosser, the fool provokes new versions of deep intersubjectivity, especially as explored in film vocabulary: *Broadway Danny Rose* in particular makes remarkable use for example of the 180-degree rule and shot design to explore the possibilities of comic espousal. This movement toward mutual appropriation, however, makes dramatic sense, paradoxically, only because Allen makes clear how unlikely it is.

Allen has impeccable credentials to prepare him for revising and repurposing (to use Rick Altman's phrase) the conventions of the fool in a kind of postmodern comedy, one that collects echoes and fragments of other forms. He is the independent filmmaker who, unlike Hitchcock, usually avoids the expectations of the classical Hollywood paradigm by casting only middling stars, and in this film even a newcomer (Nick Apollo Forte), in major roles, and tangles his viewers in a complex narrative framework and a metacommentary on Hollywood genre (the gangster film and *The Godfather*). Allen himself plays the outsider role, as the NYU dropout and one of the first American filmmakers to make a subject of his Jewishness, the rebel against Hollywood and studio control.[19]

Yet Allen, who is "suspicious of all forms of community" (Jeffrey Rubin-Dorsky's words for Allen-esque scepticism), nonetheless works through to a complex vision of espousal in *Broadway Danny Rose* (469). In this film he inserts a dance of mutually attentive subjects into a world of greed and self-regarding performance. Espousal often doesn't work in Allen—think of Cliff in *Crimes and Misdemeanors*—and the outsider sometimes isn't even very wise (Isaac can be good on other people in *Manhattan* but mostly is clueless about himself). Folly is really folly often enough in Allen, so that he has earned the right to offer in *Broadway Danny Rose* at least a folktale of love (what Sandy, the narrator, calls "the greatest Danny Rose story"): Among the major Allen films, only *Hannah and Her Sisters* and perhaps *Bullets over Broadway* are as hopeful. At the center of this hope is the fool who almost becomes the scapegoat and whose grotesque body (or perhaps clothes, in Danny's case) nonetheless is open (to use Bakhtinian imagery) to other bodies and their interior life.

The fool's double role as insider and outsider, both "allowed" (as Olivia says to Feste in *Twelfth Night*) and scorned, points to Allen's special understanding of comedy in an age of the simulacrum, of mirrors and the self as performance. The classical fool is an insider, functioning for a courtly audience as a reminder of carnival and as a voice of another kind of wisdom, a folk or perhaps even a divine wisdom, from whose vantage point outside the official world much of its business is trivial.[20] Danny's position at court, so to speak, bears the marks of this contradiction in his insiderly outsiderliness, most poignantly framed by those sad celebrity photographs on the wall of his apartment, which marginalize him exactly as he believes otherwise:

> Danny: That's Frank, Tony Bennett, and me . . . a little tiny smudge right there. . . . And there I am with Miss Judy Garland. . . .
> Tina: Where are you?
> Danny: Well, I'm right outside the frame. (249)

Furthermore, Danny does not perform this gap, he does not dramatize or thematize it. Danny Rose is, in Walter Kaiser's terms, a natural fool, not an artificial one: He does not perform fool-ness consciously as a role with which to torment or enlighten his audience. For Kaiser, in the self-awareness of the artificial fool "the licence of the natural fool was appropriated for the artificial fool; his naturalism [was turned into] anarchy, his frankness into satire" (88). In contrast, Danny's rare performances of shtick, as at Johnny Rispoli's mansion ("H-how old are you, Johnny?" ["Forty."] "That's unbelievable. Wha—Are you an Aries? Just, just tell me. Are you an Aries?"), are unselfconsciously desperate, in this instance because Johnny's mob family is closing in on Danny "White Roses" (217). Danny's relative diffidence about audience (unless he's talking to a buyer), despite his early career as a stand-up

FIG. 4 *Broadway Danny Rose*. Orion Pictures 1984.
DVD © Orion Pictures 1984.

comic, mark him as an inhabitant of a more innocent stage of the carnivalesque, in which, according to Bakhtin, "the carnival does not know footlights, in the sense that it does not acknowledge any distinction between actors and spectators." Indeed, Bakhtin's words for traditional clowns and fools suit Danny Rose remarkably well: "They stand on the borderline between life and art, in a peculiar mid-zone as it were; they were neither eccentrics nor dolts, neither were they comic actors" (*Rabelais* 7–8). Allen's warehouse scene is one such midzone, where Danny and Tina flee among the Macy's Thanksgiving Day parade floats, unconsciously inhaling helium until their voices become comic-strip parodies of a chase scene. Completely unaware of their performances, lovers and pursuing thugs become reminders of a cartoon world whose innocence might not be so distant.

But if Danny's fool is a relatively uncomplicated role (uncomplicated by self-awareness as fool), then Allen's deepening of this narrative archetype into a kind of deep intersubjectivity is an important new effect in our study. Against all logic and precedent, Danny becomes part of a quiet, interior interweaving of what Merleau-Ponty called interworlds. Against logic and precedent, because fools' stories are not supposed to be deeply intersubjective, and Allen's "loser" and "nebbish" characters have been seen typically as one dimensional. As Peter Bailey observes, "The 'loser' tag so uncritically applied to Allen's characters may have done more to blind reviewers and critics to the nuances of Allen's vision than any other misperception" (108).

Allen makes deeper claims for Danny partly by framing his face literally to recall the faces of other fools in film history. The most important shot of Danny occurs when Tina returns, during the final Thanksgiving dinner, after she has been, uncharacteristically (she thinks), so unable to shake her memory of the way she betrayed him (see figure 4). The close-up at Danny's door of his face, stilled by Tina's apology, echoes Isaac's face in the last shot of *Manhattan*: another black-and-white film, a plaintive face with glasses like Danny's, another artist pursuing the desirable shiksa. Yet Ike never begins to embody Tracy's gestures: When she voices her hopes, "Not everyone gets corrupted. You have to have a little faith in people," Ike's eyebrows never drop into belief: He cannot move beyond his own desire (Allen's screenplay claims "he breaks into a smile," but to me the smile is deeply unconvinced) (271).[21] Allen's focus on Ike's uncertain smile itself echoes the ambiguities of the most famous close-up of that earlier hapless and natural fool, Chaplin's Little Tramp, in the last shot of *City Lights*. The Tramp's nervous smile admits that to be seen (in this case by the formerly blind flower girl) is to be exposed. The opportunity for reciprocal gazing becomes a humiliation. The Tramp can only receive, not return the girl's gaze, and similarly Isaac can only receive, not return, Tracy's gaze and trust, nor can Danny, at the moment of Tina's apology, embody her gesture.

The humiliations and betrayals differ in these three films, and Allen's mise-en-scène certainly suggests differences as well as similarities. The power issues for example are different: Chaplin's Tramp is much more vulnerable than the older, successful Isaac, and Tina comes back to Danny, despite his "loser" (her word) wardrobe. Still, in all three moments, shot/reverse-shot sequences create unbridgeable distances between bodies and gazes. No appropriation crosses the divide between subjects and the shots that isolate them. Hence the profound importance of the medium long shot at the end of *Broadway Danny Rose*, in which the miracle of suture occurs inside the frame, when Danny and Tina share the camera's gaze at the same moment in front of the Carnegie Deli.

The other image of the fool's ambiguity that echoes in *Broadway Danny Rose* is Cabiria's crying/smiling face in the last moments of another film by one of Allen's beloved Italian masters, Fellini's *Nights of Cabiria* (another, because later I discuss the shadows of *The Bicycle Thief* in this film). Cabiria repeatedly trusts when reason tells her she should not, and repeatedly her lovers humiliate her. Cabiria falls quickly, despite her protests, under the spell of the hypnotist in the music hall, as does Allen's insurance detective in 2001's *Curse of the Jade Scorpion,* and Danny, who has managed a hypnotist, knows that trust is dangerous. In Danny's case, the hypnotist has lost his subject (at least the husband cannot awake his entranced wife and is not comforted by Danny's offer to take him to "the restaurant of your choice" if his wife doesn't wake up). But the dream of trust is precisely the wisdom of folly, and sometimes the dream does get incarnated in the world: Chaplin's Tramp gets the girl in *The Gold Rush* and "lives happily ever after," according to Chaplin's narrator. Cabiria awakes from her trance in the music hall to the audience's scornful laughter, as she has played herself young, virginal, and beloved in the hypnotist's scenario; nevertheless, Fellini gives her hopefulness the last look (if not word) in the film's final sequence, when Cabiria's face lights up again, looking out of the frame into her future, moving down the highway with the musicians who have materialized out of the forest. Danny's fool incorporates the ambiguities of these images; by all odds he should be as isolated as these other fools, alone looking out of their frames in each of these shots. Reciprocity should be only a wan hope, if not an illusion. But Danny (and Tina) are fools in a different story.

In fact, their wise folly works magic. The form of their folly is a collision figured in words and bodies, in dialects and gestures, particularly of hands and eyes. It is a collision of interworlds, of individual and cultural histories, and of networks of embodied and social intentionalities. To begin with, Danny and Tina gesture different narratives and embodiments of the subject. Both live in their hands, but Danny more so than Tina, and his extravagant gestures are accompanied by a wealth of other signs—hunched shoulders and eyebrows, hands moving with fingers unclenched and palms upward, tacky sports coats—that assure Danny's audience he is not threatening, not imposing, not authoritative. In contrast, Tina's body is focused on a target (even when she is confused), her gestures are sharp, her hands move quickly at angles to her body, and a certain glitziness in her clothes and hair promises a hardness and an authority: Tina makes claims for herself, as Danny rarely does.

Two lines point toward the difference in these embodied narratives of authority: Tina's "Do it to the other guy first," and Danny's "You need to suffer." Tina's surface seems only to reflect others; there's no depth to incorporate gestures and words and intentions, much less to gesture back, with an effort to catch the next reflected embodiment of her response. Her glasses are shaded just so that the movement of her eyes is invisible. The gaze of the other bounces back, with no marking gesture in Tina's look and even less of a mirroring and reinflection intended for the other to re-see. Danny's language of the gaze is very different. His narrative of suffering could equally block appropriation, and narcissism threatens him as it engulfs most of the film's other characters. Nonetheless, Danny's story of suffering is intimately entangled in others' stories—Aunt Rose's, Uncle Sydney's, and Barney Dunn's. And the lenses of his glasses are clear, set in heavy, square, unfashionable black frames. These spectacles help us see Danny's seeing and to see Danny seeing others' gazes as they respond to his seeing. He indeed never seems to notice the next betrayal looming, but among the blindnesses in the world of *Broadway Danny Rose*, his is the more generous and the more generously intersubjective, as he adopts and reworks the gestures and stories of his "loser" clients—the blind xylophone player, the one-armed juggler, the woman that plays the glasses, and, most important, Tina.

Eyes are significant throughout Allen's work, most famously in *Crimes and Misdemeanors*, but nowhere is Allen's suggestiveness richer than here, where Tina's and Danny's spectacles frame different ways of participating in a world of tangled intentions. Allen's mise-en-scène emphasizes these frames of seeing by carefully juxtaposing the glasses in the composition of his frame, when Tina and Danny are tied together in the warehouse, nose to nose and eyeglasses to eyeglasses, for example, or when Danny drives Tina back to the city from Johnny's party (and they discuss how Tina's ex-husband was shot through the eyes, and he was not blind but dead because the bullets go right through). In each sequence Allen's camera aligns these faces, spectacles, and ways of seeing in order to compare them. Despite Danny's naïveté, it's Tina the cynic who has clouded vision. In the struggle to free themselves from their ropes in the warehouse, Tina's glasses get knocked off, in one of about five sequences in the film where her full face appears, and the question arises, what does she see without the mask of her glasses? And can these two gazes respond to each other and respond to that first response in a continuing series of gestures? Is the reciprocity of deep intersubjectivity another illusion worthy of Danny Rose the naif?

Tina and Danny appropriate each other's gestures and stories and even adopt each other's dream lives in their progress toward suturing an interworld of their own. Tina's movement toward Danny's story is the more obvious. Douglas Brode observes that *Broadway Danny Rose* could be called " 'The Education of Tina,' since it is about her growing consciousness, the way she becomes worthy of Danny" (240). Tina's dream life is a fundamental measure of her change and is also a medium in which Danny and Tina exchange gestures. Dreams become a sign of consciousnesses attending to each other. Tina recounts two dreams in the film: one, when she revisions Danny's apartment in a jungle design, with bamboo furniture and zebra skins ("I've always had this as a dream"), and two, when she tells Angelina at the end of the film about her bad dream in which she stands before a mirror, wanting both to find herself and to wipe away her thoughts of Danny. Significantly, when Allen films this second moment, as Tina stares at herself in the mirror in Lou's bathroom, she is not wearing her glasses. Tina's dreams now include Danny as a consciousness that sees her, and she searches that mirror restlessly, without the filter of her clouded lenses. Danny had at least entertained her dream of his life (or anyway of his apartment), and he becomes sutured into her other dreams. And so the deeply intersubjective unweaves the defenses of this unbeliever.

Tina enters Danny's dream world, too, at least as it is externalized in two significant ways in the film. The first dream form, or collection of dream forms, is the Macy's Thanksgiving Day parade floats, Doodlebug and Underdog and the rest, that Tina and Danny encounter in the warehouse sequence. In their comic grotesquerie and childhood innocence, they could be more of Danny's clients. When Tina and Danny break into the warehouse and the pursuing thugs' bullets release helium into their faces, their chipmunkish voices (like "munchkins'," says Allen's screenplay) belong to a cartoon world, too, and Tina, minus her glasses again, imitates Danny's moves and mood (275). Appropriately, then, when Tina encounters the parade figures later, on Fifth Avenue, they vex her as a reminder of Danny's embodied consciousness that both repels and attracts her.

Tina also enters and finally adopts Danny's nostalgic folk drama of extended-family fables. Danny's use of Aunt Rose and Uncle Meyer often seems evasive because his appeal to their parallel lives functions as a distraction and as scripture that has no authority to a secular audience. But Tina signals her movement into Danny's vocabulary, even into his dream-past, when, on interrupting Danny's Thanksgiving dinner, she repeats to him his quotation of the words of another ghost, his Uncle Sydney, "Acceptance, forgiveness, and love." By abandoning the cynical narcissism of Lou and her own earlier life, Tina embraces guilt and love, emotions that in Allen's world are deeply intersubjective because they require response to another's interpretations of one's gestures and intentions toward that person. As Tina and Danny interweave each other's discourses and gestures, their capacity for espousal and shame deepens their self-awareness and their grasp of their place in the world.

This interweaving works for both consciousnesses. *Broadway Danny Rose* is not only the education of Tina. Danny, too, is a dreamer, and although his imagination is largely a life-making force, it is not altogether so. He tells us what, almost godlike, he does for his clients: "I breathe life into them." Danny gives his people a style of imagination that can warm his own Thanksgiving meal, so that Barney can say, of his TV dinner's turkey, "B-b-believe me, the frozen is as g-g-g-good as the re-real" (303). Yet Danny also recognizes the dangers of the imagination and has almost come, like Quixote, to abjure his chivalric calling when he tells Tina in this scene that if things go on as they have, "I'm gonna be selling storm windows soon" (306). The imagery of Danny's language confesses his doubts: Maybe winter and the cold will overpower his breath of life, and maybe frozen isn't as good as the real. Still, Tina's return returns Danny's favor: She breathes life into his dream, she adopts his story and his Uncle Sydney. And she does so without abandoning her spectacles, the framing of her vision. Allen's use of eyeglasses articulates with considerable precision the gestures between these two consciousnesses.

Tina and Danny see most explicitly through the other's consciousness when each enters the other's dream world as brought to life in a film world. Tina's movie dream is a version of the gangster film, particularly Coppola's *The Godfather,* and Danny's film world belongs to the phantasmagorical Fellini, perhaps from his *Amarcord* (which means "I remember," an appropriate subtitle for *Broadway Danny Rose,* which after all is the comedian Sandy's memory tale). Danny enters Tina's world at Johnny's party, with all of its echoes, mostly parodic, of *The Godfather* (the horse medallion on one man's gold neck chain, for example), where Danny is quickly written into its folklore as Tina's mysterious lover Danny White Roses, who the family's matriarch says has "the evil eye." Tina enters Danny's film world of exaggerated, grotesque, or dream bodies in their flight to escape Johnny's two brothers: They stumble first onto Wonder Man filming a commercial in the Hudson River flatlands and later into the warehouse with the still, looming Macy's parade floats. But Danny's clients may be the best examples: the blind xylophonist, the one-legged tap dancer, the one-armed juggler, Eddie Clark and his penguin, and the woman who plays the glasses. Danny himself is part of the parade, with his exaggerated facial and hand gestures, his loud plaid sports coats and plaintive eyebrows. The parade belongs in spirit, comic and sad, to those in Fellini's *Amarcord,* $8\frac{1}{2}$, or *The Clowns*. This is the circus that Tina returns to join in Danny's apartment on Thanksgiving Day.

Tina returns in part because she and Danny have constructed another world of gestures, glances, and reinflected family stories. This alternative intersubjectivity (which is also a mutually attentive, deep intersubjectivity) takes shape at the end of their epic day, as Danny and Tina sit, silent, in the back of a cab on their way to Lou's appearance at the Waldorf. They look at each other and look away, without their evasive or at least habitual gestures; in this moment of stillness, the camera, in one long shot, ponders the significant space between them (literally, as each sits at an opposite end of the cab seat). This stillness returns in the moment that Danny answers Tina's knock at his door, and they face each other. Allen almost seems to invoke a third film language for the intimacies of complex intersubjectivity: here, the language of Italian neorealism, and particularly De Sica's *The Bicycle Thief* (or *Thieves,* as it is in Italian). Tina's struggle to understand herself has taken her to a neighborhood fortune-teller, the bed-ridden Angelina, in two scenes directly modeled on the fortune-teller scenes in *The Bicycle Thief,* and Allen's final tracking shot also seems to echo De Sica's film in *its* last shot, with its emphasis on a kind of bittersweet intimacy achieved by Bruno and his father on the cold streets of the profane city.

In *Broadway Danny Rose* blindness and ambition lock many characters into a flat subjectivity that struggles unilaterally with others: The forces of sterility and disease wield enormous power. Lou Canova is the best example because he is more than a caricature; his life is performing, and he must see others as a waiting audience. At the end of the film, when Tina is living with him, he cannot believe she would not accompany him to Los Angeles: "I thought you'd be happy"; after all, "my comeback's in full swing" (296). Lou cannot see the selfhood embodied (however imperfectly) in Tina's stance before her mirror or in her dream and gesture back to her, nor can he see himself in her reflection. Deep intersubjectivity's espousal and, for that matter, shame are not possible for him. Lou's narcissism is *Broadway Danny Rose*'s most destructive force because it mirrors a complementary possibility in Danny: to live in others' performances; to experience his self through those he has breathed life into (when Lou tells Danny he's leaving him, Danny protests to Tina, "This kid owes me his life"). But given the two blindnesses, Lou's and Danny's, however artificial that binary is, the film clearly prefers Danny's.

Broadway Danny Rose illustrates one fundamental change from traditional comic ritual in the komos of postmodernism. Allen's film frames its own journey as a tall tale, as what Sandy calls "the greatest

FIG. 5 *Broadway Danny Rose*. Orion Pictures 1984.
DVD © Orion Pictures 1984.

Danny Rose story." Peter Bailey sees this self-framing as another example of Allen's ambivalence about art in films that have increasingly interrogated "their own conditions of postmodern scepticism, disillusionment, and narcissistic self-reflexivity" (5). Danny both interrogates and believes: He himself defines the fantasy theme of his tale when he tells Tina, "We all want what we can't have." He and Tina want what they can't have—the glamorous shiksa and the smooth-talking man of intellect—and yet they *can* have it in this fable. The postmodern comic ritual frames its own magic and still believes in it. In this komos there are no gods, but there is guilt and love and the circle of tale-tellers at the Carnegie Deli.

Allen's shot selection emphasizes the magic of comic intersubjectivity in wonderfully rich ways: I discussed earlier the importance of the final tracking shot from a middle distance, in which the rapprochement between Danny and Tina occurs to suture the fragmentation of the earlier shot/reverse-shot sequences. Similarly, Allen gives us that circle of tale-tellers in a series of shots that also weaves a web of gazes because Allen violates the 180-degree rule repeatedly in the film's opening sequences. No less than four times Allen's camera moves across or around the table to present these figures from opposite directions, so that the first comic who was sitting on the left side of the frame is now on the right, for example. I omit the speakers' names here because the film does not identify them, and few audiences can watch the film with the published screenplay in hand; even viewing the film again with the end credits in mind doesn't help since again these frame-tale scenes do not identify speakers. The best example occurs in the published screenplay on page 148 (after the story about the hotel joke—"I have a cheap room, but you gotta make your own bed"—that failed), but the "dissolve" to "a different view of the same table" is a crossing over the axis of action without a reestablishing shot, so that the figures "dissolve" into their displacements (the originals from the previous shot are still visible) (see figures 5 and 6). A similarly disorienting reversal of direction occurs a few seconds later (page 150 of the screenplay). Confusion increases as the camera moves laterally from one end of the table to what one later figures out is its opposite end.

These camera movements, which function without any reestablishing shot, initially disorient viewers, very few of whom can identify these speakers (who it turns out are playing themselves) and so will lose sight, so to speak, of the narrating voice: Where is the guy who is talking? Even the film's primary tale-teller is sometimes difficult to locate since his placement in the frame in each subsequent return to the Carnegie Deli is different, and noticing who is talking among the six or seven figures in the frame is not easy: The viewer's eye must scan the frame while trying simultaneously to listen to the voice-over and piece together the story and the jokes.

The effect of this confusion in mise-en-scène and of disestablished camera shots is to deindividualize each tale-teller's voice and to suggest that this fable is the product of a circle of memories and consciousnesses.

FIG. 6 *Broadway Danny Rose*. Orion Pictures 1984.
DVD © Orion Pictures 1984.

It is indeed an equivalent in film's narrative form of the interconnecting of interworlds and subjects that I have been tracing in Tina and Danny's story It is a formal equivalent to Merleau-Ponty's chiasmus, which deepens the film's faith in at least the metaphor of a deeply intersubjective komos.

I write at the beginning of this chapter that Austen, Hitchcock, and Allen illuminate the disarray of modern comedy and its dependence on deep intersubjectivity for its affect and disturbance. I also say that deep intersubjectivity is the form and subject of modern comedy, and we have seen how it is investigated with such different results in *Emma, Notorious, To Catch a Thief, North By Northwest,* and *Broadway Danny Rose*. What is at stake in these stories, and the wider body of narratives for which they stand in, is the possibility of what Robert Polhemus calls "comic faith," though with a somewhat different idea.[22] Despite the broad sense in which Polhemus uses the word "religious," it does not allow well for postmodern scepticism or the experience of decentering. With the old master narratives of the dominant race, class, and gender widely discredited (though they continue to demonstrate unusual staying power), the rhythms and metaphors of a postmodern komos, in its deeply intersubjective form, take on new significance. Ancient comedy of course was once one of the master narratives, but in this new narrative practice, comedy recuperates rituals of embodiment, espousal, expurgation, and life making amidst our dying, which we may recognize as signifiers but can use, in the family and in the polis, as if they were signifieds.

Strangely enough, there is a profound role for modern anticomedy in this understanding, for stories that subvert the komos, even as a metaphor, and this subversion is the subject of the next chapter. In other words, in our project the intersubjectively rendered failure of deep intersubjectivity in Henry James and the hollowness (as I argue for it) of Howard Hawks's *His Girl Friday* are as useful as the improbably happy tall tale of *Broadway Danny Rose*.

4

Deep Intersubjectivity and the Subversion of Comedy

THE INTERSUBJECTIVE FAILURE OF INTERSUBJECTIVITY:
HENRY JAMES'S *THE AWKWARD AGE* AND THE SHADOW OF
THE BODY

> We are shut up wholly to cross-relations.
> —HENRY JAMES, The Awkward Age

> . . . bodily speaking.
> —HENRY JAMES, The Awkward Age

Henry James's late novel *The Awkward Age* is a remarkable extension of the possibilities of deep intersubjectivity in narrative. In an intricate maze of mirrorings and appropriations it traces an extraordinarily deep opacity, representing the failures of intersubjectivity among voices whose embodiments of each other they both deny and confess in the shadows of their gestures to each other. That is, the body, what might be called the intersubjective body, looms everywhere in this work, but its presence is masked. The obscurity that cloaks the Jamesian body suits the labyrinths of consciousnesses in *The Awkward Age*, and together they—the obscurity and the labyrinths—constitute the darkness on which our paradigm of complex intersubjectivity can shed light.

This darkness is a significant extension of our preceding discussions of comedy because *The Awkward Age* consistently inverts and subverts the rituals and traditions of the *komos*, as does Howard Hawks's *His Girl Friday*, I argue. The results of this subversion are multiple and offer a further study in the varieties of the deeply intersubjective in narrative. Initially, of course, the denial of comedy gets expressed as a denial of espousal, especially the espousal of the gestures of the other in that most hopeful version of Merleau-Ponty's paradigm. But the varieties of the antikomos (to be distinguished from, say, tragedy) include shame, exposure, violation, the macabre, and despair. These variations in genre practices function in tandem with the narrative practices that I discuss in chapter 2 to provide a matrix of possibilities, of which the anticomedy of James is one of the most intricate. Comedy and anticomedy sound like a binary that begs for a Derridean critique, so let me say immediately that the binary is artificial, masking the range of practices that deep intersubjectivity, itself a richly suggestive collection of strategies for telling stories, extends in important ways. The intersubjective representation of the failures of the intersubjective in James is one rewarding example.

To speak of the failure of consciousness in James, and of intersubjectivity, is not new, though what readers mean by failure has changed. Georges Poulet remarked years ago on the curious presentness of the flow of consciousness in James: These minds rarely remember, and they do not reflect on (or even record images from) their past, from their childhood, for example. Nanda Brookenham in *The Awkward Age* has even less recollection of her personal and family history than Elizabeth Bennet does in *Pride and Prejudice:* At least Austen gives us one paragraph (in volume 3) of Elizabeth's thought about the history of the Bennet marriage. Nanda offers us no such memory about her parents' life together or any other aspect of her immediate family history. For Poulet the Jamesian delimitation of time is a defensive response to the "infinity of experiences" that "Jamesian thought" must attend to once it "achieves consciousness of itself and of others" (*Human Time* 351, 350). Poulet is meditating on the special intensity of personalities in James and their narrow focus on immediate interior experience. Dorothea Krook describes similar qualities of mind in James's characters as a particular self-consciousness: "intense and minute . . . , active without intermission . . . , [always] apprehending its own apprehensions" (*Ordeal* 22).

Although they speak of Jamesian "consciousness" as a generalized phenomenon in his writing and identify gaps—failures if you will—within that consciousness, Poulet and Krook still presume a perceiving self, however circumscribed, however stylized. That self may be one or another character or a narrating voice, sometimes both. Paul Armstrong's interest in the connection in James between ethics and consciousness or between ethics and epistemology presumes subjectivities in James's characters even more clearly than Poulet does. For Armstrong, "consciousness as a creator" in the universe of James's fiction implies James's "preoccupations," which always include complex questions about freedom and love (ix). Armstrong's conclusion reaffirms his interest in a deep intentionality in James's subjects: "Although nothing *beyond* experience guarantees our meanings and values, James and phenomenology discover *within* experience the basis for a purposeful existence" (211).

Another current in James criticism, however, detaches the surface of consciousness in James's fiction, especially the later works, from psychological depth, from psychology itself, and from interiority. In this view James gives us consciousness without a self, subjectivity without a subject. Leo Bersani explains:

> [T]he grounds for what we might think of as "vertical" motive (plunging down "into" personality) eventually disappear from James's fiction. There is no reason to believe that any "obscure" motives enter into Vanderbank's refusal to marry Nanda Brookenham in *The Awkward Age*, or that an inability to be active with women explains Strether's adventures in *The Ambassadors,* or that Maggie and her father have an "unhealthy" attachment to each other in *The Golden Bowl*. (130–31)

One may wonder for whom James's stories resist psychological exploration. Certainly particular voices inside *The Awkward Age* speculate about Vanderbank's motives in a way that might give some readers a "reason to believe" the text gestures toward motives, however murky it may leave them. Bersani seems to grudgingly recognize this awkwardness in his argument when he admits to "what I suppose we have to call psychological detail" (ibid.). Sharon Cameron continues this line of thinking when she rejects "psychology" in James and instead posits "consciousness" as a force "disengaged from the self. It is reconceived as extrinsic, made to take shape—indeed, to become social—as an *inter*subjective phenomenon" (77). Cameron uses "intersubjective" in a sense that is quite different from that in this study. For her, intersubjective is really oxymoronic: Consciousness is something that occurs between people but not between subjectivities, intentionalities, or centers of reflectiveness.

Indeed, Cameron sees in James no interior self: "[A]s consciousness in James's fiction is represented spatially as being situated not 'inside' the single self but rather 'outside' 'between' persons, the very idea of a consciousness located 'within' the self (to which it nonetheless remains inaccessible or 'other') would be, for different reasons, unacceptable . . ." (174). Nevertheless, this generalized consciousness outside the individual self is not a narrator's consciousness, as Cameron specifically affirms: "[J. Hillis] Miller has pointed out that I treat James in relation to his characters as if there were no narrator. This is perhaps because I see James as standing (albeit fictitiously) in an unmediated relation to his characters" (177). Cameron goes on to explain that James's novels are narrated, in effect, by James himself—"though, of course, not technically," she says, somewhat mysteriously (177–78). So much for Wayne Booth, Gerard Genette, and forty years of narrative theory.

Cameron and Bersani seem to me to turn James's difficulties inside out and in so doing ignore logic and James's texts. The purposes of my study require the resurrection of subjectivity in *The Awkward Age,* and furthermore an embodied subjectivity, to prepare for an exploration of James's extraordinarily rich understanding of deep intersubjectivity in all of its (mostly) failures. James's narratives are some of the most intriguing examples of work in which new assumptions about mutuality function to illuminate its failures (except, as always, in the community between text and those implied readers who follow the byzantine labyrinth of failures within the narrative).

And so, before intersubjectivity, let us consider subjectivity in James. In what sense can we say consciousnesses are present in *The Awkward Age,* in order for them to be able to fail at deep intersubjectivity, in a way measured by the new narrative conventions of embodiment and appropriation? The problem attaches to at least two levels of presentation of consciousness in this novel: the talk that fills most of its pages in a drama of maneuvers that Erving Goffman calls in a different context the "dance in talk" and the narrating voice that, despite its reticence, inscribes its consciousness deeply into the narrative (*Forms* 73).

First, what implications arise in the talk itself that spins across the text? Indeed, what word can we use for the speakers of this talk? "Character," "personalities," "persons," "people": All presume exactly the presence that Bersani and Cameron doubt. Personality has depth, persons have intentions, people have consciousness and perhaps unconsciousness; "characters" can, as the alphabet pun famously suggests, be "read" as a character on a page is inscribed. Even the more neutral "speaker" or "talker" suggests an origin to talk and, with the origin, intentionality. In fact, James's talk does inscribe intentionalities because most of the talk in this novel is about motive, other people, and complex human fears and needs. In scene after scene, talk gets used and is performative in struggles in consort with one speaker or in conflict with another. The murkiness, the uncertainty, often quite radical, about the specific originating intentionality does not remove the interest in motive since the talk itself is about some *other* person's motives much of the time and therefore by implication also about the speaker's intentions, even if also never quite ascertainable.

Take for example the scene in Mr. Longdon's garden in his country home at Beccles that opens book VII. Nanda and Vanderbank, knowing that Mitchy is soon to arrive, discuss the constitution of this small garden party:

> "But what did Mr. Longdon ask him [Mitchy] for?"
> "Ah," said Nanda gaily, "what did he ask *you* for?"
> "Why, for the reason you just now mentioned—that his interest in me is so uncontrollable."
> "Then isn't his interest in Mitchy—"
> "Of the same general order?" Vanderbank broke in. "Not in the least. . . . He wasn't in love with Mitchy's mother." (XXIV, 226)

This is talk deeply, obscurely focused on motives and feelings of others, in the first instance. The nature of the obscuration tells us much about the speakers themselves and the filters between consciousnesses in James. It also tells us much about the fears and obsessions of these personalities that almost every utterance confesses or denies. Even the tiny fragment in the preceding dialogue dips into the dark questions of erotic energy that permeate the novel: Who has loved whom (in fact the past does rear its head in James: Mitchy's mother, Nanda's dead grandmother Julia, for example), and who loves whom now. Just before this exchange, Vanderbank has said, looking about the garden, "Fancy . . . his caring [Mr. Longdon] to leave anything so lovable as all this to come up and live with *us!*" (XXIV, 225) How does the love of gardens, of an idyllic life enjoying "the long confirmation of time," according to the narrator, compare to the love of people, of London people, of London people like the Brookenham circle?

All the speculation about Mr. Longdon's motives emphasizes the gap between Mr. Longdon and the speakers, yes, but also affirms Van's belief in the presence of an intentionality on the other side of the gap. Indeed, it affirms more: It affirms Van's experience of that intentionality. His experience is powerful enough to serve as a motive for him in the face of Mitchy's imminent arrival: "Thank you for reminding me. I shall spread myself as much as possible before he comes—try to produce so much of my effect that I shall be safe" (XXIV, 226). The confession of "safe" clarifies more of Vanderbank's intentions, for example, to be ironic when he responds to Nanda (about Mr. Longdon's motive for asking him to visit) that it was an "uncontrollable" interest. Van's irony cuts several ways: He knows Longdon is deeply fond of neither him nor Mitchy, but he is of Nanda, and Mr. Longdon's intentions, Nanda and Van already understand, involve vaguely large amounts of money. This uncertainty about Mr. Longdon's motives only increases when Nanda admits that she arranged the invitations for Van and Mitchy.

The talk in this small fragment of a scene is all about intention, motive, feeling, fear, love, and its absence—all about, that is, the action of consciousnesses. Part of the sense of enclosure in *The Awkward Age* is not the exclusion of economic or "practical" concerns: Anxiety about money, for example, governs much of the talk in this novel (whatever happened to the five-pound note?). What is excluded, however, is talk of a world beyond the talkers' immediate horizon. Vanderbank may work at the General Audit, but he does not discuss government policy, economic or political pressures of the 1890s, or even the future of his office under one political party or another.

Talk is about others. Talk is about perceptions of others and their perceptions of the talker. One of the best examples—because so funny and melancholy—of how talk opens a door to the other, even if as on a blank wall, occurs early in the novel, when Harold argues with his mother about their financial plight: "Don't you see that if you want me to go about you really must enter into my needs?" (CIV, 28) For Harold to seek this sympathetic appropriation of his feelings sounds like Edmund asking Lear for understanding. Still, talk has opened a door to the gestural world of deep intersubjectivity, and the obscurity with which James cloaks his talkers' chain of mutual perceptions and misperceptions needs Merleau-Ponty's understanding of complex intersubjectivity to make better sense. By "better" I do not necessarily mean tidier or more coherent; I mean we can understand more effectively the deep, sad incoherence of this group of talkers. We can understand how deeply James has imagined the failure of the komos.

If conversation in *The Awkward Age* is so securely, explicitly, and irremediably about subjectivities—intentions, motives, feelings, and fears, others' if not the talkers' in the first instance, but then of course also about the talkers'—would it matter if there were no specific rendering of consciousness(es) outside the talk (and the bodies that in part "speak" the talk), at least for establishing the claim that James's narratives render consciousness rooted in some presumed intending self? It would not, in my view. This talk is sufficient to construct its originating impulses, however stylized and oblique that construction is. In fact *The Awkward Age* offers its readers subjectivity in another way, beyond the confines of its talk.

Another subjectivity to be recuperated belongs to that remarkable narrating consciousness that, as in most nineteenth-century novels of deep intersubjectivity, makes possible and guarantees the exchange (or failed exchange) between selves. The narrator of *The Awkward Age* is not Henry James himself, as Sharon Cameron believes he is, partly because this narrator is demonstrably different from other impersonal or "omniscient" narrators in James; nor is this narrator simply a generalized consciousness existing between characters. This voice is an observing, constructing presence with its own particular character and vision that are significantly different from, say, the narrator of *Middlemarch,* in that the voice claims (somewhat ironically, I think) not to partake of the intersubjective life whose gestures *The Awkward Age* so painstakingly renders for us. This claim and its implications are part of the narrator's special character and give *The Awkward Age* and James a special place in this study.

The storyteller in *The Awkward Age* offers himself as the simple testator to real events.[1] At one moment he refers to himself as "Mr. Longdon's historian" (CXV, 130), and at another moment he is "[Mr. Van's] chronicler" (CXVI, 140). He drops into a conversational address to as it were a real reader/listener in rare moments of expansion: "You might have felt you got a little nearer to him . . ." (CV, 45), or "It was always to be remembered for him that he could scarce show without surprising you an adjustment to the smaller conveniences" (CXVIII, 161). He can even refer to himself as "I"—"a minute, I must haste to say"—though the normal word is "we" (XXXVI, 337). Nevertheless, the voice betrays itself so consistently that its "historical" intentions can make sense only as irony. The full sentence surrounding one of the previous paragraph's fragments illustrates this betrayal in all its self-consciousness:

> As Mr Van himself could not have expressed at any subsequent time, to any interested friend the particular effect upon him of the tone of these words, his chronicler takes advantage of the fact not to pretend to a greater intelligence—to limit himself on the contrary to the simple statement that they produced in Mr Van's cheek a flush just discernible. (XVI, 140)

James's narrator not only tells his readers about his own choices, but he also points to this choice's paradoxical quality. He knows what Van understands, he can measure Van's faculties, he has privileged interior information about this character. He is an omniscient narrator. Yet he chooses to draw a curtain before Van's interior consciousness and to represent to us that he is *not* pretending (to an omniscient narrator's knowledge). Yet his pretense is offered for all to witness. The only reasonable inference is to see the narrator's wink, just as we see Thackeray's narrator's wink in *Vanity Fair* when he tells his readers he will *not* describe Amelia's fair hair, dark eyes, and unheroine-like weeping (I, 14).

James's narrator's most artificial gesture is his use of a hypothetical third person to interpret scenes in full view of his readers. In its first appearance this hypothesis serves merely to note surfaces. "Yet when she spoke it was with a different expression, an expression that would have served for an observer as a marked illustration of that disconnectedness of her parts which was frequently laughable . . ." (IV, 29). Since Mrs. Brookenham's conversation with her son is being observed and narrated at precisely this moment by that narrating voice that posits what another observer *would* have observed, there is an excess of observing in this moment of text, so that observing is itself visible, observed. Soon this ghostly watcher takes on further hypothetical qualities and is able to "go behind" surfaces (to use James's own language for omniscient narration that I discuss later in this chapter) to interpret feelings and motives (*Letters* IV, 110). "An observer disposed to interpret the scene might have fancied [Mr. Longdon] a trifle put off . . ." (XI, 86). Hypotheses multiply: The observer might have a disposition, and its activity, interpretation, is also fancying, imagining. (The subject of all this imagining is, as before, one person's possible response to another person's response to him. Inside as well as outside the hypothesis is the web of deep intersubjectivity.)

Immediately after this moment the narrator's observer appears again, even more artificially: "The ingenious observer just now suggested might even have detected . . ." (XI, 87). Here the emphasis is upon difficulty, the mask of appearances, before which the observer becomes a detective, "ingenious" in deciphering the signs (or screens) of the other. Even more telling is the past participle, "just now suggested," with its evasion of agency. But the evasion is also a confession; the agent of suggestion tips his hand in his wry humor. Our narrator hides no wires in his magic act. By the third reference in four pages, the observing fiction becomes something of an inside joke: "[Van] had waited for no account of Mrs. Brookenham's health, and it might have been apparent—still to our sharp spectator—that he found nothing wonderful . . ." (XI, 89).

The transparency of the device becomes clearest when the narrator observes it as a construct of his (and our) need to understand: "Mrs. Brook, for some minutes, had played no audible part, but the acute observer we are constantly taking for granted would perhaps have detected in her . . ." (XXII, 208). This detective is indeed the agent of our desire and even the narrator's. And so the narrator essentially admits, when he confesses "we are constantly taking for granted": For the question must now arise, what is the motive for this elaborate, defamiliarized fiction of the "sharp observer"? I see here a symptomatically modernist moment, both inside and outside the comforts of conventional omniscient narration, whose powers we *want* to take for granted, even when we know we cannot.[2]

But even if ironically hypothetical and narrated by means of a fiction, subjectivity and intentionality nonetheless permeate *The Awkward Age*'s narrative texture, its "characters" and their talk, their dance of talk, and even the dance of narration that circles their talk. James's narrator makes use of a narratological device that David Herman calls direct hypothetical focalization: the "explicit . . . appeal to a hypothetical witness, a counterfactual focalizer, in setting out elements of the story" (237). For Herman, this appeal to a nonexistent consciousness who *would* have seen or understood something if this observer had existed is a "formal correlative of skepticism, detachment, even paranoia," and works to "derange" the framework of the known, though in writers like Bronte and Thackeray "we pass through salutary doubts to achieve greater certainties" (245). Herman's brief introduction to this kind of narration does not include the possibility of the witty self-deflation that occurs in James, where defamiliarizing the epistemological rewards of omniscient narration, including the intricacies of deep intersubjectivity, is exactly a sign of the narrator's desire nonetheless to retain those rewards. He doesn't believe, but he wants to continue the comforting practices of the sacraments.

Others have detected traces of a narrator's presence in *The Awkward Age*. Wayne Booth notes in *The Rhetoric of Fiction* that James did not "free the book of all signs of its authorship," did not produce "a surface cleansed of all traces of the author," nor did James intend to do so (58–59). Booth then draws his larger conclusion, that narrative cannot avoid its vice of manipulation. Even silence is a choice, a framing. In his preface James speaks specifically of his desire "to renounce that line ['going behind' a character's dramatic surfaces] utterly" (xli). He wishes to avoid "officious explanation" (xlvi) and to write a fiction like Ibsen's plays, in which "the references in one's action can only be, with intensity, to each other, to things exactly on the same plane of exhibition with themselves" (xliii). James admits to and admires other kinds of writing, even in his own fiction, that license "going behind" scene and character with commentary. In this instance, however, he will make "this special sacrifice" of fullness and explanation in order to produce a result that will have "a coercive charm" (xli). The image of sacrifice, which recalls his "renounc[ing]" earlier, is strange here, given all the pleasure James feels in the rigor and restraint of his Ibsenian fiction. Fullness seems connected to luxury, and narrative restraint is associated with "fine rigour," as if literary asceticism were a kind of moral virtue (xli). Booth may believe James did not intend to erase all traces of authorial commentary from this novel, but James's preface idealizes that erasure, nevertheless. In his letter to the novelist Mrs. Humphry Ward about "presentation" of character and *The Awkward Age* (among other novels of his), he once again allows the merit of other kinds of storytelling but defends the special value of his renunciation that, in a mysterious reference, he says he only briefly failed, apparently, to sustain in *The Awkward Age*:

> My own immortal works, for that matter, if I may make bold, are recognizable instances of *all* the variation. I "go behind" left and right in "The Princess Cassamassima," "The Bostonians" . . . just as I do it consistently *never at all* (save for a false and limited *appearance*, here and there, of doing it a *little*, which I haven't time to explain) in "The Awkward Age." (*Letters* IV, 110)

The perhaps inevitable failure of James's ideal for *The Awkward Age* reminds us that subjectivity permeates both the telling of the tale and the tale itself. James may have wished to restrain the narrating subjectivity (whatever the brief compromises his letter refers to), but his dramatic mode of telling does not erase the subjectivities *within* the tale, nor did he wish to do so. A central ideal in the preface is the notion that without the narrator, "we [readers and author] are shut up wholly to cross-relations" (xliii). This curious phrase captures some of the doubleness of James's other language ("coercive charm," for example): "[S]hut up" suggests enclosure, deprivation, and even a kind of imprisoning; "wholly" emphasizes what is absent; and "to" is a very odd preposition, in place of the "with" one would expect, as if we are facing "cross-relations" so to speak across a table, rather than being immersed in them, as Poulet would understand our situation. "To" probably carried forward James's renunciation of "going behind" character, but even without narratorial commentary, we are "between," in the midst of relation.

The choices of James's narrating voice point toward the special quality of intersubjectivity in *The Awkward Age*. "Cross-relations" are our horizon, even if a narrator is part of that horizon, and even if this narrator is highly visible (or audible), James's claims to the contrary, in ways that beg to be understood and responded to with equal wit. So, not only can we recover subjectivity in James and the complex self-reflexive construction of a narrator's voice, but we also have an extraordinarily stylized frame for rendering intersubjectivity. The way narrative commentary sometimes gets phrased in *The Awkward Age* as hypothetical in no sense removes its subjectivities; speculative intersubjectivity still adds a representation of consciousnesses to James's world. Once James's storyteller and his intersubjective temperament become fleshed out, so to speak, what is left for us to puzzle about is the intersubjective failure of intersubjectivity within the tale of *The Awkward Age* that this narrating consciousness offers us and expands by its own added layer of reflection. Considering that story brings us to the novel's speaking bodies and James's own version of the "dance in talk," as Goffman calls it.

The failure of deep intersubjectivity to achieve in *The Awkward Age* an "interworld" of authentically reciprocal gestures emerges out of a particular kind of bad faith in the milieu of James's novel. The body is both displayed and hidden, and desire is both a spectacle and a scandal. The labyrinth of intersubjectivity in James's novel winds through complex evasions of gesturing consciousnesses and their embodiments, yet these subjects intricately hover over each other even as they seek to deceive others and themselves. Paradoxically, the body and its sustenances such as money, erotic income, and power (and their frequent shadow, fear) are the subject of gestures of language and bodies themselves in the text, even those gestures of absence that are often signs in James. Furthermore, James's most remarkable twist is the claim by his circle of sophisticates that their double moves of evasion and display are a willed simplicity, an artful naturalness whose foundation is a complex intersubjectivity precisely as Merleau-Ponty understood it. The deep sadness of the book lies in the way Nanda Brookenham is the victim of this cruel intersubjectivity.

But, first, a claim for the importance of the body in these exchanges may seem perverse to readers for whom James is abstract, cerebral, and evasive of the body and its sexuality. One strand of James criticism, from Mark Spilka to Eve Kosofsky Sedgwick, claims that James's irony precisely exposes the evasions by characters and social systems whom the drama of childhood sexuality or homoeroticism frightens. In Sedgwick, for example, John Marcher, in "The Beast in the Jungle," is finally "the irredeemably self-ignorant man who embodies and enforces heterosexual compulsion," and key to the ending of that novella is "man's desire for man—and the denial of that desire" (210–11). This denial of male desire, however, is deeply embodied in the chiasmus at the graveyard, that is, is written in and on those male bodies as Marcher watches, and is watched watching, the embodiment of passion in that other man who mourns. The body in fact permeates even evasions of the body in James and as explicitly in *The Awkward Age* as in "The Turn of the Screw" or "The Beast in the Jungle." Spilka's argument that "The Turn of the Screw" shadows forth in its ghosts characteristic Victorian anxieties about children's sexuality emphasizes the body in James in a different way.[3] We may not know what words Miles used at school, but the text's avoidance of them and the bodies they evoke is profoundly defamiliarized. The scandal of the body is also fundamental to *The Awkward Age* and its drama of deeply intersubjective loss.

This scandal of the body, its wounds, and the denials they occasion, begins in the commodifying spectacle of the body, at least for those like Vanderbank, who frequent the midway of Vanity Fair. Van describes the scene of the spectacle:

> "But beauty, in London . . . staring, glaring, obvious, knock-down beauty, as plain as a poster on a wall, an advertisement of soap or whisky, something that speaks to the crowd and crosses the foot-lights, fetches such a price in the market that the absence of it, for a woman with a girl to marry, inspires endless terrors. . . . London doesn't love the latent or the lurking. . . . It wants cash over the counter and letters ten feet high. Therefore, you see, it's all as yet rather a dark question for poor Nanda." (II, 17)

Vanderbank's commodity, woman-as-display "as plain as a poster on a wall," has no interiority in which to register another's consciousness and respond to it. So Nanda is doubly unsuited to play this high-stakes game, not only because she is not (yet anyway) so bluntly beautiful, but because she exhibits consciousness and responds to others' intentions (in words and bodies) with readings of their readings of her. Van's description sabotages its own claims, though, when he speaks of a "staring, glaring" spectacle, one that "speaks to the crowd and crosses the foot-lights": This femininity is conscious, intends across the margin of its stage, and in its "glare" possesses an edginess or even anger. Beauty's performance however waives its claim to read the other, so that it does not threaten to employ a deep intersubjectivity with its consequent subversion of commodification.

This abdicating consciousness, with all its ideological significance for scripts of gender and power, mirrors the issue that most profoundly looms in *The Awkward Age*'s web of complex intersubjectivities: the costs of exposure and secrecy in a world that contradictorily intends to promote both.[4] Women pay these costs in disproportionate degree, but not only women. Sexually desiring bodies bear the brunt of both exposure and secrecy, but many subjects must traverse borderlands between classes, national and ethnic identities, and genders in the exercise of desire. The dangers of exposure appear clearly enough in Vanderbank's account of how "glaring, obvious, knock-down beauty" functions in London: the violence implicit in "knock-down," the equation of intimacy with money transactions ("it wants cash over the counter"), and the flagrancy of the self's vaudevillian stage work that must "[cross] the footlights." James's preface expands on his theme of risk and exposure when it describes the novel's core interest in Nanda's spoliation, in her premature sophistication about the world and its (sexual) mores, that is, in her move from innocence to experience. The dangers for Nanda in the "good talk" in Mrs. Brookenham's circle can be annulled only by marriage, but Nanda listens and reads without being "corrected by marriage" (xxxiv).

The effects of this spoliation are deep, multifold, and brutal. The duchess is characteristically blunt about the Brookenhams' failure with Nanda: "Of course she's supposedly young, but she's really any age you like: your London world so fearfully batters and bruises them" (XIX, 165). Mr. Longdon picks up the metaphor of the greengrocer's shop when he objects, "Why, I'm sure her mother—after twenty years of it—is fresh enough." In demurring, the duchess expands on her image: "I know what I mean. My niece is a person *I* call fresh. It's warranted, as they say in the shops." In contrast, bruised goods can be accepted, but their handling needs to be legitimized: "If a married woman has been knocked about, that's only a part of her condition. *Elle l'a bien voulu*, and if you're married, you're married; it's the smoke—or call it the soot!—of the fire" (XIX, 165). Nanda is, so to speak, bruised, without being married. But this condition of being bruised is not only "so to speak," is not only a figure, because when the duchess images Nanda's consciousness as a "knocked about" body, she also casts suspicion on the body itself. Knowing what Nanda knows has consequences for the flesh. Nanda's erotic consciousness has been a topic in the Brookenham circle, and the casual imagery that circulates for her subjectivity extends the spoliation. For example, Mitchy assumes Nanda has heard of this imagery for her response to him, and Nanda concedes: " 'Do you mention [my mother] as a way of alluding to something you guess she must have told me?' 'That I've always supposed I made your flesh creep? Yes,' Mitchy admitted" (CXI, 94). Such supposings and such imagery reenact the violation of Nanda.

Bodies are also hidden, however, as well as exposed, in *The Awkward Age,* and their hiddenness, like their exposure, fuels the labyrinthine, deeply intersubjective evasions of this world. Dead bodies are a good example. Dead children hover over these families, acknowledged in only the most oblique way. Vanderbank, for example, has a dead brother and sister, Miles and Mary, and the duchess adopts her niece Aggie in response to the death of her daughter. Yet no one, least of all Vanderbank or the duchess, acknowledges these losses. When Mr. Longdon comes across Mary's photograph at Vanderbank's, Van changes the subject by a kind of erasure:

> "This must be your sister Mary."
> "Yes; it's very bad, but as she's dead—"
> "Dead? Dear, dear!"
> "Oh long ago"—Vanderbank eased him off. "It's delightful of you," he went on, "to have known also such a lot of *my* people." (I, 7)

The logic of "but as" sweeps away the dead sister and her representation, and for "long ago" deaths Mr. Longdon's "dear, dear" is unnecessary. Sorrow acknowledges, and Vanderbank isn't acknowledging or admitting to Mr. Longdon's acknowledgment. In a particularly bitter form of Merleau-Ponty's paradigm, this scene offers a deeply intersubjective denial of feeling in Vanberbank's refusal to appropriate Mr. Longdon's response to his own loss. James then rhymes these hidden bodies with others: particularly in another foursome, the Brookenham children, two of whom are "out" (Harold and Nanda), and two younger children, also male and female, "whom," Van tells Longdon, "you mustn't [see]" (I, 6). The symmetry of the hidden children is remarkable, linking the dead and the innocent. This symmetry, like Nanda's story more broadly, suggests that children are hidden in order to be exposed, that one of this world's pleasures is the violation of innocence.

Intersubjectivity in *The Awkward Age* promises violation because the network of gesturing bodies and consciousnesses promotes certain abuses. This approach to the other follows Sartre's paradigm, appropriating to exploit. James's line from his preface, "We are shut up to cross-relations," almost begs for another Sartrean allusion to a space with no exit and where hell is other people. Bodies, exposed or hidden, connect gestures and words in a system of power in James that has deadly effects. As Mark Seltzer describes it, "The movements of power do not lie in some hidden depths" in the novel but are visible "in the microhistories and the micropolitics of the body and the social body" (24). Although Seltzer sees in James some collusion with "mechanisms of social control," he also sees a thread of defamiliarization by which the Jamesian text "protects itself against the shame of power" and "speaks out against systems of coercion" (148–49). A good example of this double move and of the Jamesian web of deep intersubjectivity is a remarkable image in *The Awkward Age* that seems to echo a famous metaphor in Isak Dinesen's "The Blank Page" that became the seed of Susan Gubar's canonical essay about the representation of women in narrative.

The moment is Mitchy's, who appropriates for his own ironical purposes Mrs. Brook's account of his marital future, a future, "Mitchy took her straight up—'with the young thing who is, as you say, positively and helplessly modern and the pious fraud of whose classic identity with a sheet of white paper has been—oh tacitly of course, but none the less practically—dropped' " (209). The defamiliarization is patent here, as Mitchy identifies the "pious fraud" that women, or at least some women, in this instance modern, London-educated women, need to consider themselves and present themselves to others as a blank page waiting to be written upon.

Susan Gubar cites many examples of the archetype of the blank page, including one from James's *Portrait of a Lady* which compares a young woman to "a sheet of blank paper," whose inexperience awaits inscribing, in contrast to the experienced woman who is "written over in a variety of hands." Gubar continues to comment, "This model of the pen-penis writing on the virgin page participates in a long tradition identifying the author as a male and the female as his passive creation" (294–95). Gubar stresses the subversion of this model by writers like Dinesen, but she could have added that James subverts the paradigm, too. In the example at hand, Mitchy's interest in what "the modern girl" knows is deeply limited. It serves primarily to provoke his defensive response about how much more *he* knows ("She doesn't know after all a millionth part of what *I* do") (CXXII, 209). Consciousness is competition. People know that other people know, and they know in turn that other people know they know, but consciousness of consciousness leads only to display, spectacle, performance, and pride of superiority.

James's master stroke of irony, however, is a brilliant turn of the intersubjective screw. Vanderbank, Mrs. Brook, and Mitchy celebrate the community of their circle precisely for its network of sensitive readings of each other, that is, for its deep intersubjectivity. It's not enough that with all their denials and objectifications they see themselves to function "with so little selfishness" because they are "sincere" (though perhaps they protest too much, in this moment: " 'If we're not sincere, we're nothing.' 'Nothing!'—it was Mitchy who first responded. 'But we *are* sincere' " [CXXII, 202]). Sincerity is only the beginning of their excellences because it functions in an interfolding of consciousnesses that they describe in language that could be Merleau-Ponty's:

> "We pay for it, people who don't like us say, in our self-consciousness."
> "But people who don't like us," Mitchy broke in, "don't matter. Besides, how can we be properly conscious of each other—?"
> "That's it!"—Vanderbank completed his idea: "without my finding myself, for instance, in you and Mrs. Brook? We see ourselves reflected—we're conscious of the charming whole." (CXXII, 202)

Not only does Vanderbank "find himself" in Mitchy, Mrs. Brook, and the duchess, but he also registers the signs in his interlocuters that they respond to his self-discovery in them, and they interpret or revise that discovery as it reinterprets their gestures. Mrs. Brook, for example, wishes to defend their consciousness as more than sincere. " 'The thing is, don't you think?—' she appealed to Mitchy—'for us not to be so awfully clever as to make it believed that we can never be simple. We mustn't see *too* tremendous things—even in each other.' She quite lost patience with the danger she glanced at. 'We *can* be simple!' " (CXXII, 203) So Mrs. Brook wills simplicity and a kind of blindness ("We mustn't see . . .") as a performance to each other as well as to outsiders, presumably those "people who don't like us."

Mrs. Brookenham's defense of this style of deep intersubjectivity doubles back on itself in a further contradiction: " 'Then you see,' Mrs. Brook returned, 'what a mistake you would make to see abysses of subtlety in my having been merely natural.' 'We *can* be natural,' Mitchy declared" (CXXII, 203). Mitchy wills to be natural, a performance that he claims is, like Mrs. Brook's, without art. The melancholy contradictoriness of these claims looms even larger when James's reader remembers that the topic of this scene is Mr. Longdon's offer of a kind of dowry for Nanda. Mitchy has phrased the matter clearly enough to Vanderbank: "He has offered you money to marry her" (CXXII, 200). Mrs. Brook objects to this directness, but not its subject: that is, not to the bribe, but to speaking of it.

James tracks the intricate routes by which power and performance convolute the interplay of consciousnesses within the Brookenham circle of intimates in *The Awkward Age*. The chiasmus of bodies and interpretations can strangle, so that the promises of deep intersubjectivity that Merleau-Ponty sought to emphasize may come to nothing; its strategies of reciprocity can be turned inside out to become strategies of exploitation. Everywhere in *The Awkward Age* reading others is a reading of bodies as well as a reading of words, and those readings become another strategic use of power. Tishy Grendon in book VIII provides an appropriate example, as her body becomes a sign decoded by almost everyone except herself:

> The sign of Tishy Grendon—as it had often been called in a society in which variety of reference had brought to high perfection, for usual safety, the sense of signs—was a retarded facial glimmer that, in respect to any subject, closed up the rear of the procession. (CXXVII, 261)

Tishy finally figures out that Vanderbank might *really* be hungry. Her slowness of reading is only one thread in this scene's intersubjective fabric, as Nanda and Vanderbank dance with embarrassment around his rejection of Mr. Londgon's offer and around Mitchy's abandonment of Nanda for Aggie, whom he has married.

What is significant for my purposes is the depth of reading bodies as signs and the reading of these readings in James's narrative. Tishy's odd dress, green yet blue but once yellow, sparks one further example that is useful in its explicitness. "Tishy's figure showed the confidence of objects consecrated by publicity; bodily speaking a beautiful human plant, it might have taken the last November gale to account for the completeness with which, in some quarters, she had shed her leaves" (CXXVII, 261). The peculiarity of her shedding draws an interpretation that "her companions could only emphasize by the direction of their eyes" (CXXVII, 261). Tishy's comedy of imperception is a sad contrast to Nanda's depth of understanding and her understanding of her consequent losses. Tishy's imperception also underscores the discourse of the body. "Bodily speaking" is both speaking of the body and the body speaking, or misspeaking in this ironic context.

The dance in talk and the talk in dancing bodies function in a darker way in James than we have seen so far in this book. Erving Goffman describes how the dance works and its dangers: "What conversation becomes then is a sustained strip or tract of referencings, each referencing tending to bear, but often deviously, some retrospectively perceivable connection to the immediately prior one" (72). The deviousness of such hermeneutical circles in talk is fundamental to James's novel. Goffman also describes the circle of misunderstandings in his dance:

> A misunderstanding, however, causes the misunderstanding recipient to expose what he thinks the speaker might have said and thereby a view both of what he thought might be expected from the speaker and what the recipient himself might expect to receive by way of a question—all this to the possible embarrassment of the definition of self and other that actually comes to prevail. (56)

Goffman's sense of how exposure functions to embarrass speakers amid the operations of power systems is positively Jamesian. What is at stake in Goffman is similar to what is at stake for James and Nanda and the Brookenham circle: "the definition of self and other that actually comes to prevail." The battle to prevail rages within the cycling of words and gestures, with their "deviously" and "retrospectively perceivable connection" to other signs. James's reader sees how power functions in the "microhistories and the micropolitics of the body and the social body," to use Mark Seltzer's language, because the language of James's narrator, in his extravagantly self-denying presence, is conscious of these functions (24). In other words, deep intersubjectivity does not fail in *The Awkward Age* in the frame tale, where appropriation and espousal—by the narrator—do occur.

Exposure, embarrassment, shame, and violation: Here, in James's narrator's story, is an archetypal example of the Sartrean version of our paradigm with its multiple layers of perception of perception, of gestures reading and appropriating gestures, that Merleau-Ponty so attentively theorized. I said earlier that deep intersubjectivity, at least as understood by the Brookenham circle, fails to achieve an interworld of authentically reciprocal gestures in the way that Merleau-Ponty hoped for. But why should espousal be more "authentic" than shame and spoliation? Merleau-Ponty imagined other outcomes to the intersubjective negotiation, as I discuss in chapter 1, and James asks in another form that imponderable question, why trust espousal, when shame can play its trump card with devastating effect?

HOWARD HAWKS'S *HIS GIRL FRIDAY:* LAUGHTER AS COMEDY'S SABOTEUR

> He sounds like the kind of guy I ought to marry.
> —WALTER BURNS, His Girl Friday

> We have not yet got so far as to be able to love our enemies or to offer our left cheek after being struck on the right.
> —FREUD, Jokes and Their Relation to the Unconscious

Shame, exposure, humiliation: These Jamesian motifs sound like a table of contents for Freud's almost-simultaneously published *Jokes and Their Relation to the Unconscious,* which develops the argument that jokes always have a target, that is, are aimed *at* (a person, less often an institution, God). Freud is the fulcrum on which the anticomic turns, when laughter becomes the saboteur of the komos. For Freud, laughter punishes, exposes, and humiliates: It does not heal, bring together, suspend time or class, or celebrate, and it is not a force for Bakhtinian carnivalesque. This laughter is the laughter of Howard Hawks's film *His Girl Friday* (1940), a screwball comedy whose conventional genre practices are so professional that audiences are bribed to accept its brutalities and humiliations. The subversion of the komos could not be more dramatic, especially since its fundamental strategies are the same narrative practices of deep intersubjectivity that promoted espousal in *Emma* and *Broadway Danny Rose.*

Hawks and Allen: Surely the casting is confused here, with the director of *The Twentieth Century* and *Bringing Up Baby* as the agent of scepticism, and the iconoclastic Allen, director of complex and ambiguously funny films such as *Manhattan* and *Purple Rose of Cairo* as the celebrant of espousal (as we discuss in chapter 3). Indeed, *His Girl Friday* and *Broadway Danny Rose* seem quite similar exercises in genre practice. Both are big-city stories about dissonant, often narcissistic lovers; both tell their tales of loss and the effort to recapture love against grotesquely funny backstories full of images of death and isolation (think of Mollie Molloy and Earl Williams's hanging tree, and of Tina's first husband—they shot him in the eyes, but "he had it coming"—and Danny Rose's pathetic clients).

In fact, these two films could hardly be more different, but with a different kind of difference from what one might have expected. It is the studio film, functioning within the star system and classic Hollywood genre codes (with not only one deadline but *two:* the nine-o'clock train to Albany and Earl Williams's execution), which narrates with such complex suturing the failure of subjects to appropriate each other's gestures of consciousness. In contrast, it is the independent film, without major stars and glamorous color photography, which, as I argue in chapter 3, suggests how a world of ambitious narcissists (think of Walter Burns) need not imprison its lovers.

Howard Hawks is the insider, the alumnus of Phillips-Exeter and Cornell, and the consummate master—but saboteur—of classic Hollywood film genres (and nobody did more better, from gangster movies *[Scarface]* to Westerns *[Red River]* to film noir *[The Big Sleep]* to of course screwball comedy); in contrast, Woody Allen is the outsider, the Jew, the rebel against the dominant Hollywood paradigm. But Hawks and Allen have traded positions in these two films. Hawks turns screwball comedy inside out, subverting what have seemed to be its comforts. That is, in generic terms, *His Girl Friday* is an anticomic comedy in ways that our discussion of *Broadway Danny Rose* and its recovery of the komos in the depths of anxiety and uncertainty prepares for. *His Girl Friday* relies on traditional genre practices in order to poison them.

The profoundly intersubjective paradox of *His Girl Friday*, which is the key to its anticomic comedy, lies in the integral relation between its intimacies and its performed-ness. Hawks's embodied consciousnesses constitute themselves by performing to each other or, more exactly, performing to that other's performances as they oddly distort and reinflect one's own act. The struggle to impose distortion on the other and to resist the reinflection of one's own gestures is a symptom of how serious a weapon deep intersubjectivity can become in a narrative of aggression. The important examples of these intimate performances of separateness occur between Hildy Johnson and Walter Burns. The clarity of their performances (Hildy's and Walter's, that is, not Rosalind Russell's and Cary Grant's) is nowhere more brilliant or complex than in their scene in Walter's office, at the beginning of the film, when Hildy returns to the *Post* to tell Walter about her engagement to Bruce Baldwin (at least she claims this is her motive, though much in the scene undercuts her claim: her long detour down memory lane with Walter, her longer delay in removing the glove that hides her ring). The remarkable quality of this scene is its intimacies, physical, conversational, and visual, and the way they are explored in the rhythms of bodies, exchanges of gestural cues, and looks that are themselves played out against a mise-en-scène whose deep focus emphasizes windows and backward-extending spaces that finally measure the distance between Hildy and Walter.

The dance of bodies in Walter's office traces these intimacies in a kind of jointly choreographed performance. Sometimes Walter's and Hildy's shoulders are touching as they sit on his desk, bodies leaning at the same angle, remembering their life together, tightly framed by Joseph Walker's camera. At other moments they touch each other's shoulder or arm during an almost ritualized banter whose sarcasm complicates the consciousness of these bodies ("Look, Walter, that's what divorces are *for,*" and "What are you playing, osteopath?"). Hildy and Walter play the song of language in their bodies as well as in the speed and sound of their voices, and their songs have the same key and beat and tempo, as Gerald Mast observes: "The two apparent antagonists speak in an identical rhythm, in identical cadences, singing perfect verbal duets," in dramatic contrast to the cadence and rhythm of the "slow Bruce" (215). The scene is thick with physical intimacies, direct and indirect: in Hildy's and Walter's gestures of smoking (the ritual of borrowing a cigarette and then a match), arguing (Walter knows just when to duck, even though his back is turned when Hildy swings her purse), and sexual innuendo ("There's been a lamp burning in the window for you, honey, here" [patting his thigh], with Hildy's reply, "I jumped out of that window a long time ago"; and just where is that dimple?). These intimacies build a complex interworld for Hildy and Walter of knitted (and knotted) languages of body and word.

The mirrorings of deep intersubjectivity shape this play of bodies and dialogue between Hildy and Walter. That is, Hawks's narrative works by way of appropriations of appropriations, as these characters read and misread their performances to each other. But the misreadings often have an element of willfulness about them, as complex intersubjectivity becomes a mode of aggression and of territorial expansion. For example, early on in this scene Hildy and Walter each propose an account of the other's consciousness ("Quiet, Duff, he's thinking," and "Been seeing me in your dreams?"). Much of the appropriating of the other's gestures of selfhood is, as we would expect, Walter's, to be resisted, with various degrees of conviction, by Hildy. Hildy has rejected Walter's world, apparently because she wants to be a "real" woman with a honeymoon, a house, and babies. So one of Walter's responses is to appropriate, even if in parody, Hildy's feminine discourse and its intendings. When blaming Hildy for his proposal of marriage to her, Walter describes her flirtatious behavior and vamps for a moment in a kind of body masquerade to illustrate how she made "goo-goo eyes" at him, and even adds in falsetto, "Oh, Walter."[5] And after Hildy has praised Bruce's different style of masculinity ("He's kind and sweet and considerate. He wants a home and children"), Walter snorts, "Sounds more like a guy *I* ought to marry."

The deep illogic of this line raises complex questions about the way gender and power shape the interplay of subjectivities. Walter doesn't want a home and children with anyone, including Bruce, since he wouldn't give them (as he puts it) to Hildy when he was married to her. So the real agenda of the line is to foreground Bruce's "femininity" and to humiliate him in Hildy's eyes. Walter's sarcasm, however, echoes down the exchanges and reexchanged definitions of gender and identity throughout the scene. After Walter's own moment of flamboyant queerness, his joke seems to license the expression of a kind of homophobic aggression, a view complicated by recent accounts of homosexuality in Cary Grant's erotic life.[6] Walter can perform as a switch-hitter, shifting genders in whatever way will humiliate the "doll-faced hick[s]," whether Hildy or Bruce.[7]

Hildy and Walter also struggle profoundly over definitions of the masculine and the feminine as they interweave in Hildy: "You're a newspaperman, always have been and always will be," versus "I want to go someplace where I can be a woman." If being a woman is a matter of being some *place,* then Walter could take the bride's place beside Bruce as well as Hildy. For Walter, gender is indeed performance, or performances, that can be contested, parodied, and reclaimed between consciousnesses intending *for,* or mostly *against,* each other. The outcome of these contendings is a deeply intersubjective narrative about two performers who read attentively and aggressively each other's routines, including the other's reading of their prior readings. The dizzying energy that propels these performances has been experienced as joyful, but it may in fact be hysterical. Marty Roth even argues that this energy is not erotic, and one could extend this thought to say it debases or erases the erotic (165).

One of the film's most complex circuits of exchange points to the effect of deep intersubjectivity in *His Girl Friday*. The image that circulates in this scene and throughout the film is the image of the window. Walter uses the image first when he invites Hildy to sit down on his lap, comparing it to a window with a burning lamp. Hildy picks up Walter's cue, extending his image in a way that is homage as well as rejection: "Oh, I jumped out of that window a long time ago." Her improvisation on Walter's improvisation is a reading of his gesture and of his reading of her intentions in visiting him (intentions that are cloudy anyway). The extraordinary extension of these readings, however, occurs in the film's mise-en-scène that frames this conversation. Burns's office walls

DEEP INTERSUBJECTIVITY AND THE SUBVERSION OF COMEDY | 185

FIG. 7 *His Girl Friday*. Columbia Pictures 1940.
DVD © Columbia Pictures 1940.

are all windowed, or at least the three walls we can see, and they continue the function of windows as ambiguous gateways. In many of the scene's two-shots, Walter and Hildy face each other across a window, through which in clear deep focus we watch figures move in another, public world. These windows measure both the closeness and distance between Walter and Hildy and raise the larger question, how sealed into a dance of two perspectives are these two subjects?

Hawks's most stunning move is a particular reaction shot, used twice. These shots are the only ones to introduce the office windows that open into the exterior world, and both complicate sequences about marriage. In the first sequence, Walter explains that if things don't work out (after Hildy returns to the paper), he and Hildy can just "get married again." Precisely on "again," Hawks cuts to Hildy's face, her comic shock framed against those exterior windows and the daylit city outside Walter's office (see figure 7). The same cut occurs later in the scene, when Walter's misunderstanding about how Hildy is betraying him (he thinks it's another newspaper) leads Hildy finally to remove that glove and show Walter her engagement ring. In the silence echoing with the words, "An engagement ring?" Hawks reframes his lovers, swiveling the camera to the right so that the daylit windows fill the space between Hildy and Walter.

These are windows that one could "really" jump out of, and they offer a sly interpretation of Hildy's claim: If she did jump out of

Walter's window, why has she returned, glove hiding her engagement ring and asking Walter for his approval (on, for example, Bruce's profession as an insurance agent: "It's a good, honest business, isn't it?")? The windows beckon, but Hildy never looks out to consider the freedom they offer. Another character does, at significant cost, and the film contributes yet a further reading of Hildy's intentions and of the window image by Mollie Molloy. Mollie actually jumps out of her window in the service of an ideal that does not have much weight in the Burns world of display.

How could the larger, deeply intersubjective structure of *His Girl Friday* subvert its comic pretenses? That argument runs against the prevailing wisdom about this film and also seems radically counterintuitive. How could *His Girl Friday*, with its speed, glittering humor, and star performances, be about betrayals and false intimacy, intricately articulated in the subtler language of deep intersubjectivity? Surely to argue such is to cast oneself as Malvolio, reentering the scene of Orsino and Viola's wedding with renewed vindictiveness instead of the promised spirit of reconciliation.

Others have puzzled about the film's undertones, however. Robin Wood for example observes that "its dazzle masks an essential heartlessness which the film seems at times to be judging but which is never, in fact, adequately 'placed' " (1981, 73). Wood admires the film's "disturbing complexity of tone" but believes it "is unable to follow through the implications," as when "we cannot feel (as the film evidently wishes us to) that Hildy has made a satisfactory choice" (76–77). Marty Roth and Lucy Fischer, as I discuss later, develop a view of the film's bitter tones. Stanley Cavell's extended account of this film also opens a door for Malvolio when he describes "the terrible darkness of this comedy" (182). Nonetheless, for Cavell, what might be read as Walter's amorality is in fact improvisation in a "heartless yet not quite hopeless world," so that his indifference to Mollie's sacrifice (he appears just as she jumps out the window) is necessary in a world of war (179–80). That is, for Cavell this comedy's darkness lies not in Walter (or even in the newspaper world itself), but in the larger world in which Hildy and Walter survive and find "home" in being together amidst its ruthlessness, deeply alive in what Cavell calls Walter's "capacity for adventure" or what another writer might call Walter's carnivalesque spirit (185). Cavell sees a sign of grace for Hildy and Walter in the reprieve, mysteriously surfacing in the hands of Pettibone, like Bruce, another innocent with an umbrella.[8]

Pettibone *is* an agent of grace, but an ineffective and deeply impaired agent in ways that clarify the fundamental pessimism of this film. Its final scenes focus on Walter and Hildy's reprieve and their celebration. Earl Williams, the reprieve's supposed beneficiary, has been long forgotten, and Pettibone comes too late to help Mollie, the only character in the film, with one brief exception, who has the generosity, however pathetic, to listen *for* another (Earl) and appropriate his gestures to mirror them back to him for him. Pettibone's childlike innocence renders him incapable of deep intersubjectivity (almost of even simple intersubjectivity): He cannot absorb others' intentionality, much less participate in any intricate network of consciousnesses. Pettibone is a blind angel. Moreover, his blindness, though more complete than Walter's, is like Walter's measured against the possibility of genuine reciprocities in the network of embodied, gesturing consciousnesses, like Mollie's and Earl's, and the narrating camera eye's, which records the dance of bodies I discussed earlier between Walter and Hildy and frames an interworld of complex intersubjectivities that they perceive, if at all, only to turn away from.

Hildy's blindness, however, is the most significant in *His Girl Friday* because it is drawn in the most deeply intersubjective matrix. That is, her perception of perceptions and of others' (mostly Walter's) imperception of responding gestures is the most interestingly blocked, like Jane Austen's Emma early in that novel. The film offers evidence that this blockage is willed in some way because Hildy is at moments the exception to not listening *for* that I referred to above: She has some sympathy for Mollie in the newsroom scene where Mollie denounces the other reporters (the camera keeps cutting to Hildy, looking up from her typewriter to listen to Mollie), the story she has written narrates a version of Mollie's feelings, and she is much more concerned about Mollie's fate after she leaps from the window than is Walter, who walks into the newsroom immediately afterward and is concerned only about removing the rolltop desk where Williams is hiding.

The more important moment of apparently genuine listening, however, occurs in Hildy's interview with Earl, where Hawks's close-ups emphasize an intimacy in contrast to the high establishing shots that frame the cell as isolated and cold. The two-shots of Hildy and Earl separate them from the jail, as Hildy asks questions about Earl's past; she seems to enter his memories, his life-world, even his body-world, in a stunning moment of apparent being-with, when she passes her cigarette to Earl and apologizes for the lipstick. But this being-with is deeply mistaken, if not itself a strategy in Hildy's performance of attentiveness. Earl is even taken in by the gesture until a few seconds later he remembers, "I don't smoke." One of the saddest—and funniest—twists (itself deeply intersubjective) in the scene is the pleasure with which Earl seizes upon Hildy's narrative of his own behavior: Yes, that must have been why I did it, he says with obvious relief. Hildy has the capacity to attend to another's gestures to her and to respond with yet another version of those gestures: Merleau-Ponty would hope for a happier result, the weaving of an interworld. But Hildy doesn't listen as well as Mollie, though of course ironically her work frees Earl. Nonetheless, her moment of intimacy with Earl is also a kind of performance, distorted by gender and class assumptions (of course Earl would smoke) and by her loyalty to the *Post* and Burns.

Unlike Emma, then, Hildy does not become more attentive to the fabric of consciousnesses around her. She grows only to a resigned acceptance of "love" as display, not mutual appropriations. The essential moment, which reveals the subtlety of Hildy's blindness, occurs when she begins to cry, for the first time in the film, upon learning that Bruce has been arrested yet again, this time for passing counterfeit bills. Hildy's tears are overdetermined because they express both relief and sadness: relief that Walter has not abdicated to Bruce, despite his speech of renunciation that precedes Bruce's phone call, and sadness that Walter's only gesture for love is the trickster's masquerade. Hildy's tears are instantaneous in Hawks's pacing of the scene: She threads the labyrinth of Walter's deceptions immediately, grasping that his scheme to renege on his promise (to repay her the $450 she used to bribe the sheriff) expresses not only his contempt for Bruce but also his desire for her. Once again Walter can express his interest in her only through aggression and pranks. To what exactly is Hildy then acceding with her ambiguous tears? Is the answer the model for female desire that Irigaray offers, which we discuss in chapter 5? Is it to Walter's desire she accedes, though in desiring his desire she abdicates her own?

Moreover, what is the nature of Walter's desire in *His Girl Friday*? His passion for Hildy is not at all trivial or peripheral. It is a recurrent and powerful reading of Hildy. From the first scene of the film we know that Walter cannot forget Hildy's rejection, and his subsequent subterfuges all reflect his perception of her flight to and from him. What makes *His Girl Friday* a remarkable example of a special genre, the deeply intersubjective anticomedy, is both the function of this web of consciousnesses to outline Walter's refusal to espouse Hildy's gestures of an inner life and his use of the web of their interpenetrating intentionalities as a weapon against Hildy. Walter wants Hildy as partner in their fast-paced world of the news as a game, but her position as "girl

FIG. 8 *His Girl Friday*. Columbia Pictures 1940.
DVD © Columbia Pictures 1940.

Friday" will always serve his authority: Even in the last frame, Hildy is burdened by coat and suitcase as Walter precedes her down the stairs, and the film's last line is Walter's advice to her, "Why don't you carry that in the other hand?" (see figure 8). At the least Hawks's image of Friday recalls issues of slavery, although it may not be clear how deeply the Defoe echo works (is the authorial audience to remember that Friday was much wiser than Crusoe at times, asking questions about God's goodness in a world of suffering, for example?).

Whatever Walter's virtues as an adventurer in a particularly bleak world of play, with the Chinese earthquake—"a million dead"—and Hitler and the Polish corridor on page 6, his aggressive, adolescent narcissism can never appropriate Hildy's consciousness or its gestures that shadow forth her inner life, much less reflect them back to Hildy for her to absorb and reinterpret for him. Walter can duck, his back turned to Hildy, when she swings her purse at him, but his knowledge is flat, self-focused, and blind to Hildy's life of feeling. His inability to grasp in the simplest form Hildy's impulse toward family (however sentimental or culturally constructed) is one example of the profound effects of gender on the interplay of consciousnesses. In fact, the problematics of gender raise more questions about Hildy's ambiguous tears.

For example, is Walter's blindness to Hildy's domestic and maternal interests his, or is it the film's? Lucy Fischer's powerful (and idiosyncratic) critique of *His Girl Friday* in *Cinematernity* argues that it is the film's blindness. She sees a "suppression of the maternal" as inherent in classical film comedy and traces across this film its many figures of the mother as grotesque, ludicrous, or dead(ly) (116). Walter swears at one point on the grave of his mother, who Hildy reminds him is still alive; Bruce's mother is the object only of disdain; and the film's audience is invited to laugh with the newsroom at the vision of Hildy with babies, " 'singin' lullabies and hanging out didies' " (117). Most important, for Fischer, Hildy relinquishes her life-making capacity, while Walter's are freed (he takes credit, after all, for making Hildy into a newspaper reporter in the first place). Fischer's critique is persuasive to me, with one reservation: The film frames these elements itself, for the most part. That is, the blindness of the newsroom and of Walter to Hildy and Mollie (and Earl and even Bruce) is not the blindness of the film.

Other modes of consciousness (other than the dominant mode of control and display, which might be associated with certain styles of masculinity) live in this interworld of intentionalities, but Walter cannot receive them as modes of feeling and experience. Marty Roth explains it this way: "Walter is an extravagant image of primary narcissism. Our first sight of Walter is of him looking at himself in a mirror and wearing a bib under his chin. Walter . . . inhabits an unlimited subjectivity that is proof against otherness" (169). Other centers of experience—Mollie, Earl, and Hildy—are not for Walter occasions for reciprocal gestures and reception but for contestation. Walter's failure to move beyond intersubjectivity as performance and control explains why the film's conclusion is so hollow. So we return to Hildy's tears. Why does she submit finally to Walter's narrative?

The best clue is Hildy's line explaining her tears in that final scene: "I thought you were on the level for once" (when Walter explained that he had been jealous of Bruce for giving Hildy the life he—Walter—couldn't give her). Hildy is grateful that Walter was *not* on the level. She is grateful that Walter's "sincere" abdication was yet another gambit. So she chooses the story she will live in, which is Walter's. Hildy's tears and shrug of resignation signal her willingness to live in Walter's world of surfaces, with no more intimate a mirroring of her subjectivity than Walter's mock version of her life with Bruce in Albany. For Hildy, either counterfeit money in some odd way is the genuine article, or this counterfeit currency is worth more than the genuine article, or, most likely in this film, the genuine thing is not an option for Hildy because gambits are all you get in a life with another.

Is this, the genuine thing, the loss that Hildy's tears mourn? The preceding story gives us some other possibilities: Perhaps it is the babies Hildy mourns, or the ambiguous idyll of domesticity, or perhaps the relationship with Bruce, in which she was the dominant partner. It might even be a certain integrity that she has sacrificed in order to play even second-string with the big boys, the editors and mayors and governors. Maybe in 1940 the price is worth it for this woman to be somehow in the big time.

The gender politics, implicit or explicit, in screwball comedy is not always clear. I cite Ed Sikov's subtle discussion of these films in chapter 3 as an especially complex form of ambiguity. "In screwballs, unmarried people are put through a sort of courtship by ordeal. . . . But what makes the genre strange, what gives it its lasting punch, is that the ordeal continues for married people as well" (32–33). The framing terms of the ordeal are power relations, and these mostly 1930s films do not approach the classical Hollywood paradigm with its dominant male gaze, for example, in a simple way. For some viewers, like Lucy Fischer, cited earlier, these romantic comedies finally naturalize traditional assumptions, even matrophobic assumptions. Others, like Tina Olsen Lent, see a force for redefining power in sexual relationships:

> Through its discourse on the ideal relationship, the screwball comedy created a heightened awareness of the new expectations for love and marriage. While not a blueprint for actual gender relationships, the screwball comedy was part of the new liberal ideology that redefined gender relations and focused on the sexual and companionable components of intimacy. (331)

In generalizing, however, Lent categorizes *His Girl Friday* too easily and simply observes, "The harmony of Hildy and Walter's movements showed that these two characters were perfectly complementary" (328–29). "Perfectly" ignores the undertow of narcissism and the failure of espousal that we have discussed. Lent cannot help us understand Hildy's tears, but at the same time her sense of context can remind us that, for 1940, Hildy achieves a significant degree of power and freedom, and for some viewers that achievement will be more significant than the price she pays for it. But for me the tears are stubbornly important, and I see here another version of Erich Segal's death of comedy, the loss of the "rule-breaking revel in the flesh," which is a kind of "thinly disguised reenactment of the rebirth of the world" (9, 13). There is indeed a remarriage in *His Girl Friday,* but it is one that will reenact the failures of the first marriage, sans honeymoon, sans graciousness, sans liberty for the subaltern (Friday still carries her own bags), and sans rebirth (whether or not actual babies).

Whatever the loss Hildy mourns, its consequence is to make *His Girl Friday* a brilliant study of the failure of the komos and the triumph of surfaces. The presence in the film of so much dazzling humor and so many high-octane jokes is not a contradiction to this view, as we return to our starting point in Freud: Most of *His Girl Friday*'s wit is about aggression, melancholy, loss, and death, from Hildy's opening exchange with the *Post* advice columnist ("How's your cat?" "She just had kittens." "It's her own fault.") to Walter's wisecrack over the handcuffs that he shares with Hildy ("This is the tightest spot we've been in since the night Archie Leach cut his throat"). Of course only a few viewers in 1940 knew that Archie Leach was Cary Grant's birth name, but the line links to others that mark loss and fragmentation.

I always laugh hardest at the exchange between Hildy and Louie over the "very blond" blonde who has landed Bruce in jail the second time: "Ohhh, you and that albino of yours." "Evangeline? She ain't no albino. She was born right here in this country." Behind this wonderful moment of linguistic vertigo, however, is a series of melancholy questions about outsiders, marked and monstrous women, and belonging (even Louie wants to belong—or wants his women to belong). For Freud, at the heart of all jokes are unanswerable questions about anger, sexuality, human suffering, or resistance to the dominant class's moral ideas. He cites as a typical example the story of the alcoholic who stopped drinking so he could hear again but went back to drink. "So long as I didn't drink I was able to hear. But nothing I heard was as good as the brandy." Freud comments on the simple technique and the deeper issue: "Technically this joke is nothing other than an object-lesson: dialect or skill in narrative are necessary for raising a laugh, but in the background lies the sad question, may not the man have been right in his choice?" (114) Louie may have it wrong about albinos, but he also has it right, sadly, because being on the right side of boundaries matters a lot, with the Red Army on the way (according to the mayor's campaign rhetoric), and after all it is 1940.

His Girl Friday is a powerful reminder that narratives may employ strategies of deep intersubjectivity to explore the embodiment of blindness, aggression, masochism, and the abandonment of hope. The film also reminds us that this exploration may use all the devices of the komos, sabotaged by a laughter whose mentor is Freud, not Bakhtin (and anyway Bakhtin believed that true carnival is no longer possible).

5

Deep Intersubjectivity and Masquerade

> *Womanliness therefore could be assumed and worn as a mask....*
> —JOAN RIVIÈRE, "Womanliness as a Masquerade"

> *I think the masquerade has to be understood as what women do in order to recuperate some element of desire, to participate in man's desire, but at the price of renouncing their own.*
> —LUCE IRIGARAY, This Sex Which Is Not One

> *Jean: I'd give a lot to be—well, I mean, I—I'm going to be exactly the way he thinks I am, the way he'd like me to be.*
> —PRESTON STURGES, The Lady Eve

The notion of masquerade is an important conceptual knot, a chiasmus perhaps, of paradoxical and interwoven reflections about subjectivity (and intersubjectivity). It has reappeared in gender and narrative theory, from Joan Rivière's foundational essay of 1929, through, to name a few writers, Lacan, Irigaray, and Mary Ann Doane, to a recent example such as Richard Meyer's wonderful study of Rock Hudson's beefcake studio publicity in the 1950s, a "starbody" narrative of the mostly unclothed star that performs heterosexuality in a deeply ambiguous sequence of images (259). But masquerade has been employed in widely divergent and sometimes confusing senses in recent theorizing about subjectivity and identity, especially about performance and gender. To prepare for the argument about deep intersubjectivity and masquerade in *Jane Eyre* and Hitchcock's *Marnie* that follows and to emphasize the difficulties before us, let me discuss four uses of this word that begin to outline a phenomenology of masquerade as a narrative practice. One angle of this discussion, which is new in masquerade theory—my emphasis on the possibility that masquerades can operate in bad faith—underscores the benefits of understanding complex intersubjectivity itself as a group of narrative practices, in this case because it helps us think better about opacity and betrayal, as well as more intricate forms of insight and espousal.

In the first and oldest sense, "masquerade" is, strictly speaking, not disguise. Its performance does not seek to screen from its audience the deceptiveness of its surface. Masquerades in this sense admit to being chosen and even display that choice and so are offered to their audience as choices in costume, defamiliarized as it were. The "true" or prior identity of the masker may remain hidden, but the act of hiding behind the constructed surface is itself displayed. The *Oxford English Dictionary* (*OED*) defines this oldest kind of masquerade as "an assembly of people wearing masks and other disguises (often of a rich or fantastic kind) and diverting themselves . . . ," and an early example (1653) of this usage emphasizes the principle of play: "He loved such Representations and Disguises in their Maskaradoes as were witty, and sudden." Stephen Heath makes clear the disruptive potential of such play or display as a defamiliarization of the performance of "femininity" in this comment on the Dietrich persona in *Morocco:* "Dietrich wears all the accoutrements of femininity *as* accoutrements, does the poses as poses . . . and so *proffers* the masquerade . . . , not [as] a defense against but [as] a derision of masculinity (remember the bric-a-brac of male attire that Dietrich affects in her most famous poses—top hat, dress jacket, cane)" (57–58). One significant subset of this notion requires the professionalization of the masker and the institutionalization of the display in the discipline of the theater. Theatricality subtly alters the phenomenology of masquerade because the intentionality behind the mask changes, and reciprocity from the audience changes its form, too. Intersubjectivity is certainly possible, but the circle of touched touching, the embodiment of embodiments, is much more rigidly governed by social protocols. It is not accidental that theatricality is an important metaphor in Foucauldian theory since the theater becomes a useful version of the panopticon, and the discipline of the mask serves as another example of the construction of the "individual."

This oldest sense of masquerade as a confessed costuming is also its most contemporary, even postmodern, sense and might be called "masquerade-as-signifier." A second sense of masquerade points to impersonations that may function as disguise, that is, as performances whose intent is to deceive their audience and might usefully be called "masquerade-as-signified." The important distinction between these two forms of masquerade sometimes gets erased. In phenomenological terms, the difference lies in the intention of the first masker, who articulates her or his pretense as a kind of metatext before others, who are expected to read this intention and respond in kind. The second masker not only does *not* confess to the pretense but consciously seeks to hide it to naturalize his or her performance.

Of course, few masquerades, however explicitly acknowledged, can fail to contain seeds of deception or bad faith in their performance. Deception often seeps into the relation between masker and audience because neither party in this deeply intersubjective relationship may be clear about boundaries between the performed role and the performing subject. That is, the performer cannot always be clear to herself or himself or to the audience, where the claim to pretense ends and where the authority of the prior "self," the intentionality that in some sense initiates the masquerade, begins. Even if attempting to function in good faith, the masker may not possess the self-knowledge (or the illusion of the same) to draw those lines clearly. What *are* the intentions of those 1950s Rock Hudson studio photographs (wherever one might locate intentionality—in the performer, the photographer, the studio apparatus, the reception industry, or some combination of these)? One could tease out a series of possibilities, from a conscious effort to deceive in a performance of unambiguous straightness (but perhaps sabotaged by various subterranean energies), to a "camp" performance of bisexuality or gay eroticism for certain knowing audiences. However, the possibility of not performing in good faith suggests other scenarios in which the intent to exploit and abuse may predominate and for which the phenomenology of the intersubjective would be quite different. In these scenarios, reading the gesture of the other is not a prelude to Merleau-Ponty's appropriation as gesture of mutuality but to appropriation as an act of aggression. The knottedness of embodiments thus becomes even more dizzyingly intricate when masks and disguises, or masquerades-as-signifier and masquerades-as-signified, complicate the circulation of gesture and countergesture.

Further confusion looms when, in its third use, masquerade refers to the wearing of a mask whose donning the performer has forgotten and whose alteration of the wearer's performance has become naturalized to the actor; when, in other words, the mask deceives the masker. The roots of this confusion lie in a process that is worth marking, a shift in the actor's intent so that what began as wearing a mask (in an act of either confessed masquerade or disguise) becomes another version of the subject's self-understanding. Joan Rivière, in her classic essay, moves back and forth across this boundary when she identifies womanliness as a masquerade that "women who wish for masculinity may put on . . . to avert anxiety and the retribution feared from men" (35). Rivière's double perspective surfaces in her language of choice, on the one hand, for some maskers, as in the preceding sentence, when she writes that women "may put on . . ." or when she claims that "womanliness therefore could be assumed and worn as a mask" (38); on the other hand, in her diagnosis of compulsion in other maskers, as in the university lecturer on "an abstruse subject which seldom attracts women" whose inappropriately flippant behavior during her lectures "caused comment and rebuke": "She has to treat the situation of displaying her masculinity to men as a 'game,' as something *not real,* as a 'joke.' She cannot treat herself and her subject seriously . . ." (39). Rivière emphasizes the masquerade as behavior that women in some marginal sense choose but whose deeper structure of fear and evasion the maskers have not understood. Masquerade in this approach becomes a complex form of intersubjectively driven self-blinding. *Jane Eyre* is a particularly rich example of this possibility. In its most sceptical form, this sense of masquerade applies to all imperfectly self-recognizing subjects and may describe the donning of "manliness" as well as "womanliness," as I discuss later.

Finally, in the fourth approach, the image of masquerade may seem to contain a kind of logocentric implication of a "reality" behind the surface of a "true" self that could be (and perhaps should be) unmasked. The twofold narrative implications of this notion for gender studies are, one, that if "femininity" or "masculinity" or "queerness" are performances, then there may be an authentic identity behind the mask that in conventional narrative is bound to be revealed somehow to someone (even if not to the masker); this "truer" and more "authentic" self typically serves as a standard to measure "healthy" performances of a self. A second implication, working in the opposite direction, asks, if these genders and sexual orientations are *only* performances, what has happened to the body that puts on the mask? What is the narrative prequel to the masquerade? In what sense are the body and its desires constructed by the performance? Judith Butler, in *Bodies That Matter,* has articulated an approach that honors the materiality of the body and also places its regulation and performances into an overdetermined matrix of cultural supervision. "That the body which one 'is' is *to some degree* a body which gains its sexed contours in part under specular and exteriorizing conditions suggests that identificatory processes are crucial to the forming of sexed materiality" (17; my emphasis). Such an approach admits the power of social regimes in gender performance, while allowing for the materiality of a body that dons the mask.

In an analogous fashion, I want to steer a course between the extremes of social construction and platonic essentialism, allowing for an embodied consciousness with that faculty of "critical agency" that Butler also wishes to rescue from a too austere "cultural determinism" (*Bodies* x). In so doing I want to problematize, without entirely discrediting, the narrative assumption in this fourth conception that masquerade promises revelation, whether to the performing self and/or to its audiences. I prefer to suggest that "masquerade" and "disguise" point to choices of performances by a *prior* embodied consciousness (prior to the performance), itself shaped by a lifetime of gesturing to others and embodying their responding gestures. Narratives often do evaluate these performances. In Hitchcock's *To Catch a Thief* and *Marnie*, for example, there are better and worse masks. Certain roles are healthier than others. Jane Eyre also comes to decide, in a complicated interplay between ideological understanding and evasion, that some performances will make her happier than others. Such evaluation however need not posit an essential, idealized self and certainly not a gendered essence, but equally it need not abandon the incarnated subject whose field of consciousness includes other bodies, gestures, languages, choices, and social agendas.

The masquerade, in all of its guises, has been a valuable notion in theorizing female spectatorship of film especially and helped move this work beyond the simpler subject positions presumed in 1970s film criticism. These reflections about audience are also helpful in rethinking the reception of written narrative. If watching (or reading, for that matter) can be conceived as a donning of a mask, women spectators no longer are restricted either to identification with women or therefore simply to roles as targets of the male gaze in either a voyeurist or fetishist negotiation. Building on Joan Rivière, Mary Ann Doane critiques the classic Freudian notion, reworked by Irigaray, that women lack the distance from their bodies that men achieve early in life by means of the gaze at their sexual body, remarking its phallic signifier and the identity it confers. Quite the reverse, Doane argues, women soon learn to perform femininity, and "the masquerade, in flaunting femininity, holds it at a distance" (81). Jackie Stacey comments on the significance of this fluidity of identity formation for theories of female spectatorship in for example Teresa de Lauretis's argument in *Alice Doesn't* for a "double identification" with "the active masculine gaze and with the passive feminine image" (26). If this ability to bracket, defamiliarize, and play with subject positions surfaces in women (and men) as spectators, so must it in women (and men) as performers.

My interest in masquerade lies in its value for exploring representations of the intricate interplay among consciousnesses of all genders, both watching and performing, *within* narrative. The significant angle of Doane's thought for this work is her contention that masquerade can be a subversive performance. "The masquerade's resistance to patriarchal positioning would therefore lie in its denial of the production of femininity as closeness, as presence-to-itself" (81). One project in my discussion is the tracking of these resistant performances in their intersubjective networks of preceding and subsequent performances, but in *Jane Eyre,* not in Brontë's readers; in Hitchcock's films, not in Hitchcock's audiences. My interest is the *representation* of intersubjectivities, not the negotiation between text and audience, to the extent one can separate those subjects. It might be fairer to say that my interest is the representation of intersubjectivities for, in Peter Rabinowitz's terms, the authorial audience.[1]

The masquerade, however, is not only resistant. Its other functions are also important in understanding *Jane Eyre* and *Marnie.* For Doane masquerade can indeed be consciously iconoclastic, intending to shock its audience out of a comfortable reading of gender, as Stephen Heath claimed Marlene Dietrich so intends in *Morocco.* Rivière's different approach suggests masquerade's apparent complicity in dominant gender systems, since masquerade could be a ploy, half intentional and half compulsive, to defuse male anger and fear at a powerful woman's intrusion into supposedly masculine terrain. Judith Butler notes what she takes to be a revealing move here in Rivière to desexualize the masquerade (*Gender* 52). One virtue of Rivière's approach, however, is to make explicit the ambiguous politics of the masquerade. Rivière notes how often the mask slips; one might add how it almost always slips, whether consciously or not, to reveal itself as ploy. One result of this revelation is to incite greater fear in the male audience, which "suspects some hidden danger" behind the mask (43).

Masquerade then for Rivière functions as both subconscious compulsion and gender critique. Butler picks up this point in Rivière and ponders the multiple "interpretations of what precisely is masked by masquerade" (*Gender* 47) or indeed whether anything is so masked. Is the masquerade a "performative production," constructing gender, or is there a femininity prior to the performance (ibid.)? These multiplicities are consistent with Butler's larger approach to subject positions as fluid. Among those positions that might be performed by the masquerade, Butler's notion of a kind of constitutive defiance is especially useful: "Or is masquerade the means by which femininity itself is *first* established, the exclusionary practice of identity formation in which the masculine is effectively excluded . . . ?" (*Gender* 48). Here masquerade becomes an origin for consciousness, at least for feminine consciousness.

In other words, Doane, Rivière, and Butler point to an array of negotiations within the mask wearer, and between her and her audience, that may be revealed when the mask slips: self-deception; an effort to reconstruct one's own subjectivity, especially by incorporating figures of loss; a bribe to the powerful; resistance; or even public defiance.[2]

These four stories of masquerade have profound implications for intersubjective narratives of gender—whether that gender is feminine, masculine, bisexual, or some other version of sexual intentionality. In the emerging masculinity studies of the 1990s, similar assumptions and imagery appear, as in Gaylyn Studlar's examination of male Hollywood stars of the 1920s, which she calls *This Mad Masquerade: Stardom and Masculinity in the Jazz Age*. Studlar's study of masculinity as cultural construction includes, most interestingly for our own discussion of *Jane Eyre,* an extensive look at the star of the "monstrous," Lon Chaney, one of the most influential of Hollywood figures, who declared in a fan magazine of 1922, "Acting is masquerade" (9). For Studlar, narratives of masculinity articulate contradictions and fears as narratives of the feminine have for critics from Sandra Gilbert and Susan Gubar—or Joan Rivière—to Laura Mulvey and Susan Fraiman. About Chaney, for example, Studlar comments, "[His] depiction of the body-monstrous may be read as a symptomatic instance of the anxiety surrounding masculinity and the male body during this postwar period" (210). Peter Lehman traces similar indirections in his essay on male nudity in late-1990s' films, as he untangles some of the power issues in the unmasking of what he calls "the melodramatic penis" in films like *The Crying Game*. In that film the penis is neither the all-powerful penetrator of hard-core pornography nor a source of shame (because it's always too small) but still an occasion of privilege. "The discourse of the melodramatic penis still seeks to block a penis from merely being a penis" (39). To foreground masculinity as performance, even masquerade, is not to suggest only equivalence or symmetry with studies of womanliness. I want to acknowledge the significantly different questions about privilege and authority in these different arenas of gender studies, while rescuing a way of thinking about narrative—deeply intersubjective masquerade—that helps us approach stories that articulate gendered subjectivities.

Interestingly, none of these theorists includes the Sartrean possibility for the masquerade-as-signified: that it can be a disguise donned with the intent to exploit, an aggressive act in bad faith, or a violation. Adding this angle emphasizes the possibility of agency for the masker, even at the cost of admitting to the significant harm that the masker may inflict. Masquerade as aggression, anger, or abuse opens up once again the dark side of deep intersubjectivity, but perhaps in an oddly celebratory way, if it imagines more choices for the subjectivity behind or inside the mask. For Jane Eyre, for Marnie, as for Ralph Ellison's invisible man and Paul Laurence Dunbar's masked poet in "We Wear the Mask," the knotted consciousnesses of masquerade are versions and translations of complex energies (including the economic and political). Deep intersubjectivity helps us see more clearly some of the threads that make up the knots of masquerade.

MASQUERADE, MONSTROSITY, AND *JANE EYRE*

"Why!—am I a monster?" I said.
—Jane Eyre

Something of masquerade I suspected.
—Jane Eyre

Monstrousness and the masquerade: Here are two profound subjects in feminist theory and in the history of storytelling that dramatize how much is at stake in deeply intersubjective narrative practices. Selfhood itself is contradictory and puzzling enough for women (and in other ways for men) in Brontë (and the Gothic generally), but *Jane Eyre* adds to the tradition of women as monsters a new angle: the paradoxes of monstrousness explored as a narrative of masquerade. Jane both seeks and fears this masquerade because it gives shape to a set of contradictions in her journey toward maturity. This notion of a journey through the monstrous has been well explored in the rich body of *Jane Eyre* criticism. Important contexts for that journey emerge from the history and myth of women as monstrous and have been explored by critics like Sandra Gilbert and Susan Gubar (the writing-woman as monster, with the Frankenstein-like progeny of her rage), Nina Auerbach (the "ambiguous holiness" of the Victorian woman as demon [1]), and Dorothy Dinnerstein, who works with archetypes such as the "Dirty Goddess," who is "the carnal scapegoat-idol," and woman as "the Earth Mother [who] engulfs the bones of her children," who is "night in the entrails of the Earth" (124). What is new and useful about the linkage of monstrosity to masquerade is the exploration of the phenomenology of both as a narrative practice, with significant rhetorical and political implications. In its deeply intersubjective form, the monstrous becomes, for example, a series of embodiments of embodiments, whether defamiliarized as "witty and sudden," in the *OED*'s 1653 language about "Maskaradoes," or disguised to audience or indeed to masker.

Jane is initially monstrous because she is a woman writing and, even more subversively, a woman writing her own life. Gilbert and Gubar cited many years ago Gerard Manley Hopkins's infamous explanation for why a woman writing is unnatural: The artist's "most essential quality is masterly execution, which is a kind of male gift, and especially marks off men from women, the begetting of one's thoughts on paper, on verse, or whatever the matter is" (3). Only men beget *on*, and the feminine is one of those "matters" (like the blank page) that receive the begetting. The image of a woman writing her self, her identity, was inherently perverse in 1847 and still is, according to Susan Stanford Friedman, because that woman, or the representation of her, struggles through a deep alienation whose roots for Friedman lie in history, as she distances herself from Lacan, too:

> Alienation is not the result of creating a self in language, as it is for Lacanian and Barthesian critics of autobiography. Instead, alienation from the historically imposed image of the self is what motivates the writing, the creation of an alternate self in the autobiographical act. Writing the self shatters the cultural hall of mirrors and breaks the silence imposed by male speech. (41)

Friedman's and Felicity Nussbaum's studies of women's autobiographies illuminate as well the fictional narratives of women writing themselves, for these representations must navigate the same cultural environment as autobiographies. The "creation of an alternate self" is the project here, and the barriers for Jane are similar to those for Lady Mary Worley Montagu and Mrs. Thrale.

Nussbaum describes some of the contradictions and assumptions of the "dominant male culture and its constructions of the figure of woman" in eighteenth-century England that formed a context for women's own writing for a long time:

> Eighteenth-century women who represented their subjectivity in text, even private texts, were inevitably caught in mimicking male definitions of themselves. . . . Eighteenth-century women were labeled lustful, vain and inconstant; yet they were also judged capable of "overcoming" the "natural" tendencies of their sex to display the "manly Soul" of Swift's Stella or to become a "softer man" like Pope's Martha Blount in "Epistle to a Lady." ("Commonplaces" 154)

What is the phenomenology of mimicry in narrative, if even "private" texts perform masculine versions of the feminine? In Rivière's terms, what intention drives the assumption of these masks? When the pre-twentieth-century masker embodies the Other's signals that would shape her body and subjectivity, is she an eager or conflicted collaborator, a saboteur, a masochist, or an early artisan of camp, a subtle ironist? How do the contradictions of the dominant ideology appear in these masquerades? What effects should we look for in deep intersubjectivity's construction of selves amidst others in a sequence of mutual appropriations (or denials)? How do shame, exploitation, and espousal look different under the pressures of gender politics and masquerade? These questions suggest how the shift toward deep intersubjectivity has profound consequences for the gendering of narrative and for shaping the ideological confusions and mystifications of gender, both femininity and masculinity.

To explore the phenomenology of the masquerade in *Jane Eyre,* I begin with the monstrousness of the woman writing herself and with the first stage of that self-writing, which is self-knowing. How does Brontë's subject construct her subjectivity, her self, by way of others? What is the nature of her intersubjective self-framing, and what are its implications for her authority? In chapter 2 I explore the encounter of the self with another, and our topic here is closely connected: how self-knowledge and then its self-narrativizing are represented as being constituted in the shadow of the Other, and what the implications are of the gendering of these representations for the politics of intersubjectivity. The shadow of the Other takes on special power when Jane is tempted by the masquerade of the monstrous.

The seeds of the monstrous lie in Jane's writing and in the very structure of the subjectivity she seeks to write. What Jane knows about herself, or fears to know, or knows she does not know is constituted by means of deep intersubjectivity. That is, not only do these fears and knowledges exist in the environment of relations to others, but their inner fabric is also shaped by mutually appropriated gestures, by the chiasms and the crisscrossing of intentions embodied in those gestures in response to other gestures. What this narrative practice constitutes is a profound example of the classic paradigm of woman as monster. A useful illustration is Jane's tormented meditation on her selfhood at the end of chapter 27:

> Oh, that fear of his self-abandonment—far worse than my abandonment—how it goaded me! It was a barbed arrowhead in my breast; it tore me when I tried to extract it; it sickened me when remembrance thrust it further in. Birds began singing in brake and copse: birds were faithful to their mates; birds were emblems of love. What was I? In the midst of my pain of heart, and frantic effort of principle, I abhorred myself. I had no solace from self-approbation: none even from self-respect. (XXVII, 316) [3]

Jane imagines her consciousness to be penetrated by Rochester's consciousness or at least by her awareness of his inner life as she has observed it in his words and actions. Rochester's subjective world is not "over there," on the other side of a space across which she could, as for example Richardson's Clarissa did, expose herself, wittingly or not. Her perception (in this case, expressed as fear) of Rochester's subjectivity is instead a "barbed arrowhead in my breast," that is, an intentionality experienced inside Jane's body. Jane has an idea about what lies behind Rochester's behavior because she seeks behind his gesture the consciousness it begins to embody, however imperfectly, to Jane, not only of its own intentionality, but also of its version of its own earlier absorption of Jane's gestures. Rochester's "self-abandonment" is of course a response to Jane's rejection, in the immediately preceding scene, of Rochester's plea that she stay with him, even though he is already married to Bertha, and that abandonment, as Jane reads its exterior sign, calls to her own self that she has conceived and written, which she images in her body ready to be broken open. The chiasmus of subjectivities here affects even Jane's grammar: The "it" above, introducing the arrowhead, specifically refers to Jane's *fear* about what Rochester will do to himself, but "self-abandonment" lies closer to the pronoun and is easier to remember when Jane says "it tore me when I tried to extract it." The pronoun's referents get tangled, I believe, as bodies and fears mirror each other, intertwining Jane's perceptions of herself and Rochester, and his of her, and earlier yet hers of him.

The image of Rochester's mentality as embedded in Jane's body (or in her fears as if in her body) is a quintessential example of what Merleau-Ponty meant by appropriation. The arrowhead buried in

Jane's breast furthermore tears at that body, so that the incarnation continues the series of touchings in that circle of the touch that Merleau-Ponty described. The intimacy of deep intersubjectivity's stories of mutual appropriations could hardly ask for more vivid an expression. Jane's climactic, agonized question, "What was I?" grows out of a network of expressions of consciousnesses embodied between subject and another in an extended series of reenactments. Jane's question appropriates, as her body has, Rochester's appropriation of her refusal to live with him. Furthermore, Jane's question extends itself intersubjectively. She specifically rejects the traditional self-sufficiencies that in her moral tradition might console her: her principle, self-approbation, self-respect. Jane abhors herself; she is a horror; she is a monster. Because how the self knows itself is intimately connected to what it knows of what others know it knows, Jane has lost what makes her human to herself. Already, then, the monstrous and what will be its masks begin to take shape, as in her self-abhorrence, Jane asks not "who" she is, but "what?" She echoes her earlier espousal of the Reeds' view of her as a "noxious thing." But in this phase of her self-perception of other's consciousness of her as monstrous, Jane finds the strength she lacked as a child, however precocious, to gesture back to Rochester.

The chiasmus of the monstrous articulates its paradoxes, its consolations and depredations, in the body of this narrative about bodies gesturing to each other. Jane's self-narrativizing reveals the contradictions of gender in what she images as a most intimate, hidden place within the subject. That is, Jane's self-writing exposes the scaffolding of an ideological project, exactly in its intersubjective complexity. Deep intersubjectivity becomes a strategy for tracing the phenomenology of monstrosity as embodiment among warring or even espousing subjectivities. One reason Jane thinks of herself as monstrous is that others have seen her so, and she has absorbed that version of herself and mirrored it back to others or even attempted to revise that version, only to experience another affirmation of her monstrosity. Indeed, Jane's reading of the politics of attractiveness in children is an astonishing exposure of the intersubjective appropriations that dominate space in the Reed family:

> I was a discord in Gateshead Hall; I was like nobody there. . . . They were not bound to regard with affection a thing that could not sympathise with one amongst them; a heterogeneous thing. . . . I know that had I been a sanguine, brilliant, careless, exacting, handsome, romping child—though equally dependent and friendless—Mrs. Reed would have endured my presence more

complacently; her children would have entertained for me more of the cordiality of fellow-feeling; the servants would have been less prone to make me the scapegoat of the nursery. (II, 28)

Jane's understanding, crossing class barriers to include the servants who read Mrs. Reed's reading, tracks this network of consciousness of consciousnesses, noting the Reeds' response to one who could not "sympathise" with them, and grasping that "fellow-feeling" may be cancelled by an experience of difference. This exposure of difference (of gender and class) makes Jane's story a confession of the politics of subjectivities' interconnection, as well as a forgetting of that politics, when Jane's "monstrousness" comes to seem natural to her.

This naturalizing of the monstrous occurs because throughout the novel Jane has appropriated others' images for herself as less than human, often as an animal, especially a hysterical one ("Hold her arms, Miss Abbott; she's like a mad cat" [II, 24]), but animals share some closer link to the human, unlike the "thing" that Jane sees herself to be in internalizing others' views of her: "They were not bound to regard with affection a thing that could not sympathise with one amongst them; a heterogeneous thing . . . ; a useless thing . . . ; a noxious thing" (II, 28). Jane's understanding of the monstrous is already deeply intersubjective because it is a response to the Reeds' response to what they experience, in Jane's view, as *her* "inability to sympathise" with *them*. In an odd way Jane sympathizes with the Reeds' interpretation of her stance *for* them. Jane may even provoke their affirmation of her outsiderly position and feeling and if so extends the monstrous further.

In fact, I think Jane embodies the monstrous exactly as Kafka's Gregor does, as the "ungeheures Ungeziefer" in "The Metamorphosis": "ungeheures Ungeziefer" means unclean and exiled from the family; the monstrous is unnatural precisely because it lies outside the charmed circle of love of parents and other children.[4] In the novel's circle of consciousnesses, beginning with Jane's first abandonment, so to speak, by the parents who died so early, it is impossible to say which is the first touch, whether in Brontë's tale the insiders first excluded, or whether the excluding child provoked its exclusion. According to Jane's assumptions, however, in her narrative model of the deeply intersubjective, the "natural" lies within the family circle, and the outsider is the monstrous. The "natural" woman, to return to our earlier discussion, is the woman without a pen, who can be the blank page; the woman who writes is another kind of outsider, outside the family (since a woman with a pen cannot be begotten *on*), and so yet again monstrous.

This tangle of meanings to the monstrous mirrors Jane's own contradictory desires: She rejects the dominant sense of "natural" (the adult Jane certainly revels in her craft as author of her text), yet deeply seeks some integration with nature and her own womanliness (whether defined culturally or biologically); she fears the monstrous (most clearly in Bertha's madness), yet is deeply attracted to it. These contradictions have been well examined by Brontë students, though emphases differ, of course, in locating Jane as victim, collaborator, or rebel in relation to the dominant ideologies of her world, as more or less distanced from Bertha's more or less attractive anger, as insightful or deluded in her marriage to Rochester.[5] What is important for my purposes here is the phenomenological complexity of Jane's consciousness of her monstrosity and how it links as a narrative paradigm to masquerade. The thread between these notions, as we will see, is the figure of woman writing.

Her monstrosity also comes to seem natural to Jane because women's monstrosity serves the dominant gender system of Brontë's time by naturalizing its profound contradictions about gender, female and male. Some of those contradictions are certainly expressed in material circumstances, although I do not believe that economic and social circumstances are only causes (they can also be effects), or are the only causes, or in some cases are even the primary causes of ideology. Mary Poovey illuminates an important aspect of Jane's monstrosity by unthreading the complex tapestry of contradiction in the Victorian governess's role and identity:

> Because the governess was like the middle-class mother in the work she performed, but like both a working-class woman and man in the wages she received, the very figure who theoretically should have defended the naturalness of separate spheres threatened to collapse the difference between them. (127)

The governess articulated not only contradictions of class in a way that could strike at the heart of the middle-class conception of motherhood and femininity, but she also came to threaten exposure, not erasure, of "the governess trade" (to quote Jane Fairfax in *Emma*) as it took on political significance all out of proportion to the actual number of governesses in the 1850s (25,000 out of 750,000 domestic female servants, according to Poovey):

> That discussions of the governesses' plight had dovetailed, by the mid-1850s, with feminist campaigns to improve both employment opportunities for

> women and women's education reveals the critical role representations of governesses played, not, as conservatives desired, in defending the domestic ideal, but in capitalizing on the contradiction it contained. (127)

This narrative of contradictions exposed rather than erased mirrors the double narrative of masquerade that I discuss at the beginning of this chapter, in Rivière's notion of the mask that hides and then slips. There is also the double value of monstrosity, a marking to be feared and embraced. The phenomenology as well as the politics of monstrosity point to a profound ambivalence with a long history. As Dorothy Dinnerstein emphasizes, woman as monster is an ancient nightmare, one of whose roots is men's and women's fascination with and fear of women's rage.

Jane's strategy to shape these contradictions is to write and by writing to wear the monstrous in what becomes a complex masquerade, in effect to rescript monstrosity, so that she can authorize her self in a newly independent narrative that is deeply intersubjective in form and substance. There are two scripts that Jane rewrites: The first is Bertha's story and the form of consciousness it articulates, adopting and adapting another's embodiment of madness, anger, and women's experience of abuse. This recasting of Bertha's story is well recognized, but I want to add a new framework to its elements, as deep intersubjectivity knits new appropriations in that rewriting: In Jane's version Bertha's story becomes a study in masquerade. Jane, in the arrowhead sequence discussed earlier, is both wounded like Bertha and wounded like Bertha's victims. She has the opportunity to respond with Bertha's madness and fury but chooses a different gesture that also distances her from her prior notion of herself as loyal and passionate: "Birds were faithful to their mates; birds were emblems of love. What was I?" (XXVII, 316). This is a new version of Jane.

The mask image becomes clear in another appropriation of Bertha's appropriation of Jane, by means of the veil. Jane watches Bertha mirror a secret Jane for her before Jane's mirror, tearing the veil of that Jane who had defined her own fearful consciousness earlier ("I have a veil—it is down"). Bertha exposes to Jane the problematics of identity that she has yet to grasp, which confronts her again on her wedding day in the "robed and veiled figure, so unlike my usual self," and which she sees again in her mirror (XXII, XXVI, 244, 284). There's a wonderful vertigo for the reader spinning between these two images because it's not clear who is mirroring whom: Is the veiled Jane an embodiment of the veiled Bertha (veiled because hidden, now and when she married Rochester, and paradoxically veiled as a bride, too: hidden and exposed), or is Bertha's veil-play a mockery of *Jane's* hidden self and/or Jane's bride-self? Perhaps the two scenes together suggest the repulsion and attraction pulsing between Bertha and Jane, as each seeks a mutual embodiment and exposure.

These unmaskings or remaskings finally help Jane retell her story and Bertha's, who, as Gilbert and Gubar wrote in the classic study of Jane's rage, "is Jane's truest and darkest double . . . , the ferocious secret self Jane has been trying to repress ever since her days at Gateshead" (360). Madness and hysteria have always lurked inside Jane's anger. At Lowood Jane even speaks in these terms about her humiliation on the stool in classroom: "I mastered the rising hysteria" (VII, 76). Whatever Bertha's original masquerade, herself duped or duping, when Rochester married her, her multiple performances (organized by some narrative, whether rational, psychotic, or something else) embody for Jane versions of her own passion, anger, and desire; these mirrorings of mirrorings, in a deeply intersubjective chiasmus of appropriations, are fundamental to *Jane Eyre*'s study of gender and selfhood. All of the possibilities in our opening discussion lurk here: from the playful, self-conscious, postmodern "Maskaradoe" or the self-duped and naturalizing masker, to the masquerade as aggression and even abuse.

The function of the journey in *Jane Eyre* and the retrospective narrator who seems to be the goal for the young Jane's maturation point to that faith we discussed—that behind the mask a truer, better, healthier self could be disclosed. Many critics note, however, the novel's complex qualifications on this confident narrative arc, not the least of which are the sacrifice of Bertha, who has given much to Jane, the humiliation of Rochester, and the imperial subsidy for Jane's new fortune. So we cannot yet, at least, decide whether Jane ever fully disowns her Bertha-mask.

Jane Eyre studies the phenomenology of the masquerade not only in the masks women wear but also in the masks men wear. Indeed, Brontë suggests that the gestures of the masculine, like those of the feminine, may be adopted or intended for some audience. Rochester performs the most explicit masking in the novel in the gypsy fortune-telling episode and raises the most explicit questions about gender as performance:

> [H]er hat brim partially shaded her face, yet I could see, as she raised it, that it was a strange one. It looked all brown and black: elf-locks bristled out from

beneath a white band which passed under her chin . . . ; her eye confronted me at once, with a bold and direct gaze. (XIX, 198)

"Her" voice is "as harsh as her features," too (198), so that the feminine that Rochester has chosen to mimic is disturbing, partly because its "masculine" elements (the direct gaze that "confront[s]") imply violation, partly because it reverses genteel feminine standards of beauty (the "brown and black" face, the locks that "bristle"). Earlier Sam the footman has reported her to be "a shockingly ugly old creature . . . as black as a crock" (XVIII, 194). Rochester's feminine is thus anti-"feminine," even antisexual, and monstrous in its implications. Not only does its appearance shock, but this figure can also see penetratingly and dictates to Rochester's guests their role: She insists on seeing only young unmarried women and seeing them alone, much to the consternation of Blanche's mother, who senses the erotic charge in this sibylline encounter.

Rochester's masquerade, then, is part of a complex drama of sexual and narrative romance, provoking an interchange of deceptions among the Thornfield guests. Rochester's disguise is an example of a masquerade of aggression and bad faith: He wants to hear secret intimacies from each subject, not just from Jane. The purpose of his game is also to discover what kind of interest Jane may have in him, and she is the prime target of his aggression (though Blanche is a target, too): "Is there not one face you study? One figure whose movements you follow with, at least, curiosity?" (XIX, 174). From the first moment of their encounter, Jane suspects something: "if Sybil she were . . ." (XIX, 197).

Yet Jane immediately addresses this figure as "mother" and does so again when she recalls the sybil to the purpose of their interview: "But, mother, I did not come to hear Mr. Rochester's fortune: I came to hear my own, and you have told me nothing of it" (XIX, 202). Despite the primary meaning of "mother" in this setting, referring to an elderly woman of a lower class, the word echoes across *Jane Eyre,* with its many versions of the abandoned child's mother-wound, and this complex scene is followed immediately, in the first paragraph of chapter 20, with another of Jane's encounters with the maternal moon. Jane's investment in this masquerade surfaces in her confusion when Rochester's mask slips (how consciously he drops the mask is not clear): "Where was I? Did I wake or sleep? . . . The old woman's voice had changed: her accent, her gesture, and all were familiar to me as my own face in a glass—as the speech of my own tongue" (XIX, 203). In some perverse logic, Rochester's masquerade has revealed to Jane how deeply she has appropriated Rochester's face and voice, which are as intimate for her as her reflection in a mirror, as her own tongue's words (note that word requires here the body, the "tongue" it is grounded in).

Rochester's embodiment is also seductive, manipulative, and threatening because his intentions are obscure to him as well as Jane. The breathtaking tour de force of Brontë's scene is the way Rochester loses control of his masquerade, and in a moment of stunning ambiguity the sybil's own language oscillates between effect and agent of the disguise. In the long paragraph in which the sybil speaks for Jane's conscience, the power of the adopted voice overpowers Rochester's intent to deceive, and suddenly Jane's "I" becomes Rochester's "I": Her speech becomes the speech of Rochester's own tongue:

> [M]y harvest must be in smiles, in endearments, in sweet—That will do. I think I rave in a mind of exquisite delirium. I should wish now to protract this moment *ad infinitum;* but I dare not. So far I have governed myself thoroughly. I have acted as I inwardly swore I would act; but farther might try me beyond my strength. Rise, Miss Eyre: leave me; "the play is played out." (XIX, 203)

The broken syntax and swiveling dash signal the change: "in sweet—That will do."[6] The shift in voice is clear only on rereading; initially the "I" of "I think I rave" appears still to be the mimicked Jane, so that in a way the pronoun is at least serially intersubjective (first sybil as Jane, then only Rochester). For a couple of lines Rochester's language mirrors exactly Jane's throughout her story. The confusions of syntax and reference open up the labyrinths of masquerade. Rochester's play has allowed him to be Jane, her eye, mouth, and brow, to speak for her integrity, and also to "rave" in an "exquisite delirium" that he tries to "govern" and that recalls the "hysteria" Jane has sought so often to "master."

Where is the dominant power in this chiasmus of masquerades, as Rochester's mask slips? Who holds the mirror? Jane says later that "I had been on my guard almost from the beginning of the interview. Something of masquerade I suspected" (though she thought the perpetrator was Grace Poole), and so the masquerade may function primarily to expose Rochester rather than Jane (XIX, 204). The immediate effect of the charade, however, is to bring Jane closer to Rochester, as she confesses, when Rochester staggers at the news of Mason's visit: "Can I help you, sir?—I'd give my life to serve you" (XIX, 205). Here, as throughout the novel, Jane struggles with her Christian idealism because service is both lack of power (and so an especially dangerous ideal for women) and a triumphant choice. Choice and power become deeply intersubjective webs of response to response and embodiments of embodiments, sometimes self-deceiving and in any case wondrously fluid. I do not mean to suggest the performances of masculine and feminine, by women or men, are similar options for politically equivalent subjects; the asymmetries of power are clear in the fact that Rochester has much more authority to assume the feminine than Jane would have to play the masculine. Indeed, the masquerades of gender illuminate these contradictions with enormous richness. To see the threadings of subjectivities in the narrative practice of deep intersubjectivity illuminates the tangles of gender even better, but especially the contradiction between the gendered subject as a construct and also as a (prior, Merleau-Ponty would say) embodiment.

One particular thread of *Jane Eyre* criticism underlines this paradox. In this approach, these masquerades are disruptive *theatrical* practices within a carceral society of surveillance: In the tradition of Foucault, Judith Butler, and Eve Kosofsky Sedgwick that I discussed earlier, masquerade is a resistant, carnivalesque response to the power of the panopticon. Joseph Litvak's study of *Jane Eyre* in *Caught in the Act: Theatricality in the Nineteenth-Century English Novel* emphasizes selfhood as performance and how for Jane performing the governess imposes a deep discipline. In Litvak, for example, the gypsy scene is not a very good instance of a liberating carnivalesque because it is Rochester who can cross-dress and violate boundaries. "Rochester may play the gypsy, but Jane must play the spectator." Litvak agrees with my view that Rochester's masquerade externalizes complex contradictions of gender. But "this festive destabilizing of sexual, racial, and generic categories comes oddly to seem the exclusive right of the powerful" (68–69). The notion that the carnivalesque may in some way be implicated in the "official" world it inverts is, of course, a notion implicit even in Bakhtin, whose work has stimulated most contemporary theoretical work on the carnivalesque. Mary Russo provides an important early critique of Bakhtin's utopian ideal of carnival when she points out the unspoken gender assumptions in Bakhtin: "In what sense can women really produce or make spectacles of themselves?" Russo continues, citing Le Roy Ladurie, "Jews were stoned, and there is evidence that women were raped during carnival festivities. In other words . . . certain bodies, in certain public framings, in certain public spaces, are always already transgressive—dangerous, and in danger" (217).

There *is* a politics of gender to the carnivalesque, in *Jane Eyre* as in Rabelais, and Litvak teases out the variations of complicity, disciplinary oversight, and telltale "bad acting" as he calls it, moments of matrix-mocking performance by Jane (71). Helena Michie's study of power relations between bodies in *Jane Eyre* emphasizes some similar notions:

> Throughout the novel both Jane and Rochester try on a series of disguises and personae that grow more and more complex at the point of apparent unveiling. Jane's "discovery" that Rochester is the gypsy, for example, only complicates matters and generates new questions about their respective roles. For Jane, even more than Rochester, the novel is a series of costume fittings that focus on the central contradictions between heroine and dependent. (49)

Body is closely tied to class for Michie, who earlier sees that *Jane Eyre* gives us "a heroine caught between two bodies; at various times in the novel she tries on the body of a leisure-class heroine and of a worker, but realizes she can completely fit into neither" (48). What is missing in the focus on "costume fittings" and Litvak's use of the "trope of theatricality . . . to unpack subjectivity as performance" (xii) is the novel's representation both of consciousnesses within the masks and of intentionalities manipulating and appropriating, sometimes at complex cross-purposes, within the matrices of surveillance that Litvak (and Foucault) quite properly identify. That is, theatricality, in this sense, performs to the other/Other, who at the best observes sympathetically, at the least without investment, and at the worst threatens, in the Sartrean paradigm I discuss in chapter 1.

What Merleau-Ponty added to this paradigm was the possibility of the touched touching, the circle of hands gesturing to hands gesturing. Merleau-Ponty's image of the circle obscures the problem of power: Women and men do not occupy equally privileged places around this circle in *Jane Eyre*. Nevertheless, because of variations in supervision's rigor, these players have room to play to each other behind their masks. Neither Litvak nor Michie discusses, for example, in *Jane Eyre*'s gypsy scene, the interplay of gestures between these consciousnesses that I worked with earlier (Rochester's version of the monstrous, which he offers to Jane for her response; his adoption of her language, which then takes control of his performance, spoiling the masquerade). There is still room, even when supervised by the panopticon's guards, for wit, aggression, deception, and espousal: for agency. This use of Merleau-Ponty's phenomenology to define a degree of priority for the embodied agent, who is not only the disciplined subject, points to a belief that will not be shared by those readers for whom even "Jane's inwardness . . . performs a specific kind of cultural work" (Litvak 57). That is, my approach to the phenomenology of masquerade allows us to look closely at a margin in the spaces between the threads of the chiasm where intersubjectivity, our texts suggest, writes more than a disciplinary narrative.

Rochester himself reads monstrosity in ways that begin to question those ruling assumptions about gender and identity that discipline narrative. When the boundaries between Jane and Bertha blur in chapter 27 and Jane replies to Rochester that she does not think he would love her if *she* were mad, Rochester's reply reflects his grasp of Jane's appropriation of Bertha from his life:

> If you flew at me as wildly as that woman did this morning, I should receive you in an embrace, at least as fond as it would be restrictive. I should not shrink from you in disgust as I did from her; in your quiet moments you should have no watcher and no nurse but me; and I could hang over you with untiring tenderness, though you gave me no smile in return; and never weary of gazing into your eyes, though they had no longer a ray of recognition for me. (XXVII, 297)

One reason for Rochester's intricate interweaving of Bertha and Jane in this metanarrative is his desire to assure Jane he can love her, her Bertha-ness. With this evidence of Rochester's perception of her self-perception, his adaptation of her mirroring from his nightmare to hers, no wonder that Jane feels so connected to Rochester's "self-abandonment," incorporates it into her body as a "barbed arrowhead," and perceives herself yet again as a horror.

Rochester's version of Jane's nightmare contains at least some cross-gendered images, of himself as "watcher" and "nurse" for example; thus some of the boundaries of gender get marked as such and questioned in an echo of the gypsy-disguise scene. Perhaps Rochester's most remarkable moment of intersubjective appropriation (and here that word's undertow about power fits because Rochester's rights as master figure in this adoption of Jane's mentality) occurs in his tale of watching her (himself unobserved) the day after his return to Thornfield:

> You listened to the sobbing wind, and again you paced gently on, and dreamed. . . . The voice of Mrs. Fairfax wakened you: and how curiously you smiled to and at yourself, Jane! There was much sense in your smile. . . . It

seemed to say, "My fine visions are all very well, but I must not forget they are absolutely unreal. I have a rosy sky, and a green flowery Eden in my brain; but without, I am perfectly aware, lies at my feet a rough tract to travel." (XXVII, 308–9)

Rochester reads Jane's body, eye, and gestures of intention and reads their readings of her interworld in her obedience to Mrs. Fairfax and to him, in her mothering another "motherless child"; within the boundaries of that experienced world she finds a space to imagine (he imagines) and to be her own spirit. This narrative, with its construction of Jane's consciousness of others, of course serves Rochester's rhetorical purpose in the great debate of chapter 27. Its larger function, however, is part of the rewriting of the monstrous in *Jane Eyre,* a project that requires a recasting of ideologies of the masculine as well as the feminine. Rochester's part in this project is his adoption of Jane the monster as Jane the powerful. His ability to do so does not reshape the dominant gender system of the novel in all ways, but it demonstrates how, in both form and content, deep intersubjectivity can promote a new politics of gender by means of chiasmic reversibility. That "weave of consciousnesses," which Irigaray notes can be imprisoning, can also, paradoxically, let in air and light.

A final twist on the possibilities of masquerade in *Jane Eyre* is to conceive Jane's role as narrator as a kind of mask. This notion emerges from a feminist narratology that has raised important new questions about narrative strategies that are significantly gendered. Alison Case, for example, describes how the female narrator in the eighteenth and nineteenth centuries confronted a tradition that suspected "plotting women," women who were in control of their story and capable of manipulating its rhetoric, narrative shape, and thematic direction. As Case puts it, "female narrators always run the risk of being associated with female plotters of another and more unsavory sort" (15). To insulate female narrators from such suspicion, Case argues, "feminine narration is characterized by the restriction of the female narrator to the role of narrative *witness;* that is, by her exclusion from the active shaping of narrative form and meaning" (4). Case finds in this novel "the marks of Brontë's negotiation with the convention [of feminine narration] most clearly both in Jane's struggle against the negative image of her as a plotting woman and the projection of those qualities onto Bertha Mason and also in her shifting of the agency for moving her plot forward at crucial moments onto an external, supernatural force" (106). Case's archetypal example of this last evasion is Brontë's use of the maternal moon to call Jane away after Rochester's appeal that she live with him as his mistress. One way of phrasing Case's argument is to say that Jane must wear a mask of deference, in this instance to displace responsibility for her choice to flee onto an external force. Jane as storyteller must also make certain narrative moves to disarm her conventional readers, given the troubling substance of much of her tale.

To see Jane the narrator as a figure wearing a mask opens up rich angles in our study of monstrosity and masquerade, especially in light of Joan Rivière's essay that we discussed at the beginning of this chapter. What is the nature of this masquerade? How consciously does Jane the narrator adopt it? Does she let the mask slip, and, if so, how purposefully and for what purposes? To what extent does the mask become a forgotten garment in Jane's self-understanding? In an important example that Case cites, Jane prides herself on her artistry. In this instance, it is her skill as a lover to manipulate Rochester that Jane revels in: "I knew the pleasure of vexing and soothing him by turns; it was one I chiefly delighted in, and a sure instinct always prevented me from going too far: beyond the verge of provocation I never ventured; *on the extreme brink I liked well to try my skill*" [my emphasis] (XVI, 161). The remarkable note here is Jane's focus on the "extreme" brink, the edge of a precipice on which she *likes* to dance, delighting in her consciousness of control in a moment of intense risk. Does Jane expect or hope Rochester will see her remarkable delight? And to delight in her delight? How deeply intersubjective is this drama? Jane describes herself as performing a kind of masquerade: "retaining every minute form of respect, every propriety of my station, I could still meet him in argument without fear of uneasy restraint." In *her* perception Rochester sees to some degree behind the mask: "[T]his suited both him and me" (XVI, 161). Jane believes Rochester enjoys their performance of charged repartee and therefore must at least desire that he enjoy her pleasure too (although there is a less cheerful view of Jane, say, Richard Chase's, that would suggest that what "suits" Jane is a more cruel game with Rochester). Nonetheless, this display of a woman's rhetorical power surely compromises the safely deferential role of feminine narration; it defamiliarizes the masquerade and points to choices Jane has consciously made. That is, Jane is *not* Rivière's disguised woman who has forgotten that she donned the mask of womanliness.

For Case there is a parallel between this self-confessed manipulation and that of the "retrospective narrator" (100). To me the parallel is so extensive that it suggests a "witty Maskaradoe," to recall the *OED*'s language, because the older Jane repeatedly frames her narration by drawing attention to her acts of interpretation through metaphor ("emblem" is Jane's word) and editing and even in the act of memory itself. In her role as the backstory narrator, Jane openly admits to and even celebrates her pleasure in the storyteller's craft and so repeatedly undermines the strategy of disarming, as in well-known moments such as the opening to chapter 10, when she announces "This is not to be a regular biography: I am only bound to invoke memory where I know her responses will possess some degree of interest" (91); or the equally self-confident and manipulative opening to chapter 11, "when I draw up the curtain this time, reader, you must fancy you see . . ." (101); or even in Jane's confession of an internal life of passionate storytelling: "Then my sole relief was . . . to open my inward ear to a tale that was never ended—a tale my imagination created, and narrated continuously . . ." (XII, 116).

In other words, our study of masquerade theory suggests the possibility that Jane's deferentiality may itself be a mask that is marked to its audience as a choice and whose function is to be witty about gender politics or, to echo Rivière, to be subtly terrorizing or at least subtly aggressive. Behind the mask lives an intentionality that modulates her voice, edits her text, and controls—at the diegetic level—the representation of her own subjectivity. This Jane, confidently holding the pen, can engage in the game of deference, partly to lull the conventional reader and so to increase the shock value of her more subversive manipulations. Critics may disagree about how much insight or blindness we should expect in that authorial audience, but at least one contemporary reviewer, the infamous Elizabeth Rigby, was not blinded by Jane's deference, in her critique of "the little Jane, with her sharp eyes and dogmatic speeches," and of the older Jane, who has "the strength of a mere heathen mind which is a law unto itself" (441–42). I see Jane's posture as the more conventionally feminine narrator to be a complex masquerade that for some readers would be so convincing that they would see no disguise but that other readers would see immediately as a choice either to denounce or enjoy.

Jane's posture, however, is not thoroughly self-aware, and indeed throughout *Jane Eyre* much self-recognition is imperfect behind one's mask. One deeply problematic angle of Jane's voice is its assumptions about race and class. Susan Lanser extends Gayatri Spivak's critique of *Jane Eyre*'s imperial values by noting how validating Jane's voice entails silencing others whose class and ethnicity do not authorize their words. "*Jane Eyre* legitimates female authority as essentially white.

Indeed, authoritative voice in *Jane Eyre* is even more parochial, for it belongs finally only to white educated Christian Englishwomen of the middle class" (192).[7] Jane does not adopt or even attend much to important other voices: Bessie's, for example, or Hannah's, the servant at Moor House, or especially Bertha's, whose specificity gets exploited as myth by both Rochester and Jane. The speed and ease with which Jane's language takes on the privileges of her newly endowed position, once she learns of her West Indian inheritance, is remarkable. She sets her class of schoolgirls at Morton into a retrospectively defined overview that makes many assumptions about nationality and class:

> [My best scholars:] as decent, respectable, modest, and well-informed young women as could be found in the ranks of the British peasantry. And that is saying a great deal; for after all, the British peasantry are the best taught, best mannered, most self-respecting of any in Europe: since those days I have seen paysannes and Bäuerinnen; and the best of them seemed to me ignorant, coarse, and besotted, compared to my Morton girls. (XXXIV, 380)

That evaluating tone, confident in its cultural judgment, requires an assurance new for Jane. The narrative voice that evaluates retrospectively has occurred before and in fact threads through the novel, as in this comment on the ten-year-old Jane's anger by the adult Jane: "A child cannot quarrel with its elders, as I had done, cannot give its furious feelings uncontrolled play, as I had given mine, without experiencing afterwards the pang of remorse and the chill of reaction" (IV, 48). But Jane's class posture after she learns of her inheritance is new. To what extent is this posture another performance and how marked is it by Brontë's text?

These questions link up with vexed questions about the final, troublesome three paragraphs of the novel that serve as a kind of epitaph for St. John Rivers. Given the text's critique of Rivers's effort to seduce Jane into marriage by appealing to her masochism and also its dramatization of Rivers's will to power, how can her narrative of his heroic self-sacrifice in India be consistent? I think Jane distances herself considerably from Rivers; I hear a firm note of irony, despite her genuine admiration of him, when she says, "his [was] the ambition of the high master-spirit, which aims to fill a place in the first rank of those who are redeemed from the earth—who stand without fault before the throne of God . . ." (XXXVIII, 440). Without fault indeed. And is Paradise a race, with winners and losers? What happened to the notion that the first shall be last?

But Jane is not sarcastic about Rivers's efforts in India: "[H]e hews down like a giant the prejudices of creed and caste . . ." (XXXVIII, 440). Jane is now a citizen of the empire and assumes its vocabulary, allied to her Christian idealism, in a complex new self-annunciation. This narrative voice, in other words, continues to take on a posture, so to speak, whose notions about power are not defamiliarized. We see Jane don these masks, and perhaps we see her forget the donning and so naturalize the new costume, or maybe we see Brontë's text move to naturalize it. The uncertainty occurs because the masks of gender and the monstrous, especially the mask of Bertha, get more attention in *Jane Eyre* than masks of class and national privilege. This uncertainty only emphasizes that Jane's journey to maturity has brought neither full self-understanding of her postures and choices of vocabulary nor a clear grasp of exactly what masquerade is and what the embodied consciousnesses are that precede it. I say "are" because masquerade cannot be a solitary performance; it is always an embodiment for, against, between, or among bodies and consciousnesses.

The phenomenology of masquerade in *Jane Eyre* opens up a labyrinth of subjectivities, especially in their multiple relations to gender and the monstrous. I asked at the beginning of this discussion what intentionalities and negotiations of power drive these mimicries, but I asked the question about a female imposter, so to speak. *Jane Eyre* asks these questions about male imposters, too: Rochester and Rivers as well as Jane, Bertha, and Grace Poole are at different moments eager or conflicted collaborators, saboteurs, masochists, or subtle ironists, playing with "witty and sudden Maskaradoes," though as I have emphasized women and men do not have equal stakes or resources in the game.

What the masquerade adds to the phenomenology of narrative in this book is the *explicit* play with disguise, in all the forms that we have discussed, that echoes down through deeper issues of selfhood, self-knowledge, and community. Chiasmus is initially a rhetorical device, and it functions as an image in different ways for different critics. For Joseph Litvak it is a metaphor for a "rhetorical schematization of exchange" (72) in which, to give one example, "marginalized groups" acquire "disruptive eloquence," and in contrast the "economically powerful, trading eloquence for elegance, surrender their linguistic hegemony and assume a corrupt idiom that is itself 'merely' conventional" (56).

In Merleau-Ponty, however, chiasmus becomes almost a visual image for the overlapping and reversal of bodies and consciousnesses, to capture the Mobius strip of an intersubjective interworld. Perhaps no other moment in the nineteenth-century novel explores better than Rochester's sibylline performance for Jane how deep intersubjectivity tells stories of violence and betrayal amid slippery negotiations between different kinds of power, and also tells stories of mutual appropriations between contesting yet possibly espousing subjects. This scene gives us Brontë at her most profound, in that uncanny moment when Rochester as prophetess speaks for and against Jane's body (the forehead), "So far I have governed myself thoroughly," and in midstream he loses the thread of his performance. In this moment of loss lies the (intersubjectively driven) terror and hope of masquerade.

HITCHCOCK'S *MARNIE*, THE MATERNAL GAZE, AND MASQUERADE

> *Mother, Mother, I am ill*
> *Send for the doctor over the hill*
> *Call for the doctor, call for the nurse*
> *Call for the lady with the alligator purse*
> —CHILDREN PLAYING IN THE STREET, Marnie

Terror and hope: These are the final notes in our discussion of Brontë's *Jane Eyre*. However serious the dangers of betrayal and violence in that novel and however unselfaware Jane is finally of her postures as heiress and white upper-class Englishwoman, and however muted the novel's resolution is by its setting in the hidden, safe retreat of Ferndean, the struggle through the masquerades of gender and identity is reasonably hopeful for most readers of *Jane Eyre*. Alfred Hitchcock's important late film *Marnie* (1964) addresses many of these issues with more terror and less hope, in a different example of the phenomenology of masquerade.

Masquerade in Hitchcock is a triumph in the deployment of deep intersubjectivity in narrative because it maps so intricately the network of gestures between subjects and their efforts to embody or to deflect another's interpretative gestures. Masquerade can promote intimacy, as in *To Catch a Thief* (or *Twelfth Night*), but it more often separates in Hitchcock's films, whether in a series of defensive or aggressive moves, and often a character becomes confused about which identity to perform to which audience and with what degree of display to defamiliarize the mask for that audience. Hitchcock's use of masquerade in *Marnie* emphasizes what is so powerfully at stake in some modernist narratives of complex intersubjectivity: the desire for a mutually enunciating performance of subjectivities that can protect and heal. The yearning for such healing is deep in *Marnie,* but so is the film's fear that these performances might be only a fantasy, partly because constituting the subject is so problematic for modernism.[8] For the comic Hitchcock, which chapter 3 explores, the dance of the *komos* surrounds very similar elements of despair: Nothingness, after all, lurks at the center of the self (Thornhill's "ROT"), too, in *North by Northwest.* But the komos exorcises or at least limits the damages of despair, and Thornhill can doff his dark glasses and change his act. The sorrow that almost dominates *Notorious* returns in Hitchcock's late films, especially in the trilogy of despair, *Vertigo, Psycho,* and *The Birds,* although Hitchcock looked unblinkingly at these elements of sadness—the exposed or empty self, the artificiality of social performance, the tangle of sexuality and anger—in films as early as *The Lodger* and *Blackmail.* The profoundly tragic studies of masked performances in Hitchcock are probably *Shadow of a Doubt, Vertigo,* and *Marnie.* As the last in the series, *Marnie* combines the interests of its predecessors in the effects of masquerade on the web of family life and on the drama of sexual desire.

Defamiliarized and denied, flaunted and forgotten, metatext and buried text, resistant and complicit and violating, *Marnie*'s masquerades embody complex confessions and deceptions that function in the film's network of gestures among angry, wounded, violent, and compassionate consciousnesses. The dilemmas of sexual desire are partly what this network articulates and mystifies, but I argue that the wound that most importantly motivates Marnie's masquerades is a loss of the maternal gaze and touch. Bernice's body is the shadow behind Marnie's performances. To the degree that the film reveals Bernice and her story (not really the one about the sailor, but the one about Billy) as the hidden energies in Marnie's story, it is an example of our fourth kind of masquerade narrative, the one that believes there is agency behind the mask, that it can be known, by someone anyway (whether or not the masker herself), and that this recognition usually leads to some change in behavior since some masks and some performances are better than others. But this revelation narrative, linked to what Robin Wood calls the "therapeutic" theme in Hitchcock, is problematized in many ways by *Marnie,* so that its experience of suffering and loss becomes even sadder (1989, 71).

Marnie's masquerades, as both buried text and metatext, reveal desire as a labyrinth that is deeply and blindingly intersubjective. To begin understanding this enigmatic subject, it is important to see that Marnie has two kinds of masquerades, two kinds of performances.

Laura Mulvey observes in her classic essay on the gaze that "Marnie, too, performs for Mark Rutland's gaze and masquerades as the perfect to-be-looked-at image" (24). But Marnie is the "perfect to-be-looked-at image" for two different audiences, in two different masquerades—those she scripts and those Mark scripts—and the issues of power and desire are significantly different in each. Marnie's performances of her own scripts entice the male gaze only to manipulate and finally baffle it. Mark Rutland remembers Marnie, at the beginning of the film, as "Oh, the brunette with the legs"; however, Marnie's *dis*interest, once trapped by Mark, in faking the sexual feelings that he manifestly wishes to see in her is one of her most attractive qualities. It illustrates the depth of a kind of integrity and resistance in her. She *has* displayed the legs, calling attention to them while performing modesty, demurely pulling down her dress. If Marnie's intent, however, was to play the "perfect to-be-looked-at image," that intent was not to be observed as a surface that gestured back a reciprocating consciousness; that is, the image was not designed to enter, or even to pretend to enter, a network of gazes and gestures exchanged and reexchanged from the depth of her or others' intention. It was not supposed to initiate a conventional narrative of desire. These appearances—Marian Holland, Mary Taylor—were designed precisely to block the intersubjective gaze and the narrative it engenders. That's why Marnie is genuinely mystified by Mark's pursuit of her and why, in the "You're dying to play doctor" scene, she asks Mark, "Why can't you leave me alone?" She doesn't attend to the rules of the game that has followed from her masquerade as Mary Taylor, young widow in the modest but well-cut suit.

Marnie's masquerade—that is, the one she devises—is not about desire conceived in the way that Irigaray or Jean Harrington in Preston Sturges's *The Lady Eve* conceive it, as a desire to be desired (sexually that is, by one whose desire she would seek to embody). Marnie's performance enacts the blockage or deflection of desire, and I explore later how this deflection mourns for Bernice, the damaged mother. The strategic indirection of Marnie's disguise is reflected in Marnie's performance as a respectable businesswoman, which has two distinct audiences: Mark Rutland, Strutt, and a class of men who like to look; and her mother, Bernice Edgar. For both of them, Marnie's performance as smooth professional woman is initially about class and about "decency," as both Marnie and her mother call it. Marian Holland, Mary Taylor, Margaret Edgar, and the other names on the Social Security cards behind the mirror in Marnie's compact are above all respectable. Their narratives, like that of Mary Taylor to her new employers, distance Marnie from the port of Baltimore, sailors, and sex (for hire or for free). They distance her as well from even her mother's later world (after the murder) of Baptist hymns.

Yet "Mrs. Taylor" as a class masquerade has a contradictory strain: It offers enough hints at a covert sexuality (willingness to work late hours, a discreet underscoring of the commodity of her attractiveness, in perfect makeup and stylized body movements, for example) to blind prospective employers, among whom Marnie seems to be most successful with susceptible men. At one level Marnie's masquerade of decency is contradicted by its criminal intent, but it masks (or reveals) a deeper contradiction—between its intent to violate (with overtones of revenge) and what Mark claims is its plea for love. To echo our discussion at the beginning of this chapter, Marnie's masquerade begins as a disguise, a masquerade-as-signified, which its audience is to take as the "real" thing; yet it also functions to remedy wounds that Marnie does not understand or has forgotten. That is, Marnie needs the mask to be the real, the natural Marnie. In Hitchcock's world these desires are contradictory: The subject cannot simply rewrite itself. This impossibility defamiliarizes the masquerade-as-signified so that it surfaces, in a kind of revelation, as only a signifier. It could then be inserted into a healthier, more functional, narrative, but given the politics of patriarchy in *Marnie*, what would that narrative be? The film endorses no answer to that question (it certainly does not endorse Mark's).

Marnie's performance fails to sustain "decency" and fails to deflect Mark's desire because of these contradictions between its anger and neediness and between its surface and a covert sexualization. The cost of these contradictions appears throughout the first half of the film, as in the opening sequence, when Marian Holland walks down the train platform: The cost is the brittleness of Marnie's body. She moves awkwardly on her high heels as if teetering precariously on an edge. Her body, or at least its clothed surface, is a costume that she manipulates jerkily with levers and pulleys from some safe place inside. (Here, as in *The Birds*, Hitchcock uses Tippi Hedren's awkward inexperience—she was a model, with no acting training—brilliantly.[9]) This same brittleness or flatness occurs when Mary Taylor looks at Mark or Susie or the office manager, Mr. Ward; she receives but does not respond to or reinflect their gestures. She embodies no intention to embody; she will not espouse the other, and so every gesture is masked. The cost is a kind of hemorrhaging inside Marnie.

The secret of Marnie's masquerade and the explanation for its design and cost is Bernice. She is its motive and audience: Marnie's brittle, tensed body is an angry, resisting embodiment for and about her mother. The ache behind Marnie's blank stare is the pain and violation that Mrs. Edgar embodies and that have a power to attract and repel Marnie. Hitchcock's film does work in a manner similar to Madelon Sprengnether's *The Spectral Mother: Freud, Feminism, and Psychoanalysis* as it seeks to recover the absent maternal. Sprengnether observes that Derrida's approach to Lacan's view of the mother-infant has the disadvantage "that it erases the body of the mother," and Sprengnether wants to recover that maternal body (9). For her, consciousness is profoundly embodied and "may be understood as an elegiac construct, the product of an internalized loss, . . . always implicitly the loss of a mother." This loss, which is profoundly carnal, cannot be repaired: "[T]he mother's body becomes that which is longed for yet cannot be appropriated, a representative of home and not home, and hence, in Freud's terms, the site of the uncanny" (ibid.). Sprengnether's tangle of loss and yearning and of mourning the spectral mother while fearing her is exactly the tangle of Hitchcock's film. In one of *Marnie's* deepest ironies, Mark Rutland believes that he (and male sexuality) are the motive behind Marnie's masquerade and that it is, as Rivière theorizes, a type of defense. But Mark and men are only passing figures in the drama (and therefore this masquerade is indeed "resistant" in Mary Anne Doane's sense, that is, resistant to the dominant gender system).

The drama's key players are Marnie and her mother. Ann Kaplan has a sense of this core, even though she sees *Marnie* too narrowly as reductively patriarchal, seeking to tame the excesses of women's love and the blurring of boundaries that Marnie and her mother threaten. Kaplan admits, however, that Bernice is not simply the demon mother of the Hitchcock stereotype (Mrs. Sebastian in *Notorious;* Mrs. Bates in *Psycho*). "She occupies some other terrain—more mysterious, more ambiguous and contradictory," so that the film's pity for Bernice "leaves us confused as to how we are to position her" (136). If Marnie's masquerade incorporates a loss or emptiness, to borrow the language of both Judith Butler and Madelon Sprengnether, that lack is the mother, not the phallus or any Rutland. Marnie's final reunion with Bernice, however fleeting, emphasizes this double function of masquerade: to confess to and compensate for emptiness. Hitchcock's deeply intersubjective narrative traces the chiasmus of these revealings and concealings with a careful attention to the ironies of what Mark believes to be Marnie's "cure."

However, before looking at Marnie's reunion with her mother, we need to examine the significance of Mark's function (which in most ways is different from what he thinks it is) and to reflect on Marnie's second masquerade. The key to understanding that masquerade, as Mark's fiancée and then wife, is to recognize that it is not Marnie's script but Mark's, written for her to perform as payoff for Mark's blackmail. This script tells Mark's story about who Marnie should be and embodies his desire for her to desire him. The depth of Marnie's resistance is testimony to both her illness/"illness" and to her courage. I use illness in both forms (that is, also without scare quotes) to avoid a sentimentalizing of Marnie's pain and brittleness; her suffering is more than ideological resistance, and she is more than a victim of patriarchy. Nevertheless, a fundamental mystery in Marnie's masquerade as Mrs. Rutland is Mark, for in a sense the script he writes for her is *his* masquerade, and there is a remarkable parallel between Rochester's disguises (especially as sybil) and Mark's: Both externalize gender contradictions; both fail to sustain the mask at key points; and both adopt, in a deeply intersubjective move, gestures of their lovers' consciousness, embodying versions of Jane and Marnie for them to reembody, but in quite different (I think) uses of power. A measure of the difference among readings of *Jane Eyre* might be the greater resemblance some would see between Mark and Rochester.

Mark Rutland's double role in *Marnie* as predator and lover or even caretaker is one of the film's richest achievements, especially because Mark is finally an outsider in Marnie's drama. The contrary currents in Mark's characterization have been traced by previous critics: Mark as collector, trainer of wild animals, and sexual adventurer who is aroused by Marnie's secret life as a thief; or Mark as patient husband, offering Marnie books to learn about herself and helping her to understand her past in order to exorcise its effect now, so that she can love without paralyzing panic. Readers of the film have wanted to choose one or the other, Mark as savior or Mark as exploiter. For Robin Wood, Mark "represents a new stage in the development of Hitchcock's heroes: not only is he unusually free of inner compulsions . . . , he sees clearly and accepts the fact of the inextricability of good and evil—. . . that we have seen as one of the essential components of Hitchcock's moral sense" (182). But for Michele Piso, Mark is, despite a thread of genuine compassion, finally an agent of power who believes "he can possess Marnie too, violate her, break her down, and then build her back up . . . in much the same way that he rebuilt the Rutland business" (298). The question left for Piso is the degree to which the film endorses Mark's violation of Marnie as part of her "cure" or frames it as a symptom of the disease of class and privilege.

Hitchcock's script and camera emphasize Mark's doubleness in several ways. Twice Marnie, returning to the moment of childhood trauma, mistakes Mark for the sailor whom she killed, so that as Mark approaches her, she recoils in fear. The second time this happens, on the stairs in her mother's home, Mark asks Marnie, "Who am I?" The question echoes through the film, as does Marnie's earlier, unanswered question, "Why won't you leave me alone?" Like the sailor, Mark would divide Marnie from her mother and come between them in the maternal bed, though to have sex with Marnie, not her mother. The motive for Mark's persistence, however, is never clear: Sexual desire, even for a thief, seems inadequate, for example, to explain his patience in postponing consummation; similarly, the sailor's motive in the primal drama is not clear. At the moment Bernice reenters her living room during the thunderstorm, is the sailor trying to comfort Marnie or to molest her? Robin Wood believes the former, that the sailor "is gentle and kind" and that Bernice attacks him because she is "a hysterical, neurotic woman, a prostitute so filled with disgust at her work that she frantically beats with both hands the sailor who is trying to soothe and comfort her little girl" (1989, 177). But the sailor's gestures are ambiguous in intent, especially when he leans over Marnie's neck: Is he trying to speak to her or to kiss her in a sexualizing way? What consciousness does the body embody in the sailor or in Mark in these ambiguous moments, and how do we read the reading of traumatized children in recoil? What is significant here is not the promise of recovering a buried story of childhood abuse (less a cliché in 1964 than now), but the difficulty of disentangling the interknitting of violence and love in these sexualized bodies of mother, daughter, and client and, years later, in the rhyming body of the savior/husband.

Hitchcock's camera articulates the same double vision of Mark as predator and protector by its framing of his body and its sexualizing intentions in the film's violation scene on the honeymoon cruise. In some frames Mark is the embodiment of menace, especially in the high-contrast close-up of his eyes, one half of his face a mask of darkness, closing in on Marnie (this would seem to be a point-of-view shot, if Marnie's gaze were not so catatonic). In other frames Mark softens, especially when he covers Marnie's body with his robe in repentance for his exposure of her. In the stylized images that record his effort then to rouse her, asking her to play her part in the masquerade he has written for them, their juxtaposed bodies cannot read each other. Marnie's brittleness becomes even more rigid unclothed, as she retreats from her surface into some inner safe haven, leaving her body behind to be manipulated like a doll's. Hitchcock's camera frames the couple from above and below to trace Mark's caresses over the surface of the absolutely still mannequin. Marnie's paralysis *is* her reading of Mark's reading of her, her gesture in a network of deeply intersubjective embodiments between them. It is a consequence of Mark's ambivalent character that we cannot be sure about the subsequent violation (whatever it is exactly that occurs behind the camera, when Marnie is lowered in her stiffness to the bed); is it to his mind, however misguidedly, a part of the "cure," or an act of rage, or some combination of both? Hitchcock knows that the intersubjectivity of the masquerade makes the interknottings of embodiments even more multiple in function.

In the masquerade Mark designs for Marnie, the intersubjective gaze for which Merleau-Ponty had such high hopes fails, and this failure is one of the saddest strands in the film. Her rebellion against Mark's script underscores the politics of the masquerade for Marnie. In the shipboard bedroom scene, Marnie's eyes never move, never blink, never engage with Mark or his world (see figure 9). One effect of the stunning frame that places Marnie's head against the room's porthole (within its circle) is to emphasize the rhyme between Marnie's dead eye and the porthole, open to the sea and the moonlight, but equally still and unresponding. No interknitting of consciousnesses or their gestures will occur in this dead space, where only Mark's desire can move.

The same failure occurs elsewhere in the film. In the free-association scene (also in a bedroom), Marnie defends herself valiantly against Mark's invasive, controlling compassion. Even in her pain and vulnerability, she suspects that Mark is not the healing agent she needs, or that he thinks he is. When she loses the free-association game, as her rage ("women are feeble and stupid and men are filthy pigs") and fear ("death"/"me") overpower her, she crumbles into Mark's arms, with the cry, "O God, help me, help me, somebody help me." Marnie has still evaded Mark here, with some vestige of an instinct for self-preservation. Her gaze is focused far away from Mark and the Rutland mansion, and her cry for "*some*body" to help her is another form of escape or rejection, given Mark's repeated insistence that *he* is her white knight. Marnie's body never gestures back to Mark's, incorporating its sexuality in hers; her eyes never move into his, they only receive his look. The one instance when she almost reciprocates occurs when she looks at Mark on the driveway at the Rutland estate, when he brings Forio to her. Nevertheless, every move by Mark that solicits espousal and every effort to model a gesture for Marnie to embody and return from within her intentionality is stymied because his notion of espousal is com-

DEEP INTERSUBJECTIVITY AND MASQUERADE | 227

FIG. 9 *Marnie*. Universal Pictures 1964.
DVD © Universal Studios 2000.

promised by assumptions of class and privilege and because Marnie's sexual energy is circulating in another story that has little connection to his narrative. Marnie's rigid child-body never softens for Mark, and her child's gaze never sexualizes Mark's.[10]

The passion that drives Marnie's labyrinthine and sometimes desperate masquerades is not Jean Harrington's, who, early in Preston Sturges's *The Lady Eve*, articulates this more common motivation for sexual masquerade: to perform the subjectivity that a lover wants to love. Does Jean participate in Charley's desire at the cost of renouncing her own, as Luce Irigaray's paradigm, cited at the beginning of this chapter, suggests? Is it possible that Jean espouses her desire *and* Charley's desire in her masquerade? Or maybe she just believes she can. Jean, the shipboard gambler and witty con artist converted by love, seems to believe she can be "the way" Charley, wealthy and naive heir to the Pike beer fortune, wants her to be, as if being is only a way, a style. Her fractured, defensive syntax gives her doubts away: "I'd give a lot to be—well, I mean, I—I'm *going* to be exactly the way he thinks I am, the way he'd like me to be." Jean nonetheless describes with uncanny precision the network of perceived perceptions in the midst of which her disguise functions. Charley Pike has constructed a view of the way Jean is, which is the way he'd like the "real" Jean to be; she grasps his construction and expects to will to become this character, as

Mark expects Marnie to will to become "Mrs. Rutland" and his lover. The mask for Jean is so to speak a mask of the soul, of an inner life that will be embodied somehow—by means of the mask—for Charley.

Seeing Charley see her in this performance promises a powerful fulfillment for Jean, and for us the question is to what degree her pleasure functions by means of a displacement, a sort of making love in a series of mirrors, or an espousal through the disguise. Her mask, however, like those of others, is imperfect; it doesn't cover everything. And when it slips, Charley, as Joan Rivière predicted, fears even more deeply whatever the mask may have hidden. Jean's desire, to perform the subjectivity her lover desires, is also Judy's desire in *Vertigo*. Judy consents to be Madeleine for Scottie when she despairs of attracting his love as only Judy. But Judy hopes that her Madeleine, like Jean's other masquerade as Lady Eve, will not only be, in Irigaray's words, "an alienated version of femininity arising from the woman's awareness of the man's desire for her to be his other" but will also *reveal* Judy and will bring Scottie back to her (220). This argument presumes, in contrast to much *Vertigo* criticism, that *Judy* is the body and spirit that gets reshaped by the mask of Madeleine, that is, that Madeleine is a version of Judy, not merely a mask devised by Gavin Elster that his mistress wears. In the logic of this reasoning, Scottie has fallen in love with Judy from Salinas but is *also* drawn to the safely distant and safely mysterious Madeleine, partly as an evasion of the embodied and immediately present Judy. In comedy, masquerade can function to liberate; the mask is a device of the fluid self, as chapter 3 illustrates in *To Catch a Thief,* for example; there masquerade is not a strategic move in the endgames of gender. But *Vertigo* is not a comedy, and in pursuit of her desire Judy gives away Judy.

Marnie is not a comedy either, but Marnie will not give Marnie away to save herself, however contradictory and self-sabotaging she might otherwise be. The masquerade Mark writes for Marnie and blackmails her into performing appears therefore to be hollow and mechanical. Marnie's desperate resistance to Mark's strategies testifies not only to the depth of her pain and her sense of being trapped in a cul-de-sac but also to her courage. The masquerade that Marnie *has* incorporated into her body's gestures, even while defying it, is her mother's. The climax of the film is about the relation between the disguises and bodies of mother and daughter. This time, looking—and looking at looking—achieves that reciprocity, however limited its reexchange, that Merleau-Ponty hoped for in the chiasmus of the intersubjective gaze.

Marnie's own masquerades conceal and reveal her drive toward and repulsion from Bernice's gaze. These masquerades perform "decency," the refusal to be sexually active, at least in a technical sense, in as thorough a sense of her word "decent" as Bernice could wish for, but this performance is an act of both respectful and furiously self-punishing obedience. Marnie seeks to write the script of the good daughter as Bernice conceives good but will also demonstrate to her mother how limited and painful this version of the good is. As Marnie says at the end of the film, "Oh, Momma, you surely have realized your ambition. I'm decent all right; of course I'm a cheat and a liar and a thief; but I am decent."

Marnie's masquerade is also a defiance of men's power to look and penetrate surfaces, yet she needs Mark's desire for her (whatever its components) to help her return to the mother. Although the masquerades are furthermore an erasure of Baltimore and the port and men's touches and her mother's working-class milieu, they still carry the mark of the world they seek to erase. (These traces of class origins are especially clear in the mise-en-scène of Hitchcock's shots on the night of the free-association game, when the camera includes Marnie and Lil in the same frame: Marnie's polish is manifestly an effort, a surface; Lil moves *with* her clothes, her robe, where Marnie moves parallel to but at a distance from hers, as if she is a half second behind them, the same way she moves parallel to Rutland luxury in general, next to it but not part of it.) The brittle body of the disguised Marian/Mary/Peggy is Bernice's body—not the earlier sexually caressed body, but the damaged one, moving stiffly on its cane/suitcases/stilts of high heels. It is the body of the daughter who fears and yearns for the mother's touch, the body of the daughter who has appropriated and rejected the mother's gestures that have (she feels) formed and rejected her. This knot of blockages and adoptions is one of the most subtle examples of the circle of the touched touching and of deep intersubjectivity in this book and perhaps the most sorrowful one.

Marnie's recovery, with Bernice, of a story they can tell together is the film's climactic study of the gaps and linkages performed by masquerade. Hitchcock's scenario externalizes the intersubjective gaze in this recovery sequence in one direct way, when Marnie sees the past in its fullness as her mother does. In recovering the sights of the night of the sailor's death, Marnie and Bernice can stand before that landscape, to borrow Merleau-Ponty's image from chapter 1, and gesture to each other and see that the other sees and, further, that the other espouses her gestures of seeing and embodying what the other has already seen. This recovered-memory sequence is a rare example in film where the illogical effect of a film's point-of-view camera in a flashback scene works—all of us see the past; we—Mark and Bernice and the film's viewers—see what Marnie is seeing, forgetting that technically she is only telling us what she sees. This illogical effect works thematically because it is in formal terms exactly the moment of the intersubjective gaze.[11] Hitchcock's most poignant frame to articulate this movement between mother and daughter is the moment, after Marnie's immersion in her memories on the staircase, in which Marnie and her mother face each other, heads and eyes absolutely level, seeing for the first time the act of the other seeing her seeing—and acknowledging being seen.

Marnie is rewarded in this sequence with more than the memory of killing the sailor. She hears the story of her birth and her mother's first violation: *This* story is the heart of her matter, not the sailor story. This story, told without the visual pyrotechnics of the earlier memory tale, takes Marnie into her mother's life, behind the dark mask (most brilliantly imaged early in the film during Marnie's first visit home, when Bernice, shadowed as to be faceless, slowly descends the staircase, after Marnie's nightmare). Bernice's face is now fully lit, and her story needs no visual reannunciation: Her face embodies her teenage innocence. Billy's betrayal is the wound that Bernice wants to make sure Marnie does not experience, so that the daughter's body will be different from her mother's, intact and looking forward to a different narrative.

Of course Marnie's body does reembody Bernice's wounds, as we have discussed, in her stilted walk and the link in the free-association game to lameness, and to the end Hitchcock never sentimentalizes these wounds or hints at a healing that has not, and perhaps cannot, occur. To participate with Bernice in her tale of betrayal and reward is Marnie's closest approach to healing and recovery of the lost intimacy of her childhood. For Bernice, two treasures bought with her innocence remain. The first is something to wear, something that will mark her as another person and that, for the naive high school girl, is a transfiguring costume: "I still got that basketball sweater" (Billy the high-school star traded it for her fifteen-year-old's virginity). The second treasure is also transfiguring but, in comparison to the first, in a deeper way (and Hitchcock's film does make these judgments): "And I got you, Marnie." When Bernice finishes, "You're the only thing I ever did love," Marnie's reply tells us how close, and distant, her recovery of that intimacy is: "You must have loved me, Mama." Marnie can acknowledge her mother's narrative of love without feeling or remembering the feeling of being loved. She knows the mask is down, but cannot remember or feel what preceded it.

Masquerades reveal and conceal incompletely, and the web of consciousnesses shapes various and contradictory forms of espousal,

FIG. 10 *Marnie*. Universal Pictures 1964.
DVD © Universal Studios 2000.

shame, aggression, evasion, or bad faith. The relationship between Marnie and Bernice is a remarkable example of such a web. Bernice for example also yearns to touch Marnie, as Hitchcock shows in his close-up of her hand tentatively reaching out to caress Marnie's hair. Yet Bernice cannot let Marnie rest on her body and asks her to move away ("Get up, Marnie, you're aching my leg"). The ache is real in several ways and sharp enough that Bernice cannot find another way to touch Marnie. For her, their bodies cannot embody each other; the experience of loss and shame is too deep. Yet the pleasure they feel in telling the same story now is manifest; they both weep in one common response at enfolding the tale, if not at enfolding each other.

Hitchcock's final shots of Bernice in the film isolate her in the frame; sitting, seeing into her past, she does not look at the departing Marnie. When she says, "Goodbye, sugar-pop," it's not quite clear which Marnie she's bidding farewell to. In its mix of two-shots and close-ups, of touching and aching, of embodiments and loneliness, this sequence of Marnie's return to her mother traces the interlocking of evasions and embodiments in the web of two deeply wounded consciousnesses reading each other and reading their readings in that narrative of perceiving perceptions that I call deep intersubjectivity. I can think of few examples of intersubjective narrative about which both Sartre and Merleau-Ponty could both be so accurate in tracing the phenomenology of shame and espousal.

Uncertainty afflicts Mark and Marnie's final sequence as well, especially because for Mark Marnie is still playing her part in the masquerade he has written for her. On the steps of Bernice's house, they stand on opposite sides of the frame, without touching (see figure 10). Marnie's final two clauses collide, but not in her ears; she speaks with a childlike dependency, without sarcasm: "I don't want to go to jail, Mark; I'd rather stay with you." Mark's smile and his last line in the film, a question, "Had you, dear?" seem to recognize how wan the logic is that renders him preferable to prison. Or perhaps it is the smile of triumph at caging the wildcat at last. Whatever Mark's degree of compassion for Marnie as hurt child rather than as "the criminal female" and however indebted Marnie is to Mark for restoring her mother's story to her, there is a sense in which at this moment the cell door clicks shut. In all its outrageousness, Bernice's earlier cry, "She's lucky, she's plain lucky" not to experience sexual pleasure, speaks some sad truth about Marnie. As Mark puts his arm around Marnie's shoulder, neither body moves in or for the other. They cannot espouse each other, in this film, while playing roles in Mark's masquerade.[12]

These complications in *Marnie* echo those of Hitchcock's two other profound studies of masquerade and identity, *Shadow of a Doubt* and *Vertigo*. Charlie in *Shadow of a Doubt* is not sure exactly who she is once that foundational model for her identity, Uncle Charlie, is unmasked. The pieties of both Jack Graham (her faithful detective lover) and the minister's eulogy, which like the children's rhyme in *Marnie* completes the film from an off-screen space, are ineffectual reassurances. Hitchcock's final shot of Charlie, troubled face outlined against the church's white walls, echoes his final shot of Scottie in *Vertigo*, who also has not found peace in the "truth" about the beloved imposter. Scottie, like young Charlie, desires in part not to be enlightened so that he can live in the world of the masquerade, but a masquerade that is naturalized, where no mask can slip and terrify. The real inversion of the komos is the link of sexual energy to death in these films. The lover Scottie thinks he wants keeps dying, perhaps because in ways he cannot understand he wants her to die; the only erotically potent male for Charlie is a man who is not only a family member but also despises the feminine, so that her safe alternative for love in the limited world of Santa Rosa is a romantic link to Jack, dull, unimaginative, and nonerotic.[13] For Marnie, too, there is no way to be sexual that is not damaging or even deadly. Marnie's experience of the masquerade seems more constructive than Scottie's and Charlie's because reapproaching the mother was more feasible than bringing into the light either Scottie's fantasy lover or Uncle Charlie, the dark twin, the subject of the family romance that Charlie and her mother Emma weave. If *Marnie* is more hopeful than *Shadow of a Doubt* or *Vertigo,* that hope lies in Marnie's return to Bernice that Mark promises. But *Marnie* may also be less hopeful, also because of Mark's promise. Charlie and Scottie are freed of their illusion, however shattering that freedom, but Marnie is still dependent on Mark's power to grant and deny.

Masquerades in all three films are a network of gestures, gazes, and embodiments by means of which subjectivities read each other's readings of each other, or misread them, in an experience of the power circulated in gender and family systems. In Hitchcock's study of this circulation, the strategies of deep intersubjectivity track the operation of power in narratives of shame and embodiment. *Marnie*'s poignance lies in its study of the suffering that we see incarnated in both Marnie's brittle body and Bernice's and that make visible their narratives of loss. In this film Hitchcock's web of complex intersubjectivities recalls in its multiple threads Irigaray's account of knottedness, of the chiasmus, in Merleau-Ponty: "Energy plays itself out in the backward-and-forward motion of a loom. But weaving the visible and my look in this way, I could just as well say that I close them off from myself. The texture becomes increasingly tight, taking me into it, sheltering me there but imprisoning me as well" (*Ethics* 183). The web, like the mask, shelters and imprisons. Its comforts exact a price, like that wall of Merleau-Ponty's that connects and separates.

Hitchcock's importance as a storyteller lies partly in his ability to give us this double movement of complex intersubjectivity (which is both the form and subject of his narrative) in both a comic edition and a more sorrowful edition. The contrast between Hitchcock's Grant films in chapter 3 and *Marnie* rehearses the quarrel between Sartre and Merleau-Ponty: Is the promise of deep intersubjectivity more typically shame or espousal? Indeed, is its promise a promise, threat, or some intricate reciprocal rethreading—a chiasmus—of both?

Epilogue

CONCLUDING THEORETICAL REFLECTIONS

We live in a general Disguise, and like the Masquerades, every Man dresses himself up in a particular Habit.
—DANIEL DEFOE

The body contains the life story just as much as the brain.
—EDNA O'BRIEN

It is, nonetheless, with an assertion of the look's potentially transformative powers that I end this book. The eye can confer the active gift of love upon bodies which have long been accustomed to neglect and disdain.
—KAJA SILVERMAN, The Threshold of the Visible World

These heavy epigraphs for a brief epilogue underscore some of the key motifs in this book. Defoe reminds us that we began and ended with masquerades, Moll's and Marnie's: There's a deep gender politics at work here, as well perhaps as a Pygmalion flaw in this male writer who frames his study with figures of women. O'Brien offers another way to see how the body of consciousness and consciousness in the body undergird all intersubjectivity. Many readers must hope that Kaja Silverman is right, that our seeing doesn't always turn other selves to stone but can confer "the gift of love," although Silverman says elsewhere in her book that "none of us is released from the imperative of looking ethically by the fundamental impossibility of that task" (5).

What is missing in all of these lines, and what has been so hard to see and conceptualize about in the structure of consciousness in narrative, is what I call deep intersubjectivity, that chiasmus, to borrow again Merleau-Ponty's word, of consciousness of consciousness felt, registered and rerepresented, of perception of perceptions perceived and interpreted and sometimes espoused, sometimes violated.

This book has argued for two ideas about deep intersubjectivity: first, that there is a change in the way stories narrate human consciousness, particularly in the way they narrate human consciousness*es*, that becomes visible in the time of Jane Austen; second, that there are better ways to read representations of human consciousnesses, regardless of whether they take the form of deep intersubjectivity. These better strategies of reading arise out of what I call a poststructuralist phenomenology. These two ideas are intertwined throughout this study because the change in narrative practices for which I argue would not be visible without the newly ground, or at least newly reground, lens of phenomenological reading. Indeed, the real project here is to open the door to a new phenomenology of narrative.

Let me say a word about what I have and have not attempted in this book in the effort to open that door. Phenomenological criticism has taken several paths in the past, some seriously discredited, as I discuss in chapter 1, and I have no interest in reviving the transcendental idealism of those critical practices. Instead I have sought to define and defend an approach to representations of consciousness, agency, and intentionality that avoids on one hand a kind of mystical idealism and on the other hand a reduction of subjectivity to material causes. The last step in that reduction was the erasure of the subject altogether, as if critics were playing, ironically, a kind of phenomenological trump card; in some paradigms, like the Lacanian (as commonly understood), the subject remains, but only as a series of fragments or even absences. These outcomes may now appear to be dead ends, at least to some readers, and so I find Kaja Silverman's 1996 book, *The Threshold of the Visible World,* poignant and profound as it works within its austere Lacanian framework, "with the greatest difficulty," to find legitimacy for, in Silverman's words, "the gift of love" (227). Silverman's hopes for what she calls the "productive look" seem to me an antidote to postmodern isolation and are a good example of deep intersubjectivity's comic predilection. However, even Defoe finds disguises everywhere, and I have struggled throughout this book to be fair to a phenomenology of deception, failure, and violation. Maybe the bias toward comedy is simply mine. In another direction lies a current of phenomenological thinking that leads to meditations on readers' experiences of reading and to reader-response theory. I have not worked closely with theories of readership here, and such an inquiry would be one important way to pursue the implications of deep intersubjectivity.

Finally, I have not addressed the topic of origins: If my argument seems reasonable, then why did deep intersubjectivity as a form of narrative emerge at the end of the eighteenth century, at least in narratives in English? This is a subject for another book and another critic. However, it is clear to me that this emergence must be overdetermined, and selecting the key strands from the tapestry of cultural history must be somewhat arbitrary, or at least personal. This claim is especially likely to be true because forms of consciousness, even if forms of consciousness*es*, are Mobius strips of the inner and the external, of human feelings and circumstances. If one must make choices, a place to start would be the sharpest and most economical outline I have seen of the array of forces that come together in the eighteenth-century novel, in Helene Moglen's introduction to *The Trauma of Gender: A Feminist Theory of the English Novel*. Moglen traces both sides of the Mobius strip, the power of new class, economic, and gender systems, along with the power of a "new structure of consciousness," individualism (4), and then she outlines how material circumstances and this new structure of consciousness each shaped the other. Material conditions must have some force, and I remember Ian Watt's claim years ago that the eighteenth-century novel's emphasis on private experience had one of its roots in the shift in domestic space from common living and sleeping areas to a new compartmentalizing in, for example, "separate sleeping quarters for every member of the family, and even for the household servants" (188).

Yet I am wary of trusting too much to such material causes as explanations. Cultural studies and contemporary neuroscience share the desire to link the world and the body to inner consciousness as its prime movers, but these linkages are fraught with gaps, as David Lodge explores in *Consciousness and the Novel*. Lodge, citing the neuroscientist Gerald Edelman, writes, " 'Consciousness is a first-person phenomenon,' which science, oriented to impersonal observation and the formulation of general laws, finds difficult to cope with" (29). Or, to put it another way (this is Lodge again): "Jane Austen's *Emma* could not have been written by anyone else, and never will be written by anyone else again; but an experiment demonstrating the second law of thermodynamics is and must be repeatable by any competent scientist" (11).

Accounts of material circumstances can describe changes in gender systems and economic privileges, but they cannot explain why *this* bankrupt merchant wrote *Moll Flanders* or why *that* genteelly impoverished clergyman's daughter wrote *Jane Eyre*. At the risk of promoting a Carlylean heroine worship, I suggest that one important force in the emergence of deep intersubjectivity was Jane Austen's profound mastery of narrative rhetoric, especially what narratologists call the free indirect style (the trick of narrating a character's interior consciousness as if grasped by another observer, as in this from *Emma:* "Her own conduct, as well as her own heart, was before her in the same few minutes She saw it all with a clearness which had never blessed her before. . . . What blindness, what madness, had led her on!" (370).[1]

So I have not done many things: I have not sought to resuscitate the old transcendental phenomenology or explored connections to reader-response theory or inquired into the origins of the shift in narrative practices at the end of the eighteenth century that I describe. What I have done, I believe, is to explain how a newly self-conscious and rigorous phenomenological reading might work, with examples of that reading that support my claim for a change in narrative practices between Defoe and Austen. My examples are a first effort to explore narrative practices under the lens of deep intersubjectivity. My choices make use of a couple of frameworks: first, a historical one, using eighteenth- and nineteenth-century British novels, and second, a framework of genre practices: comedy, anticomedy, and masquerade, with written and film narratives as examples. I have chosen these stories and these schema because, to be honest, I like them. At the same time I also think they are broadly representative of narrative practices, and I think others might like them, too.

A new phenomenology of narrative has many avenues to explore. There is the matter of origins, and there is the rhetoric of narrative, for example, which could call for a much deeper study either of deep intersubjectivity and the free indirect style or of the role of intersubjectivity in counterfactual narrative. I am interested in the way novel series construct an intersubjective world (say, in Trollope's Palliser novels). I am also intrigued by questions of film form and deep intersubjectivity: For example, how does suture work as a form of human consciousness(es)? Suture theory has largely been the province of Lacanian film criticism, which has yielded profound insights into the tragic domain in film experience, as in Silverman's exploration of the "castrating coherence" of the shot/reverse-shot paradigm (*Subject* 205). Still, this approach seems significantly limited precisely by its acceptance of images of absence as constituting subjectivity, and it might be useful to work out a theory of deeply intersubjective suture that avoids the mystical echoes of idealist phenomenology.

Much more remains to be done on the politics of intersubjectivity, too; I have given some attention to class, gender, and ethnic assumptions,

EPILOGUE

but not enough. Finally, there are questions with the largest reach, situating a phenomenology of narrative in the landscape not only of the rhetoric of narrative but also of narrative's epistemology and ontology, the kinds of questions raised by, for example, Garrett Stewart in *Between Film and Screen,* Stanley Cavell (among other works) in *The World Viewed,* and Frank Kermode in *The Sense of an Ending.*[2]

This study, then, is I hope a beginning.

CONCLUDING PERSONAL REFLECTIONS

> *Daddy, did you know that you can feel the earth spinning in your heart?*
> —KATE RATLIFF, *age 4, May 2002*

As a student of deep intersubjectivity in narrative, I believe we link our stories together with threads of words and gestures that others return to us for us to embody and to return these threads again to them, and yet again, in the weave of a tapestry. My project here has been to understand the representation of those threadings. I have also performed another task as rigorously as I could, before, during, and after composing my own writing: the task of framing my own framing of those signs in the narrative of my life that I am always writing. Do I believe in the belief or disbelief of *Broadway Danny Rose* or *His Girl Friday*? Why do I care so much about the subversions of self and agency, or at least of their conventional forms, in Lacanian film studies and cultural studies in the shadow of Foucault? I confess that I want to believe in the rituals of modern and even postmodern comedy; I want to believe in a self with some capacity for continuity and integrity. Those beliefs inevitably, perhaps even usefully, color this work.

Those beliefs, moreover, have a story, of course. I began this book years ago, when I was young. Its ripeness coincided with my late '40s and early '50s, particularly in a four-year period when my wife had seven miscarriages before our daughter was born. It felt like there was a deep and obscure (or maybe not so obscure) parallel between book and child, as if our lives were an unimaginative sequel to *Hedda Gabler.* My wife was stubborn beyond reason, or perhaps, as she would put it, since she is more metaphysical than I, it was our daughter who was stubborn, insisting beyond reason on getting herself born. Kate is here nonetheless, joyful, alert, and certainly stubborn, and I use her words for the last image of a link in our consciousness between world and body: "Daddy, did you know you can feel the earth spinning in your heart?" I can still hear Kate's voice piping up from the back seat of the car as we turned a corner, and I turn that moment into a story for you. And now I know that you know that I know this is a story, constructed and rehearsed and retold. Can we thus spin our narratives back and forth between us, webbing stories about stories and embodiment of embodiments for a more conscious, more deeply intersubjective life together (or not together, if we so choose)?

Sometimes the threads of these stories we tell and retell to each other bear up under enormous pressure, and sometimes the threads snap. What seems more remarkable to me now is not how often they snap, but how often they don't.

Notes

Notes to Chapter 1

1. Maurice Merleau-Ponty (1908–1961), contemporary and sometime friend of Sartre and Lacan, was a professor at the Sorbonne and later at the Collège de France. Among his important works are *Phenomenology of Perception* (1945; English tr. 1962); *Humanism and Terror* (1947; English tr. 1969); *Adventures of the Dialectic* (1955; English tr. 1973); *Signs* (1960; English tr. 1964); and the posthumous *The Visible and the Invisible* (1964; English tr. 1968). Paul Ricoeur called Merleau-Ponty "the greatest of the French phenomenologists" (Audi 484).

   Phenomenology itself, with its interest in the nature and structure of perception, has close links to existentialism and, like it, comes in various flavors and brands. Merleau-Ponty wrote as part of a conversation and quarrel with earlier and contemporary phenomenologists like Husserl, Heidegger, and Sartre of course. Links to later thinkers like Levinas and Derrida are also important. I include Derrida, although according to Evans and Lawlor, "Derrida has said repeatedly that he did not read Merleau-Ponty in order to avoid his influence" (19).

2. For accounts of this work, see Sarah Lawall, *Critics of Consciousness* (1968); J. Hillis Miller's essay, "The Geneva School"; Daniel Schwarz, *The Humanist Heritage;* and Frank Lentricchia, *After the New Criticism,* chapter 3, especially pp. 62–78.

3. I am indebted for my understanding of the Lacanian self to Lee's book *Jacques Lacan.*

4. Here is Lentricchia's account of that loss of credibility: "The effect of Jacques Derrida's attack on Husserl's theory of signs in *La voix et le phénomène* is to force us into a reappraisal of the whole phenomenological movement. After Derrida we cannot avoid asking whether there is such a thing as phenomenology: whether the attack, in the name of intentionality, on the dualistically isolated, self-sufficient, and enclosed substance of Descartes's subject is anything but the most self-deluded of anti-metaphysical moves in the history of philosophy which succeeds only, as Derrida shows in the case of Husserl, in reinstituting a Cartesian minimum under the guise of the 'phenomenological voice' " (79).

5. One example of this yearning occurs in Sobchack, who wants to see film itself as projecting a kind of subjectivity: "That is, in terms of its performance, it is as much a *viewing subject* as it is also a *visible* and *viewed object*. Thus, in its existential function, it shares a privileged equivalence with its human counterparts in the film experience.

This is certainly *not* to say that the film is a *human* subject. Rather, it is to consider the film a *viewing* subject . . ." (21–22).

These transcending agents of seeing, however, do *not*, for Sobchack, ever erase the boundaries between them: "[C]inematic vision in the film experience is articulated by *both* the film *and* the spectator simultaneously engaged in *two* quite distinctly located visual acts that meet on shared ground but never identically occupy it" (23).

Even Merleau-Ponty is not free of the occasional trace of transcendental idealism, as in this language that follows the earlier account of watching a landscape together: "[I]t is not *I* who sees, not *he* who sees, because an anonymous visibility inhabits both of us, a vision in general, in virtue of that primordial property that belongs to the flesh, being here and now, of radiating everywhere and forever, being an individual, of being also a dimension and a universal" (*Visible* 142).

Even here, however, Merleau-Ponty wants his "universal" and general vision to be a property of the flesh.

6. A letter from Husserl quoted by Donn Welton in *The Other Husserl* (67). Welton is one such scholar who argues that, for example, the Husserl that Derrida wrote from and against is a deeply partial Husserl (Derrida was writing in the 1950s, before the late unpublished manuscripts and notebooks became available). For Welton, Husserl's method "as a whole," "properly reconstructed," "dismantle[s] precisely those implicit metaphysical elements that, according to Derrida, would be its undoing" (396).

7. For more on this debate, see Stewart's *Between Film and Screen*, chapter 3 and pp. 123–32, for example, on Cavell and the phenomenology of film "versus" photographs; for Cavell, see *The World Viewed*, as in chapter 3, on the "phenomenological frame" of film "that is indefinitely extendible and contractible" (25). Further meditations on Cavell and Bazin and claims for film as somehow a "fuller" version of "the world" appear in Rothman and Keane's *Reading Cavell's "The World Viewed": A Philosophical Perspective on Film*, as in their reflections on film's response to, in Cavell's view, "our wish for presentness" (90). Bazin's own (to my mind contradictory) thoughts about "the ontology of the photographic image" stress both how cinema satisfies "our appetite for illusion by a mechanical reproduction in the making of which man plays no part" and also "the pseudorealism of a deception aimed at fooling the eye" (12).

8. Throughout chapter 6 ("The Impossible Real") of his book, Jonathan Lee demonstrates that a disproportionate emphasis on Lacan's mirror-phase (and the role of *méconnaissance*) loses sight of Lacan's later interest in "the real," which does allow for the influence of the body. Interestingly, Lee's citation about the "speaking body" comes from 1973, the year of Laura Mulvey's influential essay in film theory that builds on Lacan's earlier thinking. However, it seems to me that Lacan's interest is still in fragments and in critiques of claims to wholeness (toward which he, like Sartre, thought Merleau-Ponty tilted).

9. For Silverman, see her *Threshold of the Visible World*, where she seeks to move beyond Lacan's focus on the "fantasy of the 'body in bits and pieces' " (20) and the "currently fashionable notion of a perpetually mobile subject" (11). Silverman wants to allow for a "productive look," which, even in a world ruled mostly by cruel and objectifying gazes, can negotiate another kind of consciousness of the other that, however "precarious," makes possible the gift of love (173). She argues for the "principle of the self-same body" (25) to ground her approach to subjectivity and to this degree shares the emphasis of my work, though she criticizes Merleau-Ponty (erroneously, I think) for his notion of "an absolute symmetry and reciprocity of seer and seen" (245). See my discussion later in this chapter.

10. Whether Austen's novels reflect the kinds of deep cultural shifts that Lionel Trilling alluded to or whether they in some way help to write the culture of consciousnesses that Sartre and especially Merleau-Ponty try to describe makes a nice question.

11. George Levine wrote in *Victorian Studies*, for example, "Having adopted Miller's method of analysis . . . , we would probably discover that much of the fiction we know could be regarded as Victorian" (429).

12. For example, from *Discourse in the Novel:* "Prior to this appropriation, the word does not exist in a neutral and impersonal language (it is not, after all, out of a dictionary that the speaker gets his words!), but rather it exists in other people's mouths . . . : it is from there that one must take the word and make it his own" (293–94).

Carol Rifelj, explaining her approach to the Other, makes a useful distinction between Bakhtin's primary interest in "the question of alterity, the voice of the other . . . , the different voices *of* the novel" and her concern with "the problem of the other explicitly represented *in* the novel, including the characters' thoughts and feelings and their relations with each other" (25). Neither Bakhtin nor Rifelj moves into the denser layers of subjectivities responding to each other that characterize the work of Austen and her successors.

For another approach to talk—and gesture—as complex intersubjectivity, see Erving Goffman's *Forms of Talk:* "If language is to be traced back to some primal scene, better it is traced back to the occasional need of a grunted signal to help coordinate action in what is *already* the shared world of a joint task than to a conversation in and through which a common universe is *generated*" (141). Goffman's image combines the languages of Merleau-Ponty, when he hopes that, by studying behaviors of talk among subjects, "the dance of talk might finally be available to us" (74).

13. For Burney's self-cannibalizing, see Julia Epstein, *The Iron Pen:* "If however the agony is very great, you may, privately, bite the inside of your cheek, or of your lips, for a little relief . . . with that precaution, that if you ever gnaw a piece out, it will not be minded, only be sure either to swallow it, or commit it to a corner of the inside of your mouth till they are gone—for you must not spit" (30).

14. Husserl describes the idea more fully thus: "Thanks to them [the further explications of this chapter], the *full and proper sense of phenomenological transcendental 'idealism' becomes understandable* to us for the first time. The *illusion* of a solipsism is dissolved, *even though* the proposition that everything existing for me must derive its existential sense exclusively from me myself, from my sphere of consciousness retains its validity and fundamental importance" (150).

15. Kaja Silverman's extended reflections on Sartre's use of *le regard* have a similar direction and open toward my discussion of Merleau-Ponty below: "Sartre misses the crucial opportunity implicit in the concept of the looked-at look—the opportunity to theorize it in relation not to objectivity, but to subjectivity" (1996, 166), and I would say to *inter*subjectivity. Silverman also comments on an issue of translation: that in French there is only one word, *le regard*, for what in English we can name "the look" or "the gaze." She wishes to follow Lacan in distinguishing between a "look," which refers to the physical action of the eye, and a "gaze," which may include a camera's seeing, and observing, which is not only optical (167).

16. For more on the study of embodiment and the politics of the body, see, among many possibilities, Foucault, *Discipline and Punish;* Gallagher and Lacquer, eds., *The Making of the Modern Body;* and Helen Michie on women's bodies in Victorian fiction, in *The Flesh Made Word: Female Figures and Women's Bodies*.

17. Work on the gaze and the construction of subjectivity in film began with Hitchcock, in the seminal work of Laura Mulvey and Raymond Bellour. Critics have continued to return to these films, from Slavoj Zizek to Jackie Stacey to Ayako Saito, in their effort to understand the politics of spectatorship, selfhood, and affect in film.

Notes to Chapter 2

1. Paul Hunter, in *The Reluctant Pilgrim,* describes the tradition of Puritan spiritual autobiographies, within which Moll's journey to penitence gains credibility. Virginia Woolf and more recent feminists find Moll's ability to survive attractive for other reasons. In contrast, Maximilian Novak, in chapter 4 of *Realism, Myth, and History in Defoe's Fiction,* believes Moll's inconsistencies are the text's signals of dramatic irony and judgment. Dorothy Van Ghent agrees in *The English Novel: Form and Function* that Moll is deeply inconsistent but sees those inconsistencies as symptoms of the *novel*'s amorality. A fourth approach is G. A. Starr's, who sees Moll as both heartless and disarming (in *Defoe and Casuistry*).

2. See Hunter's *The Reluctant Pilgrim* for discussion of the Puritan traditions of the emblematic reading of events and casting people in typological roles (pp. 99–101, for example).

3. Arguments abound, as I suggested before, over irony and rhetoric in *Moll Flanders*. However, I do not believe that limitations to the fundamental nature of perception in Moll the character are themselves ironic commentary, primarily because these limitations operate in other Defoe novels and in other authors' narratives before our paradigm shift.

4. "Depth" is a notion also offered by Erich Kahler in defining the movement toward interiorizing in fiction (24–26, 67, e.g.). By the "depth of psyche," which early modern fiction newly renders, Kahler means the novelist's more minute observation of the inner workings of individual minds, not an observation of layers of exchange that Merleau-Ponty allows us to theorize.

5. On the blush as an embodiment, see Mary Ann O'Farrell's *Telling Complexions*. O'Farrell's project is similar to mine as she studies the speaking body. Her framework is predominantly Foucauldian, however, and she places the contrary pressure of Barthian "pleasures of narrative *within* an examination of the novel as an institution" (7; my emphasis). Nonetheless, she sees her work as negotiating between "two positions," one that emphasizes the regulatory power of ideology (even or especially within narrative), and the other, which sees in narrative "opportunities . . . to formulate alternatively powerful resistance" to hegemonic forces (148–49).

6. Sedgwick, in *Between Men,* conceives homosociality as a continuum of male friendships, from "bonding," mentorship, and rivalries, to explicitly homosexual (genital) relationships, a continuum that may include intensely homophobic behaviors. There is a "potential unbrokenness" of this continuum "from homosocial to homosexual," but it has been "radically disrupted" by the gender systems and politics of desire in the last two hundred years (1–2). Sedgwick's studies of Dickens in chapters 9 (*Our Mutual Friend*) and 10 (*Edwin Drood*) point to structures of desire (triangulations of men to women via men, of men to men via women; the links between repression of male desire for men, homophobia, and misogyny) that are other important versions of deep intersubjectivity.

7. "School[ing] men's bodies in normative heterosexual touching" seems excessive

NOTES

to me, suggesting the novel's role solely as collaborator with convention, and with a convention interested only in schooling homoerotic energy. Cohen's interest in the minute operations of erotic regulation sometimes leads him to overreach metonymically, so to speak. Hands everywhere suggest masturbation, whatever their other functions. Biddy, for example, is self-evidently another masturbator, for Cohen: "Also like Pip, Biddy exhibits a hand replete with the dirtying signs of both manual labor and onanistic indulgence: 'Her hands always wanted washing' " (62). But the logic of Cohen's colon is obscure.

8. See Patricia Meyer Spacks for a review of these critiques and her own reply: "It can be argued that Pamela's artfulness is, in fact, an integral part of her virtue" (211). Spacks argues, and believes Richardson argues, that Pamela's "pervasive theatricality" is not hypocrisy but self-respect in a world in which "external judgment" (and finally God's) is the key context for virtue's enactment (209).

9. One critic who develops this point of view, from different angles, is Mark Spilka. Here is one thread from Spilka's complex analysis: "*The Turn of the Screw* can be seen as a step toward a recognition of the impossibility of an adult life which excludes sexuality in the name of ideal innocence, a recognition of the impasse which his own cultural assumptions made inevitable. . . . That James valued [the governess's] saintliness and recognized the reality of what she fought [sex-ghosts], yet foresaw her inevitable failure, is a tribute to his artistic grasp of his materials" (110). That is, Spilka balances nicely an admiration in James for the governess, with a recognition of her inability to accept sexuality in children or herself. Hence the psychocultural "reality" of the ghosts.

10. William Empson celebrates Jenny's "deep generosity" that responds profoundly, especially in this letter, to other's experiences, even if not in quite the interplay of readings that adds up to deep intersubjectivity (891).

11. See Suzanne Graver's article on feminisms in *Middlemarch* for a review of different disappointments with Eliot's so-called conservatism and of various recuperations of the novel for a more progressive politics (in Blake 64–74).

Notes to Chapter 3

1. Cornford on Attic comedy, Kenneth Reckford on Aristophanes; C. L. Barber on Shakespeare's festive comedy; Freud on humor and anxiety; and Bakhtin on the carnivalesque in Rabelais (1984) provide the theoretical framework for my approach to comedy. The Cambridge Ritualists have returned to academic favor to some degree and provide useful approaches to ancient comic rituals. See Jeffrey Henderson's introduction (Cornford), Robert Ackerman, and Reckford.

In *The Death of Comedy* Erich Segal reviews two other theories about the origin of the word "komos," in dream and agricultural communities, but his conclusions, also linked to Bakhtin, are not dissimilar from mine: "Perhaps with 'holiday humour' we can entertain all three proposals and argue that Comedy, the mask that launched a thousand quips, is named with as provocative an etymology as Helen of Troy: a dreamsong of a revel in the country" (9).

2. James Phelan's reading of this scene emphasizes these words and the element of *action* (139–40) that Anne reads. For Phelan, what matters in *Persuasion* is the rhetoric of plot and events in support of his contention that style is "significant, but not all-important" in this novel (147). Phelan comments that *readers* understand in this scene that Anne's and Wentworth's "two minds are meant for each other" (141), and one

promising approach would ask his kinds of rhetorical questions about deep intersubjectivity's webs of consciousnesses.

See also Kay Young's discussion of the language of bodies in this scene in her essay on *Persuasion*, "Feeling Embodied." I especially like Young's description of Wentworth's "embodied attunement" to Anne's body (2003, 85).

3. The cancelled final chapters offer one luminous version of the gaps: "There was time for all this to pass, with such interruptions only as enhanced the charm of the communication . . ." (268).

4. See Barbara Hardy's discussion, in a chapter on social groups, of the Box Hill picnic (113–16). Hardy's is the best study to date of Austen's representation of consciousness. Although not strictly phenomenological, Hardy demonstrates how Austen's "flexible medium" promotes a representation of more intricate intersubjectivity.

5. Kay Young's *Ordinary Pleasures: Couples, Conversations, Comedy* examines the intricate ways language creates intimacy for lovers, from *Pride and Prejudice* to *The Thin Man* and *I Love Lucy* (2001). Her readings often complement mine, with her interest in people's "acknowledgement" of each other in the genre of deeply intimate conversation.

6. For other takes on these issues, see Judith Mayne, who is more willing to believe in class and gender heterogeneity than to allow for the freedom of active viewers to dismantle "the fantasies of regression and fusion" that cinema promises (53). Paul Willemen argues that "the academic practice of close reading begs the question of how semantic values are constructed, read, and located in history" (58). For him, to see film as less than a cultural construction is a kind of bourgeois mystification.

These studies then also posit the construction of subjectivity not only *within* film, but *by* film, of real viewers' consciousnesses.

7. Jane Shattuc criticizes a too-easy move "against the grain" to construct usefully oppositional viewing positions. She observes, about "tearjerkers" of the kind that *The Color Purple* may typify, "Ultimately, rather than champion the feminine, racial and political content of these tearjerkers, feminists have preferred to defend melodramas based on their ironic or contradictory value . . ." (149).

8. See Rabinowitz (29ff) on the complexities of "authorial" audience. It is even more difficult to do "authorial" reading when a narrative, like a film, has in some sense multiple authors.

9. Brill observes at the beginning of his book, "This conception of Hitchcock reverses the one shared by most commentators. At the center of the greater part of his movies I find an affectionate, profoundly hopeful view of fallen human nature and the redemptive possibilities of love between men and women" (xiii). I share some of Brill's approach but find the hopefulness characteristically shadowed by an equally profound sense of the fragility of human connection.

10. By "Hitchcock" I refer not only to a historical figure and to an authorial intention or implication of a narrating intelligence within a film text, but also to a collection of creative energies, including screenwriters, cinematographers, and production designers, whose work shaped what we see in the frame of a film.

11. See Modleski, chapter 5, especially p. 85. For Carol Clover, see *Men, Women, and Chainsaws*, chapter 1 ("Her Body, Himself"): "The willingness and even eagerness (so we judge from these films' enormous popularity) of the male viewer to throw in his emotional lot, if only temporarily, with not only a woman but a woman in fear and pain, at least in the first instance, would seem to suggest that he has a vicarious stake in that fear and pain" (61).

NOTES 247

Despite the risk of committing "textual idealism," as Judith Mayne calls it (29), I will not concentrate here on "real" spectators and the tangle of theories about where their gendered response to film originates and how it functions. These speculations have split along two lines, as Jackie Stacey argues, one emerging from psychoanalytic theory, the other from the ethnographic and cultural study of specific audiences. This quarrel between feminist theory and cultural studies is not immediately germane to this book. I concentrate on *representations* of intersubjectivity within films and have outlined in chapter 1 the assumptions about subjectivity that underlie this work. See Stacey's *Star-Gazing*, chapter 2, for a review of approaches to the gaze and spectatorship in the last twenty-five years.

12. A new and important version of intersubjectivity in film is Vivian Sobchack's notion that film, embodying an intention, looks back at an audience, so that the cinema is a site of interlocking gazes, "a *shared* space of being, of seeing, hearing, and bodily and reflective movement performed and experienced by both film and viewer" (10). Sobchack makes extensive use of Merleau-Ponty as well, especially his notion of "chiasmus" as an intertwining of the address of eyes, the spectators' and film's: "[T]here are always two embodied acts of vision at work in the theater," and so there is a reversibility of perception as well (24). Of course, however reversible by implication may be film's vision, response to responses to prior gestures cannot occur within the movie theatre (except as a fantasy within a film like Woody Allen's *The Purple Rose of Cairo*).

13. Many Hitchcock critics have discussed theatricality; see for example Lesley Brill on role-playing and theatricality in Hitchcock's romance (e.g., 15–18); Stanley Cavell (1981, 763–67); and George Wilson's chapter on the problem of appearances, in *Narration in Light*.

Theatricality is a widely used image that needs some problematizing. In chapter 5 I discuss the important Foucauldian use of the image for disciplinary performances under supervision, in an extension of the "vision" metaphors from *Discipline and Punish*. For Foucault, the world *is* a stage, a vast panopticon, and those inquiries that seek to study the "individual" (or "soul") performing on that stage participate in an illusory project since the individual is a technology evolved by the matrix of powers that precede knowing itself. "This is the historical reality of this soul, which . . . is born rather out of methods of punishment, supervision and constraint" (29).

My use of theater downplays a literal application of the image, with professionals (or at least persons marked as "actors") performing in a space demarcated in some clear way from an audience that pays to watch the delivery of (usually) an announced script. These elements serve well the Foucauldian use of the theater image. My use points to what Erving Goffman calls "relations in public" (in his book of that title), that is, the rituals of performance that allow for a range of more rigid or flexible embodiments between intentionalities across more permeable membranes in what Merleau-Ponty called their "interworld."

14. There is, of course, a fourth Cary Grant film that offers a pattern inverse to the other three: In *Suspicion* (1941) the knowing Cary Grant male seems to threaten a woman innocent of the world and its sexual ways. Although problems of gender and gaze overlap in all four films, *Suspicion*'s heroine is so different in the kinds of authority and gaze she proposes that I put that film aside in most of this chapter. See Mark Crispin Miller's argument for *Suspicion*'s critique of its Hollywood genre, an argument that seems to me to overvalue "the influence of Lina's gaze" (1179).

15. See Robin Wood's contrast between the James Stewart characters, with their disturbing "masculine power/impotence," and the Cary Grant characters, who allow for more gender-role ambiguity and equalization between women and men (1989, 364–65).

16. On the subject of Thornhill's maturation, see Robin Wood (1989, 139) and Cavell (*Critical Inquiry*, xxxx). George Wilson argues that Thornhill is too thin a characterization "to make his personal transfiguration a matter of great moment or serious concern" (64). Richard Millington adds the idea that Thornhill's education includes the powers of ideology: "The maneuvers that Thornhill teaches himself, then, not only describe a tactics of self-recovery but define a stance toward the experience of living within American culture, a strategy for the reclamation of 'American character' " (150).

17. Interestingly, the original screenplay called for a different backdrop for the titles: It was to be the night scenes of the robberies that follow the titles in the film.

18. I disagree with Robin Wood that Devlin *does* return Alicia's kiss, though Wood is correct to point out Andrew Britton's error (that Devlin cynically trapped Alicia *before* Sebastian saw them) (1989, 325). Devlin plots the kiss to explain their presence to the husband, who has already spotted them.

19. See *American-Jewish Filmmakers*, by David Desser and Lester D. Friedman, chapters 1 and 2, for a discussion of the Jewish American film context and Woody Allen's movement through his films into the topic of Jewish experience.

20. For discussions of the fool in medieval and Renaissance culture and literature, see Bakhtin's book on Rabelais, Enid Welsford, Walter Kaiser, and C. L. Barber.

21. Compare Sam Girgus's take on this final moment: "Ike's sad face provides the film's perfect final image of vulnerability. . . . Ike's ambiguous smile beautifully epitomizes the tension of desire and despair" (69).

22. In *Comic Faith: The Great Tradition from Austen to Joyce*, Polhemus defines his subject as "a tacit belief that the world is both funny and potentially good; a pattern of expressing or finding religious impulse, motive, and meaning in the forms of comedy; and an implicit assumption that a basis for believing in the value of life can be found in the fact of comic expression itself" (3).

Notes to Chapter 4

1. It is James's text that genders its narrator as male in, for example, the passage cited on the next page of this chapter: "[Mr. Van's] chronicler takes advantage of the fact not to pretend to a greater intelligence—to limit himself on the contrary to the simple statement that . . ." (140).

2. As George Levine cogently argues in *The Realistic Imagination*, it would be naive to think that the great nineteenth-century practitioners of omniscient narration were themselves unaware of the assumptions, perhaps faith, on which it was founded.

3. See Mark Spilka, "Turning the Freudian Screw: How Not to Do It," who argues that the evasions of the body that pervade "The Turn of the Screw" are not only, or even primarily, the governess's, but those of her social world: "[The governess] enables James to establish something more important [than her flaws]: the inevitable failure of Victorian domestic sainthood in coping with erotic horror. . . . At some point in their lives Victorian children will meet their sex-ghosts: there is no real alternative in the tale, no way to save them from damage . . ." (107).

4. Typically such a consciousness has been read to interiorize structures of power,

as in Foucault, *Discipline and Punish,* in Nancy Armstrong's *Desire and Domestic Fiction,* and more recently in Judith Butler's *The Psychic Life of Power.*

Butler's work is especially interesting because she struggles to allow room for contesting agency amidst the formidable influence of the contingent world. She wants to argue that even "the subject produced as continuous, visible, and located is nonetheless haunted by an unassimilable remainder, a melancholia that marks the limits of subjectivation," though she admits that "such a formulation can hardly be the basis for an optimistic view of the subject or of a subject-centered politics" (*Psychic Life* 29). My own argument stresses the possibility of agency, to avoid what Butler calls "the dismissal of the subject as a philosophical trope" and in an analogous fashion to allow for the capacity of the text to revise as well as collude (ibid.).

5. This moment ("Oh, Walter"), like so many other telling details in *His Girl Friday,* was improvised. The script ends with "goo-goo eyes for two years, till I broke down" (13). Mast cites Russell's account in her autobiography of the contest over improvising lines on the set of the film, so that the filmed result is often significantly different from the final revised studio script (see Mast 229 and 376, fn.14).

6. See Brendan Gill, "Pursuer and Pursued: The Still Untold Story of Cary Grant," in *The New Yorker* (June 2, 1997), 84–88. Gill recounts the story of Grant's male and female lovers and adds that Grant's comic performances were often "a bisexual parody that is comic precisely because it is a parody—a genial mocking of the conventional heterosexual relationship" (87).

Gill's notion of parody is helpful for many instances in Grant's career (one thinks of *Bringing Up Baby*), but "genial" does not seem like the right word for Walter's performance and certainly not for his ridicule of Bruce in this moment.

7. The classic account of the narrativizing of this panic over the boundaries of sexual identity is Eve Kosofsky Sedgwick's chapter on Henry James's "The Beast and the Jungle," in *The Epistemology of the Closet,* 182–212.

8. My disagreement with Cavell over *His Girl Friday* should not obscure the significant common ground in our approaches to narrative as consciousness, as a network of "acknowledgment" (to use the word from *The World Viewed*) in "our existence with others in the world" (1987, 185).

Notes to Chapter 5

1. See Rabinowitz's discussion of the status of authorial reading (29–30). I share his balanced view that the authorial reading is neither singular and fully authoritative, nor simply one among many competing readings with no greater claim to persuade.

2. Mary Russo offers another fruitful connection—of masquerade to the carnivalesque. Although Russo is wary of the benefits of Bakhtin's carnival for marginalized populations, for whom the season of disorder is often only a temporary release from the official hierarchy, she praises the defamiliarizing and antiessentializing elements of a carnivalized masquerade: "Nonetheless, the hyperboles of masquerade and carnival suggest, at least, some preliminary 'acting out' of the dilemmas of femininity' " (225).

3. All *Jane Eyre* citations are from the 1996 Bedford edition.

4. Stanley Corngold discusses the implications of Kafka's German in the famous first sentence of "Die Verwandlung": "Ungeziefer" ("bug," "vermin") refers originally in middle high German to "an unclean animal not suited for sacrifice," and "ungeheur" originally suggests "without a part in a family" (66).

5. On the issue of Jane's return to a feminized Rochester, Dianne Sadoff has a useful summary of interpretations, from Richard Chase's 1947 accusation that Jane wants Rochester castrated (or even, by way of her Bertha-self, castrates him herself), through various defensive responses to Chase (Adrienne Rich, Sandra Gilbert, and Susan Gubar, for example), to her own judgment: "It is time, I think, for feminist critics to stop apologizing for Bronte's narrative punishment of Rochester; his punishment indeed represents a 'symbolic castration,' one that does not signify 'equality' but rather a fear of sexual difference and masculine power" (184).

Gayatri Spivak initiated the inquiry into Jane as collaborator in a world of empire, and class and ethnic privilege. Gilbert and Gubar investigated the push/pull that Jane feels with Bertha, and the kind of distancing from her rage and the patriarchal world that the novel's retreat to Ferndean at the end may offer as a comfort to the wounded and rebellious couple.

6. Brontë's punctuation of this key transition varied across the early editions for reasons difficult to determine. She felt insecure on this score, as she wrote to her publishers on September 24, 1847: "I have to thank you for punctuating the sheets before sending them to me, as I have found the task very puzzling, and, besides, I consider your mode of punctuation a great deal more correct and rational than my own" (*Jane Eyre* 1969, xv). Our modern Brontë editors, Jane Jack and Margaret Smith, track a variety of changes between Brontë's manuscript and the first edition and on through the second and third editions and cannot be sure which are Brontë's changes, printing errors, or publisher's changes.

Here are the various versions of the line I'm looking at: manuscript: "in sweet— that will do;" first edition: "in sweet.' That will do." Second and third editions: "in sweet.—That will do." The Clarendon Brontë: "in sweet—that will do." (1969, 252) The Bedford edition that I am using has another solution: "in sweet—That will do." (1996, 203) I thank Beth Newman for drawing my attention to these textual irregularities.

Perhaps the best conclusion to draw is that the intersecting performances of identity here, which deep intersubjectivity outlines so well, are indeed "puzzling," and "rational" punctuation (whatever that would be) might be counterproductive.

7. Spivak's critique of *Jane Eyre*'s "unquestioned ideology of imperialist axiomatics" (248) is extended by Firdous Azim in *The Colonial Rise of the Novel* to Jane's plans to educate members of "lower" classes in both England and India (180–81).

8. Chapter 1 includes a discussion of this problematic subject, in light particularly of Gabriele Schwab's approach to modernist and postmodern agency by way of what she calls "subjects without selves."

9. See Spoto for the story of Hitchcock's recruitment of Hedren after spotting her in a television diet drink ad. Hitchcock knew from the beginning of course that she had no acting experience (Spoto 474–77).

10. Lucretia Knapp argues that Marnie's "resistance to compulsory heterosexuality" points to another possible circulation of sexual energy, although Knapp carefully resists identifying Marnie as a lesbian character (265). Resistant sexualities do become a possibility when Lil says to Mark, "I'm queer for liars." But Lil's queerness is an emotion offered not to Marnie but to Mark, who is also a liar. I see less a narrative, even a displaced one, of homosexual desire than a narrative of the mother's abandonment intercut with heterosexual violation. Active sexual desire of any kind is not yet a safe option for Marnie.

11. Another example of flashback narration might be Joe Gillis's story in *Sunset*

Boulevard, where we of course *see* everything, details on vases and tapestries, that he does not narrate (and could not have), but the voice-over narrator regularly reminds us he is narrating this tale. However, the plenitude of the visual image seduces audiences away from the limits of a first-person narrator, and the camera comes to feel omniscient. Seymour Chatman has reflected on these narrative conventions and concludes that the pressure of film narration reduces the differences I refer to: "Film narrative contains a plenitude of visual details . . . , but . . . narrative films do not allow us to dwell on [them]. Pressure from the narrative component is too great" (126).

12. In other words, I see none of the promise of healing that Robin Wood sees in this moment. Or, if there is a promise, it comes from Marnie and Bernice, not from Marnie and Mark. Another motif is the children's rhyme "Mother, mother, I am ill," which, repeated at key moments in the film, frames Marnie's "cure" but in uncertain ways. Perhaps Marnie's story is another repetition of the folk motif folded into the ancient story of the doctor over the hill and the lady with the alligator purse.

13. Truffaut complained to Hitchcock about the casting of Macdonald Carey for the role of Jack (154), but I think the casting is essential for its contrast to Joseph Cotton's Uncle Charlie, so that Jack will not offer erotic intensity to Young Charlie, and at the end of this film there is no promise of fulfillment for her, only safety.

Notes to Epilogue

1. For more on the free indirect style, see Lodge, 44–47, Gerald Prince's *Dictionary of Narratology*, 34–35, or H. Porter Abbott's *Cambridge Introduction to Narrative*, 190–91.

2. For the larger issues in the rhetoric of narrative, see for example Wayne Booth and, more recently, James Phelan's *Narrative as Rhetoric*. On counterfactual narrative ("If I had not gotten stuck in the traffic jam, I would probably have arrived in class on time), see *Counterfactual Thought Experiments in World Politics*, eds. Tetlock and Belkin. For suture theory, see William Rothman, "Against 'The System of Suture,' " and Kaja Silverman's history of the classical quarrel spawned by Lacan, Alain Miller, and Jean-Pierre Oudart, along with her original contributions in *The Subject of Semiotics*, 201ff.

Bibliography

Narratives

Allen, Woody. *Four Films of Woody Allen* (*Annie Hall, Interiors, Manhattan, Stardust Memories*). New York: Random House, 1982.
———. *Three Films of Woody Allen* (*Zelig, Broadway Danny Rose, The Purple Rose of Cairo*). New York: Random House, 1987
Austen, Jane. *Emma,* ed. R. W. Chapman, 3d ed. London: Oxford University Press, 1933.
———. *Mansfield Park,* ed. R. W. Chapman, revised by Mary Lascelles. London: Oxford University Press, 1934.
———. *Northanger Abbey and Persuasion,* ed. R. W. Chapman, 3d ed. London: Oxford University Press, 1969.
———. *Pride and Prejudice,* ed. R. W. Chapman, 3d ed. London: Oxford University Press, 1965.
Brontë, Charlotte. *Jane Eyre,* ed. Jane Jack and Margaret Smith. Oxford: Clarendon Press, 1969.
———. *Jane Eyre,* ed. Beth Newman. New York: St. Martin's, 1996.
Burney, Frances. *Evelina,* ed. Edward Bloom. Oxford: Oxford University Press, 1968.
Collins, Wilkie. *The Moonstone,* ed. J. I. M. Steward. Harmondsworth: Penguin, 1966.
Defoe, Daniel. *Moll Flanders,* ed. Edward Kelly. New York: W. W. Norton, 1973.
Dickens, Charles. *Great Expectations,* ed. Angus Calder. Harmondsworth: Penguin, 1965.
Eliot, George. *Middlemarch,* ed W. J. Harvey. Harmondsworth: Penguin, 1965. Fielding, Henry. *Tom Jones,* ed. R. P. C. Mutter. Harmondsworth: Penguin, 1966. James, Henry. *The Awkward Age,* ed. Vivien Jones. Oxford: Oxford University Press, 1984.
———. *The Complete Notebooks of Henry James,* ed. Leon Edel and Lyall Powers. New York: Oxford University Press, 1987.
———. *Letters,* ed. Leon Edel, vol. IV. Cambridge, Mass.: Harvard University Press, 1984.
———. *The Turn of the Screw,* ed. Peter G. Beidler. New York: St. Martin's Press, 1995.
Kafka, Franz. *The Metamorphosis,* tr. and ed. Stanley Corngold. New York: Bantam Books, 1972.

Richardson, Samuel. *Pamela*. 2 vols. London: Dent, 1962.
Thackeray, William M. *Vanity Fair*, eds. Geoffrey and Kathleen Tillotson. Boston: Houghton Mifflin Co., 1963.

Theory, Criticism, and Philosophy

Abbott, H. Porter. *The Cambridge Introduction to Narrative*. Cambridge: Cambridge University Press, 2002.
Ackerman, Robert. *The Myth and Ritual School: J. G. Frazier and the Cambridge Ritualists*. New York: Garland, 1991.
Allen, Jeffner, and Iris Marion Young. *The Thinking Muse: Feminism and Modern French Philosophy*. Bloomington: Indiana University Press, 1989.
Altman, Rick. *Film/Genre*. London: British Film Institute, 1991.
Armstrong, Nancy. *Desire and Domestic Fiction: A Political History of the Novel*. New York: Oxford University Press, 1987.
Armstrong, Paul B. *The Phenomenology of Henry James*. Chapel Hill: University of North Carolina Press, 1983.
Audi, Robert, ed. *The Cambridge Dictionary of Philosophy*. Cambridge: Cambridge University Press, 1995.
Auerbach, Nina. *Woman and the Demon: The Life of a Victorian Myth*. Cambridge, Mass: Harvard University Press, 1982.
Azim, Firdous. *The Colonial Rise of the Novel*. New York: Routledge, 1993.
Backscheider, Paula R. *Daniel Defoe: His Life*. Baltimore, Md.: Johns Hopkins University Press, 1989.
Bailey, Peter. *The Reluctant Film Art of Woody Allen*. Lexington: University Press of Kentucky, 2001.
Bakhtin, M. M. *The Dialogic Imagination*, tr. C. Emerson and M. Holquist. Austin: University of Texas Press, 1981.
———. "Discourse in the Novel," in *The Dialogic Imagination*, tr. Caryl Emerson and Michael Holquist. Austin: University of Texas Press, 1981, 259–422.
———. *Rabelais and His World*, tr. H. Iswolsky. Bloomington: Indiana University Press, 1984.
Barber, C. L. *Shakespeare's Festive Comedy*. Princeton, N.J.: Princeton University Press, 1959.
Bazin, André. *What Is Cinema?* tr. Hugh Gray. Berkeley: University of California Press, 1967.
Bellour, Raymond. "Hitchcock, the Enunciator." *Camera Obscura* 2 (Fall 1977): 66–91.
———. "Le Blocage Symbolique." *Communications* no. 23 (1975).
Bender, John. *Imagining the Penitentiary: Fiction and the Architecture of Mind in Eighteenth-Century England*. Chicago: University of Chicago Press, 1987.
Bernheimer, Charles. "The Uncanny Lure of Manet's *Olympia*," in *Seduction and Theory*, ed. Dianne Hunter. Urbana: University of Illinois Press, 1989, 13–27.
Bersani, Leo. *A Future For Astyanax: Character and Desire in Literature*. Boston: Little, Brown, 1976.
Blake, Kathleen, ed. *Approaches to Teaching Eliot's "Middlemarch."* New York: MLA, 1990.
Boone, Joseph. "Vacation Cruises, or, The Homoerotics of Orientalism." *PMLA* 110, no. 1 (January 1995): 89–107.

Booth, Wayne. *The Rhetoric of Fiction*. Chicago: University of Chicago Press, 1961.
Brill, Lesley. *The Hitchcock Romance: Love and Irony in Hitchcock's Films*. Princeton, N.J.: Princeton University Press, 1988.
Brode, Douglas. *Woody Allen: His Films and Career*. Secaucus: Citadel Press, 1985.
Butler, Judith. *Bodies That Matter*. New York: Routledge, 1993.
———. *Gender Trouble*. New York: Routledge, 1990.
———. *The Psychic Life of Power*. Stanford, Calif.: Stanford University Press, 1997.
Cameron, Sharon. *Thinking in Henry James*. Baltimore: Johns Hopkins University Press, 1989.
Case, Allison. *Plotting Women*. Charlottesville: University of Virginia Press, 1999.
Castle, Terry. *Masquerade and Civilization*. Stanford, Calif.: Stanford University Press, 1986.
Cavell, Stanley. "North by Northwest." *Critical Inquiry* (1981): 761–77.
———. *Pursuits of Happiness: The Hollywood Comedy of Remarriage*. Cambridge, Mass.: Harvard University Press, 1981.
———. *The World Viewed*. Cambridge, Mass: Harvard University Press, 1979.
Chatman, Seymour. "What Novels Can Do That Films Can't (and Vice Versa)." *Critical Inquiry* 7, no. 1 (Autumn 1980): 121–33.
Clover, Carol. *Men, Women, and Chain Saws: Gender in the Modern Horror Film*. Princeton: Princeton University Press, 1992.
Cohen, William A. *Sex Scandal: The Private Parts of Victorian Fiction*. Durham: Duke University Press, 1996.
Cohn, Dorrit. *Transparent Minds: Narrative Modes for Presenting Consciousness in Fiction*. Princeton, N.J.: Princeton University Press, 1978.
Cornford, F. M. *The Origin of Attic Comedy*, ed. T. H. Gaster. Introduction by Jeffrey Henderson. Ann Arbor: University of Michigan, 1993; original edition, 1914.
Craft-Fairchild, Catherine. *Masquerade and Gender: Disguise and Female Identity in Eighteenth-Century Fictions by Women*. University Park: Pennsylvania State University Press, 1993.
Damrosch, Leopold. *God's Plot and Man's Stories*. Chicago: University of Chicago Press, 1985.
De Lauretis, Teresa. *Alice Doesn't: Feminism, Semiotics, Cinema*. Bloomington: Indiana University Press, 1984.
Derrida, Jacques. "Structure, Sign, and Play in the Discourse of the Human Sciences," in *The Structuralist Controversy*, ed. Richard Macksey and Eugenio Donato. Baltimore, Md.: Johns Hopkins University Press, 1972, 247–65.
Desser, David, and Lester Friedman. *American-Jewish Filmmakers*. Urbana: University of Illinois Press, 1993.
Dinnerstein, Dorothy. *The Mermaid and the Minotaur*. New York: Harper and Row, 1976.
Doane, Mary Ann. *The Desire to Desire*. Bloomington: Indiana University Press, 1987.
———. "Film and the Masquerade: Theorising the Female Spectator." *Screen* 23 (September–October 1982): 74–87.
Doyle, Laura. *Bordering on the Body: The Racial Matrix of Modern Fiction and Culture*. New York: Oxford University Press, 1994.
Durgnat, Raymond. *The Strange Case of Alfred Hitchcock*. Cambridge, Mass.: MIT Press, 1974.
Empson, William. "Tom Jones," in *Tom Jones*, ed. Sheridan Baker. New York: Norton, 1973, 869–893.

Epstein, Julia. *The Iron Pen: Frances Burney and the Politics of Women's Writing*. Madison: University of Wisconsin Press, 1989.

Ermarth, Elizabeth Deeds. *Realism and Consensus in the English Novel*. Princeton, N.J.: Princeton University Press, 1983.

Evans, Fred, and Leonard Lawlor, eds. *Chiasms: Merleau-Ponty's Notion of Flesh*. Albany: State University of New York Press, 2000.

Felman, Shosana. "Turning the Screw of Interpretation," in *Literature and Psychoanalysis*, ed. S. Felman. Baltimore, Md.: Johns Hopkins University Press, 1982, 94–207.

Fischer, Lucy. *Cinematernity: Film, Motherhood, Genre*. Princeton, N.J.: Princeton University Press, 1996.

Flitterman-Lewis, Sandy. "To See and Not to Be: Female Subjectivity and the Law in Hitchcock's *Notorious*." *Literature and Psychology* 33, no. 3–4 (1987): 1–15.

Foucault, Michel. *Discipline and Punish*, tr. Alan Sheridan. New York: Random House, 1979.

Fraiman, Susan. *Unbecoming Women: British Women Writers and the Novel of Development*. New York: Columbia University Press, 1993.

Freedman, Barbara. *Staging the Gaze: Postmodernism, Psychoanalysis, and Shakespearean Comedy*. Ithaca, N.Y.: Cornell University Press, 1991.

Freud, Sigmund. *Jokes and Their Relation to the Unconscious*, tr. James Strachey. New York: Norton, 1960.

Friedman, Susan Stanford. "Women's Autobiographical Selves: Theory and Practice," in *The Private Self: Theory and Practice of Women's Autobiographical Writing*, ed. Shari Benstock. Chapel Hill: University of North Carolina Press, 1988, 34–62.

Gallagher, Catherine, and Thomas Lacqueur. *The Making of the Modern Body*. Berkeley: University of California Press, 1987.

Geuens, Jean-Pierre. "Visuality and Power: The Work of the Steadicam." *Film Quarterly* 47 (1993–1994): 8–17.

Gilbert, Sandra, and Susan Gubar. *The Madwoman in the Attic: The Woman Writer and the Nineteenth-Century Literary Imagination*. New Haven, Conn.: Yale University Press, 1979.

Gill, Brendan. "Pursuer and Pursued: The Still Untold Story of Cary Grant." *The New Yorker* (June 2, 1997): 84–88.

Gillis, Christina Madsen. *The Paradox of Privacy: Epistolary Form in "Clarissa."* Gainesville: University Press of Florida, 1984.

Girgus, Sam. *The Films of Woody Allen*. Cambridge: Cambridge University Press. 1993.

Goffman, Erving. *Forms of Talk*. Philadelphia: University of Pennsylvania Press, 1981.

Gomery, Douglas. *The Hollywood Studio System*. New York: St. Martin's Press, 1986.

Gubar, Susan. " 'The Blank Page' and the Issues of Female Creativity," in *The New Feminist Criticism*, ed. Elaine Showalter. New York: Pantheon, 1985, 292–313.

Hardy, Barbara. *A Reading of Jane Austen*. London: Peter Owen, 1975.

Havelock, Eric. *Preface to Plato*. Cambridge, Mass.: Harvard University Press, 1963.

Hayes, John Michael. *To Catch a Thief: Screenplay*. Hollywood, Calif.: Script City, 1954.

Heath, Stephen. "Joan Rivière and the Masquerade," in *Formations of Fantasy*, ed. Victor Burgin, James Donald, and Cora Kaplan. London: Methuen, 1986.

Hecht, Ben. *Notorious: Screenplay*. Hollywood, Calif.: Script City, 1946.

Herman, David. "Hypothetical Focalization." *Narrative* 2 (October 1994): 230–53.

Hollinger, Karen. " 'The Look,' Narrativity, and the Female Spectator in *Vertigo*." *Journal of Film and Video* 39: 18–27.

Hunter, J. Paul. *Occasional Form: Henry Fielding and the Chains of Circumstance.* Baltimore, Md.: Johns Hopkins University Press, 1975.
———. *The Reluctant Pilgrim: Defoe's Emblematic Method and Quest for Form in "Robinson Crusoe."* Baltimore, Md.: Johns Hopkins University Press, 1966.
Husserl, Edmund. *Cartesian Meditations,* tr. Dorion Cairns. The Hague: Nijhoff, 1973.
Irigaray, Luce. "The Invisible of the Flesh: A Reading of Merleau-Ponty, *The Visible and the Invisible,* 'The Intertwining—The Chiasm,' " in *An Ethics of Sexual Difference,* tr. C. Burke and G. C. Gill. Ithaca, N.Y.: Cornell University Press, 1993 [French edition, 1984], 151–84.
———. *This Sex Which Is Not One,* tr. Catherine Porter and Carolyn Burke. Ithaca, N.Y.: Cornell University Press, 1990.
Johnson, Charles. *Being and Race: Black Writing since 1970.* Bloomington: Indiana University Press, 1988.
Johnson, Claudia. *Jane Austen: Women, Politics, and the Novel.* Chicago: University of Chicago Press, 1988.
Kahler, Erich. *The Inward Turn of Narrative,* tr. Richard Winston and Clara Winston. Princeton, N.J.: Princeton University Press, 1973.
Kaiser, Walter. "The Wisdom of the Fool," in *Comedy: Developments in Criticism,* ed. D. J. Palmer. London: Macmillan, 1984.
Kaplan, Deborah. "Representing Two Cultures: Jane Austen's Letters," in *The Private Self: Theory and Practice of Women's Autobiographical Writings,* ed. Shari Benstock. Chapel Hill: University of North Carolina Press, 1988.
Kaplan, E. Ann. *Motherhood and Representation: The Mother in Popular Culture and Melodrama.* London: Routledge, 1992.
———. *Women and Film: Both Sides of the Camera.* New York and London: Methuen, 1983.
Keane, Marian. "A Closer Look at Scopophilia: Mulvey, Hitchcock, and *Vertigo,*" in *A Hitchcock Reader,* ed. Marshall Deutelbaum and Leland Poague. Ames: Iowa State University Press, 1986.
Kent, George. *Blackness and the Adventure of Western Culture.* Chicago: Third World Press, 1972.
Kermode, Frank. *The Sense of an Ending.* Oxford: Oxford University Press, 1967.
Klinger, Barbara. *Melodrama and Meaning: History, Culture, and the Films of Douglas Sirk.* Bloomington: Indiana University Press, 1994.
Knapp, Lucretia. "The Queer Voice in *Marnie,*" in *Out in Culture: Gay, Lesbian, and Queer Essays on Popular Culture,* ed. Corey K. Creekmur and Alexander Doty. Durham, N.C.: Duke University Press, 1995, 262–81.
Krook, Dorothea. *The Ordeal of Consciousness in Henry James.* Cambridge: Cambridge University Press, 1962.
Lanser, Susan. *Fictions of Authority: Women Writers and Narrative Voice.* Ithaca, N.Y.: Cornell University Press, 1992.
Lawall, Sarah. *Critics of Consciousness: The Existential Structures of Literature.* Cambridge, Mass.: Harvard University Press, 1968.
Lee, Jonathan. *Jacques Lacan.* Boston: Hall, 1990.
Lehman, Ernest. *North by Northwest.* New York: Viking, 1972.
Lehman, Peter, "Crying Over the Melodramatic Penis: Melodrama and Male Nudity in Films of the 90's," in *Masculinity: Bodies, Movies, Culture,* ed. Peter Lehman. New York: Routledge, 2001.

Lent, Tina Olsen. "Romantic Love and Friendship: The Redefinition of Gender Relations in Screwball Comedy," in *Classical Hollywood Comedy,* ed. Kristine Karnick and Henry Jenkins. New York: Routledge, 1995, 314–31.

Lentricchia, Frank. *After the New Criticism.* Chicago: University of Chicago Press, 1980.

Levine, George. Review of J. Hillis Miller, *The Form of Victorian Fiction. Victorian Studies* 13 (1969–1970): 429.

Liddell, Henry, and Robert Scott. *A Greek-English Lexicon.* Oxford: Oxford University Press, 1968.

Litvak, Joseph. *Caught in the Act: Theatricality in the Nineteenth-Century English Novel.* Berkeley: University of California Press, 1992.

Lodge, David. *Consciousness and the Novel.* Cambridge, Mass.: Harvard University Press, 2002.

Lyotard, Jean-François. "Can Thought Go on without a Body?" *Discourse* 11, no. 1 (Fall–Winter 1988–1989): 74–87.

Macksey, Richard, and Eugenioe Donato, eds. *The Structuralist Controversy.* Baltimore, Md.: Johns Hopkins University Press, 1972.

Mast, Gerald. *Howard Hawks, Storyteller.* New York: Oxford University Press, 1982.

Mayne, Judith. *Cinema and Spectatorship.* London: Routledge, 1993.

McElhaney, Joe. "Touching the Surface: *Marnie,* Melodrama, and Modernism," in *Alfred Hitchcock: Centenary Essays,* ed. Richard Allen and S. Ishii Gonzales. London: British Film Institute, 1999.

McKeon, Michael. *The Origins of the English Novel, 1600–1740.* Baltimore, Md.: Johns Hopkins University Press, 1987.

Merleau-Ponty, Maurice. *Adventures of the Dialectic,* tr. Joseph Bien. Evanston: Northwestern University Press, 1973.

———. *In Praise of Philosophy and Other Essays,* tr. J. Wild, J. Edie, and J. O'Neill. Evanston: Northwestern University Press, 1988.

———. *The Phenomenology of Perception,* tr. Colin Smith. London: Routledge and Kegan Paul, 1962.

———. *The Primacy of Perception,* ed. James Edie. Evanston, Ill.: Northwestern University Press, 1964.

———. *Signs,* tr. R. McCleary. Evanston, Ill.: Northwestern University Press, 1964.

———. *The Visible and the Invisible,* tr. Alphonso Lingis. Evanston: Northwestern University Press, 1968.

Meyer, Richard. "Rock Hudson's Body," in *Inside/Out: Lesbian Theories, Gay Theories,* ed. Diana Fuss. Routledge: New York and London, 1991, 259–88.

Michie, Helena. *The Flesh Made Word: Female Figures and Women's Bodies.* New York: Oxford University Press, 1987.

Miller, J. Hillis. *The Disappearance of God.* Cambridge, Mass.: Harvard University Press, 1963.

———. *The Form of Victorian Fiction.* Notre Dame: University of Notre Dame Press, 1968.

———. "The Geneva School," in *Modern French Criticism,* ed. John F. Simon. Chicago: University of Chicago Press, 1972.

Miller, Mark Crispin. "Hitchcock's Suspicions and *Suspicion.*" *Modern Language Notes* 98 (December 1983): 1143–86.

Millington, Richard. "Hitchcock and American Character: The Comedy of Self-Construction in *North by Northwest,*" in *Hitchcock's America,* ed. Jonathan Freedman and Richard Millington. New York: Oxford University Press, 1999.

Modleski, Tania. *The Women Who Knew Too Much: Hitchcock and Feminist Theory*. New York and London: Methuen, 1988.
Moglen, Helene. *The Trauma of Gender: A Feminist Theory of the English Novel*. Berkeley: University of California Press, 2001.
Mulvey, Laura. *Visual and Other Pleasures*. Bloomington: Indiana University Press, 1989.
Newman, Beth. " 'The Situation of the Looker-On': Gender, Narration, and Gaze in *Wuthering Heights*." *PMLA* 105 (1990): 1029–41.
Novak, Maximillian. *Realism, Myth, and History in Defoe's Fiction*. Lincoln: University of Nebraska Press, 1983.
Nussbaum, Felicity. *The Autobiographical Subject: Gender and Ideology in Eighteenth-Century England*. Baltimore, Md.: Johns Hopkins University Press, 1989.
———. "Eighteenth-Century Women's Autobiographical Commonplaces," in *The Private Self: Theory and Practice of Women's Autobiographical Writings*, ed. Shari Benstock. Chapel Hill: University of North Carolina Press, 1988, 147–71.
O'Farrell, Mary Ann. *Telling Complexions: The Nineteenth-Century English Novel and the Blush*. Durham, N.C.: Duke University Press, 1997.
Perkins, David. "Literary Classifications: How Have They Been Made?" in *Theoretical Issues in Literary History*, ed. David Perkins. Cambridge, Mass.: Harvard University Press, 1991, 248–67.
Pfister, Joel. *Staging Depth: Eugene O'Neill and the Politics of Psychological Discourse*. Chapel Hill: University of North Carolina Press, 1995.
Phelan, James. *Narrative As Rhetoric*. Columbus: The Ohio State University Press, 1996.
———. *Worlds from Words: A Theory of Language in Fiction*. Chicago: University of Chicago Press, 1981.
Piso, Michele. "Mark's Marnie," in *A Hitchcock Reader*, ed. Marshall Deutelbaum and Leland Poague. Ames: Iowa State University Press, 1986.
Polhemus, Robert. *Comic Faith: The Great Tradition from Austen to Joyce*. Chicago: University of Chicago Press, 1981.
Poovey, Mary. *Uneven Developments: The Ideological Work of Gender in Mid-Victorian England*. Chicago: University of Chicago Press, 1988.
Poulet, Georges. *The Metamorphoses of the Circle*, tr. Elliott Coleman and Carley Dawson. Baltimore, Md.: Johns Hopkins University Press, 1966.
Prince, Gerald. *A Dictionary of Narratology*. Lincoln: University of Nebraska Press, 1987.
Rabinowitz, Peter. *Before Reading*. Ithaca: Cornell University Press, 1987. Columbus: Ohio State University Press, 1998.
Reckford, Kenneth. *Aristophanes' Old-And-New Comedy*. Chapel Hill: University of North Carolina Press, 1987.
Rifelj, Carol. *Reading the Other: Novels and the Problem of Other Minds*. Ann Arbor: University of Michigan Press, 1992.
Rigby, Elizabeth. Rev. of *Jane Eyre*, *The Quarterly Review*, December 1848. Reprinted in *Jane Eyre*, ed. Richard J. Dunn. 2nd ed. New York: Norton, 1987, 440–443.
Rivière, Joan. "Womanliness as a Masquerade," in *Formations of Fantasy*, ed. Victor Burgin, James Donald, and Cora Kaplan. London: Methuen, 1986 [orig. pub. 1929].
Roof, Judith, and Robyn Wiegman, eds. *Who Can Speak? Authority and Critical Identity*. Urbana: University of Illinois Press, 1995.
Roth, Marty. "Slap-Happiness: The Erotic Contract of 'His Girl Friday.' " *Screen* 30, no. 1–2 (1989): 160–75.

Rothman, William. "Against 'The System of Suture.' " *Film Quarterly* 29, no. 1 (Fall 1975): 45–50.

———. *Hitchcock: The Murderous Gaze*. Cambridge, Mass.: Harvard University Press, 1982.

———, and Marian Keane. *Reading Cavell's "The World Viewed": A Philosophical Perspective on Film*. Detroit: Wayne State University Press, 2000.

Rubin-Dorsky, Jeffrey. "Perversions or Perversity? Woody and Me," in *People of the Book: Thirty Scholars Reflect on Their Jewish Identity*, ed. Jeffrey Rubin-Dorsky and Shelley Fisher Fishkin. Madison: University of Wisconsin Press, 1996, 456–71.

Russo, Mary. "Female Grotesques: Carnival and Theory," in *Feminist Studies/Critical Studies*, ed. Teresa de Lauretis. Bloomington: Indiana University Press, 1986.

Sadoff, Dianne. *Monsters of Affection: Dickens, Eliot and Bronte on Fatherhood*. Baltimore: Johns Hopkins University Press, 1982.

Said, Edward. *Culture and Imperialism*. New York: Knopf, 1993.

Saito, Ayako. "Hitchcock's Trilogy: A Logic of Mise-en-Scène," in *Endless Night: Cinema and Psychoanalysis, Parallel Histories*, ed. Janet Bergstrom. Berkeley: University of California Press, 1999, 200–248.

Samuels, Robert. *Hitchcock's Bi-Textuality: Lacan, Feminisms, and Queer Theory*. Albany: State University of New York Press, 1998.

Sartre, Jean-Paul. *Being and Nothingness*, tr. Hazel Barnes. New York: Simon and Schuster (Washington Square Press), 1966.

Scarry, Elaine. *The Body in Pain: The Making and Unmaking of the World*. New York: Oxford University Press, 1985.

Schwab, Gabriele. *Subjects without Selves*. Cambridge, Mass.: Harvard University Press, 1994.

Schwarz, Daniel. *The Humanist Heritage: Critical Theories of the English Novel from James to Hillis Miller*. Philadelphia: University of Pennsylvania Press, 1986.

Sedgwick, Eve Kosofsky. *Between Men: English Literature and Male Homosocial Desire*. New York: Columbia University Press, 1985.

———. *Epistemology of the Closet*. Berkeley: University of California Press, 1990.

Segal, Erich. *The Death of Comedy*. Cambridge, Mass.: Harvard University Press, 2001.

Seltzer, Mark. *Henry James and the Art of Power*. Ithaca, N.Y.: Cornell University Press, 1984.

Shattuc, Jane. "Having a Good Cry over *The Color Purple:* The Problem of Affect and Imperialism in Feminist Theory," in *Melodrama: Stage, Picture, Screen*, ed. Jacky Bratton, Jim Cook, and Christine Gledhill. London: British Film Institute, 1994.

Sikov, Ed. *Screwball: Hollywood's Madcap Comedies*. New York: Crown, 1989.

Silverman, Kaja. *Male Subjectivity at the Margins*. New York: Routledge, 1992.

———. *The Subject of Semiotics*. Oxford: Oxford University Press, 1983.

———. *The Threshold of the Visible World*. New York: Routledge, 1996.

Smith, Murray. *Engaging Characters: Fiction, Emotion, and the Cinema*. Oxford: Oxford University Press, 1995.

Sobchack, Vivian. *The Address of the Eye: A Phenomenology of Film Experience*. Princeton, N.J.: Princeton University Press, 1992.

Spacks, Patricia Meyer. *Imagining a Self: Autobiography and Novel in Eighteenth-Century England*. Cambridge, Mass.: Harvard University Press, 1976.

Spilka, Mark. "Turning the Freudian Screw: How Not to Do It." *Literature and Psychology* 3 (Fall 1963): 105–11.

Spivak, Gayatri. "Three Women's Texts and a Critique of Imperialism." *Critical Inquiry* 12 (Autumn 1985): 241–61.

BIBLIOGRAPHY

Spoto, Donald. *The Dark Side of Genius: The Life of Alfred Hitchcock*. New York: Ballantine Books, 1984.
Sprengnether, Madelon. *The Spectral Mother: Freud, Feminism, and Psychoanalysis*. Ithaca, N.Y.: Cornell University Press, 1990.
Stacey, Jackie. *Star Gazing: Hollywood Cinema and Female Spectatorship*. London: Routledge, 1994.
Stam, Robert, Robert Burgoyne, and Sandy Flitterman-Lewis. *New Vocabularies in Film Semiotics*. London: Routledge, 1992.
Starr, G. A. *Defoe and Casuistry*. Princeton: Princeton University Press, 1971.
Stewart, Garrett. *Between Film and Screen: Modernism's Photo Synthesis*. Chicago: University of Chicago Press, 1999.
Studlar, Gaylyn. *This Mad Masquerade: Stardom and Masculinity in the Jazz Age*. New York: Columbia University Press, 1996.
Tanner, Tony. "Introduction," in Jane Austen, *Sense and Sensibility*. Harmondsworth: Penguin Books, 1969.
Tave, Stuart. *Some Words of Jane Austen*. Chicago: University of Chicago Press, 1973.
Tetlock, Philip and Aaron Belkin,eds. *Counterfactual Thought Experiments in World Politics*. Princeton: Princeton University Press, 1996.
Travis, Molly Abel. "*Beloved* and *Middle Passage*: Race, Narrative, and the Critic's Essentialism," in *Narrative* 2, no. 3 (October 1994): 179–200.
Trilling, Lionel. "Mansfield Park," in *The Opposing Self*. New York: Viking, 1955.
Truffaut, François. *Hitchcock*. New York: Simon and Schuster, 1967.
Van Ghent, Dorothy. *The English Novel: Form and Function*. New York: Rinehart, 1953.
Watt, Ian. *The Rise of the Novel*. Berkeley: University of California Press, 1957.
Welsford, Enid. *The Fool: His Social and Literary History*. London: Faber and Faber, 1935.
Welton, Donn. *The Other Husserl*. Bloomington: Indiana University Press, 2000.
Willemen, Paul. *Looks and Frictions*. London: British Film Institute, 1994.
Williams, Linda, ed. *Viewing Positions: Ways of Seeing Film*. New Brunswick: Rutgers University Press, 1995.
Wilson, George M. "Alfred Hitchcock's *North by Northwest*," *Narration in Light: Studies in Cinematic Point of View*. Baltimore, Md.: Johns Hopkins University Press, 1986, 62–81.
Wood, Robin. *Hitchcock's Films Revisited*. New York: Columbia University Press, 1989.
———. *Howard Hawks*. London: British Film Institute, 1981.
Woolf, Virginia. *A Room of One's Own*. New York: Harcourt Brace, 1929.
Young, Kay. "Feeling Embodied: Consciousness, *Persuasion*, and Jane Austen." *Narrative* 11 (January 2003): 78–92.
———. *Ordinary Pleasures: Couples, Conversation, Comedy*. Columbus: Ohio State University Press, 2001.
Zizek, Slavoj. *Looking Awry: An Introduction to Jacques Lacan through Popular Culture*. Cambridge, Mass.: MIT Press, 1991.

Film Narratives

Annie Hall. Director: Woody Allen. Screenplay: Woody Allen and Marshall Brickman. Featured players: Woody Allen (Alvy), Diane Keaton (Annie). Released by United Artists, 1977.

The Bicycle Thief. Director: Vittorio de Sica. Screenplay: Cesare Zavattini, with Oreste Biancolo, Vittorio de Sica, et al. Featured players: Lamberto Maggiorani (Antonio), Enzo Staiola (Bruno). Produzioni De Sica, 1948.

Broadway Danny Rose. Director: Woody Allen. Screenplay: Woody Allen. Featured players: Woody Allen (Danny), Mia Farrow (Tina). Released by Orion Pictures, 1984.

City Lights. Director: Charles Chaplin. Screenplay: Charles Chaplin. Featured players: Chaplin (the Tramp), Virginia Cherrill (the Blind Girl). Released by United Artists, 1931.

Do The Right Thing. Director: Spike Lee. Screenplay: Spike Lee. Featured players: Danny Aiello (Sal), Bill Nunn (Raheem), Spike Lee (Mookie). Released by 40 Acres and a Mule Filmworks and Universal Pictures, 1989.

His Girl Friday. Director: Howard Hawks. Screenplay: Charles Lederer, based on "The Front Page" by Ben Hecht and Charles MacArthur. Featured players: Cary Grant (Walter Burns), Rosalind Russell (Hildie). Released by Columbia Pictures, 1940.

The Lady Eve. Director: Preston Sturges. Screenplay: Preston Sturges. Featured players: Henry Fonda (Charley Pike), Barbara Stanwyck (Jean). Released by Paramount Pictures, 1941.

Manhattan. Director: Woody Allen. Screenplay: Woody Allen. Featured players: Woody Allen (Isaac), Mariel Hemingway (Tracy), Diane Keaton (Mary). Released by United Artists, 1979.

Marnie. Director: Alfred Hitchcock. Screenplay: Jay Presson Allen. Featured players: Tippi Hedren (Marnie), Sean Connery (Mark), Louise Latham (Bernice). Released by Universal Pictures, 1964.

The Nights of Cabiria. Director: Federico Fellini. Screenplay: F. Fellini, Ennio Flaiano and Tullio Pinello. Featured players: Guilietta Masina (Cabiria), Amedeo Nazzari (Alberto). Released by Rialto Pictures, 1957.

North By Northwest. Director: Alfred Hitchcock. Screenplay: Ernest Lehmann. Featured players: Cary Grant (Thornhil), Eva Marie Saint (Eve), James Mason (Vandamm). Released by MGM, 1959.

Notorious. Director: Alfred Hitchcock. Screenplay: Ben Hecht. Featured players: Ingrid Bergman (Alicia), Cary Grant (Devlin), Claude Rains (Sebastian). Released by RKO-Radio Pictures, 1946.

Shadow of a Doubt. Director: Alfred Hitchcock. Screenplay: Thornton Wilder, Sally Benson and Alma Reville. Featured players: Teresa Wright (Young Charley), Joseph Cotton (Uncle Charley). Released by Universal Pictures, 1942.

To Catch a Thief. Director: Alfred Hitchcock. Screenplay: John Michael Hayes. Featured players: Cary Grant (Robie), Grace Kelly (Frances). Released by Paramount Pictures, 1955.

Vertigo. Director: Alfred Hitchcock. Screenplay: Alec Coppel and Samuel Taylor. Featured players: James Stewart (Scottie), Kim Novak (Judy/Madeleine). Released by Paramount Pictures, 1957.

Index

Agee, James, 100
Alcoff, Linda Martin, 100
Allen, Woody, 107, 122–23; *Annie Hall,* 107; *Another Woman,* 151; *Broadway Danny Rose,* 29, 36, 122, 127, 151–62, 181–82; *Bullets over Broadway,* 127, 152; *Crimes and Misdemeanors,* 152, 156; *Curse of the Jade Scorpion,* 154–55; *Hannah and Her Sisters,* 152; *Manhattan,* 152, 153–54, 181; *The Purple Rose of Cairo,* 181, 247n12; *Sleeper,* 127; *Take the Money and Run,* 127
Althusser, Louis, 132
Altman, Rick, 105–6, 151
Amarcord (Fellini), 158
Annie Hall (Allen), 107
Another Woman (Allen), 151
anticomedy. *See* comedy and anticomedy
anxiety, 108–21, 122, 151
appropriation of appropriations, 30, 83, 128; in *The Awkward Age,* 163; in *Great Expectations,* 50–58; in *His Girl Friday,* 183, 188; in *Jane Eyre,* 203–4, 207–8; in *Middlemarch,* 93, 97; in *Moll Flanders,* 42, 44, 46; in *Persuasion,* 112–13; in *Tom Jones,* 76–77; in *The Turn of the Screw,* 70. *See also* espousal
Armstrong, Nancy, 11–12, 65, 109–10
Armstrong, Paul, 164–65
As You Like It (Shakespeare), 150
audiences, 8–10, 17, 89–90, 123–26, 132, 197–98; reader-response theory and, 22, 85, 236, 238

Auerbach, Nina, 200–201
Austen, Jane, 25–26, 35, 50, 84, 109–10, 122, 238; *Emma,* 29, 31, 36, 109, 113–21, 181, 187, 238; *Mansfield Park,* 24–26, 29, 35, 109; *Persuasion,* 3–4, 26, 29, 32, 110, 112–13; *Pride and Prejudice,* 109–12, 164
authority, female, 37, 136, 214–17
Awkward Age, The (James), 29, 36–37, 120, 128, 161–80

Backscheider, Paula, 47–48
Bailey, Peter, 153, 160
Bakhtin, Mikhail: appropriation and, 83; the body and, 23, 152; carnival and, 122, 153, 181, 192, 211–12, 245n1, 249n2; language exchanged and, 4, 27, 33–34, 81–83
Barber, C. L., 245n1
Barchester Towers (Trollope), 82
Bazin, André, 22
"Beast in the Jungle, The" (James), 174
Bender, John, 84–85
Bernheimer, Charles, 32
Bersani, Leo, 165
Bicycle Thief, The (De Sica), 154, 159
Birds, The (Hitchcock), 220, 222–23
Blackmail (Hitchcock), 137, 220
Bleak House (Dickens), 85
blushes, 50–51, 80
body, the: comedy/anticomedy and, 37; consciousnesses and, 5–6, 14, 16, 19–24, 27–28, 55, 99, 235, 237; film narration and, 127–28; gestures and, 34, 69–70; intentionality and, 19,

22–23; masquerade and, 196–97; in *The Awkward Age*, 163, 173–80; in *Broadway Danny Rose*, 152; in *His Girl Friday*, 37, 182–83; in *Marnie*, 222–23, 225, 229–31; in *The Turn of the Screw*, 174
Boone, Joseph, 16
Booth, Wayne, 85, 116–17, 166, 171–72
Brill, Lesley, 130
Bringing Up Baby (Hawks), 181
Britton, Andrew, 248n18
Broadway Danny Rose (Allen), 29, 36, 122, 127, 151–62, 181–82
Brode, Douglas, 156
Brontë, Charlotte, *Jane Eyre*, 27, 29, 37, 196–98, 200–219, 224
Brontë family, 12
Browning, Robert, 11
Bullets over Broadway (Allen), 127, 152
Burgoyne, Robert, 124
Burney, Fanny, 27, 58–62
Butler, Judith, 34, 196–99, 211, 223, 248n4

Cambridge Ritualists, 106, 245n1
camera angles/movements. *See* shot selection/editing
Cameron, Sharon, 165–66, 169
Carey, Macdonald, 251n12
carnival, 122, 153, 181, 192, 211–12, 245n1, 249n2
Case, Allison, 37, 214–16
Cat People (Tourneur), 140
Cavell, Stanley, 22, 186, 239
Cervantes, Miguel de, 38
Chaney, Lon, 199
Chaplin, Charlie, 153–55
Chase, Richard, 215, 249n4
Citizen Kane (Welles), 128
City Lights (Chaplin), 153–54
Clarissa (Richardson), 69, 92, 203
class identities. *See* social class consciousnesses/identities
Clover, Carol, 131
Clowns, The (Fellini), 158
Cohen, William, 53–54
Cohn, Dorrit, 25
Collins, Wilke, 58, 61–62
comedy and anticomedy, 35–37, 106–8, 132, 162–64, 236; Austen and, 110, 113, 116, 121; film, 122–23, 128–29; Freud and, 36, 181, 192; *The Awkward Age* and, 163; *Broadway Danny Rose* and, 36, 122, 127, 151, 159–60, 181–82; *Emma* and, 36; *His Girl Friday* and, 37, 122, 127, 163, 181–92; *Middlemarch* and, 94–95; *Tom Jones* and, 79
community, 16, 35–36, 82, 97–99, 120–22, 151
conduct books, 109–10
Confessions of Nat Turner (Styron), 99–100
consciousness: abstraction of, 10; the body and, 5–6, 16, 19–24, 27–28, 55, 99, 235, 237; cultural contexts/history and, 10–13, 16–17, 19–20; James and, 164–65; mirrorings and, 5, 19–21, 46, 64; transcendency/transparency and, 4, 6, 8–17, 21–22, 25–26, 30, 236, 238. *See also* self and other
Cooper, James Fenimore, 37
Coppola, Francis Ford, 158
Cornford, F. M., 37, 106–7, 113, 245n1
Cotton, Joseph, 251n12
Crimes and Misdemeanors (Allen), 152, 156
Crying Game, The (Jordan), 199
cultural contexts, 10–13, 16–17, 19–20, 24, 35, 123–25, 132, 237
Curse of the Jade Scorpion (Allen), 154–55

Damrosch, Leopold, 93
Daniel Deronda (Eliot), 100
Dastur, Françoise, 21
deconstructionism, 8, 10, 17, 18
Defoe, Daniel, 38, 47–48, 58, 235; *Moll Flanders*, 36, 39–48, 56–57, 62, 70, 74, 85, 92; *Robinson Crusoe*, 189
De Lauretis, Teresa, 197–98
depths, 49, 64, 65–66
Derrida, Jacques, 17, 99, 164, 223, 241nn1, 4
Descartes, René, 6, 27, 99
De Sica, Vittorio, 154, 159
desire, 11–12, 57, 91–92, 220–21, 244n 6

INDEX

Dickens, Charles, 124–25; *Bleak House*, 85; *Great Expectations*, 29, 36, 39–40, 49–58, 70, 80, 125; *Little Dorrit*, 17; *The Mystery of Edwin Drood*, 244n 6; *Our Mutual Friend*, 26, 244n 6
Dietrich, Marlene, 194, 198
Dinesen, Isak, 177
Dinnerstein, Dorothy, 201, 207
Doane, Mary Ann, 193, 197–98, 223
Do the Right Thing (Lee), 127–28
Doyle, Laura, 16, 23
Dunbar, Paul Laurence, 200

Edelman, Gerald, 237
editing. *See* shot selection/editing
8½ (Fellini), 158
Eliot, George: *Daniel Deronda*, 100; *Middlemarch*, 36, 88–90, 92–101, 128, 169; *The Mill on the Floss*, 85; *Romola*, 100
Ellison, Ralph, 200
Emma (Austen), 29, 31, 36, 109, 113–21, 181, 187, 238
Empson, William, 245n10
Ermarth, Elizabeth, 25, 36, 98–99
erotic play, 134–35, 137, 140–43
espousal, 24–38, 106–8, 129; gazes/glances and, 133; masquerade and, 202; relations in public and, 143; theatricality and, 134, 136; in *The Awkward Age*, 163; in *Broadway Danny Rose*, 151–52, 156–59, 181; in *Emma*, 113–21, 181; in *Great Expectations*, 51–56; in *Marnie*, 227, 232; in *Persuasion*, 112–13; in *Pride and Prejudice*, 110–12; in *To Catch a Thief*, 147–48; in *Tom Jones*, 91
ethnicity, 10, 12–13, 15–16, 65, 238. *See also* racial consciousnesses/identities
Evans, Fred, 21–22
Evelina (Burney), 58–62

Fellini, Federico, 154–55, 158
Fielding, Henry, 38, 69, 92; *Tom Jones*, 36, 49, 74–79, 81, 85–88, 90–94
film criticism, 22, 33, 123
Fischer, Lucy, 186, 189–91
Flitterman-Lewis, Sandy, 124, 139
Fonda, Henry, 137

fool, the, 151–62
Foucault, Michel, 82; the body and, 34; cultural regulation/demystification and, 11, 54, 56; panopticon and, 84–85, 97, 110, 194; power and, 35, 66, 113; theatricality and, 194, 211–12, 247n13
Fraiman, Susan, 109–10, 199
Frankenstein (Shelley), 26
Freedman, Barbara, 132
Frenzy (Hitchcock), 150
Freud, Sigmund, 20, 31–32, 36, 181, 192, 197, 223, 245n1
Friedman, Susan Stanford, 201

gazes and glances, 27–28, 235; espousal and, 133; in film, 123, 129–33; gender and, 31–33, 35, 37, 131, 135, 197–98; power and, 116, 130–31, 135–36; in *The Awkward Age*, 170–71; in *Broadway Danny Rose*, 154–56, 160; in *Emma*, 31, 109–10, 114–16, 120–21; in *Evelina*, 59; in *Mansfield Park*, 24–25, 35; in *Marnie*, 219–33; in *North by Northwest*, 135–36; in *Notorious*, 37, 144, 148–49; in *Persuasion*, 3–4, 32, 110; in *Pride and Prejudice*, 110; in *To Catch a Thief*, 135, 148–49; in *Tom Jones*, 77–78; in *Vanity Fair*, 79–80
gaze theory, 33
gendered consciousnesses/identities, 8, 10–12, 15–16, 65, 235, 238; comedy and, 107; defiance of, 111–12; female authority and, 37, 214–17; formation of self and, 109–10; gazes/glances and, 31–32, 35, 37, 131, 135–36, 197–98; gestures and, 35; masculinity and, 16, 135; masquerade and, 194, 196, 198–99; monstrosity and, 37, 200–7; omniscient narration and, 99–100; power and, 46–47, 131, 136, 175, 177, 184; in *His Girl Friday*, 184, 189–91; in *Jane Eyre*, 200–219; in *Marnie*, 223; in *Middlemarch*, 95; in *North by Northwest*, 136, 139; in *Notorious*, 136–37; in *To Catch a Thief*, 135–36

Genette, Gerard, 166
genre theory, 105–6
gestures, 5, 14, 18, 28, 30, 34–35, 69–70, 95; in *Broadway Danny Rose*, 155; in *Emma*, 117–18; in *Evelina*, 60–62; in *Great Expectations*, 50; in *North by Northwest*, 146; in *Pamela*, 69–70
Geuens, Jean-Pierre, 123
Gilbert, Sandra, 199–201, 208
Gill, Brendan, 249n6
Girgus, Sam, 248n21
God, disappearance of, 27, 82, 84
Godfather, The (Coppola), 151, 158
Goethe, Johann Wolfgang von, 37
Goffman, Erving, 18, 23, 36, 166, 173, 179–80, 243n12, 247n13
Gold Rush, The (Chaplin), 155
Gomery, Douglas, 123
Granger, Farley, 137
Grant, Cary, 137, 140, 184, 192
Gravity's Rainbow (Pynchon), 85
Great Expectations (Dickens), 29, 36, 39–40, 49–58, 70, 80, 125
Gubar, Susan, 177, 199, 200–201, 208

Halloween (Carpenter), 131
Hannah and Her Sisters (Allen), 152
Hansen, Miriam, 33
Hardy, Barbara, 246n4
Hardy, Thomas, 85
Havelock, Eric, 25
Hawks, Howard: *Bringing Up Baby*, 181; *His Girl Friday*, 37, 122, 127, 129, 140, 163, 181–92; *The Twentieth Century*, 181
healing. *See* pharmakos
Heath, Stephen, 194, 198
Hedren, Tippi, 222–23
Herman, David, 171
His Girl Friday (Hawks), 37, 122, 127, 129, 140, 163, 181–92
Hitchcock, Alfred: Cary Grant films of, 37, 133–50; casting by, 137, 222–23; comedy and, 122–23, 129–30, 220; gazes in films of, 37, 130–33, 144, 150; masquerade in, 37, 130, 150; *The Birds*, 220, 222–23; *Blackmail*, 137, 220; *Frenzy*, 150; *The Lodger*, 220; *Marnie*, 29, 37, 130, 134, 137, 140, 150, 197–98, 219–33; *Murder!*, 135; *North by Northwest*, 17–18, 132, 135–36, 138–44, 146, 150, 220; *Notorious*, 37, 129, 133, 136–44, 148–50, 220; *Psycho*, 150, 220; *Rear Window*, 131, 133; *Saboteur*, 146; *Shadow of a Doubt*, 220, 232–33; *Stage Fright*, 135; *Suspicion*, 136–37, 247n14; *To Catch a Thief*, 37, 129, 135–36, 139–41, 145–49, 197, 220, 228; *Vertigo*, 36, 128, 132, 220, 228, 232–33
homosociality, 53–54
Hopkins, Gerard Manley, 9, 201
Hudson, Rock, 193, 195
Hunter, J. Paul, 92–93, 244n1
Hurston, Zora Neale, 100
Husserl, Edmund, 11, 21, 30, 33

Ibsen, Henrik, 171–72
intentionalities, 9–10, 18–19, 24, 66, 85, 124, 166–68
interworlds, 13–15, 56, 153, 188, 247n13
Irigaray, Luce, 29, 188, 193, 197, 214, 227–28, 233
Iser, Wolfgang, 85

James, Henry, 9–10, 163–65, 171–72; *The Awkward Age*, 29, 36–37, 120, 128, 161–80; "The Beast in the Jungle," 174; *Portrait of a Lady*, 177; *The Turn of the Screw*, 36, 63, 66, 70–73, 76, 80–81, 85, 174
Jane Eyre (Brontë), 27, 29, 37, 196–98, 200–219, 224
Johnson, Charles, 12–15
Johnson, Claudia, 109–10

Kafka, Franz, 34, 205
Kahler, Erich, 25, 244n4
Kaiser, Walter, 152
Kaplan, Ann, 133, 223
Keller, Gottfried, 37
Kent, George, 15
Kermode, Frank, 239
Knapp, Lucretia, 250n9
Krook, Dorothea, 164
Kuleshov, Lev, 127

INDEX

Lacan, Jacques, 193, 201; the body and, 20, 23, 223; mirror phase and, 5, 7, 19–20, 64; self and, 5, 7, 23–24, 27, 64, 99, 124–25, 132, 236; suture theory and, 125, 238
Laclos, Pierre-Ambroise-François Choderlos de, 37
Ladurie, Le Roy, 212
Lady Eve, The (Sturges), 128, 221, 227–28
Lakritz, Andrew, 100
Lanser, Susan, 37, 217
Lawlor, Leonard, 21–22
Lee, Jonathan, 7, 23
Lee, Spike, 127–28
Lehman, Peter, 199
Lent, Tina Olsen, 191
Lentricchia, Frank, 9, 241n4
Let Us Now Praise Famous Men (Agee), 100
Liaisons Dangereuses, Les (Laclos), 38
Little Dorrit (Dickens), 17
Litvak, Joseph, 211, 218–19
Locke, John, 5, 49
Lodge, David, 237
Lodger, The (Hitchcock), 220
Lyotard, Jean-François, 9

Manet, Édouard, 32
Manhattan (Allen), 152–54, 181
Mansfield Park (Austen), 24–26, 29, 35, 109
Marnie (Hitchcock), 29, 37, 130, 134, 137, 150, 197–98, 219–33
masculinity, 16, 135–36
masquerade, 36–37, 109, 130, 150, 193–200, 235; in *Jane Eyre*, 196–97, 200–219, 224; in *Marnie*, 37, 197–98, 219–33; in *Shadow of a Doubt*, 232–33; in *The Lady Eve*, 227–28; in *To Catch a Thief*, 197, 220, 228; in *Twelfth Night*, 220; in *Vertigo*, 228, 232–33
Mast, Gerald, 183
Mayne, Judith, 246n6, 247n11
Melville, Herman, 37
Mentoria (Murray), 110
Merleau-Ponty, Maurice, 116, 125; appropriation of appropriations and, 30, 44, 46, 49, 53, 56, 77, 83, 93, 112, 128, 176, 195, 204; the body and, 5–7, 14, 19–21, 55–56, 99; "chiasm" of, 4–5, 14–15, 17, 21, 29, 44, 50, 64, 70, 73, 97–98, 121, 134, 137, 143, 162, 168, 179, 219, 233, 235–36, 247n12; comedy/tragicomedy and, 20; consciousness and, 6–7, 20; espousal and, 26–28, 32, 55–56, 91, 106, 163, 180, 232; gazes/glances and, 32–33, 78, 114–15, 149, 226, 229–30; gendering and, 34; gesture and language in, 14, 28, 30; interworlds/intercorporeity and, 13–15, 88–89, 95, 97–98, 134, 153, 188, 247n13; Johnson's misreading of, 12–15; Sartre and, 14, 21, 24–38, 110, 233; self and other in, 19–22, 24, 26, 28–30, 42, 49, 73, 114, 132; as theoretical model, 4–6, 10–11, 16–17, 23–24, 84, 132, 173, 213; touch/touching and, 6–7, 34, 53, 55, 88, 204, 212; transcendentalism/transparency and, 14, 16–17, 21–22, 30; wall imagery of, 14, 28–29, 33, 58, 72, 93, 98, 120–21, 233
Metamorphosis, The (Kafka), 205
Metz, Christian, 126
Meyer, Richard, 193
Michie, Helena, 212
Middlemarch (Eliot), 36, 88–90, 92–101, 128, 169
Middle Passage (Johnson), 13, 15
Miller, J. Hillis, 8–11, 26–27, 30, 81–84, 99, 165–66
Mill on the Floss, The (Eliot), 85
mirrorings, 5, 7, 19–21, 46, 55, 64, 127. *See also* appropriation of appropriations
modernism, 220
Modleski, Tania, 131
Moglen, Helene, 237
Moll Flanders (Defoe), 36, 39–48, 56–57, 62, 70, 74, 85, 92
Moonstone, The (Collins), 58, 61–62
Morocco (von Sternberg), 194, 198
Mulvey, Laura, 31–33, 131–32, 199, 221
Murder! (Hitchcock), 135

Murray, Ann, 110
Mystery of Edwin Drood, The (Dickens), 244n 6

naming/renaming, 52, 134, 137–39
narrative voices: female, 214–15; in film, 127–28; first-person, 49, 62–66; flashback scenes and, 230; geopolitical language and, 11–12; James and, 166, 169–73; omniscient, 27, 64, 73, 81–86, 94, 99–100, 127; structural change in, 25–26, 35–38, 65, 236–38; in *Broadway Danny Rose*, 161; in *Emma*, 238; in *Jane Eyre*, 214–18; in *Middlemarch*, 89–90, 99, 169; in *Tom Jones*, 86–88; in *Vanity Fair*, 170
Newman, Beth, 32
Nights of Cabiria (Fellini), 154–55
North by Northwest (Hitchcock), 17–18, 132, 135–36, 138–44, 146, 150, 220
Notorious (Hitchcock), 37, 129, 133, 136–44, 148–50, 220
Novak, Maximillian, 244n1
Now Voyager (Rapper), 126
Nussbaum, Felicity, 65, 201–2

O'Brien, Edna, 235
O'Farrell, Mary Ann, 244n5
Olympia (Manet), 32
O'Neill, Eugene, 65–66
Othello (Shakespeare), 150
other, the. *See* self and other
Our Mutual Friend (Dickens), 26, 244n 6

Pamela (Richardson), 36, 63, 66–70, 72, 77, 81, 92
panopticon, 84–85, 97, 110, 194, 211
Peck, Gregory, 137
Peeping Tom (Powell), 131
Peregrine Pickle (Smollett), 94
performance, 18, 134–35, 193. *See also* theatricality
Perkins, David, 106
Persuasion (Austen), 3–4, 26, 29, 32, 110, 112–13
Pfister, Joel, 65–66
pharmakos, 107, 113, 220, 230–31
Phelan, James, 245n2
phenomenological criticism, 4, 7–17, 21, 236, 238
Piso, Michele, 225
Poe, Edgar Allen, 11
Polhemus, Robert, 162
Poovey, Mary, 12, 109–10, 206–7
Portrait of a Lady (James), 177
postructuralism, 4, 18, 236
Poulet, Georges, 8–11, 30, 164, 172
Powell, Michael, 131
power, 11, 35, 40, 66, 113; gazes/glances and, 116, 130–31, 135–36; gender and, 46–47, 131, 136, 175, 177, 184; theatricality and, 136–43; in *The Awkward Age*, 175, 177–80; in *Broadway Danny Rose*, 154; in *City Lights*, 154; in *Emma*, 115–16; in *Great Expectations*, 70; in *His Girl Friday*, 184, 191; in *Jane Eyre*, 37, 210–12; in *Marnie*, 137, 229; in *Moll Flanders*, 47; in *North by Northwest*, 136, 139; in *Notorious*, 136–37
Pride and Prejudice (Austen), 109–12, 164
Psycho (Hitchcock), 150, 220
public, private relationships in, 113, 143–50, 247n13
Purple Rose of Cairo, The (Allen), 181, 247n12

Rabinowitz, Peter, 126, 198
racial consciousnesses/identities, 8, 10–11, 12–15, 217–18. *See also* ethnicity
reader-response theory, 22, 85, 236, 238
readers and reading. *See* audiences
Rear Window (Hitchcock), 131, 133
Reckford, Kenneth, 245n1
renaming. *See* naming/renaming
Return of the Native, The (Hardy), 85
Richardson, Samuel, 38; *Clarissa*, 69, 92, 203; *Pamela*, 36, 63, 66–70, 72, 77, 81, 92
Rifelj, Carol, 25, 243n12
Rigby, Elizabeth, 216
Rivière, Joan, 193, 196, 198–99, 202, 207, 215–16, 223, 228
Robbe-Grillet, Alain, 38
Robinson Crusoe (Defoe), 189
Romola (Eliot), 100

Roth, Marty, 184, 186, 190
Rubin-Dorsky, Jeffrey, 151
Russo, Mary, 211–12, 249n2

Saboteur (Hitchcock), 146
Sadoff, Dianne, 249n4
Samuels, Robert, 132
Sartre, Jean-Paul: gazes/glances and, 31–32, 77–79, 149; Johnson's misreading of, 14; masquerade and, 200, 212; Merleau-Ponty and, 14, 21, 24–38, 110, 233; self and other in, 26, 31, 176–77; shame/fear and, 26, 28, 31, 55, 106, 112, 180, 232
scapegoats, 36, 107, 113, 129, 152
Scarry, Elaine, 34
Schwab, Gabriele, 18, 36
Schwarz, Daniel, 10
screwball comedies, 127, 129, 191
scripting, 134, 136–37; in *Emma*, 116–17; in *Marnie*, 140, 224–27, 229, 232; in *North by Northwest*, 139–40; in *Notorious*, 139; in *To Catch a Thief*, 139–40
Sedgwick, Eve Kosofsky, 15–16, 53–54, 173–74, 211
Segal, Erich, 191, 245n1
self and other, 5–7, 15–16, 19–27, 28–31, 42; formation of self within, 109–10; loss/fragmentation of self within, 10, 18, 23–24, 109; in *Broadway Danny Rose*, 157–59; in *Emma*, 114, 117–18, 121; in *Evelina*, 58–62; in *Great Expectations*, 49–58, 80; in *His Girl Friday*, 190; in *Jane Eyre*, 202; in *Middlemarch*, 88–90, 92–101; in *Moll Flanders*, 36, 39–48, 56–57; in *The Moonstone*, 58; in *Pamela*, 63, 66–70, 72, 77, 81; in *The Awkward Age*, 166–68; in *The Turn of the Screw*, 63, 66, 70–73, 76, 80–81, 85; in *Tom Jones*, 74–79, 85–88, 90–94; in *Vanity Fair*, 79–81. *See also* consciousness
Seltzer, Mark, 177, 180
sexual consciousnesses/identities, 8, 15–16, 193, 195–97; in *The Awkward Age*, 173–74; in *Great Expectations*, 53–56; in *Marnie*, 227; in *The Mystery of Edwin Drood*, 244n6; in *Our Mutual Friend*, 244n6; in *The Lady Eve*, 227–28
Shadow of a Doubt (Hitchcock), 220, 232–33
Shakespeare, William, 132; *Othello*, 150; *Twelfth Night*, 107–8, 132, 152, 186, 220; *The Winter's Tale*, 150–51; *As You Like It*, 150
shame, 24–38, 55–56, 106–8, 129; masquerade and, 202; relations in public and, 143–44; theatricality and, 134, 136; in *Broadway Danny Rose*, 157; in *Great Expectations*, 51, 57; in *Middlemarch*, 93; in *Pride and Prejudice*, 110–12; in *Tom Jones*, 79
Shattuc, Jane, 246n7
Shelley, Mary Wollstonecraft, 26
shot selection/editing, 124, 127, 238; in *The Bicycle Thief*, 159; in *Broadway Danny Rose*, 151, 153–54, 159–62; in *City Lights*, 153–54; in *His Girl Friday*, 182–85, 187; in *Manhattan*, 153; in *Marnie*, 225–26, 229–31; in *Notorious*, 141–42, 144; in *To Catch a Thief*, 141, 146–47
Sikov, Ed, 129, 191
Silence of the Lambs, The (Demme), 131
silences, 34, 51–52, 80, 100, 159
Silverman, Kaja, 19, 23, 125, 235–36, 238, 243n15
Sleeper (Allen), 127
Smith, Murray, 126, 132
Smollett, Tobias, 94
Sobchack, Vivian, 8–9, 20–22, 24, 241n5, 247n12
social class consciousnesses/identities, 8, 10–12, 15–16, 95, 238; omniscient narration and, 99–100; in *Great Expectations*, 54–56, 70; in *Jane Eyre*, 205–7, 212, 217–18; in *Marnie*, 222, 229; in *Middlemarch*, 65
Spacks, Patricia Meyer, 245n8
Spilka, Mark, 173–74, 245n9
Spivak, Gayatri Chakravorty, 100, 217, 250n4
Sprengnether, Madelon, 223
Stacey, Jackie, 197, 247n11
Stage Fright (Hitchcock), 135

Stam, Robert, 124
Starobinski, Jean, 9
Starr, G. A., 244n1
steadicams, 123–24
Stendhal, 37
Sterne, Laurence, 26, 38
Stewart, Garrett, 22, 239
Stewart, James, 137
Studlar, Gaylyn, 199
Sturges, Preston, 128, 221, 227–28
Styron, William, 99–100
subjects, 5–7, 9–11, 17–24, 63–66, 236
Sunset Boulevard (Wilder), 250n10
Suspicion (Hitchcock), 136, 137, 247n14
suture theory, 125–26, 238

Take the Money and Run (Allen), 127
Tanner, Tony, 109
Tave, Stuart, 109
Thackeray, William Makepeace, 79–82, 86–87, 170
theatricality, 37, 130, 134–43, 194, 211–12
"The Blank Page" (Dinesen), 177
To Catch a Thief (Hitchcock), 37, 129, 135–36, 139–41, 145–49, 197, 220, 228
Tom Jones (Fielding), 36, 49, 74–79, 81, 85–88, 90–94
touches and touching, 6–7, 34, 88; in *Great Expectations*, 53–55, 70; in *Jane Eyre*, 204, 212; in *Marnie*, 229, 231
Travis, Molly Abel, 15

Trilling, Lionel, 109
Tristram Shandy, The Life and Opinions of (Sterne), 26
Trollope, Anthony, 82, 238
Truffaut, François, 251n12
Turn of the Screw, The (James), 36, 63, 66, 70–73, 76, 80–81, 85, 174
Twelfth Night (Shakespeare), 107–8, 132, 152, 186, 220
Twentieth Century, The (Hawks), 181

Valéry, Paul, 32
Van Ghent, Dorothy, 244n1
Vanity Fair (Thackeray), 79–82, 86–87, 170
Vertigo (Hitchcock), 36, 128, 132, 220, 228, 232–33
viewers and viewing. *See* audiences

watchers and watching. *See* gazes and glances
Watt, Ian, 237
Welles, Orson, 128
Willemen, Paul, 246n6
Williams, Linda, 33
Winter's Tale, The (Shakespeare), 150–51
Wood, Robin, 186, 221, 224–25, 248n18, 251n11
Woolf, Virginia, 109, 244n1
Written on the Wind (Sirk), 126

Young, Kay, 246nn2, 5

Zizek, Slavoj, 23, 132

THE THEORY AND INTERPRETATION OF NARRATIVE SERIES
James Phelan and Peter J. Rabinowitz, Editors

Because the series editors believe that the most significant work in narrative studies today contributes both to our knowledge of specific narratives and to our understanding of narrative in general, studies in the series typically offer interpretations of individual narratives and address significant theoretical issues underlying those interpretations. The series does not privilege any one critical perspective but is open to work from any strong theoretical position.

Misreading Jane Eyre: A Postformalist Paradigm
JEROME BEATY

Invisible Author, Last Essays
CHRISTINE BROOKE-ROSE

Bloodscripts: Writing the Violent Subject
ELANA GOMEL

Narratologies: New Perspectives on Narrative Analysis
Edited by DAVID HERMAN

Telling Tales: Gender and Narrative Form in Victorian Literature and Culture
ELIZABETH LANGLAND

Matters of Fact: Reading Nonfiction over the Edge
DANIEL W. LEHMAN

Breaking the Frame: Metalepsis and the Construction of the Subject
DEBRA MALINA

Framing Anna Karenina: Tolstoy, the Woman Question, and the Victorian Novel
AMY MANDELKER

Surprised by Shame: Dostoevsky's Liars and Narrative Exposure
DEBORAH A. MARTINSEN

Politics, Persuasion, and Pragmatism: A Rhetoric of Feminist Utopian Fiction
ELLEN PEEL

Narrative as Rhetoric: Technique, Audiences, Ethics, Ideology
JAMES PHELAN

Understanding Narrative
Edited by JAMES PHELAN AND PETER J. RABINOWITZ

Before Reading: Narrative Conventions and the Politics of Interpretation
PETER J. RABINOWITZ

Narrative Dynamics: Time, Plot, Closure, and Frames
Edited by BRIAN RICHARDSON

The Progress of Romance: Literary Historiography and the Gothic Novel
DAVID H. RICHTER

A Glance beyond Doubt: Narration, Representation, Subjectivity
SHLOMITH RIMMON-KENAN

Psychological Politics of the American Dream: The Commodification of Subjectivity in Twentieth-Century American Literature
LOIS TYSON

Ordinary Pleasures: Couples, Conversation, and Comedy
KAY YOUNG

Having a Good Cry: Effeminate Feelings and Pop-Culture Forms
ROBYN R. WARHOL

www.ingramcontent.com/pod-product-compliance
Lightning Source LLC
Chambersburg PA
CBHW030109010526
44116CB00005B/161